Divided Loyalties
in a Doomed Empire

Divided Loyalties in a Doomed Empire

The French in the West
from New France
to the Lewis and Clark Expedition

Daniel Royot

DELAWARE

Newark: University of Delaware Press

Associated University Presses
2010 Eastpark Boulevard
Cranbury, NJ 08512

The paper used in this publication meets the requirements of the American National Standard for Permanence of Paper for Printed Library Materials Z39.48-1984.

Library of Congress Cataloging-in-Publication Data

Royot, Daniel.
    Divided loyalties in a doomed empire : the French in the West : from New France to the Lewis and Clark Expedition / Daniel Royot.
        p.   cm.
    Includes bibliographical references and index.
    ISBN-13: 978-0-87413-968-6 (alk. paper)
    ISBN-10: 0-87413-968-6 (alk. paper)
    1. French—West (U.S.)—History.   2. Frontier and pioneer life—West (U.S.)   3. West (U.S.)—Discovery and exploration.   4. West (U.S.)—History. 5. West (U.S.)—Ethnic relations.   6.   Canada—History—To 1763 (New France)   7. Lewis and Clark Expedition   (1804–1806)   8. France—Colonies— America.   9. French—North America—History.   10. North America—History. I. Title.
F596.3.F8R695   2007
978'.0100494—dc22   2006030920

SECOND PRINTING 2008

Contents

Foreword

Wᴀɪʟᴇ ᴀᴍᴇʀɪᴄᴀ ɪs ᴄᴇʟᴇʙʀᴀᴛɪɴɢ ᴛʜᴇ ʙɪᴄᴇɴᴛᴇɴɴɪᴀʟ ᴏғ ᴛʜᴇ ʟᴇᴡɪs ᴀɴᴅ Clark expedition, this book is an attempt to trace the lifeline of the French community in the West, from the territorial expansion of New France to the subjection of the defeated colonial empire to the Spanish or English rulers, before the Louisiana Purchase eventually Americanized the descendants of the earlier bourgeois and coureurs des bois. I have devoted several decades of my life to the study of the American West, and as a Frenchman, my aim has been to convey something of my transatlantic experience. In completing this task I derive great pleasure from acknowledging my numerous intellectual and personal debts.

I owe much to my private corps of discovery. My wife Yvette, my daughter Muriel and grandson William patiently accompanied me on some of my western journeys, and I am particularly grateful to my son-in-law Jean-Michel who drove me all along the Lewis and Clark trail with admirable equanimity.

My fieldwork was greatly facilitated by grants from the Fulbright Committee, the Commission française d'échanges universitaires in Paris, the Canadian Research Council and the Research Center on North American Cultures, Université Montaigne, Bordeaux, whose director Christian Lerat offered me decisive support. My heartfelt thanks also go to the Robert H. Smith International Center for Jefferson Studies at Monticello for the fellowship I was offered in 1998. I was greatly stimulated by my contacts with Douglas Wilson who was then in charge. My deep obligation is also owed Daniel Jordan, Executive Director of the Thomas Jefferson Foundation. His encouragements have always been precious to me.

Among the institutions that provided me with useful information along the Lewis and Clark Trail, I wish to acknowledge the Interpretive Center at Great Falls and the Clatsop National Memorial in Oregon. I equally like to remember my conversation with Ranger Kevin Peters, at the Nez Percés National Historical Park, Spalding, Idaho. To his information on Native Americans, he added references to the bee engraved in the Laguiole knives from Auvergne, which made

me conscious that this is a small world. Last but not least Roy Good-
man gave me helpful assistance at the American Philosophical Society in Philadelphia.

In the seventies I was fortunate and honored to be initiated into
the discovery of the major landmarks in westward expansion by Ray
Allen Billington at the Huntington Library. James C. Austin, who
was a dear friend at Southern Illinois University, Edwardsville, introduced me to John F. McDermott at a meeting of the St. Louis West-
erners. They both told me about the French presence in the
Midwest, especially when we visited St. Genevieve and met a lady
who had my grandmother's maiden name.

My argument takes its departure from insights originally provided
by Edward Geary at Bowdoin College and Joe Vital-Ouellette, an old
French-American logger from New Brunswick who took me to the
Maine woods and taught me a lot on bears, moose, mosquitoes, and
fish. I became so much part of the environment that in Brunswick,
French-speaking policemen once mistook me for an unidentified
runaway Indian. They called me « un sauvage», which for them was
by no means derogatory .

Many scholars have been instrumental in keeping my interest in
American studies over the years. They are Stephen Whitfield, Kevin
J. Hayes, Thomas Inge, Leonard Frey, Norman Fruman, Michael
Adams, Kermit Vanderbilt, and Glen Love among others whom I
feel guilty about overlooking here. Clarence Sandelin guided me
through New Mexico. At the University of Texas, Austin, Americo
Paredes kindly answered my queries on Spain in America. Editor
and author in Quebec, Denis Vaugeois also deserves thanks for helping me define my project. As president of the French Canadian Association, Recteur Jean-Michel Lacroix, gave me full support for my
wandering in Western Canada.

Philippe Jacquin and I had coauthored several books in French
on the American West before his sudden death in September 2002.
He was the foremost French expert on Native Americans and French
coureurs des bois. I owe him an incalculable debt for delving into
virgin grounds. François Duban, Professor of American Studies at
the Université de la Réunion and Océan Indien, is both an authority
on the ecology of the Pacific West and an expert at word processing.
His skillful treatment of my manuscript allowed me to meet the requirements of American editing practice.

J. A. Leo Lemay has been a close friend ever since we hit upon a
Gila monster on the slopes of Tonto National Monument in the
Spring of 1987. My debt to him is so immense that a full chapter
would be needed to acknowledge it. Don Mell has also been a

thoughtful, precious adviser. He saved me from hazardous lapses when I was completing my manuscript. I wish to express my deep gratefulness to him and to Karen Druliner at the University of Delaware Press.

At the University of Delaware, this book has benefited from an expert appraisal by Michael Edson, who read the manuscript with a critical yet sympathetic eye. His perceptive views on style and composition made his comments and suggestions invaluable. I owe him a special debt for his steady, conscientious revisions in the summer of 2005.

Christine Retz has been an admirably patient, kindly managing editor at Associated University Presses and I am also thankful for the editorial work of Beth Ann Stuebe.

I have striven for synthesis considering the awe-inspiring amount of outstanding scholarly studies bearing on two centuries of American and European history of the westward movement. The material had to be necessarily, sometimes painfully, selective, never to depart from the original argument contained in my title. Subjective though my judgments may sometimes appear, I simply tried to remain a candid observer of a past that may implicitly reveal much of the present.

N.B., French words such as Sainte Geneviève take an accent in the context of New France; otherwise the accent is dropped.

Introduction

IN THE JOURNALS OF THE LEWIS AND CLARK EXPEDITION, THE TERMS "French" and "Frenchmen" refer to French Canadians, French Spaniards, and French Americans, never to French citizens. Strikingly, Meriwether Lewis only once uses Canadian French to comment on the 450 inhabitants of St. Charles. On the other hand, he never pointed to the possible links between the Creoles in Upper Louisiana and the former Acadians down south. After the loss of Canada, the so-called few acres of snow snubbed by both Voltaire and the French court, the former subjects of His Majesty Louis XV changed their nationalities but somehow retained their habits and culture. The British and Spanish colonies of Canada and Louisiana inexorably became multicultural. The French also kept their language in most underpopulated regions but their enclaves now cut off from the homeland evolved along different lines. The French Canadians and French Spaniards did not face the same issues as the Parisians in the late eighteenth century. The echoes of the Revolution reached Montreal and St. Louis, and sometimes spurred patriotic feelings. Yet French colonists, or at least their descendants, were more familiar with the values of the ancien régime than with those of the Republic or the Consulate.

Compared with the British, the French had the advantage of seniority on the new continent. The main incentive to exploration was the fur trade. As early as 1615 Samuel de Champlain not only followed Indian trails but established a whole network of waterways. Within a century, New France extended to Lake Winnipeg, Hudson Bay, Lake Michigan, Ohio, Illinois, and the shores of the Gulf of Mexico. The forts built on the strategic locations stood as landmarks for new adventurers. Cartographers worked hand in hand with explorers and missionaries. The westward movement of the French seemed irresistible. It was not only grounded in the lust for profits from the fine furs and pelts but involved drifters, deserters, and farmers discontented with the feudal system imposed on them. French colonization was, however, fragile. Few were the French who crossed the Atlantic with their families. New France was a man's

11

country. Interracial relations and miscegenation were inevitable. A French subject soon found his allegiance divided between Indian tribes, fur traders, and his homeland. The pressure of the British westward movement was too strong by the mid-eighteenth century for New France to withstand attacks from all sides. The French population was divided between Spain and Britain on each side of the Mississippi River after the Treaty of Paris in 1763. What did French mean then? What was at stake for the French communities when the rebels fought British hegemony in the War of Independence? Louisiana was later used as a pawn in a diplomatic struggle under Bonaparte's régime.

This essay is intended to follow the evolution of the French in the West. It emphasizes the crucial moments when epoch-making changes occurred, and their impact on mentalities. In terms of American studies it also consists of an approach to view the history of North America from a specific French perspective.

Divided Loyalties
in a Doomed Empire

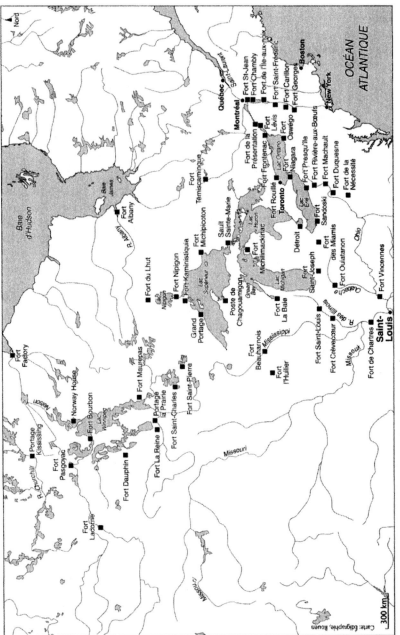

New France Expansion: Northwest. Map courtesy of Édigraphie.

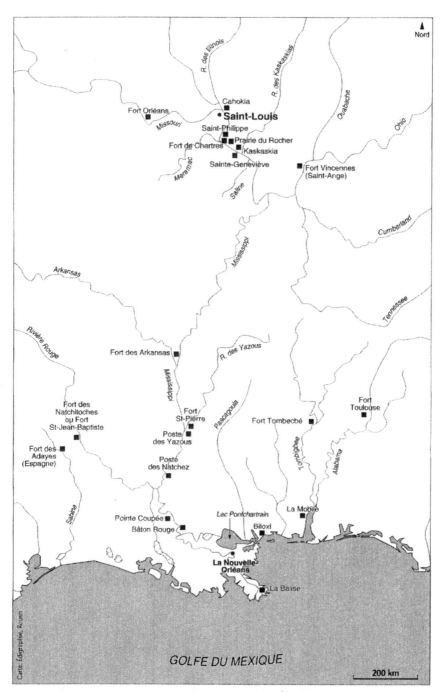

New France Expansion: Southwest. Map courtesy of Édigraphie.

1

From Quebec to the "Pays d'en haut"

SIXTEENTH-CENTURY FRANCE KNEW LITTLE ABOUT NORTH AMERICA. Explorers roaming the new continent encountered a linguistic barrier and struggled to learn significant geographical data from the natives. When Jacques Cartier returned from his third voyage to Canada in 1542, he also conceded that relations were strained with the Iroquois Indians despite his goodwill. The same year, King Francis I did not fully realize the prospects opened by Jean-François de la Rocque de Roberval's exploration of the Ottawa territories as far as the Lachine rapids. At that time the monarch was paying more attention to his conflicts with Britain and Spain. Meanwhile, fishermen from Brittany continued to gather what information they could from the Newfoundland waters where they spent months every year. The fur trade still involved a small minority of hunters and merchants. The inhabitants of Normandy sometimes came across deported Indians destined to entertain the court, such as were seen by Henry II and Catherine of Medicis when they visited Rouen in 1550. In August 1626 Amantacha, a young Huron, was baptized by Archbishop François de Harlay in the Rouen cathedral where a crowd had gathered, believing that the Indian was Samuel de Champlain's son. Amantacha was named Louis de Sainte Foi in homage to the king.[1]

In the early years of the colony, discouraged survivors of the Canadian winter who came home gave frightful accounts of their experience in the New World, hence the necessity for the authorities to compel beggars and convicts to migrate to those inhospitable regions. Meanwhile, official reports on explorations remained confidential for fear they might come to the ears of Spanish, Portuguese, or English spies. Besides, financiers could not be satisfied with pelts and furs alone. The crown needed to replenish the treasury with gold, but undermined by internecine religious and political quar-

17

rels, could not afford to take risks overseas. Yet the publication of several books on America attracted attention, as exemplified by Cartier's accounts of his travels in 1545, and at the turn of the century, in *Les Grands Voyages* by Théodore de Bry and his sons. Montaigne, who was fascinated by the discovery of cannibals by Villegagnon in Brazil, was eager to question a sailor of his ship's company to gratify his intellectual curiosity.[2] Such readings stimulated exotic tastes as well as the inquisitiveness of investors in trading companies. Following Marco Polo's travels in the Far East, the European economy had adapted standing statutes and regulations dating back to medieval times when dealing with oriental mores, especially through the Venice merchants. Likewise in the New World, commercial relations depended on the exploitation of new resources in the hands of so-called savages.

Many regions were represented among the French who founded New France. A majority came from the maritime provinces of Normandy, Brittany, Anjou, Poitou, and Charente. The Bretons had long led a rugged life on a damp, windswept peninsula as fishermen and peasants. Of Viking stock, Normands had been used to cattle-breeding and dairy farming. On the coast of Acadia the forebears of Longfellow's Evangeline recreated the salt meadows of their native Atlantic homeland. The settlers usually lived on a riverfront with a permanent view of paddling trappers and Indians.

At the turn of the seventeenth century, Henry IV Vert Galant, recently converted to Catholicism, granted the monopoly of the fur trade to Protestant Pierre Du Gua de Monts, whose task was not only to establish the authority of the crown but to spread the faith in God. Du Gua hoped to find in Acadia a climate suitable to both agriculture and fur-trapping. His agents Samuel de Champlain and Jean de Poutrincourt first settled at Port Royal where their small settlement soon suffered from scurvy and subsequent famine. Smuggling was also detrimental to the enterprise, especially when Dutch trappers were introduced to the Indians by a French traitor named La Jeunesse.[3] The permanent threat from the English navy finally induced Champlain to retreat to the Saint Lawrence valley where he founded the Quebec colony. Fishermen and traders were familiar with Tadoussac, located at the mouth of the Saguenay, from which the canoes of the Montagnais Indians came loaded with pelts and furs. Champlain hoped to deprive them of the monopoly they staunchly kept by barring the way to the North and the West, called "Le Pays d'en Haut." In the Quebec outpost, two dozen young men were in charge of the maintenance of the storehouse through the long winter months. Through Champlain's initiative, they were visited by friendly Algonquins to whom they offered assistance against hostile tribes such as the Irinokhoiv, otherwise known as Snakes. In the spring of 1609, a military campaign launched by Champlain led him to meet the Hurons, who soon proved to be particularly hospitable. To improve links with his newfound allies, he sent young Frenchmen to live in one of their tribes and learn their language.[4] Young Etienne Brûlé volunteered to follow chief Iroquet who himself left a young Huron with the French. The following spring Etienne came back dressed like a "savage," delighted with his active wintering months and now proficient in the native tongue. The success of the experience induced Nicolas de Vignau to live among another Algonquin group. The exchange of *truchements* [interpreters], enabled the French to better understand the complex network of Indian commercial relations.[5] However, in 1613, while on a visit to Vignau, the Algonquins denied Champlain the opportunity to go northward to their stronghold on the île des Allumettes where they controlled the trade on the Outaouais river.[6]

The continual immersion of the most adventurous colonists in the native population belies long-term assumptions about its brutish practices. Pierre-Esprit Radisson was the first European to go northwest of the Great Lakes. In 1656, he remarked that the Cree tribes adorned their clothes with shells from the Atlantic, bartered for furs by the Ottawa Indians.[7] The transit of commodities from tribe to tribe over long distances thus added to the profits of exchange. The shifty Ottawas were constantly on the move, and covered hundreds of miles to contact the Winnebagos and the Sioux. Trekking to the Great Plains was subject to a toll levied by Indian tribes along the way. Safety and reciprocity depended on a code to be observed with caution. The aggressiveness of young warriors seeking prestige might well annihilate a good-neighbor policy that had been effective for years. Gifts and the exchange of young boys might also smooth over obstacles toward a renewed peace as long as interpreters were highly valued among the Algonquins who had first-rate experts in the Huron language. Tribes would also host French traders for an entire winter, offering lodging, food, and sometimes young women. Faced with such a tangled web of commercial and political relations, the colonists sometimes had to make agonizing diplomatic choices to avoid fatal errors. Any item they brought was favored by the native populations for its novelty. Deemed either magicians or demons by tribes competing for their products, the French adventurers were so eager to get furs that they offered firearms, such as the harquebus or the musket, as early as 1609.[8]

ERRANDS IN THE CANADIAN WILDERNESS

A limited number of men was enough to maintain the fur trade and thereby earn substantial profits. All those in power in the colony discouraged newcomers. Between 1608 and 1663, only 1,200 immigrants sailed across the Atlantic to Canada. Champlain and his entourage resolved to send dozens of Frenchmen to winter among the Indians until Quebec was stormed in 1629 by the British, who then occupied New France. On their return the interpreters were well equipped to serve the merchants as mediators with the Indian chiefs. Sometimes those young men incurred the scorn of civil and religious authorities, who deplored their fascination with the wilderness. Jean Manet and Gros Jean de Dieppe spent three winters with the natives, Etienne Brûlé settled among the Hurons for eighteen years.[9] In 1632 Canada and Acadia were returned to France by the Treaty of Saint-Germain-en-Laye when the Compagnie de la Nouvelle France, founded by Cardinal de Richelieu as early as 1627, had more leeway after the English left the territory. In 1642, the French occupied the island of Montreal, whose exceptional site was already known to traders. The outpost was the initial gateway to the west: the Outaouais and its tributaries led to the Great Lakes. The Richelieu river gave access to the Mohawk territories, only fifty miles away from the Dutch trading posts on the Hudson. Before 1660, a thousand settlers and *engagés* [articled servants] under contract landed on the shores of the Saint Lawrence. They received no salary but were allowed to take part in the fur trade.[10]

Meanwhile, New England was attracting far more Europeans than New France. The Dutch were increasingly attentive to the desire for firearms among the Mahicans and Mohawks along the Hudson. To strengthen ties with the native population, Champlain urged the Hurons to convert to Catholicism so the new colonists could marry their daughters and teach them crafts and arts. At first, the missionaries favored integration. The Récollets in 1615, then the Jesuits in 1625, trusted that the pagans would respond to their pleas for conversion.[11] They hoped that the settlements of whole families would deter single young men from seducing Indian girls and vanishing into the wilderness. Yet the ambition of the clergy proved at odds with the interests of discharged soldiers and immigrant bachelors, who were increasingly inclined to winter in the woods, learn Indian languages, and eke out their meager pay by trading furs. In 1645 twenty thousand pelts were stored between Lachine, Trois Rivières, and Quebec by *les hivernants* [the wintering Frenchmen] as they were now called.[12]

The Indians' craving for imported technology made it easier to infiltrate villages. While sharing their daily lives a handful of young daredevils painstakingly gained the Indians' confidence. The raw recruit from Normandy or Poitou experienced culture shock at the sight of painted faces when he first encountered savages. In their canoes on the Saint Lawrence they evoked in his memory the masks used during the Mardi Gras frolics in their native country. Equally striking was the way the Hurons styled their hair: a ponytail attached to one side or a strip of hair on a shaven head. In summer their naked bodies were tanned like the sunburnt French beggars on the Paris streets, and thus exhibited tattooed skin from head to foot.[13] Before shoving off in their canoes the natives looked the French boys up and down to assess their ability to paddle hard. The boatmen sneaked through rapids and freshets, carefully avoiding snags and iceblocks. Long hours were devoted to portage when cascades appeared insuperable. The lack of privacy on board would be a trial for the French guest when the Indians defecated in the very bowl they used for cornmeal. At the Indian camp, a surname was given to the host, in keeping with his appearance or behavior. At times he was invited to the chief's wigwam where he slept overnight in company with the whole family. He was also expected to share his food with visitors who kept delousing themselves during the meal. The warriors loved to brag about their feats while passing their *petunoirs* [pipes] from one mouth to another. If native mores were a far cry from the civilized habits of soldiers and priests, the young men of peasant stock now transplanted to the New World were by no means as inhibited as the bourgeois. Hunger and poverty had encouraged them to leave the old continent. They soon adapted to beaver, bear, porcupine, and ultimately dog meat when nothing else was available. In winter they grew accustomed to eating once every three days, sometimes living exclusively on roots.[14]

The French guests shaved once they knew that bearded men generally suffered opprobrium. In summer they wore just a piece of cloth stretched between their thighs and tied to the front and back by a belt. Their bare bodies were coated with grease to protect them from mosquitoes. In winter they wore long fur *capote* [coats] that often proved inadequate to stave off the severe cold. Indian medicine healed wounds, using a profusion of herbal teas and ointments. The spring sunlight was so intense that the reflection damaged the cornea. Whenever a young Frenchman had an eye sore that threatened to blind him, an Indian woman scraped the cornea with a blade until the infected humor was removed. However, the sweat lodge was the most popular therapy for major ailments among the

French, who huddled together with the natives in a steamroom to cure diseases that might have been fatal in France.[15]

Courage and endurance were requisites for anyone wanting to be integrated into native communities. Otherwise the Indians gibed at the newcomer's lack of strength or resilience when submitted to an ordeal. They were particularly keen on competitions, and cheered winners. Strangers claiming to be fast runners were promptly challenged. When La Vallée wrestled with a Huron and defeated him, the superior skill of the Frenchman was immediately recognized.[16] Resistance to physical pain was also tested by placing red coals under the limbs of two competitors who were eliminated as soon as they withdrew an arm or a leg. The fighting spirit was a major asset in the evaluation of individuals. The Hurons had recognized in Champlain a staunch ally wielding immense power with his gun called *tonnerre* [thunder].[17] Later they regarded missionaries with suspicion when they saw them ignoring weapons. Tribes extended military alliances to commercial relations and denounced treaties when the partner traded with an enemy. For example, Etienne Brûlé had lived for many years with the Hurons when he was captured by Seneca tribesmen after having lost his way. A violent storm broke out just as they were going to put him to death. The interpreter declared that it was divine intervention in his favor. They were so impressed that they celebrated the event and made friends with Brûlé. They also took advantage of this encounter to organize a rapprochement with the French. The Hurons never forgave Brûlé's treason and finally killed him.[18]

Interpreters immersed in native culture were keenly aware that any murder always demanded retribution in Indian society. Conversely, the Hurons themselves knew that ruthless vengeance was at odds with the religious beliefs of the whites. Emery de Caen had been commissioned by Richelieu to reoccupy Quebec in 1632 and, in compensation, offered special privileges to the fur trade. After the assassination of two Frenchmen by Montagnais in the wilderness, he wished to demonstrate his leniency by throwing a sword into a river while solemnly claiming that the crime was shrouded in oblivion just like the weapon now lying in deep water. The Hurons made fun of the way anger had abated among the cowardly whites and estimated that the death of a Frenchman would now cost only a dozen beavers.[19]

The French were possessed of a secret weapon to impose their presence on the tribes. Whether illiterate or qualified for noble tasks, they carried samples of their technical skills. The Hurons called them the "iron people," owing to their use of knives, axes, and boilers. These tools became objects of worship. An Indian woman once proclaimed that the spirit of a broken boiler had returned to the motherland of all boilers.[20]

Some magic power was generally ascribed to the most common tools. Such was also the case with pictures and printed fabrics, which also seemed to convey supernatural meanings. In 1634 Jean Nicolet explored the Lake Superior region on a quest of the Northwest Passage. When he first met the Winnebagos, his robe, made in China and decorated with flowers and birds, gave him so much prestige that he could easily engage in peace negotiations with the tribes south of Lake Michigan.[21]

The French colonists discovered a society given to oral speech, eloquence, and acting. As shown by the early use of interpreters, they felt they would exert immense power over the populations if they had a working knowledge of Indian languages. Jacques Cartier's first move was to kidnap young Indians and force them to learn French, but the method was ineffective. The Indians were able to repeat separate words like *orignal* [moose] or even oaths. But they did not care much about the language of strangers who were so eager to reach out to them.[22]

Living in isolation throughout the winter, Frenchmen were drawn to native communities to practice their own idiom by identifying objects with spoken words. But adequate translation required more than the pronunciation of individual sounds and syllables. A different stress or intonation could alter the meaning of a phrase. Metaphors were so abundant in Indian speech that learners had to be acquainted with native cosmogony, religious beliefs, and spiritual modes of thinking. Jean de Brébeuf, a missionary, spent three years practicing among the Hurons before he was fluent.[23] Sometimes illiterate trappers who had a good ear could pick up words inaccessible to learned priests. Many Frenchmen flaunted their competence as interpreters to be enlisted in the fur trade but few were reliable. As late as 1747, Governor La Galissonnière complained of the lack of qualified interpreters. Uncouth immigrants from the old continent could not expect to be knowledgeable linguists. They would themselves speak regional dialects from Anjou or Touraine, which, interpreted by natives, were incomprehensible to whoever listened to them. Communication with the natives implied a long process of assimilation. Successive generations had to fuse age-old experiences with a new cultural outlook depending on life in the wilderness.[24]

FEUDAL NEW FRANCE

New France was governed from the mother country through the Minister of Marine who was directly responsible to the king, just as if it was a province of France. A governor, usually a naval officer, was appointed by the king, with another official of equal rank, the intendant, to oversee the colony. Both resided in Quebec. The governor's salary amounted to 20,000 livres, the old French monetary unit. This high income was intended to preserve his allegiance.

The intendant was charged with independent jurisdiction over the police, justice, and finances. He might appeal to the minister in case of strong disagreement with the governor. Conversely, he could be dismissed at His Majesty's free will. He received 16,000 livres. In such an autocratic system, conflicts were inevitable between the two officials. In 1746, a controversy occurred over the right to issue orders to the officers of the royal navy, but the most common opposition arose from the intendant's objections to the governor's extravagant expenditures.[25]

A council composed of members drawn from the citizenry, the bishop, attorneys, and the agents for the Company of New France was appointed by the king to assist the governor and the intendant. Then financial crises due to both profligacy and incompetence resulted in the creation of successive companies, the *Compagnie des Cent Associés* [Hundred Associates] in 1632, and later the Company of the Indies. The council registered edicts and ordinances but its chief function was as a court of law. Judges were sent by the intendant to distant settlements where they held court in lieu of the council. Their sentences were based on the *coutume de Paris* [Paris common law] and excluded trial by jury.[26]

Canada had many religious organizations, including two seminaries, one in Quebec supervised by priests of the Missions Etrangères, the other in Montreal under the Sulpicians. There was a Jesuit college in Quebec. The Récollets monks had convents in Quebec, Montreal, and Three Rivers. They spent time among the Indians and served as chaplains with the colonial troops. Their mission was located at the Lake of the Two Mountains by the mouth of the Ottawa River. The order of the Dames de la Congrégation de Notre-Dame devoted their time to teaching and charitable works.[27]

Canada was divided into three districts: Quebec, Montreal, and Three Rivers. The district governor of Montreal stood second to the governor-general at Quebec. Each district had a military commander. Officers were appointed by the king upon recommendations by the governor who was himself under pressure from influential aristocrats interested in the promotion of a family member or a close friend. The colony had a militia organization under the orders of officers commissioned by the governor. The men were poorly equipped and trained. It was not until the eighteenth century that the militia could count on 12,000 men. The supply of muskets was scarce in the decades of penury. To avoid mutinies, the government had to ensure discipline among the military by offering land, tools, and livestock to discharged soldiers so that they would settle in the vicinity of forts. The officers' pay depended on the income of the posts from the fur trade. The man in command of a post generally held the rank of captain. The control of the fur trade was in the hands of the intendant, officers being normally excluded from the trade. Regarding the liquor traffic among the natives, the government considered it could not be banned. Otherwise the Indians would go to trade with the English. Before Bishop Pontbriand came over in 1742, the clergy was often inclined to tolerate the liquor trade, seeking only to keep down abuses.[28]

In the days following English occupation (1629–32) the Compagnie des Cent Associés was entrusted with the management of New France. It was agreed to renew the policy of truchements learning their trade among the tribes. Every summer the furs collected during the preceding winter were delivered to Quebec. Two dozen interpreters contributed to increase the profits considerably. But the Hurons, their privileged partners, were constantly at war with the Iroquois.[29] Meanwhile the crown paid little attention to the colonists, who lived sparingly on small crops but were allowed to get beaver from the natives so long as it was then purchased by the company. At first the Hurons and the Algonquins accepted a handful of nails, a small bottle of liquor, or a piece of bread for a large amount of pelts and furs. Then they raised the price by demanding an axe or a blanket. It was the lack of currency that hampered the growth of trades. The French would trade a boiler for beaver when they could afford to buy imported manufactured products. The employees of the company were not paid in cash but received the equivalent in utensils, tools, or arms, which cost 50 percent more than in France.[30]

Inequality prevailed in the social structure of New France, still submissive to hierarchies inherited from the Middle Ages. The immigrant population was dominated by a few noblemen, missionaries and wealthy merchants who had easy access to Indian communities through selected truchements. The most adventurous individuals left the villages to take a chance incognito far in the woods. Travelers observed in their accounts that the Oneida Indians wore shirts as early as 1634. The call of the Canadian forest alarmed the Jesuits, whose mission was to evangelize the natives. They blamed young Christians for living with savages, thus forsaking their faith and preventing the conversion of pagans. Indians were baffled by the attitudes of men in black robes who carried no weapons, refused women, and told incomprehensible stories. Colonial authorities answered that their priests were shamans invested with a superior power to fight enemies. The Récollets friars openly accused traders of discrediting their mission in order to control Indian minds. They also questioned the competence of interpreters who allegedly distorted the contents of sermons to entertain their hosts.[31]

After 1632 Richelieu supported the Company of Jesus (Jesuits) who now were substituted for the Récollets. The Jesuits had dreams of a New Jerusalem immune to corruption and violence. Their strategy sought to regain the confidence of the interpreters in the hope of being initiated into native culture. Not only did the latter resent such intrusion into their domain, but the Indians themselves distrusted the "black robes."

By the mid-seventeenth century the independent *coureur des bois* [woodrunner] who traded furs on his own account enjoyed a privileged status in the tribes, whereas the missionary remained a mysterious outsider. Amid the wilderness, the French were guilty of all the evil pursuits castigated by the Jesuits. Isolation in the woods was for them conducive to debauchery and atheism. The fur trade was gradually proving incompatible with evangelization, especially when the woodrunners supplied Indians with alcoholic beverages to curry favor with them.

To complete the replica of the autocratic system of New France an order of nobility was created by Richelieu in the charter of the Hundred Associates. To convince members of the lesser nobility to remain in the New World, feudal rights were granted them in *seigneuries* [seigniories] on the Saint Lawrence riverfronts. This way of apportioning land was apparently intended to avoid the evils of speculation. The tenants lived at the back of the demesne in houses on the outskirts of the forest. Extending over ten acres, their fields sloped down to the bank with a frontage of four acres. Huddled together in embattled villages along the river the settlers thus managed to retain a sense of community. Seigneurs were responsible for bringing new settlers at their own expense to clear the land. They paid low rent, about ten percent of their income. The tenant was expected to pay a rent to the seigneur and render him feudal dues, including fees on the gristmill. Within thirty years seventy-four seigneuries cropped up along the Saint Lawrence but the government had no plan to extend the system westward to areas scantily settled. The seigneurs initially had judicial power, but after 1693 they no longer had the right to hold courts of law on their domains.[32]

This colonial squirearchy was doomed to failure because the seigneurs were mere agents of the crown. They could not fully rely on their tenants and had to till the fields themselves. Some of them took to fur trading for a living. Settlers were thus shackled by legal restrictions and subject to the hegemony of influential aristocrats and merchants linked to the company.

The clergy had considerable rights under the ancien régime. The Jesuits were given free rein to hire engagés, bound to stay three years in New France before they might be manumitted. Land grants were distributed to encourage farming, but the Jesuits themselves were lured by the fur trade, which led them to use their own truchements to connect evangelization with the collection of pelts. In 1648, five fathers, one friar, three youngsters, nine workers, and eight soldiers boarded sixty Huron canoes on the Ottawa river to build the outpost of Sainte Marie in the wilderness.[33] The Jesuits' efficient network of relations in New France determined the career of Pierre Boucher, who stayed with the Hurons from the age of fourteen as an engagé. He was promoted to the rank of official interpreter in 1641 at Trois Rivières. The company offered him a demesne at Gros Bois where he was also appointed local judge. As governor of the city in 1663 he received his letters patent of nobility. He crowned his fabulous experience with a book on the history of New France published in Paris in 1664.[34] Charles Le Moyne first served the Jesuits at the age of fifteen in 1641. After living among the Indians, he was an interpreter at the village of Montreal in 1646 when the Iroquois tried to storm the local storehouses. In partnership with a wealthy trader, Jacques Le Ber (his brother-in-law), Le Moyne sold furs in association with the Jesuits and the Sulpicians. After receiving the demesne of Longueuil he was conferred a title of nobility in 1668.[35] Charles Lemoyne de Longueuil et de Chateaugay (1626–85), had twelve sons. Three of them, Charles, Pierre, and Jean-Baptiste, became prominent figures.

CANADA: THE STORM CENTER OF INDIAN WARS

Until 1641 the few French soldiers dispatched by the crown to protect the colonists could easily keep at bay small bands of hostile Indians who were occasionally shooting their stone-pointed arrows. But the capture of two interpreters, François Marguerie and

Thomas Godefroy, later became a matter of serious concern. The Jesuits resolved to call for the protection of an army unit at Sainte Marie during the winter of 1644. Left idle when skirmishes ceased, the impecunious soldiers acquainted themselves with the native population despite the reluctance of the Jesuits. A year later they sold four thousand pelts obtained from the Hurons. Yet under the pressure of the Iroquois the latter were eventually forced to end their commercial contacts with the French on the Saint Lawrence.[36]

After the Hurons had vanished from the settlements for fear of reprisals by their hereditary enemies, the governor tried hard to maintain a small garrison. Not only did he close his eyes to smuggled pelts but soldiers were allotted acres of land to cultivate, and in the long run could build farmhouses. Whatever incentives were used to avoid desertions and encourage agriculture, half a century after the landing of the first colonists the fur trade was still the only means by which the common man could achieve social success.

The Iroquois resented the privileges granted by the French to the Hurons and Algonquins. In 1639 they were provided with muskets by Flemish settlers to frighten the Hurons away from the paths to Trois Rivières. Priests were murdered during the siege of Ville Marie in 1642. The resistance of the Hurons was hampered when villages were decimated by smallpox, typhus, and cholera. Shamans who tried to apply their rituals to the cure of diseases were arraigned by the Jesuits. When the natives realized that the black robes as well as the woodrunners seemed invulnerable to contagion, they stood in awe of the alleged magic protecting the intruders. Meanwhile, Governor Charles Huault de Montmagny published an ordinance dated July 9, 1644, banning the sale of firearms to savages, whether Christian or not, thus adding to the despair of the allies of France. In the tradition of French nobility Montmagny could not refrain from doing a beau geste and at the same time weakened the defenses of New France when he symbolically made the gift of an harquebus to a Huron convert.[37] The Jesuits vindicated such liberality by suggesting that the Lord was not averse to arming new Christians to spread the faith among heathens.

In the summer of 1638, the Hurons took a hundred Iroquois prisoners to Teanaustaye, below a range of hills near the southern borders of their territory. Many of the captives were brought to the seat of the new Jesuit mission of Saint Joseph, and put to death with frightful tortures, though not before several had been converted and baptized. Despite the remonstrances of the priests, the torture was followed by cannibal feasts customary with the Hurons and the Iroquois to celebrate victories. Once, when the priests objected to such practices a cooked, severed hand was flung in at their door as an invitation to join in the festivity. As the owner of the severed member had been baptized, the Jesuits dug a hole in their chapel, and buried it with solemn rites of sepulture.

A new phase in the onslaught on the Huron nation began in 1648, lasting until 1653. Two Jesuit missionaries, Jean de Brébeuf and Gabriel Lalemant, were burnt alive by the Iroquois in 1649. Their torturers expected them to sing the ritual song of death, but instead they preached to the infidels to try to convert them. When the Indians heard them speak about baptism, they poured a kettle full of boiling water over their bodies to parody the sacrament. The hearts of the Jesuits were then roasted and eaten.

Father Isaac Jogues, who served as emissary to negotiate with the Iroquois, was also murdered. Governor Louis D'Ailleboust, who had taken over from Montmagny, was also left powerless against the havoc wreaked by the enemy. Thousands of Hurons were killed or kept in slavery to compensate for losses in Iroquois villages.[38]

The growing demands for furs had long spurred northern Europeans to open new markets. Each country had struck alliances with selected tribes. The Dutch preferred the Mahicans to the Mohawks when founding Fort Amsterdam in 1625. They produced woollen blankets and also manufactured eye-catching, though cheap wampums with Venetian glass. The young *bosch-lopers* [wood-walkers] from the Netherlands soon infiltrated the shores of the Hudson and met with the hostility from the Iroquois. The rivalry between Indian nations was exacerbated by the resulting scarcity of beaver in the Saint Lawrence Valley and around Lake Ontario. The Mohawks traded with all those who supplied them with firearms, and therefore the Dutch gave them heavy loads of rifles. As shown in Montmagny's ordinance, whenever the French appeared reluctant to comply with similar demands from the Hurons, they jeopardized their security. The rifle was an invaluable asset for the Indians despite having to resort to a blacksmith's shop for repairs. The usual scarcity of powder and bullets was also a problem. Originally intended for European battlefields, such arms often jammed in the cold season. Towards the end of the seventeenth century, hunting rifles imported from a workshop in Tulle, central France, were more weatherproof. Though excellent marksmen, the Hurons did not always take care to keep such weapons in good condition. At least the tonnerre, as the natives called it, enabled its possessor to show off his power. Warriors were actually more prone to torture and enslave their enemies than to kill them. The Iroquois remained true to their rituals and retained a sense of coherence, whereas the Hurons were weakened by the influence of the missionaries and partially forsook their ancestral beliefs. They were set apart from the pagans who demanded an eye for an eye.[39]

In 1650, six hundred Hurons sought refuge in Quebec while other survivors went west. The following decades were a long story of agonizing reappraisals. Blockades and skirmishes involved conflicting Iroquois tribes sometimes tempted them into an alliance with the French, or to be faithful to their Dutch allies. Familiar as they were with the intricacies of European politics, the representatives of the French crown at first dealt awkwardly with Iroquois chiefs who had little in common with European aristocrats. When violence erupted the embattled settlers were horrified at the atrocities committed on captives. In 1657, Governor Louis d'Ailleboust jailed all the Oneida Indians present at Quebec after the murder of three Frenchmen.[40] When Louis XIV was informed of mounting perils in Canada, he announced that he could not let a band of savages bring disgrace to the country. A regiment of a thousand men under the command of Carignan-Salières landed in 1665 and laid waste Iroquois villages. Peace was then established for a decade. During this same decade tribes migrated in great number to the Great Lakes. Indians were forced gradually to recognize European domination. The fur trade, linked to the alliance with the weakened Hurons, did not emerge unscathed from years of conflicts. Yet it remained the cornerstone of the New France economy. Therefore new modes had to be found to perpetuate the cult of "brown gold."[41]

The Early *Coureurs des Bois*

In a report to the comte de Pontchartrain, Antoine Raudot, intendant of the colonies in charge of New France was severe in his judgment concerning a century of French presence along the Saint Lawrence.[42] To explain economic stagnation, he put the blame on the colonists who deserted their fields for a life of adventure in the woods. Missionaries, travelers, and officers denounced the fur fever as a scourge afflicting populations of young aristocrats, poor immigrants, outcasts, and deserters. The maverick coureurs des bois, those woodrunners scattered throughout the Canadian forests, numbered in the hundreds. They seemed to have developed a sense of ubiquity as they could be found up to two thousand miles from Quebec, sneaking into tribal lands, expecting natives to barter their beaver for tools, arms, and trinkets. Disillusioned sons of peasants found an outlet in the West and gladly left a colony that was floundering in corruption and negligence. The movement was amplified with a new flow of immigrants between 1650 and 1670. However, the two thousand Frenchmen who then reached the shores of Canada were by no means comparable in number to the crowds of British settlers who had been crossing the Atlantic to New England since 1620. In 1628, Richelieu had closed the overseas territories to the Huguenots, who constituted an intellectual elite.[43] Most of the newcomers were from the French maritime provinces of Normandy and Anjou, where poverty and religious persecution had triggered revolts and deportations. Orphans, derelicts, and renegades, mostly underage, were hired by the clergy as engagés and their passage to America was paid. Illiterate and destitute, they hoped to make a living as carpenters or masons.[44] In 1665 four hundred men discharged from Carignan-Salières' regiment were persuaded to stay on as farmers by their officers upon the order of Minister Louvois. In French folk tales pioneers were transmuted into adventurers living off the fat of the land.

Another source of immigration was the transportation of beggars, convicts, and rebels as early as 1626. Judges often sentenced thieves to spend their lives in exile as a way to get rid of the most subversive part of the rabble. Repentant highwaymen, poachers, smugglers, and delinquent salt traders were pressed to enlist in the colonial army, as well as young libertine noblemen like François de Bouchel d'Orcival from Auvergne. In 1709, lost children were gathered in Paris and hired as engagés by the colony. The transportation of tramps to Canada sometimes aroused protest among the clergy. To ward off the perils of contagious depravity in the New World, local authorities would send convicts into exile with their families.[45]

In 1663, three thousand Canadians were living on the banks of the Saint Lawrence, stretching out over a distance of three hundred miles. Generally men were three times more numerous than women. In the fifteen- to twenty-nine-year-old age group, the population was overwhelmingly male. One third of the inhabitants were born in the colony, and only a third of them were able to find a regular occupation. Whether servants or day laborers, they would rarely keep away from the fur trade.

Whenever promoting colonization in the seventeenth century the French monarchy was faced with a dilemma. New France needed innovative methods to populate a terra incognita. On the other hand, settlements had to be organized to safeguard stability and social peace. The policy consisted of extending feudal structures by offering land to the Church and nobility. Each privileged owner thus divided his lots for tenants to clear the forests, grow crops and pay their dues. The Canadian *seigneur* levied taxes for his benefit. He also administered justice until 1693. However, too few Frenchmen responded to the propaganda of prospective empire builders. Pioneers remained constantly in want of farmhands as long as the chance of success was dim for uprooted peasants. Not only did the harsh climate and the stubborn soil of the Saint Lawrence Valley have little appeal, but isolation and Indian attacks soon resulted in discontent and desertion. Many French settlers escaped in canoes from the settlements of the Saint Lawrence and boarded fishing ships. Law enforcement proved ineffective in communities where rampant unrest prevailed. Former vagrants, unwittingly drafted from the ranks of immigrants as engagés, openly resented a status that implied long-term servitude. It took some time to realize that aristocratic standards could not be applied to an inchoate society whose members shared the dream of material success.[46]

Outside Trois Rivières, Quebec, and Montreal the region was dotted with sparse houses on the riverfront. Immense stretches of wilderness expanded beyond domains harboring only twoscore of inhabitants. It is no wonder that the roots of the woodrunner's staunch individualism may be traced to the call of the wild felt by young men who had little to lose by remaining in the service of a squire. Although confrontation with the unknown might seem terrifying to colonists awed by the threatening presence of devils, the runaways were prompted by their instinctive quest for freedom. Wild beasts, savage men, and possibly supernatural monsters did not repel them as much as the Jesuits and the wealthy landowners did. Many of the most sedate colonists were frozen with terror when remembering the witch trial in 1634 of the so-called possessed Ursuline nuns in the convent of Loudun, a small town in western France.[47] But youngsters had no intention of enlightening darkness or ordering chaos. The wilderness could be the antipode of Eden but the fugitives were prepared to face those creatures that in New England, Cotton Mather called droves of devils, dragons, and fiery flying serpents.[48] French adventurers gladly turned away from the hope of meeting smug angels in heaven. Strictness of conscience seemed to stop at the edge of the clearing as the veneer of civilization laid over the barbaric elements in the individual became thinner and thinner. In *Letters from an American Farmer* published in 1782, St. John Crèvecoeur still considered that backwoodsmen shared in the wildness of the environment and had long degenerated into primitive huntsmen.[49] In the seventeenth century the New England pioneer often tended to imagine that the wilderness was a wasteland to be overcome, otherwise a threshold that he had to cross over before reaching the Promised Land. In New France, there was no communitarian spirit to organize such tasks. Fierce and independent, averse to religious or civil authorities, the woodrunner transmuted his rebellious attitude into a hazardous enterprise of freedom, while merging the idea of self-achievement with a flight from social constraints.

2

New France Goes West

The Fur Eldorado

THE EXPANSION OF THE FUR TRADE HAD BROUGHT A FORTUNE TO THE Compagnie des Cent Associés, which ceded its rights to the Communauté des Habitants de la Nouvelle France in 1645. The oligarchy of colonial merchants preserved a monopoly that first banned competition from individuals, while arguing that profits were shared by all in the Canadian colony. Frustrated Frenchmen were scouted by the Dutch traders at Fort Orange, and their skills enabled them to smuggle thousands of pelts out of the Huron territory. But the fur trade suffered from slackening activity among Indians who had earlier sacrificed fishing and fruit picking for beaver trapping. Short of supplies in the cold months, they flocked round the military posts where they relied on colonial support. In 1648, Governor Louis d'Ailleboust appealed for volunteers to explore new regions to expand the trade and protect the Hurons. He resorted to seasoned trappers who until then had been engaged in smuggling pelts into the Dutch colony. He also allowed them to trade partly for their own benefit. Those legal independent traders were called *voyageurs* in New France and peddlers in the English colonies. In the fall of 1649, thirty-four woodrunners, guided by two Hurons, returned with 26,000 pelts. Meanwhile the standing regulations allowed 5,000 pelts to be sold independently in Quebec.[1] With the opening of the Northwest, the restrictions were lifted on the fur trade in 1656. Its spectacular expansion now reached west of the Great Lakes. According to Radisson's accounts, for a long time it had been rumored in the Cree tribes that the French were sad, arrogant beings, sometimes with a tail or a single mammal, and prone to eating thunder.[2] Yet contacts multiplied by the mid-seventeenth century. East of the Great Lakes the Ottawa Indians welcomed the woodrunners around the strait of Michilimakinac between Lake Huron and Lake Michigan.[3] They had long been trading furs for shells from the Atlantic coast with the Ojibwa and Potawatomi Indians. The latter were experts at building bark canoes, which were invaluable on lakes.

The way west was less exposed than the area of Lake Ontario to the raids of the Iroquois. In 1653, three canoes came back from Lake Superior to Trois Rivières with hundreds of pelts. Thousands were delivered until the end of the decade. The boundless expanse of western woodlands was then known as Le Pays d'en Haut.

The fur Eldorado attracted numbers of habitants—those residents who had received exclusive rights to trade. Zacharie Dupuy was given a license in 1656 by Jean de Lauzon, director of the Compagnie des Cent Associés, to exploit the Lake Nipigon region and beyond. Pierre-Esprit Radisson and his brother-in-law Médard Chouart, Sieur des Groseilliers, returned the same year from the West with a bonanza load of furs.[4] In 1659 they went round Lake Superior, up to Northern Minnesota, wintered toward Prairie du Chien and came into contact with the Mascouten, Winnebago, and Dakota tribes. Back in Montreal they signed a contract with Charles Lemoyne, another explorer, and hired ambitious young men eager to succeed in the West. But as engagés they did not hold the status of inhabitants and were banned from the fur trade. Consequently, a new class of outcasts turned away from this employment to engage in unlawful practices. By hook or by crook they wanted pelts. Sometimes they could tempt the military. In April 1660, a group led by Dollard des Ormeaux, commander of the fort at Quebec, asked permission from the governor to ambush Iroquois bands with sixteen young men from Ville Marie. He had it in mind to rob their beaver. Like everyone preparing for war or the wilderness, the group first went to church, confessed their sins to the priest, and received Communion. They reached Long Sault on the Ottawa river, where they planned to attack the Iroquois canoes. Dollard was not aware that there would be five hundred Indians against them. Besieged in a dilapidated fort where they had found refuge, most of the Frenchmen were killed or horribly tortured. The governor turned the disaster into a gallant exploit by self-sacrificing brave young combatants.[5] Nine years later four coureurs des bois reveled one night with Iroquois, then murdered a family in the tribe to seize their pelts.[6]

In the long run many realized that violence was self-defeating. The most successful of the freelance traders had their connections in villages in the backwoods where they waited for the returning canoes and paid for their contents with goods bought on credit. They transported the furs on rivers, sometimes over rapids, to deliver them to a *bourgeois* [licensed merchant]. As the woodrunner needed to buy articles to trade, he received an advance from the trader who protected himself with a contract drawn up by a notary. The coureur des bois left in the spring, wintered among the Indians, and returned the following year. The articles to barter were bought at a higher rate—almost a third more than in France. In addition, the trader's profits included the interests on the loan. Altogether the woodrunner earned twice as much as a laborer in Quebec. However, the work involved many risks: wounds, failing health, and violent death. The trader also manned several expeditions to be on the safe side. The biggest profits were made by the French wholesalers in La Rochelle or Paris, where prices were constantly on the rise. Costs were noticeably reduced when the fur trade reached the Great Lakes in Le Pays d'en Haut. Cheap articles were offered to tribes still unaware of market prices. At first they rated very highly glass beads, half a pint of brandy, and a pouch of tobacco. When less naive they would claim hoes, kettles, and guns. A half-drunk Indian would more easily part with his furs.[7]

Other elements contributed to facilitate transactions. The woodrunner now sang, danced, and fought the Indian way. At the year's end, this *mangeur de lard* [pork eater] was given loads of collected furs to convoy from lake warehouses to Quebec or Montreal. Returning winterers either saved or squandered their income. When they were running out of cash, they sold their embroidery, their lace, and even their clothes, before restarting the cycle again and rushing back to their expectant paramours waiting in a tribal haven.[8]

Now recognized as the backbone of New France economy, the beaver trade was taken over in May 1664 by the *Compagnie des Indes Occidentales* to ward off a crisis that was aggravated by the low price set on pelts by La Rochelle wholesalers.[9] The company's territory extended from Canada to the West Indies, the Amazon, and Africa. It was a private concern enjoying the full use of the lands granted by charter. Apart from exerting administrative and judicial powers, the company had to cover the expenses of the missions. Louis XIV was shrewd enough not to mention the number of immigrants to be admitted every year. This absolute monarchy was concerned protecting the vested economic interests and aristocratic privileges against the rabble, whether in France or Canada. But how could Versailles wield power over the remote Pays d'en Haut?

The achievement of the new organization turned out to be disappointing. Profits became thinner as Indians were becoming wiser. When expectations were great in the fur trade, nobles and peasants alike had engaged in the business. At least a third of the New France population was then seeking profits in peltries. Yet until 1663 colonization on the new continent had been in the hands of aristocrats

without any strict control. The political context had become so perilous that the king himself gave closer attention to ongoing changes.
A new troubled era thus opened in the last quarter of the seventeenth century with the shortage of fur supplies east of the Alleghenies. The British pushed forward to the north where the Iroquois
were occupying the Mohawk Valley, thereby playing a significant
role in the fight for the western trade. They had a long history of
rivalry with the Hurons and hatred for the French. The founding
of the Hudson's Bay Company in 1670, headed by Prince Rupert,
benefited from a grant from the English crown to trade in the regions draining into the Hudson Bay. This severe blow to French interests ignited a succession of conflicts. Intendant Jean Talon of New
France, appointed in 1665, had a shock when he heard that the British company had appropriated the Great Lakes' shores, painstakingly explored earlier by Radisson and Groseilliers. Louis XIV could
not let perfidious Albion infest the Pays d'en Haut without reacting
promptly. In 1674, he awarded the privilege of the beaver trade to a
group of financiers headed by Jean Oudiette, who had already mo-
nopolized the slave trade in Senegal.[10] In exchange for taxes on imports, the new firm was required to accept all pelts at a price
between £four and six. Traders could have expected more but they
were satisfied with this new permanent outlet that protected them
against price fluctuations. At last the king had openly taken part in
the destiny of New France to gratify his imperial aims. After missionaries and soldiers, he sent ministers and councillors to strengthen
the colony. Fur trading was now considered subsidiary to a prospective agrarian economy that also aimed at supplying raw materials to
the mother country, as well as providing both progress and har-
mony.

   In 1675 the mythical northwest passage to China was still to be
mapped out. In New France copper mines were by no means tantamount to goldfields. Yet three thousand immigrants had landed on
Canadian shores and the presence of innumerable officials testified
to the growing interest in a French empire across the Atlantic. To
vindicate their function and seek promotion, governors and intendants, who sometimes held their offices for ten years, encouraged
the agents of the crown to draft glowing reports on the state of affairs. It was a time for adventure and discovery. Jean Talon acknowledged that several explorers had followed in the steps of Radisson
toward Lake Superior.[11] In 1663 Adrien Joliet, the Jesuit Jacques Ménard, and two woodrunners, Antoine Trottier and Ponterel de Belle-
court, returned with thirty-five canoes filled with pelts after circling
the lake. Their ranks were augmented in 1665 by Nicolas Perrot and

Toussaint Baudry, who enjoyed friendly relations with the Potawatomi Indians. Exploration that included a cleric usually gained credibility. In 1665, Father Allouez accompanied six coureurs des bois in the Pays d'en Haut. In 1670, with the agreement of Jean Talon, Cavelier de la Salle left with twelve men to find a passage to the Vermillion and China, not excluding the possibility of exploring new beaver haunts.[12] Woodrunners were hired for their skills, but Talon and Frontenac often held in suspicion rovers who headed for Lake Superior.[13] The mirage of gold persisted for Louis Jolliet and Jacques Marquette, whose inroads into remote areas depended on experienced guides, lawless though they might appear.[14]

Comte Louis de Buade de Frontenac became governor of New France in 1672, three years before Talon returned to France after achieving the most ambitious expansionist policy that Louis XIV could have envisioned. Father Charles Albanel reached Hudson Bay in 1671, Simon-François Daumont de Saint-Lusson gathered fourteen Indian nations at Sault Sainte Marie in June 1671 to have them swear allegiance to the King of France.[15] Frontenac was megalomanical and intractable. Louis XIV had been glad to send him away from Versailles. The new governor was a quasi-despot until the king appointed Jacques Duchesneau intendant to succeed to Talon in 1675.

The settlement policy was slackening. A total of 4,000 colonists had left Canada since 1659. Fortunately, the birthrate remained high so that the population grew from 6,700 in 1672 to 10,000 in 1682. In Paris Minister Colbert ordered Frontenac to limit expenses drastically. The latter determined that the only way out of a slumping economy was through the fur trade. Most officials in Quebec complained of his arrogance. But on his side he had such trailblazers as Cavelier de la Salle, Henri Chevalier de Tonty, and Daniel Greysolon Dulhut. Pragmatic, Frontenac was permissive about the liquor trade with Indians, thus antagonizing the Jesuits. He replied that the priests fulfilled fake missions since they were more interested in capturing beaver than souls. In the meantime, without Colbert's agreement, Frontenac had a fort built on Lake Ontario to control the fur trade. Expansionism also had its side effects: Pierre Le Sueur, with the help of twenty-five men, had been commissioned by the king to find goldmines in Sioux territories, but he brought back buffalo robes and beaver furs. Due to lack of the precious metal, peltries were indeed a good return on investment.[16]

WEST BY SOUTHWEST

Cavelier de la Salle and Louis Jolliet could not afford to discriminate between volunteers when they set out on their long treks down the Mississippi. This voyage of discovery was expected to lead to southern shores through regions abundant in flora and fauna. In the spring of 1673, Jolliet and Marquette, who spoke several Indian languages, left Fort Michilimackinac. They were escorted by Pierre Moreau, *la taupe* [the mole], Jacques Largillier, *le castor* [the beaver], and Jean Rouxel, an elk hunter with a dubious reputation. The expedition sailed across Lake Michigan then on to the Wisconsin River aided by two Mascouten guides until they reached the Mississippi. On their way southward they passed the Missouri and the Ohio Rivers before they encountered hostile natives and threatening Spaniards. After reaching the mouth of the Arkansas in the summer. Jolliet and Marquette decided to return to Lake Michigan.[17]

In 1678, Cavelier de la Salle was granted permission to follow Jolliet's route to reach the Gulf of Mexico. Michel Accault, who spoke the Illinois language, and Guillaume Couture acted as his interpreters. In the spring of 1679, La Salle sent a party of sixteen men including Father Louis Hennepin, a Récollet priest, to the Sault de Conty, now Niagara Falls. Going beyond their former destination they met the Senecas who belonged to the Iroquois nation, and were trading partners of the Dutch and the English. The move was wise but unrewarding until La Salle himself arrived from Fort Frontenac. A shrewd observer of Indian manners, he was allowed to construct a stockade. While a boat, *Le Griffon* [griffin], was under construction to sail on the Great Lakes, a party went down the Wisconsin, then on to the Mississippi. Two hundred miles south, they stopped in the *Pays des Illinois* [Illinois Indian country] to set up winter quarters. Beset by financial difficulties, La Salle's remaining group then boarded the vessel bound for Michilimackinac in August. They reached the western outpost, which housed a Jesuit mission and a few cabins where French traders lived with Indian women. La Salle found that many members of the advance party had deserted. Some were put under arrest, others had already been hired by traders hostile to the arrival of intruders. With those that had remained faithful, he collected a huge load of furs at a French Indian village on Potawatomi Island, now Rock Island, and sent them to Sault de Conty. La Salle carried on with his journey west on Lake Michigan by canoes. At the mouth of the Saint Joseph River he had a large log cabin built, which he called Fort des Miamis. In the winter, La Salle left his men behind to explore the area, still hoping to find a route to the Gulf of Mexico. La Salle's only guide in his search for a portage was a Mohegan hunter. Later when he set out with his small party, he ignored the dangers lurking in the wilderness, believing that thirty men would ensure respect and fear from hundreds of warriors. On January 1,1680, La Salle reached a deserted village of four hundred cabins where his men took some of the corn stored in caches. His hunters had killed only two buffaloes in two weeks and all were starving. A few days later, the expedition emerged on a broad stretch of the Illinois River known as Peoria Lake. His men soon made friends with fearful Illinois Indians who had mistaken them for Iroquois. As a gesture of disapproval of La Salle's expedition, Father Allouez, who served at the mission of the Immaculate Conception, had left only a few days before their arrival. La Salle explained to the Illinois that he was intending to build a fort and also a large canoe to paddle down the river. Peoria Lake, which was the center of the Pays des Illinois, opened on to the prairies and offered a network of waterways. Within a few weeks Fort Crèvecoeur became habitable.[18] The day before the hull of a new boat was finished in February, La Salle sent a small group to meet the Upper Missouri Sioux, risking antagonizing the Michilimackinac traders now operating in the area, should commercial links be established. Michel Accault led a party of four, including Father Hennepin, in a heavily loaded canoe.[19] In the early spring, after meeting the friendly Illinois at their camp close to the Tamaroa on the Mississippi, south of the mouth of the Illinois River, they were captured on April 11 by the Sioux and saved three months later by the legendary explorer Greysolon Dulhut. Meanwhile, La Salle's hopes of sailing down the Mississippi were shattered by the desertion of half a dozen men. Realizing that he could not both keep the fort and arm a boat to sail south, on March 10 he left the place under Tonty's command and decided to return with four men to Fort Frontenac, 1,500 miles away. The prospects were gloomy for the French voyageurs forced to accept poor living conditions for a long period of time at Fort Crèvecoeur. On La Salle's request, Tonty had set out with five men, including two Récollet priests, to examine a site on a rocky promontory overlooking the Illinois River. When they came back, they realized that the remaining members of the group had deserted with tools, leaving a message scribbled on the side of a boat stranded near Fort Crèvecoeur, claiming "We are all savages."[20]

As the renegades were on their way back to Canada, after passing Lake Erie, most of them were met up by La Salle. He had been forewarned by Tonty, and later two deserters were killed in a firefight. The most rebellious of them Moyse Hilaret, a carpenter, voiced the general discontent of Frenchmen who had not been able to live up to the dreams of conquest that aristocrats had wished to instill in them. In September 1680, there were only five men around Tonty in Illinois, fighting to withstand the onslaught of Iroquois warriors trying to establish a foothold in a fur-rich region, and therefore making it impossible for the French to move south of Michilimackinac. The Illinois could arm only about a hundred men with muskets and four hundred with bows and arrows against five hundred well-equipped Iroquois braves. In a bold attempt, Tonty went up to their chief to parley. While hinting that French troops were gathered across the river, he also offered gifts as symbols of goodwill. At least the truce slowed down the Iroquois, who remained on the east bank of the Illinois. Having avoided bloodshed Tonty and his party decided to retreat to Michilimackinac in a canoe. Meanwhile the local tribes fled from the Iroquois to the west bank of the Mississippi. The rashness of the Illinois cost them heavy casualties. Four hundred women and children were burnt slowly on roasting pits and an equal number later were held in slavery.[21] On his way back, Tonty lost Father de la Ribourde, who never reappeared after a stroll to read his breviary.[22] The group suffered incredible hardships after their canoe failed them. Walking through the woods in the snow, they lived on roots and even had to melt a pewter cup to make balls for their guns. They reached Michilimackinac in early June 1681 where they finally met La Salle who told them the whole story about the rescue parties sent to meet them in the winter. He had missed Tonty on his way down the waterways, not expecting him to travel on land. Reaching Fort Crèvecoeur on December 4, he had found the place laid waste by the Iroquois. There only remained heads and bodies of women and children scattered among ashes, which convinced them that Tonty had escaped before the attack. By January 1681, La Salle was back at the Saint Joseph River fort. By no means discouraged, he planned another journey of discovery after returning to Fort Frontenac and Montreal to raise funds. Earlier he had been encouraged by the Miamis' agonizing reappraisal of their policies towards the French. Bands of Kaskaskia warriors had dealt severe blows to the Iroquois who were going back north after their raids. The Miamis now felt invigorated by the impetus of their neighbors and realized that it was time to cast their lot with La Salle.

The new expedition led by La Salle in the fall of 1681 numbered twenty-three Frenchmen, and thirty Mahican and Abenaki Indians, including some families picked out among migrants from New England earlier removed from their villages by pioneers. They had then settled along the Miami river with the local tribes. First of all, most of the route was on the frozen waters of the Chicago, Des Plaines, and Illinois Rivers. They went through the Illinois country in January 1682 via Fort Crèvecoeur. In February they reached the Mississippi where sailing was hazardous amidst drifting iceblocks. La

Salle renamed the river Fleuve Colbert to honor Louis XIV's powerful finance minister. Downstream weather conditions improved as
spring approached. Game was plentiful and Indians along the
banks, though sometimes hostile, maintained a wary distance. In
April the French canoes were finding their way to the ocean through
the bayous. Now it was time for La Salle to deliver a speech in which
he claimed for France the land extending to the Gulf of Mexico. He
named it Louisiana to celebrate the King of France, under the auspices of Jacques de la Métairie, the royal representative who had
taken part in the expedition. Ironically, neither La Salle nor France
ever realized the extent of the empire they had appropriated.[23] The
men of the expedition learned to live on oysters, crayfish, and alliga-
tors' flesh. Paddling upstream was strenuous when they headed back
north. They now faced aggressive tribes and a sultry climate. In June,
La Salle was so sick that he asked Tonty to go ahead while he spent
part of the summer at Fort Prudhomme at the Chickasaw Bluffs, in
a cabin they had built on their way south. When he had recovered it
took him a month to reach the site of Fort Crèvecoeur, then Fort
Miami in September before meeting Tonty at Michilimackinac. La
Salle was aware of a change of mood regarding political orientations
in New France. He was eager to claim recognition for planting the
flag with the fleur-de-lys on the territory of Louisiana, thereby
annexing the central part of North America. To reassure French investors it was vital to control the navigation on the Mississippi, especially as ships from France were now expected to make directly for
the Gulf of Mexico. Almost midway between the sea and Michilimackinac, the colony of Illinois had to be used as a stronghold
against the Iroquois, and as an area to store the furs of the western
tribes. Anchored in the Mississippi Valley, Fort Crèvecoeur was re-
built to serve as one of the numerous outposts to control navigation
down to the mouth of the river. But the location appeared too vulnerable to Iroquois attacks. La Salle had Fort Saint Louis built on a
rock—Le Rocher—a few dozen miles up north. La Salle and Tonty
spent the winter of 1682–83 there in the company of hundreds of
Indians in camps around the palisades. The rock towered 125 feet
above the ground. Within several years the Indian population grew
to 20,000 residents. La Salle thus demonstrated his ability to rally
natives and later attract French colonists. Saint Louis became the
first permanent French fort in the upper South.[24] Angered by La
Salle's omnipresence on the colonial scene, Joseph Antoine Le Feb-
vre de La Barre, the governor of New France who had just taken
over from Frontenac, was instrumental in hindering the explorer's
interests. Backed by Duluth, a young officer and nobleman named

Louis Henri de Baugy was commissioned to recall La Salle. So far the seigneur of Illinois had parsimoniously given out authorizations to trade on his domain, but La Barre encouraged legions of voyageurs to descend the Illinois and Kankakee Rivers. Most of them had never been south of Michilimackinac. Sixty men comprised the entire population of Illinois in early 1683, including twenty soldiers under Tonty's orders. Within months convoys of canoes brought six hundred voyageurs equivalent to half the population of traders in the back country of Canada. Most of the canoes belonged to syndicates of investors. The majority of them were to return to Michilimackinac and Montreal while the rivers were still navigable. Some of the voyageurs would remain and later go further down the Mississippi, take squaws, live in cabins near Indian dwellings, and have numerous offspring.[25]

From Louisiana, Governor de Lamothe Cadillac sent Pierre Le Sueur, a cousin of D'Iberville's, west of the Mississippi. Born in Canada, he had accompanied Nicolas Perrot to the *Baie des Puants* [Greenbay] on Lake Michigan, served the then commander of the Pays d'en Haut (Lamothe Cadillac), and had settled among the Sioux where he had Fort Chagoumigon built. As commander he had ruled over a zone extending from the source of the Mississippi to the Kickapoo or Rivière Noire, with the exclusive right of the fur trade except for beaver, though he never complied with the request. With twenty-five men, Le Sueur went up the Mississippi as far as Sault Saint Antoine in 1701. In April he paddled on the Missouri, then over a hundred miles on the Rivière Verte where he built Fort Vert (or Fort L'Huillier). He wintered there with his men, but after they left it was no longer possible to protect the fort from Sioux raids.[26]

Juchereau de Saint-Denis, born in Quebec in 1676, was also dispatched by Lamothe Cadillac to watch over the Spanish post of the Adayes near which he built Fort Saint-Jean Baptiste des Natchitoches on the Red River, thereby stopping the advance of the Spaniards toward the Mississippi. It was a mere entrenchment, not a stronghold with guns, and in complete isolation half the year due to masses of tree trunks blocking the stream. In 1715, Juchereau went across Texas and reached Mexico where he was jailed.[27] A Breton-born explorer, Jean-Baptiste Bénard de la Harpe had traveled through Peru before sailing across to Louisiana with forty colonists in 1718. He built an outpost a few hundred miles above Natchitoches in 1719 and in Texas established links with Spanish missionaries who were offered a commission on sales. When the local governor ordered La Harpe to withdraw, he was told that La Salle had appropriated Texas in 1687. It was then beyond the power of New Spain to go such a long way to dislodge La Harpe. Besides, the padres did not encourage such a move.[28] Jean Baptiste Le Moyne, Sieur de Bienville, who co-founded Louisiana with his brother Pierre d'Iberville sent him to the Red River where he built Fort Malouin. For an entire year he explored the region as far as the Arkansas River where he met Indian tribes but tried in vain to reach the Spanish territory.

In 1719, Captain Claude-Charles du Tisné left his garrison in the Illinois country at Bienville's request for a trading expedition to reach the Pawnees, but he was stopped by the Osages. In 1720 he went southwest to Oklahoma and was captured in a Pani village. When the Indians threatened to kill him he frightened them by removing the wig he was wearing, revealing the baldness that he had since his childhood. Tisné was fluent in Indian languages and he so impressed the natives that they were eager to do business with him. He finally returned to Canada with a load of furs. He was intending to meet the Comanches but the Panis remained reluctant to guide him to them. A gentleman farmer from Normandy, Etienne Véniard de Bourgmont, shed his officer's uniform in 1713 to become a coureur des bois living among the Missouri tribes. Ten years later he left Louisiana with nineteen Frenchmen and a hundred Indians for territories washed by the Kansas and Colorado Rivers. He had to determine whether the Spaniards were about to advance from Santa Fe and make an alliance with the Apaches against the French. The presence of Bourgmont's Métis son was a major asset for the Missouris and the Comanches, who were well provided with rifles, knives, and kettles by the French traders. The Indians complained that the Spaniards had only bad axes to offer. Bourgmont was so well greeted by the Comanches and the Osages that he had a delegation of them invited by Louis XV. They were so much in demand at Versailles and other mansions that Bourgmont made a fortune by showing them around. Among the Indian guests was a Missouri princess, who married one of Bourgmont's sergeants in Notre Dame Cathedral in Paris. Madame de Bourgmont was probably relieved to learn that the newlyweds had decided to return to Missouri.[29]

In 1717 the Compagnie d'Occident was entrusted with the development of Louisiana. An influx of soldiers and engagés led to the population growth in Kaskaskia, which amounted to three hundred in 1732. But this policy was not rewarding enough for investors, who soon curtailed funds. It was clear that the banks of the Mississippi would never see mushrooming towns despite a revival of Canadian migration by the mid-eighteenth century. The new village of Sainte

Geneviève then numbered eight hundred inhabitants, half of whom were black and more than one hundred of whom were Indian. In 1746, three hundred whites lived in Illinois along with six hundred black slaves.

French traders were often engaged in smuggling goods into Spanish territory. Despite the repeated orders of Spanish officials, the French coureurs des bois supplied Comanches with rifles and ammunition in their wars against the Apaches. There was a growing interest in the new markets opening in the Southwest, although illegal intrusion was severely punished by New Spain.

In 1739 Pierre Antoine Mallet, his brother Paul, and five others left Fort de Chartres, hoping to reach Texas near the upper Missouri. But on the way Indians told them they were heading northwest. Looking for the road to Santa Fe, Mallet and his party went overland to the Platte River, and struck out across southwestern Colorado. They lost their goods in a stream but reached the Spanish mission of Picouries near Taos, and ended up in Santa Fe. They were detained several months on contraband charges. Yet no proof of illegal trade was found against them, and they were finally allowed to go home.[30] In June 1750 Jacques LeGardeur of Saint Pierre left Montreal to continue the search for the western sea. He passed Michilimackinac on July 12 and in the fall arrived at Fort La Reine [Portage la Prairie, Manitoba] where he stayed for two years. His second in command was Joseph Claude Boucher de Nivervile. LeGardeur explored Red River, Lake Winnipeg, and the Lake of the Woods region. On his return he complained that Jean Baptiste De La Morinie, a Jesuit, was a useless missionary who did not even have mathematical instruments.[31]

LeGardeur and the Chevalier Boucher de Niverville exercised control over the northwestern posts until 1753. They had little success, especially as they did not understand the Indian culture of the potlatch. Meanwhile Father La Morinerie was assigned to Fort La Reine but eventually confessed his inability to make converts among the peoples of the West. In 1752 Legardeur was said to be the first person known to refer in French to the Stony or Shining Mountains as the *Montagnes de Roche* [Rocky Mountains]. He was naturally indebted to Alvar Nunez Cabeza de Vaca (1490–1557), who in 1529 called them Sierra and whose explorations were well published throughout Europe. In 1753 Louis De La Corne de Saint-Luc became commander of the Northwest territories and established Fort Saint Louis near the forks of the North and South Saskatchewan Rivers. He retained his commission until 1757.[32]

West by Northwest

Louis XV was crowned in 1715 in a country bled white by military conflicts. The Treaty of Utrecht, signed in 1713, had put an end to the War of the Spanish Succession, mostly benefiting the king of England by extending his empire overseas. The Iroquois country was now under English protectorate and free trade was allowed around the Great Lakes. It was now urgent that France keep control of the fur trade in the region. The fort built by the French in 1680 near Niagara could no longer withstand an onslaught of the Five Nations. In 1726 Governor Beauharnois and Intendant Michel Bégon had a new stone-walled fort built on the right bank of the Niagara River to protect the portage between Lake Ontario and Lake Erie. It was also a way to keep an eye on trade at the outpost of Oswego, established by the English in 1722. The French authorities started to build other forts on the route leading from the Great Lakes to the Mississippi.

In 1717 Governor Philippe Rigaud de Vaudreuil was convinced that a western effluent of Lake Superior led to the Mer de l'Ouest, opening on the Pacific Ocean. He believed the mainspring of that stream to be in the Lac des Bois or Lac des Assiniboines where he decided to establish an outpost. It was the task of Lieutenant de la Noue to find a gateway to the west by reaching the Lac de la Pluie. In the same period Louisiana was threatened in the east by England and in the west by Spain. New France was also seeking an outlet for the fur trade to fight the monopoly of the English around Hudson Bay. Pierre Gaultier de Varennes et de la Vérendrye was appointed commander of Kaministiquia on Lake Superior in 1728. Born in 1685 at Trois Rivières, he was the son of René Gaultier de Varennes who came to Canada from Anjou to fight the Iroquois as a lieutenant in the regiment of Carignan-Salières. René married Marie, the daughter of Pierre Boucher, the governor of Trois Rivières, and took over from him in 1688. Pierre chose a military career and volunteered to campaign in Europe in the Régiment de Bretagne. He was wounded and taken prisoner at the battle of Malplaquet in September 1709. After his release in 1710, he was promoted to lieutenant. He then returned to Canada where he was in command of an outpost on Lake Nipigon. He was so sure that a northwest passage would enable him to discover the Mer de l'Ouest that he persuaded Minister Maurepas to let him get the upper hand on the fur trade in the regions he would discover. In June 1731 he went west with his three sons, Christophe de la Jemerais, a nephew, and fifty men. They wintered near Lake Superior in Fort Saint Charles, hastily built at the Lac des Bois before the cold season. They proceeded in the spring of 1732, and soon discovered the boundless expanse of the prairies. La Verendrye built posts to be used as landmarks on the way. He found Indian partners in the fur trade but diplomatic moves were hazardous to the extent that an alliance with a tribe would sometimes arouse the hostility of others. La Verendrye and his party returned to Quebec in early 1733, then resumed their trek as far as Lake Winnepeg in 1734. Fort Rouge was built where the Assiniboine and Red Rivers meet. La Vérendrye was authorized to build a new outpost two years later on the shore of Lake Winnipeg. In the following decade, he obtained financial backing to build six more outposts further west. In 1736, Sioux bands attacked the expedition, killing Jean-Baptiste, the elder son, Father Aulneau de la Touche, and twenty-one men. In 1738 La Vérendrye explored Saskatchewan, northeast Montana, and northwest Dakota, then stayed at Fort La Reine on the Assiniboine. In December, he entered the main Mandan village along the upper waters of the Knife River with an escort of six hundred Assiniboines. He stood only a few miles from the Missouri River but did not bother to see it himself. He still imagined it was the "River of the West" and believed that it flowed southwest toward the Gulf of Mexico. In 1741 he was at Lake Dauphin and managed to get to the Rivières des Biches, today Portage La Prairie. But heavily in debt and harassed by creditors, La Vérendrye did not go beyond the Great Plains. He left two men with the Mandans in Dakota on his way back, and had his sons Pierre and Louis-Joseph adopted by the Crees, to whom gifts were generously distributed. In a separate expedition, La Vérendrye's sons reached the foot of the Rockies after getting across the Black Hills. Disillusioned and slandered in Quebec, La Vérendrye himself resigned from his functions before the new governor, Roland-Michel Barrin, marquis de La Galissonnière, eventually paid homage to his achievements in 1749 by awarding him the Cross of Saint Louis, one of the highest distinctions in the kingdom. As he was preparing to leave for the West again, La Vérendrye died suddenly the same year. His map of the western region proved invaluable and the forts he had built became bulwarks against English penetration. In 1743 François du Trembeau, La Vérendrye's third son explored parts of South Dakota which he named *Mauvaises Terres* [Bad Lands].[33]

The French possessions in the West now extended from Lake Superior to Lake Winnipeg, the Lac de la Pluie, Saint Charles on the western shore of the Lac des Bois, and Fort Maurepas at the mouth of the Winnipeg River. Until 1753, the occupation of new territories testified to the ambition of an almighty monarchy. Fort Bourbon, Fort Paskoyac (beyond the Saskatchewan), and finally Fort La Corne were built. In the French imagination, the forts were impregnable fortresses. The multiplication of these outposts was interpreted by the English as a massive support of the woodrunners, who were obstructing their own fur-trading operations. Those whom the English derisively called peddlers carried heavy loads on rivers and built huts covered with shingles in which goods were stored. Nearby, half a dozen or more Indians would keep watch in a small lodge for weeks.

3

The Wilderness at Stake:
The Colony at the Crossroads

IN THE LAST DECADES OF THE SEVENTEENTH CENTURY THE KING'S MEN IN Quebec still aspired to rival the New England settlements despite the slow growth of the French population in New France. Imperial schemes were exalted but in the short term it was imperative to impart new energies to the colony to make it at least self-sufficient. If agriculture was to supplant the fur trade, imports would suffer and smuggling would prosper. Major traders were untouchable unless the network of woodrunners could be dismantled to regain social control. The campaigns launched to discredit the coureurs des bois stressed their refusal to accept tasks akin to their condition, and their arrogant defiance of authority. In Quebec, the fiery intendant Talon had endeavored to safeguard the squirearchy in 1665. Seven years later, forty-six discharged soldiers and selected immigrants became seigneurs. Going a step further, Talon planned to gather loafers and force them to work for the community. Living in seclusion in the wilderness was likened to vagrancy and incurred severe punishment. By the end of the century the number of stray woodrunners decreased from eight hundred in 1680 to three hundred. Perhaps official reports were exaggerated, as agents hoped to convince the King of their power. It was equally difficult to distinguish the voyageurs transporting furs for a company from the freelance woodrunners in the Pays d'en Haut. The listings of engagés involved in travels westward amounted to three thousand between 1675 and 1745. It appeared that a quarter of the male population born at the end of the seventeenth century in New France went west at least once in their lifetime.[1]

La Barre involved the fur trade in dubious dealings when he permitted the Iroquois to loot the boats of unlicensed traders, even if it was only to avoid a new war. But in 1684, the now friendly Indians seized loads of pelts smuggled by the governor himself, who retaliated by sending nine hundred Frenchmen and nine hundred allied tribes to the Anse de la Famine, southeast of Lake Ontario, to give a display of military power. Two hundred engagés supplied by the trader Aubert de la Chesnaye reinforced the troops against the Iroquois and their allies of the Five Nations. But weakened by a shortage of food supplies and epidemics, the French accepted the enemy's conditions in the negotiations, and allowed the Iroquois to keep fighting the Illinois. Added to La Barre's hostility to La Salle, the so-called shameful peace of the Anse de la Famine aggravated La Barre's disgrace. He was then recalled by Louis XIV.[2] As new governor, Jacques-René de Brisay de Denonville had to avenge the honor of New France. In 1687, he mustered an army of eight hundred regulars, 1,100 militiamen, four hundred Indians and nearly two hundred coureurs des bois to attack the Tsonnontouans who lived south of Lake Ontario. He laid waste villages and burnt crops to demonstrate the French presence in the West. Among the Indians captured during the fights, forty were removed to France as galley slaves.[3]

The mounting tension in New France reflected the crisis in Europe, which culminated when the war between France and England broke out in May 1689. The coronation of William of Orange and the repeal of the Edict of Nantes protecting the Protestants had precipitated a conflict that had been brewing across the Atlantic. The government felt the very existence of New France was endangered by social causes such as the low marriage rate and dwindling families. In wartimes the colonial populations had to be reminded of their duties. Stringent regulations were initiated to preclude close relations with Indians. Woodrunners were also expected to produce character references stamped by missionaries when they sought employment. Denonville planned to build military outposts on rivers to control the movements of the fur trade toward the west and Louisiana. Listings of voyageurs were sent to local commanders to put outlaws under arrest. Patrols on canoes would investigate the portages and meeting points to confiscate loads of pelts.

The representatives of the king under the ancien régime received low salaries when the hardships of their exile were considered. Accordingly, governors and intendants used their influence with the commercial establishment to further their interests in the fur trade. When he was in charge of New France, Frontenac had accused the governor of Montreal of using deserters to collect furs for his own use at Michilimackinac. A coalition implicating Intendant Duchesneau against Frontenac resulted in the arrest of Pierre Moreau, known as *la taupine* [beetle], who was one of the governor's protégés. Frontenac retaliated by accusing Duchesneau of using two woodrunners, David and Faure, to send beaver furs to New Holland.[4] Such antagonisms revealed the power of local oligarchies to neutralize the efforts of the king's men, who were progressively bought off and thus rendered ineffective. Rampant corruption thus affected rulers often unable to enforce the law because of the cost to their personal dealings. Internecine rivalries and government interference had also aroused discontent among the habitants, aside from the temptation for woodrunners to go to the enemy, as new conflicts with the Iroquois were brewing. The fear that unrest might trigger revolts led rulers to appease passions. To bury the hatchet, Duchesneau appealed to Colbert to establish a system of clearance certificates authorizing seventy-five men on twenty-five canoes to trade with the Ottawas every year.[5] Discharged officers and other persona grata were granted favors like these at the expense of other individuals in straitened circumstances, who were often more in need of help. Speculators also infiltrated the happy few and easily thwarted any type of control. Traders and voyagers went as far as the Assiniboine and Sioux countries.[6] Outposts were convenient landmarks for future explorations. Earlier the Jesuits had built Sault Sainte Marie and Michilimackinac. Many tribes met at Fort Pontchartrain, Fort Duluth, and Fort Kaministiquia. Forty-four forts had been built in 1713. A few cabins sheltered an officer and a dozen soldiers stationed to protect rivermen. Isolated for months and often confronted with hostile Indians, these men illicitly cooperated with traders allegedly under their watchful eyes.

The Lure of the terra incognita

The colonial environment reflected the difficulty to communicate in the stratified French society. When aristocrats and priests were seeking information on the backwoods, they dealt with illiterate trappers whose oral reports were garbled in their native vernacular. In 1721, Pierre-François Xavier de Charlevoix, one of the most reliable chroniclers of life in New France, found many contradictions in the answers of Kaskaskia inmates when he inquired about the local situation.[7] Like Indians, the woodrunner would count time in days spent on canoes. He named locations in relation to a peculiar landscape, an incident, or an encounter with a wild animal. He memorized a mental image of the stars and found his bearings by observing moss on tree trunks. Few had a compass at their disposal. In 1741, Fabry de la Bruyère lent one to a coureur des bois who got lost in the backwoods by misusing it.[8]

Administrators often complained about the ignorance of men like Laurain, who had been up the Missouri in 1705 and was unable to describe what he had seen. Nicolas de La Salle heard that voyageurs had gone more than a thousand miles up the Missouri. He wanted an engineer to draw a map of the river in 1709 but the governor could not afford to set up an expedition. Rather than rely on the memories of woodrunners for the task, Intendant Talon made it clear that he preferred the contributions of Jesuits who had spent some time in the tribes. His objections to woodrunners stemmed from their inability to record their daily occupations in a journal.[9]

After the demise of Cardinal Mazarin in 1661, the king's major counselor who had been in disgrace for some time, Louis XIV preferred to trust pragmatic bourgeois ministers around him like Colbert, Louvois, and Pontchartrain, who let him wield his despotic power. The Sun King was averse to the exploration of remote territories that would remain vacant until the English or the Dutch had an opportunity to grab them. In the meantime the wilderness remained the refuge of deserters and renegades. But French adventurers ignored colonial policies when they were busy roaming the backwoods and prairies.

In 1681, Intendant Duchesneau distinguished two kinds of coureurs des bois. Some collected beaver furs from the Assiniboines, the Miamis, and the Illinois, being away for a period of three years at a time. Others met Indians coming down to Long Sault, Petite Nation, or Michilimackinac to get their loads of pelts. They paid them in firewater, which gradually damaged the trade by spreading drunkenness and crime.[10]

The demand for furs was such that authorities were losing control over dozens of individuals scattered throughout Indian country. Tribes also initiated young whites into hunting over long distances, and what had remained an aristocratic privilege in France was now common in the colony. The elk, the bear, and smaller game sold so well that one or two Indians were often hired for a couple of days to accompany farmers taking some time off. Hunting was essential to a beaver man's life. During his nomadic days on rivers, he carried few provisions in his canoe and had to keep dried meat, sometimes for weeks when game was scant. He maneuvered his fragile craft with skill and repaired it when needed. This transplanted Frenchman was stocky, incredibly strong, and resilient. He wore a linen shirt, deerskin leggings, and moccasins. He had a sash around his waist and a woolen cap with a tassel hanging to one side, and a bandanna around his head. Some emulated Indians and even formed up in teams to supply forts. Communities of hunters spread over Illinois and Missouri, which were teeming with *bœuf* [buffalo]. Shoving and paddling all day long they sang time-worn melodies such as "A la Claire Fontaine."[11]

François de Beauharnois, governor of New France in 1736, recognized that a vast extent of territory peopled with Indians and surrounded by English smugglers was a natural haven for deserters. Those derelicts having "neither fireside nor home" were a threat to the stability of the colony.[12] They embodied laxity and lawlessness, providing bad examples for young men who were lured away from their families by the prospects of debauchery. Discharged soldiers hardly ever took to farming. Long used to hunting for food, they still lived on buck or bear meat. Deserters could be found among those who had smuggled pelts, and lived with Indian women in their tribes. The runaways gathered in groups of four or five, and frequently got lost in the backwoods. Dissatisfied engagés, servants, and apprentices also went on the lam. Jean Gai, a woodworker, François Quenet, a locksmith, and Fortier, a servant, quit their workshops without notice. Tibierge, a miller, left with half a dozen engagés and five canoes to collect furs. All were chased by their masters and sued for breach of contract. They had little to lose in fact. There was no hope for them to start a family since women were not sufficiently numerous. At times, heads of family also responded to the call of the wild. Durantaye left his wife and five children. Jean Baptiste Patissier lived for fifteen years among the Ottawas.[13]

By the turn of the eighteenth century, fugitives from Canada found caches for stolen furs in Upper Louisiana, as was sometimes the case with soldiers who had deserted their outposts on western rivers. Altogether 150 engagés in the fur trade out of a total of 668 vanished out west. Motivations for desertion varied. One such deserter, La Montagne, withdrew in a hut, and received pelts for brandy and gunpowder. Most exiles lived in Indian villages and became indistinguishable from the natives. Traders and soldiers would sometimes come across a "white Indian" and exchange a few words with him in French. Although labeled as an outcast by the colonial power, the backwoods recluse was not isolated for long. The English and the Dutch valued his competence and enlisted his support to participate in the trade. Two woodrunners, Du Plessis and Marion Fontaine, sought revenge on the governor who had defamed them. They rallied to the English, and guided them on Lake Ontario up to Michilimackinac in eleven canoes in 1686. Johannes Ronsebon, a Dutch entrepreneur, organized a new expedition the following year.[14]

In November 1686 Louis XIV had signed a treaty with James II to maintain the status quo on the new continent.[15] But Governor Denonville, who had just succeeded La Barre, wanted to subdue the Iroquois on the grounds that they were within French territory. Fifteen thousand troops and Indians crossed Lake Ontario to Irondequoit Bay where they met the canoes manned by Duluth and Tonty. Noblemen in their breastplates, plumed headgear, and fulsome wigs were now sitting side by side with Indians whose heads were crowned with buffalo horns, while animal tails were hanging from their belts. Ronsebon's French partners who had defected to the other side were captured and taken prisoner. But most of the time clandestine woodrunners in the service of the English escaped detection, and were soon engulfed by the wilderness.

Meanwhile, aristocrats and bourgeois in Montreal had already established covert relations with the English. In 1722, the latter had Fort Oswego built on the southern shore of Lake Ontario to assist smugglers. The Seneca villages of the north shore, such as Teyaiagon, also served the same purpose as well as did the Indian villages close to Montreal and Quebec. Squaws, warriors, and whites disguised as Indians went back and forth with their discreet loads of goods destined for officers, priests, and other respectable colonists. It was well known that any interference with Indian rights was a touchy subject. Iroquois missions like Caughnawaga, near Montreal, had become independent communities, free to trade with anyone.[16]

Officials reviled Indians who acted in collusion with fugitives. Yet they had to shelter their allies against Iroquois attacks. Outlaws went west to elude squads who were in hot pursuit. Once settled in Indian country they could stay with almost complete impunity unless they offended natives. Laplace, a deserter who had found refuge among the Sioux, was killed by a warrior who had allegedly lost his mind. In 1723 Indians implored mercy for an escaped convict who had marriage bonds in the tribe. Pardon was not sought for black fugitives. In Louisiana they were promptly returned to their masters. It also happened that homesickness compelled whites to ask the governor for mercy before leaving their refuge, as exemplified in the case of Baudron who had spent years with the Shawnees.[17]

In New France families usually enforced strict discipline on offspring who found an outlet in listening to hunters' tales. The young also secretly left home to spend days in Indian communities where girls rarely kept them at arm's length. At Mardi Gras celebrations they dressed like the natives, imitated their dances, and sometimes ran naked through their villages. Young Frenchmen generally ignored social discrimination. The sons of aristocrats and merchants mixed with engagés and servants. All took part in brief expeditions to barter a few elk skins or rackets for firewater or trinkets. Youngsters in quest of temporary freedom from their families or wishing to help a widowed mother by earning extra money would accompany Indians and woodrunners to the Pays d'en Haut. They sometimes took a brother or a cousin along with them and formed teams that traditions would later honor. In the process the Desfossés and Cardinal families happened to create dynasties. Roughing it was part and parcel of education. The young nobleman did not seem to demean himself by so doing; on the contrary, most colonists considered it could mold characters. But as time passed clannish attitudes, family solidarity, and underground practices were increasingly thought subversive by colonial authorities.[18]

Woodrunners of common birth were accused of transgressing hierarchies pertaining to the ancien régime. Living independently with an income that respectable subjects might envy, they scorned farming and dressed with flashy elegance. The representatives of the crown resented this pretence of nobility and the habit of illegally assuming the title of squire. Removed from their European surroundings the coureurs des bois no longer pledged allegiance to secular traditions. When accustomed to Indian ways these men willfully borrowed native codes of behavior, thus considering daily chores such as plowing and harvesting as beneath their dignity. They also spent hours talking and smoking with tribal sachems. Such an experience in cultural hybridization seemed to bestow prestige on those who resented their plebeian condition. No wonder the government of New France saw their behavior as a threat to colonial order and a model for idlers, rogues, and vagabonds. There was also the likelihood that it could be a cover for conspirators.[19]

White Indians and Embattled Woodrunners

Westward expansion into unsettled areas was regarded by the French as hazardous to the stability of the colony. Aside from the hope for economic betterment, the beaver men acting on their own initiative were driven by a desire for change, the lure of the unknown, and the call of the wild. Sometimes they felt the urge to move for no particular reason. They craved escape from an uncongenial environment. As diplomatic relations were alien to those staunch individualists, they unconsciously meddled with the policies of the New France government. For example, Denonville blamed woodrunners for causing a breach of peace with the Iroquois after arming their enemies.[20]

As years passed it took longer and longer to reach beaver lands. Experienced coureurs des bois, now often considered as licensed voyageurs, hired youngsters as oarsmen. The hivernants among them would winter in the tribes to maintain a useful presence and curry favor with privileged suppliers. The woodrunner unwittingly became a pawn in Anglo-French relations. Should the government of New France put an end to the deviant activities of such spurned nomads, the friendly Indians would turn against the king for depriving them of their interests in the fur trade, thus harming indispensable allies against English intruders. The native protected the coureur des bois who was shrewd enough to turn his precarious status to his own advantage.

The phrase "We are all savages," read in 1680 by Tonty at Fort Crèvecoeur, bluntly revealed that some of his men had foregone civilization for a primitive life among the natives. A hundred years later the famous explorer Alexander Mackenzie stated that it took less time for a civilized man to surrender to the wilderness than for a savage to be civilized. The revolutionary leader Mirabeau who proclaimed in 1789 that he and his companions were in the Jeu de Paume room by the will of the people, and would be expelled only by the sheer force of bayonets, said that the Canadian savages had not been frenchified but had instead made savages of Frenchmen.[21] Emissaries of the crown were often stunned to learn that runaways had vanished in remote Indian villages, never to be seen again. They were at a loss to explain the conduct of such hermits who prior to Henry Thoreau had deliberately gone to the woods to escape a life of desperation. Instinct seemed to have prevailed over reason, and promiscuity happily dulled their moral sense. Guillaume Saint Jean de Crèvecoeur later wondered what the attraction was of living with illiterate, pagan, lawless, and destitute Indians. He only surmised that there must be something in their adopted way of life in the wilderness that was superior to the charms of European civilization.[22]

Captives were added to Indian communities via adoption. This way of obtaining additional kindred made up for the loss of lives especially in wartime. The Hurons, Iroquois, and other tribes along the Missouri and Mississippi renewed their human and spiritual potential through this ritual process of integration. When Governor Montmagny claimed two interpreters, Marguerie and Godefroy, in an Iroquois village, he was told that they no longer belonged to the French because the right of war had made them thoroughly Iroquois.[23] The fate of a captive was either torture and death, or full recognition as a member of a clan. A long march preceded his arrival at the camp. The prisoner was manhandled, and bound hand

and foot for the night. His first ordeal was tantamount to running the gauntlet as the inmates of the village struck him with sticks. Then his body was painted all over, and he was left to wander while tribesmen called him "the walking dead one."[24] Each of his movements was under careful scrutiny and any attempt to escape was punished by death. One such prisoner, René Goupil, was accused of witchcraft and executed after making the sign of the cross over a Mohawk child.[25] In the final stage of his initiation, a captive witnessed scenes of torture so horrifying that he had no other choice but to accept identification with his captors in order to save his life. Then a new existence began for him. A prisoner of the Oneida Indians in 1690, Pierre Millet later related that he had received a tribal name. Two women took him to a river where they washed him to rub out his whiteness and rid him of his former identity. He was given a headdress and a wampum to be ranked as a free man.[26] Pierre Radisson was adopted by a widow after his capture by the Mohawks in 1652. The woman spread grease on his body, combed his hair, removed the paint from his face and searched for lice in his clothes. Whenever she found one she would bite it delicately. Then the chief brought him before the village dwellers, and declared that now being of Mohawk flesh and blood, the white man deserved full respect and protection as the substitute for a deceased member of the clan. The attribution of the latter's name to the initiate was declared sufficient to revive him.[27]

When a young white child was captured he quickly became indianized, learned the tribe's language, and soon forgot his past. Readjustment to the French environment, if he was freed, generally implied agonizing efforts to re-assimilate. The adopted white was welcome to have a family life. Many Indian wives found themselves alone after the deaths of warriors in the successive fur wars. Sometimes it cost a captive his life if he refused overtures made by a woman of the tribe, as happened to La Liberté, a woodrunner who had repulsed an Iroquois squaw.[28]

Judgments on the mentalities of adopted whites have evolved over the centuries—from devastating accounts of cruel treatment to the glorification of life in an unspoiled environment. As usual the truth is probably somewhere in between. The younger the liberated captives were, the less adaptable to white society they became after a decade or two in captivity. In 1700 Louis Thomas Chabert de Joncaire, formerly adopted by the Senecas, admitted that whites were sometimes reluctant to return to a life of routine after years in the wilderness.[29] Perhaps the major reason for grudgingly accepting this freedom was to be found in the social background of the individuals.

The governor of New York, Cadwallader Colden, ascribed such attitudes to the difficulties the poor met with in New France under the
domination of despotic rulers.[30]

Adoption was not exclusively the consequence of a state of bellig-
erence. Missionaries knew about this mode of gaining admittance to
communities, and thereby found a way to stay among prospective
converts. Brother Gabriel was adopted by an Illinois chief who offered him hospitality and allowed him to spread his faith. After the
death of La Vérendrye's elder son in 1736, the Crees had substituted
his second son for a dead chief, as described above. Adoption could
also be instrumental in furthering diplomatic relations. Chabert de
Joncaire managed to reconcile the Senecas with the French, and
had Fort Niagara built by convincing them that he wanted a house
close to their villages. Despite such assets in colonial policies, authorities were suspicious of adopted woodrunners whose interest in
public affairs was subservient to personal choices. The fear of subver-
sion remained predominant among official observers.[31]

In the early days of the westward movement, Father Carheil, a missionary at Michilimackinac, depicted the Pays d'en Haut as a replica
of Sodom and Gomorrah. He accused the so-called fugitive voyageurs of depraving Indian women.[32] Almost half a century later Governor Vaudreuil was alert to the French habit of buying sexual favors
by surrendering goods intended for exchange. Later David Thompson, the explorer, witnessed similar leanings on the part of French
traders staying in Mandan camps. They sold off their supplies and
then spent their leisure time with girls. Indian chiefs were so baffled
by the sexual urges of the French that they wondered if the white
men had ever seen women before.[33]

In the course of his expedition to the "Great American Desert"
in the early nineteenth century, Zebulon Pike noted that the absence of white women northwest of Lake Superior discouraged male
migration there. He could not imagine the kind of the relationship
Indian women had experienced with white men since the begin-
nings of colonization in New France. Those who had the best knowledge of native sexuality were the explorers, trappers, truchements,
and wanderers generally dismissed as scoundrels.[34] The Hurons believed that sexual gratification was the best way to heal mental disorders. Sex was no sin for unmarried individuals. Conversely, sexual
preoccupations were not predominant in the state of marriage. Missionaries warned the colonists against the ignorance of sin in Indian
mentalities. They observed that girls prostituted themselves at an
early age. A husband did not care about the behavior of his wife if
she felt like offering her body to a stranger, but she had to do it

conspicuously. Young French bachelors quickly learned about the practice of *courir l'allumette* [running the match]. They went around the huts of the village, carrying torches until they met a girl who blew out the flame to signify her approval. No wonder the keepers of public order were outraged by the fascination exerted by such permissiveness.[35]

Negotiations with whites implied the offer of women to the other party. When the Récollet priests declined such gifts they antagonized the chiefs who could not comprehend that celibacy was a vocation. Not all circumstances were favorable, especially when a young warrior snarled at a white rival, and retaliated by setting fire to his wigwam.

As early as 1635, miscegenation had been favored by Champlain, who trusted in the future assimilation of Hurons, and expected their daughters to marry Frenchmen once the women converted to Catholicism. Under Louis XIV, Colbert granted a bonus of 3,000 livres for a wedding with a *sauvagesse* [Indian woman]. But the Jesuits were hostile to such unions on account of the prevailing immorality in the tribes. In frontier settlements, despite being educated by the Ursulines, Indian girls still maintained such sexual freedom. In the second half of the seventeenth century new migrants could rarely meet the moral requirements of the Church if they were to make a living in the fur trade. By 1682, government agents and religious orders agreed to investigate the practice of interracial unions. But the measure was of no avail. Because the bonds of marriage were disregarded by lovers in the backwoods, the specter of rampant lewdness haunted Father Jean de Lamberville, superior of the missions among the Onondagas. In 1709, he openly referred to the ban on interracial marriages in the English colonies as an example to follow, but only officers and officials were targeted. Soldiers in distant outposts and woodrunners were exempted de facto on account of the immense, uncontrollable territory of New France and Louisiana. When a Frenchman began negotiations with the Ottawa Indians he would take one of their young girls with her father's consent. He promised some blankets, a rifle, gunpowder, lead, and tobacco. She followed him everywhere, acted as a guide, and prepared pelts for sale. Sex was naturally included in the contract but the union was intended first of all to divide the chores on a reciprocal basis.[36]

The coureur des bois could not dodge age-old obligations, such as the payment of a dowry, when he wanted an Indian running mate. Thus evading the French law, the squaw man abided by the rules of the natives, hence the phrase *mariage à la façon du pays* [marriage countrywise]. Among the Algonquins and Hurons, the skills of the prospective husband were tested before the amount of the dowry was determined. In a matrilineal society, the rights of women had to be guaranteed before a full agreement was reached. Around the Great Lakes, the Winnebagos, the Illinois, and the Sioux gave a major role to the brother of the bride, who demanded much consideration before making a decision as to the future of his sister. Only parents had authority over their daughter in the Ojibwa, Assiniboine, and Cree tribes. In most cases, a prominent man was entitled to keep several spouses, if only to knit the family together. The alternative to marriage was slaveholding when the coureur des bois could offer no compensation. A captive was more accessible than a chief's daughter but less influential. Any transgression of the marriage ritual triggered fierce reprisals. At Fort Phélypeaux soldiers and traders were massacred by a band of Crees for detaining young women without their consent.[37]

Aside from her legendary sexuality, the squaw was also valued for her hard work. She carried heavy loads in regions where draught horses were unknown. In the Ojibwa and Algonquin tribes she could row like men and in the Illinois country, she built huts. She would also trap small game, pick wild fruit and herbs, as well as spread marrow on buffalo skins to soften them. No coureur des bois in New France was inspired by courtly love. There was no troubadour singing in the Canadian forests, but Indian women fell for young Frenchmen who might offer them a better future. Boilers, knives, and fabrics were also tokens of social success. Girls who had seen their mothers living in submission and sometimes rough handled, welcomed milder attitudes. They willingly abandoned their next-of-kin to follow their French husbands over long distances. Whatever his reactions to different circumstances, the coureur des bois lived through a fundamental paradox. Despised, even rejected by an aristocratic society, he was a Caesar of the wilderness, by turns respected, feared, and admired, one against whom, in Pierre Radisson's own words, Indians hardly ever raised their voices.[38]

Woman was an ideal agent of acculturation because she shared in the daily life of a coureur des bois and taught him the ways of her people day by day. Even though years of exile could not make a Frenchman perfectly bilingual, yet immersed as he was in a new culture he gradually assumed Indian attitudes. In 1687, Magry recalled one Provençal who went around naked, and muttered only a few words in French. He had now discarded the trappings of European society, and every day faced the common issues of the native environment and tribal norms.[39] In his records Tonty noted the syncretic meanings conveyed by tattoos on the bodies of squaw men. For instance, he recalled the pictures of the Holy Virgin and Jesus combined with that of a snake on the breast of a compatriot. Illiteracy was compensated by sign language. If the woodrunner belonged to the underclass of peasants or rivermen his taboos and superstitions were a far cry from the dogma of the Roman Church. Since childhood he had been familiar with witchcraft and magic rituals. Visions and prophecies were akin to his belief in supernatural determination through specific signs. He shared a sense of wonder when Indians shot arrows above a sacred rock or laid tobacco leaves to propitiate the spirits. Yet few traces have been left of these experiences except for the meager records of Jesuits who had to rely on partial testimonies.[40]

Frenchmen had a reputation for boasting when they were fluent enough to do so. They loved playing lacrosse and gambling, even staking their spouses. Near Detroit they were seen to compete in races a distance of a mile and a half long. A Canadian runner named Campo was so fast that Indians banned him from their games. Singing and dancing were favorite entertainments to which hosts were invited. Fiddlers and viola players enthralled tribes who capered around on old French tunes, as exemplified in anecdotes told by one Pénicault in Margry's records.[41]

The French coureur des bois had an advantage over the English and the Spaniards. He did not find it beneath his dignity to be sized up at great length, touched, rubbed, and painted. He gave up acquired tastes to eat unattractive food and got used to endless discussions in smoky lodges. Above all he kept in mind that the Indian was intractable without an exchange of gifts, especially as objects had a symbolic significance depending on the rank and prestige of those concerned.

Any trader intending to barter with the tribes had to comply with a ceremony entailing speech-making and showing off. This solemn occasion sealed a contract and was to be renewed at each new encounter. The gifts of highly symbolic objects substantiated the significance of the meeting. Any defaulter was subject to recrimination on the part of the chiefs who might wreck the transaction out of spite.

The coureur des bois had two ways to obtain pelts. The easiest consisted of obtaining the very clothing the Indians wore in winter. They stitched together beaver skins to make a robe in which they wrapped themselves, worn with the fur facing inside. Within several months, the fur was so impregnated with grease that it was used in the making of felt for hatters. Indians set a high price on beaver robes as they were in great demand. Otherwise, the trader had to escort the tribesmen to their hunting grounds. This was called *courir la drouine*.[42] After wintering with them he painstakingly negotiated to get the best lots. When several coureurs des bois came by, villagers were aware of their conflicting interests, and raised the bidding. As a last resort the offer of firewater made it easier to consummate the deal.

In the last decades of the seventeenth century the development of the fur trade had been backed by massive imports of axes from Biscay, as well as boilers and knives from ironworks in central France. The Foxes and the Sioux always badgered agents for rifles, gunpowder, and lead while the coureurs des bois were training warriors from all the tribes within the French settlements. They would also set up a blacksmith shop near camps to repair the all-too-frequent defects in their materials. Even traders sometimes discovered that bullets did not fit the guns. Nevertheless, it was easy to trick natives who likened a gun report to witchcraft and believed that powder was grown in fields and harvested like corn.

Governor Frontenac recognized the power of brandy well before it became the major instrument of the trade. In 1739 twelve thousand pounds of beaver belts were gathered, despite the ban on liquor. Incapable of resisting temptation, Indians drank barrels of brandy as soon as it was available to them, and would be under the influence for a couple of weeks after the arrival of traders. The Jesuits came upon campsites strewn with dead bodies after orgies that were followed by brawls and murders. Once he was sober again an Indian often believed that the spirits had made use of his arm to strike.

When brandy was not available, the woodrunner had other ways to make the most of Indian credulity. He promised to drive back ghosts and enemies, all the while magnifying his powers through tales about outlandish places and peoples. On the other hand his mimetic habits resulted in a transmutation that surprised French travelers. He wore the *capote* [beaver robe], a hooded blue coat, in winter, and went bare-breasted in summer with tattoos all over his body. Availing himself of his paramount ascendancy over the natives, he was able to dictate codes of behavior. The guns, medals, and clothes that he delivered allegedly bestowed prestige on the beneficiaries. A hunter rose in the clan hierarchy in proportion to the number of presents he received. Meantime the woodrunner was careful not to offend a chief in terms of decorum.

Alive to the common dangers of the environment, the woodrunner had learned how to prevent friendly tribes from plundering canoes before murdering and scalping the occupants. The motivations

for such tribal habits were various. The spirit of revenge was ingrained in the Indian mentalities, and a feud might extend over generations. French interference in such conflicts also aroused hostility,
as shown in the slaughter of Jean Baptiste de la Vérendrye after his
father had supplied arms to the Crees and Assiniboines in the mid-
eighteenth century.

The French who found refuge in the wilderness were not expecting to be redeemed by prelapsarian purity. In their midst, despera-
does, robbers, and slavers had long transported Indian captives and
children to put them up for sale in Montreal or Quebec. Slaves were
in great demand throughout the English colonies because the ocean
trade did not provide enough Africans for their plantations. West of
the Mississippi, Pawnees, Ojibwas, and Osages were favorite targets
of coureurs des bois, who risked their lives if they were caught in the
act by fellow tribesmen of the captives. Before the mid-eighteenth
century, a coureur des bois's life in the backwoods or in the prairies
seemed to be somehow out of time. Free from social restraints he
felt relieved from the inhibitions thwarting his instinctive urges in a
colony under strict Catholic observances. Moreover, he had little access to books such as *Robinson Crusoe* (published in 1719) and the
term "noble savage" would have sounded hilarious to him. Aware
that he appeared as a degenerate in the eyes of bourgeois, he was
far from imagining the fashionable primitivism displayed in Parisian
aristocratic circles.

In wartime, however, history caught up with the woodrunners. In
1684 the Knight of Troyes enlisted them to storm English outposts
on James Bay. In the same way Pierre Le Moyne d'Iberville attacked
Port Nelson in 1687. Both waged guerrilla warfare on the enemy.
Stalking the Redcoats in their light moccasins, while holding a small
axe, the French and their Indian companions carried their powder
pouch in otter bags, with their guns slung across their shoulders.
They furtively scattered and vanished in the forests before the bewildered English troops in their garish uniforms were sighted and waylaid.[43]

Since 1668 the mouths of rivers from James Bay to Hudson Bay
had been protected by English forts, such as Moose Factory, Fort Albany, Fort Charles, Fort Churchill, and Fort Chipewyan. With its network of waterways to the forts, the Hudson's Bay Company had
attracted French traders such as Radisson, Groseilliers, Elie Gri-
mard, and an interpreter nicknamed Le Parisien.[44]

In 1717, a garrison under lieutenant Zacharie Rebutel de Noue's
command settled on the south of Lake Nipigon. The French presence around the Great Lakes was thereby officially asserted. The

woodrunners were ideal scouts to precede forays into Indian country. Although the Treaty of Utrecht had banned the French from those territories the Canadians who still controlled the major trails and streams deterred Indians from reaching the trading posts of the Hudson's Bay Company. They scared them with rumors of epidemics or threats of war with the Sioux. In 1728 they mendaciously warned the tribes about an attack on Albany by the Mohawks. Acting as henchmen for officers, the woodrunners intimidated the most vulnerable of the tribesmen and terrorized Assiniboine families. They also allied with Sioux bands to raid a Cree camp near the trading post of Lac de la Pluie. Some treacherous white Indians were also in the habit of informing the English troops. In 1732 Joseph Delestre reached unarmed Fort Albany with his squaw and went over to the British. Were these men traitors? Sometimes they had no other choice. For instance, at Fort Bourbon Nicolas Jérémie was the sole survivor of a party of woodrunners invited to feast with a tribe that slaughtered them when drunk. Whenever a man like him felt ostracized or threatened, he sought safety at any cost. A woodrunner had little chance to be welcomed back by colonial society after he had vanished in the wilderness for years. At least he could offer his skills to the highest bidder, whether French or English.[45]

4

Life in the *Pays des Illinois* at Mid-Eighteenth Century

COLONIAL POLICIES

DURING THE FIRST YEARS OF HENRI DE TONTY'S COMMAND AT THE END OF the seventeenth century, the population of the *Pays des Illinois* [Illinois Territory] consisted of transplanted Canadians of Louis Jolliet's generation who, like him, were born in New France. They had long been confronted with the wilderness and had little in common with the pioneers of the English colonies with their large families. Most of residents in Illinois were bachelors. No wonder that the bourgeois voyageurs, the coureurs des bois, and the military rank and file would seek the company of Indian women, free as they were from the restraints of social observances and the duties of family life. So far the missionaries had been instrumental in having edicts drafted to ban promiscuity. But they were hardly ever enforced by commanders. Interracial unions were numerous and most often seasonal.[1]

Winter ice restricted navigation on the Great Lakes from late November to April. The long voyage home took ten weeks with days of paddling on streams and through rapids in birch-bark canoes. When the river ceased being navigable, a portage was necessary. Traders had to unload hundred of pounds of furs and trade goods, and then carry them backpack style from one stream to another. The portage could be long and toilsome when, for instance, it was necessary to bypass the Niagara Falls.

When Kaskaskia was founded in 1703 the fur traders were indispensable to the economy.[2] As time passed tilled land and grazing cattle changed the landscape. Married couples came from the east and orphan girls sponsored by royal authorities [*Filles du Roy*] were transported from France to replenish the settlement but they still far outnumbered the bachelors. The Illinois territory could no longer be likened to an extension of New France when it was made part of

Louisiana in 1717. For the previous decade only a score of settlers and traders had been living on the stretch of fertile land between Kaskaskia and Cahokia. They were all married to Indian women. By 1750, fields across the Mississippi were cultivated by the Kaskaskia, Fort de Chartres, and Cahokia communities along the banks of the Illinois. A score of salt workers, hunters, and traders now gathered in the new township of Sainte Geneviève.[3]

Houses were huddled together in long lots on riverbanks. Farmers grew crops of wheat, corn, barley, and tobacco. A new class of pioneers arose from the rural community but their mode of life had little in common with that of the English yeomen. The Illinois habitant was known for a joie de vivre that would have baffled self-righteous Puritans, who likened his Catholic rituals to pagan ceremonies. He danced on Sunday after Mass, then sat back on his porch or at the local tavern to sip his brandy while smoking his pipe. Upper Louisiana became a refuge for migrants from New France. They did not resent the extremes of a new climate after the hardships of the long Canadian winter. Happy with their modest lots, they never imagined themselves in the Promised Land. Although they went to church they often paid lip service to the priests' injunctions. Their modest peasant origins made them aware of the abuses of monarchy, especially after Louis XV, first called the *Bienaimé* [beloved], became so unpopular in the mother country that his coach had to bypass Paris on its way back to Versailles in times of war.

During the first decades of the eighteenth century, western New France inhabitants shifted progressively from northern to southern attitudes. Canadian authorities had to administer a region now identified as both the Illinois and Upper Louisiana. In keeping with the times, the law was harsh. Imprisonment for debt was frequent and torture often used to draw out confessions, especially under the Black Code now enforced from down south up to Kaskaskia.[2] A slave was generally sentenced to be whipped for committing larceny. In New Orleans a slave who was guilty of manhandling a soldier in 1742 had his right ear cut off and he had to carry a six-pound ball on his foot the rest of his life.[4]

The government heavily subsidized the Jesuit, Ursuline, and Sulpician orders by 1742. Missionaries among the Indians were granted six hundred livres per year by the king. In return for these allowances the French crown expected strict obedience. In case of controversy over Church property the king could simply annex a house or land to his domain. Meanwhile the government unfailingly supported the Church against its enemies. Heretics and profaners were severely punished. A fortune-teller using a crucifix could be sentenced to three years in the galleys.

The governors turned a blind eye to the liquor traffic to preserve the interests of the fur trade, but spoke out against abuses. They knew that should the Indians turn to the British to sell their pelts, it would be harmful to the Catholic Church, for the natives might adopt Protestant heresies. Henry du Breuil de Pontbriand, who was Bishop of Quebec, condemned the laxity of officers in the outposts, and proclaimed that dealers delivering *eau de vie* [brandy] to the savages should never be absolved of their sins in Confession. Yet the colonial economy was at stake in the issue. In 1748, Abbé de l'Isle Dieu stated in a letter to Pontbriand that the Indian tribes of the Tamaroas mission in the Illinois were given daily supplies of brandy by voyageurs and threatened to rebel when deprived of it. In 1747 the Jesuits had to abandon the Choctaw mission after riots were started by drunken Indians. Nevertheless, the Company of Jesus had long kept the natives loyal to the French and hostile to the British. In 1749 the order had fifty-one members in New France, thirty-four of whom were located among the tribes.[5]

In New France, colonial finances were supplied through the Treasurer General of the Navy. The circulating medium was generally restricted to card money exchanged with bills on the treasury at Rochefort or against the local treasury. Due to the balance deficit, coin remained scarce. In Louisiana, paper money was withdrawn by the king's ordinance in 1744. Military operations, especially those against the Chickasaw nation in the Mississippi Valley, put such a strain on colonial finances that card money was depreciated. The Spanish pistole became popular during the economic boom prompted by the war of 1744–48, but it declined in value after peace was restored.[6]

Aside from the regular expenses involved in the salaries of officials, the subsidies to the Church and the investments for fortifications, credits went first to the military in wartime and the Indian administration. Paid out of the proceeds from licenses to traders, local expenses were weighed down by gratuities to missionaries, interpreters, surgeons, and the almoner. The governor's approval was expected in financial matters but the intendant had considerable leeway to trim down the budget whenever he found fault with financial choices.

Louisiana was returned to the crown by the Company of the Indies in 1731. Within a highly centralized system, the king supplied the storekeeper of the colony with goods. This kind of process was under the supervision of the intendant and the farmer general of the revenues. The expenditures were heavy due to unexpected costs of the Chickasaw campaign of 1739–40. In 1743, they covered the great outlays needed for fortification. Paper money being discredited, a plan was offered to soak up the deficit. This implied sending more than six hundred black slaves to the Illinois on the king's account, each being sold for 1,800 livres, but it was eventually rejected by the minister.[6]

The sum required for Indian presents was constantly increasing. It amounted to 54,000 livres in 1746, four times the sum allocated in 1731. The threats of uprisings in the Pays de Illinois was a strong motivation to offer gifts to maintain alliances or subsidize war parties. The funds were supplied by purchases from traders at the posts, and generally at high prices. The costs of freight added one-third to the value of commodities. Another cause for excessive spending was the convoy of supplies sent to the Arkansas, Natchitoches, and Illinois posts very year. The boats were manned by slaves escorted by soldiers. Traders going to the backwoods took advantage of the convoy, which was safer than using *pirogues* in the Indian country. But on the way, goods were sometimes given away by corrupt members of the crews. In 1749, the convoy under the command of Lieutenant de Montchervaux made slow progress toward the Illinois. He had left the Indian gifts behind at New Orleans, buying others at an exorbitant price to trade with officers in the posts along the river. In 1750, an investigation led to taking the trade out of the hands of the military, and leaving the king's goods on the care of private individuals under contract.[7]

The non-Indian population of Louisiana was close to 9,000 in 1745. It extended from the Gulf of Mexico to the Illinois, with small settlements on the Missouri, the Wabash, and the Arkansas Rivers. There were 1,500 women and children and almost 5,000 black slaves, including mulattoes. Most people came from Canada, and New Orleans had several hundred inhabitants. Posts were scattered near the mouth of the tributaries of the Mississippi. The Arkansas post had a garrison of fewer than twenty soldiers. A dozen settlers hunted buffalo and bear. They salted the meat and sent it down to other posts. They also raised tobacco and sold it to traders or Indians.

There were four villages in the Illinois: Kaskaskia, Prairie du Rocher, Saint Philippe, and Cahokia, numbering in all about a thousand whites and 350 slaves. Few inhabitants were located at Fort de Chartres and Sainte Geneviève on the Missouri side. They all grew some corn but were mostly engaged in hunting and fur trading.

The government relied more on the high birthrate than on immigration to increase the number of colonists. Dissatisfied settlers were firmly deterred from returning to the homeland as they would have set a bad example among their fellow Frenchmen already skeptical about prospects in the New World. Detroit had a population of 1,500 by 1750.[8] Other French communities were now stabilized around Michilimackinac and River Saint Joseph. Houses were built with notched logs. They had dirt floors and no glass in the windows. The roof was made of wooden shingles fastened with wooden pins since nails were scarce in the western country. On the inside, walls were whitewashed with lime. Like the natives, the whites relied chiefly on fish, venison, and corn for food. Wine and brandy were drunk freely when obtainable. In the mid-eighteenth century the French suffered from poor health in Louisiana. Smallpox had been spread by slaves from Africa but the *grippe* [flu] was the most prevalent disease, along with the mumps.[9]

FRENCH COMMUNITIES

French society in the Illinois did not share the expectations of the English pioneers in the Appalachians. The centralized administration gave few opportunities to colonists eager to go westward and plant new settlements. Most of the concessions were held under grants from the king whose 1716 edict had redistributed lands to eliminate speculators. Each new plot of about sixty acres had a free tenant if the concessionaire agreed to submit to seigneurial rights. In 1743, Governor Beauharnois had been in power for seventeen years. A new common for pastures was carved out on the peninsula formed by the Kaskaskia and Mississippi Rivers. But incentives to cattle breeding and agricultural development could never divert the inhabitants from their interest in trading. Chevalier Charles de Bertet, who was commander in the Illinois in 1742, sent convicted salt smugglers to work in lead mines. On the other hand, Pierre François Rigaud de Cavagnol, Marquis de Vaudreuil the new governor of Louisiana in 1743, was anxious to ban the transportation of slaves to the Illinois, claiming that their large numbers in the fields would turn the farmers away from their tasks. He had the last word against inhabitants who felt victimized compared to their fellow Englishmen in the South.[10]

Corn grew well in the alluvion deposited by the Mississippi although farming was still dependent on wooden plows drawn by oxen while horses were generally intended for portage. The Illinois became the granary for Louisiana and the French Antilles. But the efforts to develop extensive farming were hampered by the lack of available land. The Jesuits leased fields, and supplied seeds and implements at Detroit. Crops were shared in halves with the owner— except for corn that the tenant kept. In return, he plowed for the Jesuits, and his wife took care of their laundry.[11]

On the Great Plains, the French pioneers hunted the buffalo for the wool of its neck, which was sold to stocking and hat manufacturers. When he was appointed governor of Canada in 1747, Roland-Michel Barrin La Galissonnière went west to watch buffalo herds that he believed inexhaustible.[12] He imagined having them rounded up and slaughtered for their salted meat to be shipped to Europe. Illinois salt was produced in great quantities near Kaskaskia. It was an example of the resourcefulness of a population too sparse to envisage broader prospects but on the whole happy with their lot.

La Galissonnière was deeply concerned with the future of the French West. He felt that jealous neighbors might soon plan to strip France of her colonies. At any rate they could not compete forever with the fast-developing English settlements. The fur trade was now less lucrative because the difficulties of navigation in the vast interior kept the resources often too far apart. However, La Galissonnière saw the West as the future home of a numerous population that would hopefully offset on land the superiority the English had on sea. He was equally interested in the demographic growth around the Great Lakes. He calculated that a thousand farmers would be enough to keep the upper lakes region and the Illinois safe from foreign intrusion. La Galissonnière's geopolitical schemes consisted of keeping the English at a distance to prevent them from winning the Indians over to their cause by dismantling either Canada or Louisiana. He thought of sending men as soldiers to the Illinois and discharging them after a short term of service. The settlement of the West would be accomplished by immigration from Canada, while the Illinois would, in turn, help with the population growth of Louisiana.

La Galissonnière was not always consistent in his statements about the Illinois. In 1748, before the outbreak of the French and Indian War, he contended that the region would never become prosperous. Three years later, he acknowledged that the Illinois could steadily ship grain downriver as far as New Orleans despite all the naval forces in the world.[13]

THE BROWN GOLD

In 1743, Cadwallader Colden observed that the French employed men of great abilities in the fur trade.[14] But their supremacy was gradually threatened by the initiatives of their English rivals. France believed in strict regulation, and did not tolerate free trade in open competition. In the farming system the monopoly of the fur trade could be granted to individuals or companies at public auction. They thus received a lease for three years to exploit a post. Not only choosing the amount of goods to exchange, including liquor, and loading canoes, farmers were also expected to transport cargoes for the officer in charge of the post and to supply him with firewood. The farmer would sometimes hire engagés and an interpreter to deal with Indians. Under the license system the voyageur bought a *congé* [clearance certificate] indicating the number of canoes and engagés allowed for his business, as well as the route taken to reach a remote site in the Indian country. The engagés under contract were paid in peltries on their return. By 1742 a royal ordinance banned the fur trade by the officers at the posts because they neglected their official duties when they devoted time to profit making, sometimes bordering on corruption. By 1743 all the posts except for Michilimackinac and Detroit were converted to the farming system and let out at auction. Officers in command were now paid a percentage of the proceeds of the posts. Charles de la Buache de Beauharnois, appointed governor in 1726, had vainly objected to the royal edict by pointing to the risk of exorbitant prices owing to higher bids by farmers. In the previous system officers had also a much smaller share of the profits and the Indians paid less for the goods they bought.[15]

The war with the English allowed no time to revise the trade regulations but the rising cost of goods hastened the defection of the Indians from the French of the upper country, in places like *La Baye* [Green Bay] and River Saint Joseph. When he took office in 1747, Governor La Galissonnière recommended that posts such as Nipigon, Kamanistiquia, and Chequamigon might be left with the farmers, as they were too far from the English to face any danger. On the other hand, officers were to receive a fixed payment instead of revenue based on production.[16]

The coureurs des bois were still considered to be illegal intruders. When they could not get their supplies in Illinois they defected to the enemy by seeking cooperation with the English in exchange for pelts. During the war years those outlawed, double-dealing backwoodsmen on the run grew in number and prosperity when the supply of French goods ran short in the west. Between Canada and Louisiana, Illinois was a convenient refuge for deserters who, being on the outskirts of the two colonies, could not easily be claimed by justice. Voyageurs licensed in Canada often ignored local authorities to gain access to remote Indian furs thanks to the coureurs des bois' schemes. When Vaudreuil and Beauharnois were asked by the French minister to chase lawless traders the Canadian governor was jealous of the possession of the Illinois by Louisiana, and was in no mood to cooperate prior to the establishment of clear boundary lines.

Traders from Montreal sent convoys to deliver goods to Indians, especially to get beaver, the main market in the Illinois. The canoes returned home loaded with furs and pelts, either before bad weather or after wintering. Apart from utensils like kettles and boilers, tools such as awls and needles, and the usual paraphernalia of ribbon, mirrors, and colored rateen for moccasins and beads, Indians were mostly interested in gunflints, powder, steel for striking fire, knives, and hatchets as well as brandy and tobacco. In the competition with the English, the French market was weak on *ecarlatine,* the cloth used for blankets and petticoats. The ban on brandy also went against French traders in the 1730s. When Indians were suspected of delivering beaver to the agents of the Hudson's Bay Company with the complicity of the coureurs des bois, French raiding parties in the neighborhood of Oswego in 1746 slackened the English fur trade, which was again thriving in 1749. Stringent measures were then taken to oppose woodrunner infiltration and reconcile regular voyageurs with the farmers who had also been prone to encroach upon one another's right in the competition for pelts. It was equally essential to deter Indians from trading with the British once and for all. Convoys were to be put under military command by Jacques-Pierre de Taffanel de La Jonquière, the new governor in 1749. Yet to be made secure against English competition the trading area of beaver had to be extended to the northwest after La Vérendrye's expeditions had opened new avenues.[17]

WAR AND PEACE WITH THE INDIANS

In the early eighteenth century France was endeavoring to build an empire by strengthening the middle colony of the Illinois as a buffer zone between Canada and Louisiana. As Spaniards and Englishmen were pushing toward the Mississippi, the French had to rely on allies among Indian nations to support them against the intruders. But the good neighbor policy turned into harsh reprisals when the natives did not comply with France's schemes. In the South the proud Natchez who refused to cede their lands attacked Fort Rosalie in 1729 and killed the members of the garrison. Etienne

Boucher de Périer, the new governor of Louisiana after Bienville had left the office, enlisted the Choctaws to destroy the Natchez, who two years later numbered only about a hundred. They were rescued by the Chickasaws who lived throughout the Mississippi Valley after expanding their hunting grounds to obtain more skins and pelts for the British trade. When the French realized that the Chickasaws were cutting off Louisiana from the Illinois they pressed their Choctaw allies to intimidate the intruders by scalping their warriors, and paid them accordingly. The French eventually won the Choctaws' allegiance by arming them with guns to fight the Creeks and the Chickasaws. Aside from such strategic moves, France highly valued the deerskins available in the Choctaw villages. Both French and English agents labored to retain their influence while innumerable local chiefs were played off against the European rivals.[18]

In the Pays d'en Haut the Foxes, who first lived in eastern Wisconsin, were pushed south to northern Illinois by the Ojibwas. They stood between the French and the Sioux on the Upper Mississippi and fiercely defended their land against invasion by keeping away traders from the Minnesota and Des Moines routes. Many years before, in 1701, Antoine de Lamothe Cadillac had built a new fort at Detroit and asked the local tribes to settle in Michigan, close to what he called the Paris of America.[19] A decade later the Foxes, Sauks, Mascoutens, and Kickapoos turned down his relocation offer. In 1712, after Cadillac had been relieved of his command at Detroit, the Foxes attacked the fort but the French replied by laying siege to their fortified village. The Indians suffered heavy losses. However, they continued to fight the occupant until 1716.[20]

The conflicts between the Foxes and the Illinois appeared detrimental to the fur trade especially when water transportation was needed through Fox regions. In 1727 Beauharnois declared war on the Foxes, who threatened to ally with the Iroquois and the Sioux. French agents infiltrated neighboring tribes to divide the enemy. Feeling isolated, a band of a thousand Foxes sought to find refuge in the Seneca country. But a whole army of Creole traders and Illinois Indians as well as bands of Miamis, Potawatomis, and Sauks, led by Nicolas Antoine Coulon de Villiers, besieged them in northern Illinois. When the Foxes attempted a breakout in the dark after three weeks, they were chased by more than a thousand French and Indian pursuers who caught up with the men, women, and children. Beauharnois was pitiless. Except for fifty of them, all were stabbed or tortured and burnt alive. The eradication of the Foxes lifted the barrier on the Mississippi and the Sioux country. The survivors moved to Green Bay, then to the lower Rock River.[21]

The French government was determined to preserve Indian alliances in the upper Mississippi regions at all costs. Yet tribes did not share the same status with regard to the administration. There were Indians living at western posts, those in or around settlements and village communities, and lastly free Indians ranging the woods and the open country. The Illinois tribes were progressively Christianized by Jesuit or Sulpician missionaries who expected them to assist the French in their wars. The governors of Canada and Louisiana met delegates from the tribes each spring at Montreal and Mobile to strengthen ties and encourage commercial cooperation by distributing presents. Ruling over nations often in conflict was, however, no easy matter. At Detroit the Hurons were tired of being harassed by the Ottawas and in 1739 thought of moving to the Ohio Valley or joining some southern tribe. Negotiations with Jesuit Father La Richardie on behalf of Beauharnois failed when Nicolas, a Huron chief, led his people to the south shore of Lake Erie. La Richardie then opposed the plan to remove the tribe to Sault Saint Louis on account of Iroquois hostility in the area. He was, in fact, suspicious of the influence of the Sulpician order there. The commandant at Detroit also hoped that the Hurons would join friendly nations to wage war on the Chickasaws. Beauharnois sent his nephew to Detroit in the summer of 1741 to help find a solution. But his mission to the Huron village on Lake Erie failed utterly. The Jesuits thwarted the governor's plan to settle the tribe at Montreal. La Richardie was accused of being under English influence through his connection with the Iroquois. The new commandant at Detroit, Pierre Jacques Payan, Sieur de Noyan, complained to the minister that Beauharnois was striving to rule Detroit from Quebec. His nephew's mission had deprived the commandant of his power over the Hurons. Despite the support that De Noyan received from the French court, Beauharnois was strong enough to remove him from Detroit. The Hurons eventually settled at La Grande Terre below Detroit.[22]

At Michilimackinac the Ottawas aimed to seek better lands for their crops by moving to the Wisconsin region. Pierre-Joseph Céloron, Sieur de Blainville, who was commandant of the post, managed to have the Ottawas return after they had spent the winter of 1740 on the banks of the upper Mississippi. When the Ottawas addressed Beauharnois to counteract Céloron he assigned two possible sites for relocation and left them to make their own choice. One site was at the head of Lake Huron, and the other on the northwest corner of the Michigan peninsula. Céloron's obstinacy was rewarded when the Ottawas decided to move to L'Arbre Croche, a stone's throw from Michilimackinac, ultimately heedless of the governor's promise of more brandy if they accepted his offer.

In 1740 the Sioux increased their raids against isolated Ottawa communities and French runaways from the forts. They also led brutal attacks against Illinois tribes. In retaliation, the latter killed several Foxes on the Wisconsin River, mistaking them for Sioux. New fights flared up when Sacs avenged the Foxes by killing nine Illinois. It was only later that the Illinois recognized they had been confused about their target. In 1742, the Sioux seemed to be ready to negotiate an agreement—a move that appeared credible after the La Verendrye expedition had received promises of a return to peace among nations on the Great Plains.[23]

Since 1739, Beauharnois had relied on Pierre Paul Marin de la Malgue, an Indian agent whose task was to return the Sacs and Foxes back to La Baye in Wisconsin after their unexpected inroads in the Illinois in support of English traders. When Marin went back to France on business in 1743, he was succeeded by Paul Louis Dazenard, Sieur de Lusignan. As the Sioux were seeking an alliance with the Foxes, the minister, who was supported by the king, ordered Beauharnois to oppose it, but the governor openly disagreed because he thought that any effort to separate them would bring war. His determination was finally rewarded by the withdrawal of the minister's instructions.[24]

On his part Lusignan was weak with the Sioux. When several of them murdered three Frenchmen in the Illinois, they were carelessly released. It was probably a display of leniency to relieve tension but the decision hurt the farming population. Many other incidents occurred in the same period. Probably stirred up by some coureurs des bois, in 1740 the Missouris organized a war party against the Arkansas who had sided with the French.

In 1745 De Bertet decided to farm out the Missouri fur trade to a person likely to support French interests. Sieur Paul Deruisseaux, a Canadian seigneur, was offered the monopoly for five years. He built a fort and a storehouse, paid bribes to officers, transported effects for the garrison, and gave presents to the Indians. Beaver and marten were to be shipped to Canada, but Louisiana could receive other products. Long-term peace seemed to be established. De Bertet happily informed Vaudreuil that Deruisseaux's achievement had put an end to the unrest caused by straggling coureurs des bois and their Indian henchmen in the area.[25]

The Shawnees triggered new conflicts when they migrated from the Allegheny River to the lower Ohio, then to Shawneetown in the Illinois. They were known as pro-French but had connections with

English traders in Pennsylvania especially through their chief Peter Chartier, a French half-breed. Unable to provide goods to retain their loyalty, Vaudreuil thought of removing them to the west but they soon broke up. Some of them settled in Ohio to serve English interests. The burden of supporting Indian allies was becoming unbearable by 1745. Hordes of them were clustering around posts to collect food and presents when convoys arrived.[26]

In the southwest colonies, the Chickasaws still remained in a position to limit French expansion. In 1739, forces from both Canada and Louisiana were mustered by Bienville at Fort Prudhomme on the Mississippi to crush the Chickasaws, but bad organization, in addition to diseases among the troops, doomed the campaign to failure, so a doubtful truce was signed hurriedly with the enemy. In the following years, the Chickasaws ventured into Ohio to push back the northern raids that the Canadian government permitted. Bienville's mishandling of the Chickasaw crisis had dealt a significant blow to French prestige. But the fear of an upheaval in the Illinois by dissatisfied natives ultimately prompted Bienville to annihilate the Chickasaw presence along the Mississippi. Their tribes were so decimated by heavy casualties that they could hardly survive their defeats. Another reason for the French victory had been the decision to support Choctaw warfare against an hereditary enemy. But the Choctaws themselves were tempted to defect to the English under the leadership of chief Red Shoe and his brother Mingo. Eventually the delivery of adequate supplies by the French authorities persuaded the faithful population to rise up against Red Shoe and his followers.[27]

Except for the Pays des Illinois in 1718, and Detroit by the mid-eighteenth century, French expansion amounted to occupation without population. There were trading posts and villages, but no stable colonial society. Paradoxically, the king's entourage delighted in utopian wishful thinking by enthusiastically outlining an empire of the West involving noble savages and aristocrats addicted to primitivism.

Friendly western Indians were not subject to economic or military pressure. Their political independence was fully recognized. Seen from forts and Indian villages, the imperial presence boiled down to a handful of missionaries, farmers, and woodrunners. French lives depended on the goodwill of the allied nations toward the often transient residents. Instead of coercion, the French chose to make themselves indispensable to the locals by providing them with tools, food, and medical care. Under the appearance of equal treatment they obtained allegiance through gratitude whenever chiefs did not know better. As the French moved around in Indian communities, missionaries emulated shamans, and officers were inspired by chieftains' ceremonials. The French underclass experimented with marginality whereas dignitaries relied on the support of the natives with somewhat feigned humility. Whereas the British colonist was first a surveyor, the French habitant was seen as a simple blacksmith to whom the natives ascribed magic power. Miscegenation and social interaction resulted in a composite culture in which forts, outposts, and lodges harbored new but problematic interracial ways of life.

Around the Great Lakes, Detroit was not considered as safe as Michilimakinac, owing to the close relationships between the British and the Iroquois. Improvisation, makeshift, and the spirit of adventure were major factors in the survival of partially integrated French patterns of settlement. The freedom enjoyed in the wilderness was conducive to an alternative process of colonization well beyond government control. The monarchy considered the French presence in the west as a bulwark, apt to hold back the flow of British immigration. It was primarily a defensive task, for France could not afford to control a new continent. Yet delusions of grandeur could conceal the harsh realities of a country unreasonably clasping her dreams of supremacy, just as France was becoming nostalgic about the receding Grand Siècle.

5

Shifting Identities

THE EMPIRE IN JEOPARDY

BACK EAST, NEW FRANCE FELT THE SHOCK WAVE OF THE EUROPEAN WAR OF Austrian Succession (1740–48), during which the English had been severely defeated at the battle of Fontenoy by French troops. When the first ranks of the English column stopped fifty yards from the French guards, officers saluted each other. Lord Hay shouted, "Have your troops shoot first" but the Comte d'Anterroches replied, "No, Sir, after you." The beau geste cost the loss of the French front lines on the battlefield. Gallic bravado was to pay a much higher price in the following decades.[1]

Now England was turning toward the new continent to build an empire, starting with the storming of Louisburg. The French government launched an offensive in the hope of rousing the city's population against its British occupiers. But the fleet sent from Rochefort with 3,500 soldiers never attained its goals. The newly appointed governor, La Jonquière, was then sailing to Canada on a ship that was scuttled by the royal navy. In 1748 the Peace of Aachen established a compromise by which Louisburg was returned to France.[2] It was only an elusive truce. The two European powers had been preparing a major confrontation in which the possession of Ohio and the Mississippi Valley was at stake. The French built Fort Vincennes to protect the Ohio and Wabash Rivers. From the French view, the vital alliance with the Miamis had been threatened since 1743, when English traders had crossed the Appalachians and settled at Pickawillany. From the English point of view, the Ohio River was the only outlet for their expansionist policies.

Meanwhile the French West was set ablaze. In Detroit and Michilimackinac news was spread of a rebellion among the Potawatomis and the Ottawas. In 1748 Indians surrendered the murderers of several Frenchmen. When they were shackled and transported to Quebec there was an uproar among the natives. Three prisoners escaped and killed the soldiers who were escorting them.[3] Despite the Indians' plea for leniency the colonists demanded merciless punishment for the culprits.

The Pays des Illinois was a key position, though dangerously distant from both Quebec and Louisiana. When De Bertet took command in 1742, Fort de Chartres was in bad repair and could hardly become the stronghold of resistance to foreign invasion as initially planned. De Bertet abandoned the fort in 1747 to concentrate troops and most of the settlement at nearby Kaskaskia. Because of the nature of the English threat, the decision was made to leave the Illinois country to the care of Louisiana and to supply Vaudreuil with military support from the southern garrisons. It was only in 1751 that Monsieur de Macarty-Mactigue took command of Fort de Chartres with six companies as reinforcement. François Saucier, an engineer from Mobile, Alabama, was called to draw the plans of a new fort. He had to overcome innumerable obstacles before the fort, though unfinished, imposed its stone walls in the landscape of the Mississippi River plain in 1757.[4] His son François had been commander of Portage des Sioux since 1799, when Lewis and Clark were preparing their expedition at nearby Camp Dubois in the winter of 1803–04.

In 1748 the French lost the support of the Miamis whose rapprochement with Pennsylvania constituted an asset for the contemporaries of Benjamin Franklin. A delegation of Ottawas implored the Miamis to remain in the French alliance. Their refusal was considered as a betrayal, liable to harsh retribution. The Miami chief Memeskia, known to the French as La Demoiselle, had promised rewards for the scalp of the commandant of Detroit, Baron Paul Joseph Lemoyne de Longueuil. The local French fort had been burnt in 1747 and Frenchmen killed or held prisoners. When Joseph Guyon Dubuisson, Longueuil's emissary, was sent to negotiate he could do little more than hold his position, neither repairing the damage or punishing the assassins. A year later, La Demoiselle received plentiful supplies of merchandise to reward his newly proffered ally. In fact, he was still an archenemy of the French.[5]

To demonstrate his unflinching attitude, La Galissonnière sent Pierre-Joseph Céloron in command of two hundred and fifty French soldiers and thirty Indians to the Ohio in the middle of June 1749.[6] They reached Niagara, made a portage around the falls, then another to the upper Alleghenies. Near present-day Warren, Pennsylvania, Céloron buried leaden plates declaring that the Ohio and its tributaries were French. On his way he saw the English flag flying and noted that the natives were hostile to the French. After ascend-

ing the Great Miami, the party stopped at the village of La Demoiselle where they obtained his promise to return to the Miami post
with his tribe the following spring. On their way back Céloron's men
reached the Detroit River in October and descended to Montreal in
the middle of December. By 1750 a new threat of rebellion was rumored in the Illinois: Kaskaskia and Cahokia were targeted by a coalition of Miamis, Osages, and Sioux won over to the English side by
the promise of cheap goods.[7]

As the showdown between France and England known as the
Seven Years' War drew closer, the French West seemed to be weakened in several ways. The ancien régime was unfit to overcome the
difficulties caused by maintaining new posts or settlements in the
wilderness. The ambition to rule colonial life from Paris through
Michilimackinac and Detroit remained utterly impracticable. Besides, the scant means allowed was not equal to the imperial ambition of the French government. Colonial funds were not only
insufficient but rarely available in times of urgent need. Yet ironically, the yearly colonial expenditures in Canada and Louisiana did
not even amount to the pension of a Versailles courtier. The quest
of prestige was priceless and debt immeasurable in the kingdom of
France. The New York colony had twice the population of both Canada and Louisiana in the eighteenth century. Immigration to New
France was inadequate to meet the demands of territorial expansion, especially to pacify Indian tribes and retard the flow of English
migrants. Even after the ban on non-Catholic immigrants had been
lifted, pioneers were outnumbered by officials crowding the administration and the armed forces, aristocrats seeking glory and favors,
convicts transported from France, discontented deserters, and outlawed adventurers in the wilderness.

In the mid-eighteenth century the French fur trade could still
prosper in the upper Mississippi and the Northwest after the British
had invested the lower Great Lakes region and the Upper Ohio. As
beaver was diminishing in number, La Galissonnière predicted the
inevitable decline of the trade and once more stressed the necessity
to turn to farming. Meanwhile the French alliance with the Indians
was recognized by Europeans as outstanding and inimitable, considering the expanse of land to control and the permanent shortage of
goods to offer in the fur trade. The noblemen in charge of diplomatic relations generally fared well with the natives. French pater-
nalism was comparable to the manners of early planter society in the
Old South. But, averse as they were to the rabble, the colonial rulers
could also be ruthless when Indian behavior reminded them of the
peasant upheavals known as the *jacqueries.*

The French population in the West was aware of the power and the wealth of British colonial America. To thwart an impending invasion inordinately depended on the alliance with Indian nations, and also on the willingness and capacity of the mother country to save her colonies in North America. The French pioneer population was socially divided, out of touch with the centralized government, and subject to officers who had no stake in the future of the transatlantic colonies.

THE FRENCH AND INDIAN WARS

As opposed to previous European conflicts, the Seven Years' War (1756–63) began with skirmishes in Ohio before spreading to the other continents. It involved Europe, North America, India, and the West Indies. Back in the mid-1750s the wars had a strong impact on European minds owing to their exotic attraction and the fratricidal conflicts between Indian communities more than ever before dependent on their English or French allies for food, clothing, and weapons. Most Indian populations sided with France, but the situation was singular in a confrontation taking place in a context far different from European battlefields.

French voyageurs were enlisted to participate in guerrilla warfare against the English troops and their agents, who were eager to infiltrate the Ohio and the Great Lakes. The English strategy to divert the Indians from their French alliance was obstructed when 150 voyageur brigades from the Northwest reinforced Detroit while rallying Huron, Potawatomi, and Ottawa tribes. Meanwhile, numbers of Miami and Huron allies of the French defected to join a coalition masterminded by the English commander. The lack of communication between Canada and Louisiana contributed to demoralize the Illinois population. Yet the firing power of the English troops was overrated through unfounded rumors. In the Northwest, the Crees warned the Hudson's Bay Company against thirty Canadians in seven canoes who were trying to intercept the furs of the Assiniboines. Indians were often prevented from reaching their usual trading posts on the tributaries of the Albany River by Canadian traders. It was thus in the interest of the company to provoke the Crees into fighting the French.

At the outbreak of the war with England, French colonists were in low spirits. Under the administration of Governor La Jonquière and Intendant François Bigot, corruption had spread to the west where, for instance, the La Baye post made huge illicit profits. Most farmers called up in the militia had to leave their fields in the care of their wives. Meanwhile their sons elected to retreat into the woods among Indian tribes. Major Macarty-Mactique was appointed commandant of Illinois in 1750 and promoted to the coveted rank of chevalier de Saint-Louis.[8] He led a convoy of keelboats and canoes upstream from New Orleans in August 1751. A band of Miamis had come to Fort de Chartres a few days before his arrival. They planned to make a foray into Kaskaskia on Christmas Day when the faithful came back from Mass. Being aware of the plot, Macarty's men sent out a few colonists on horseback, who deceived the ambushed Miamis by suddenly rushing back to the fort, thus raising a false alarm. Believing they were discovered, the Indians disbanded under the fire of the French troops. Thirty Indians were killed and a few others taken prisoner. When he was informed on the event, Governor Vaudreuil sent back orders to release the prisoners who then confessed they had been misled by the English.[9]

In March 1752, Macarty was in trouble over the rebellion of young recruits who refused to chase deserters. He put a young man under arrest but he was pardoned upon the insistence of officers' wives, who feared riots in the community.[10] The inhabitants of Fort de Chartres faced another ordeal in June 1752, when a coalition of Sauks, Sioux, and Kickapoos came down the Mississippi on Corpus Christi Day to retaliate on Cahokia Illinois who had captured and killed Fox hunters. The Foxes set fire to a village, slaughtered men, women, and children and led away the rest as captives. Back in their canoes the warriors passed by Fort de Chartres, and hoisted the French colors in defiance of Macarty. Being allies of the two nations, the French would have imposed their mediation before the bloodshed had they been forewarned. It remained for the emissaries of the governor to treat with the Foxes concerning the ransom of the Illinois.[11]

At La Jonquière's death in 1752, Ange de Menneville, marquis de Duquesne, was appointed governor of New France. His one aim was to push back the English from the Ohio frontier. The same year veteran Céloron sent Ottawa chief Charles Langlade with 250 of his kin and coureurs des bois to raid Pickawillany. The Miami renegade La Demoiselle was killed, butchered, and eaten.[12] The English traders were spared but the Miami population slaughtered. The survivors had to bow to French authority and for some time the axis of communication between Canada and Louisiana was secured.

Duquesne raised an army of a few hundred regulars, two thousand militiamen, and two hundred native tribesmen. Pierre-Paul de la Malgue "born with a tomahawk in his hand" was in command.[13]

In 1754 Fort Duquesne was built at the fork of the Monongahela and Ohio Rivers by a Montreal expeditionary corps. The English troops were ill-prepared to prevent the French from preserving the Ohio Valley for themselves. Lieutenant Colonel George Washington was in charge of a detachment designed to contain the French advance. Accompanied by Iroquois Chief Tanaghrisson. he attacked the French camp on May 28, and ordered firing on a party whose commanding officer, Ensign Joseph Coulon de Villiers de Jumonville, was killed before he had time to read the demands by the English to leave the lands of the king. All the French soldiers were shot and scalped. The French counteroffensive compelled Washington to surrender.[14] When the news of the event reached France, an indignant Voltaire stated: "I was English at heart but am no longer so, when they murder our officers in America."[15] This was typical Gallic jingoism. Native guerrilla warfare was considered as a valuable asset on the French side, but denounced as a treacherous practice in English strategy.

In the west the French and Indian forces first won significant battles. Louis Joseph Marquis de Montcalm Gozon de Saint Véran became Major General of New France. His second in command was Gaston François, Chevalier de Levis. Montcalm captured the British Fort Oswego on the south shore of Lake Ontario in 1756. He also took Fort William Henry in the upper valley of the Hudson and strengthened the defenses of Fort Carillon (Lake George, New York), also known as Ticonderoga. As a result, the French momentarily weakened the Iroquois power in Oneida country. Smallpox ravaged the Great Lakes region where the Potawatomis were living. It swept through northern Ontario, Rainy Lake, and Red River, wiping out three fourths of the Ojibwas and ninety percent of the Chippewas. In 1759 Louis Césaire Dagneau, sieur de Quindre (1704–67) led a militia from Detroit that included his brother Major Guillaume Dagneau and François Marie Le Marchand de Lignery in an attempt to relieve Fort Niagara, which was under attack by the British. But Dagneau was taken prisoner and the operation fizzled. In July 1759 the French commander of Fort Niagara, Pierre Bouchot, surrendered to the British force. Lignery was ambushed, wounded, and captured. He died a few days later.

Louis Antoine, comte de Bougainville, acknowledged that Niagara was the gateway to the west. He was a clear-sighted, realistic officer with outstanding scientific knowledge, who served as Montcalm's aide-de-camp. He could have been a Meriwether Lewis to a French sovereign, eager to conquer the terra incognita of the empire. He deplored the way the colonial officials despised the rank and file while fawning on Indian tribes. He soon realized that governors were doting "great fathers," who depended too much on the whims of their savage children. He sensed the irreconcilable antagonism between the French occupants and the Canadian residents. Bougainville was not allured by the exotic habits of the natives, but tried to adapt to them as a strategic choice. He was adopted by Mohawks and sang war songs reluctantly. He painfully admitted that the Canadians had no other option than to ambush, scalp, and torture their enemies. But he was also aware that their victories were short-lived because they preferred to share their time between skirmishes and hunting, and had no broad perspectives. Long campaigns were thus incompatible with their carefree way of life. In the long run, Bougainville found that French guerrilla warfare was self-defeating.[16]

As a token of their friendly spirit the Louisiana colonists supported the war efforts. Coulon de Villiers escorted a convoy of food supplies to Fort Duquesne from the Illinois and raided Fort Granville near present-day Altoona, Pennsylvania. In 1755 a new British expedition to capture the fort under Major General Edward Braddock and George Washington with 2,000 men was ambushed by a French force of 250 militia men and 600 Indians led by Captain Daniel de Beaujeu. Most of the English troops were captured or massacred by Indians who looted their convoys. In June 1756, Fort de Chartres was threatened when Charles Philippe Aubry came from New Orleans to build a fort on the Ohio (across from present-day Paducah, Kentucky). In operation a year later, it was called Fort Massac. The triumphant mood was short-lived. The English pressure on the west had much intensified by 1758. Aubry left Fort Duquesne with troops and supplies to withstand the advance of seven thousand English regulars and colonial volunteers. Despite a few successful delaying actions, the French withdrew and burned Fort Duquesne. Aubry and his detachment retreated to Illinois before a new contingent was organized. In the spring of 1759 Aubry sailed up the Ohio and the Wabash to reach Fort Niagara. Close to his destination, he was attacked by General William Johnson, lost a hundred men, and was captured.

Ohio tribes were receptive to English offers of cooperation. The peace that was struck enabled General Forbes to make progress toward Fort Duquesne. He was convinced that the preservation of the west depended on maintaining Indian alliances. In the spring of 1759 the French troops who remained in the Ohio Valley were so poorly armed that their Indian allies felt that they bore the brunt of the offensive.

The Battle of the Plaines d'Abraham in Quebec sealed the fate of

New France on September 14, 1759. A year later the Illinois was still independent of English rule. Its population was apprehensive of an invasion daily as enemy troops were often sighted in the vicinity of Saint Joseph. After the surrender of Quebec, the commander of Michilimackinac had decided to retreat to Fort de Chartres with a hundred troops where their presence was welcome. Within a few months the French-Indian alliance had been disrupted. In the summer of 1760 western Indians met at Fort Pitt to pledge allegiance to the English crown. By the fall of 1761 only Illinois was not under the British flag. Captain Pierre Joseph Neyon de Villiers took over from Macarty, who had left for New Orleans.[17]

Once the peace returned after the Treaty of Paris in 1763, not all the Indians were prone to accept the English in the place of the French who had been driven out of their lands. Throughout the negotiations leading to the treaty, the French monarchy was concerned about maintaining a time-honored alliance with the Spanish branch of the Bourbon family. French diplomats contended that Canada included neither Ohio nor the Illinois, and wanted to shore up defenses with a neutral Indian state near the Mississippi. Yet the treaty ratified by Louis XV gave to Britain all the lands of the Illinois. In 1762 the French king had already ceded Louisiana to his cousin Carlos III of Spain but the population continued to live as before. Neyon de Villiers, the commander of Illinois, was then at the head of a territory under the Union Jack but with no British troops in sight. The despondent French Canadians had a frustrating sense of betrayal by the crown. The deportation of the Acadians and their exile in Louisiana, called *le grand dérangement* [removal], in addition to the bitterness of a forsaken people vindicated the phrase *les maudits français* [the damned French] applied to their unworthy mother country.[18]

The Ottawas, led by Chief Pontiac, felt they could organize a coalition of Indian nations to repel the British forces. With the help of groups of humiliated Frenchmen who were still eager to demonstrate their aspiration to independence, the Indians first tried to take Detroit by surprise, then stormed Fort Michilimackinac on June 2, 1763, among other guerrilla actions. Fort Venango (Franklin, Pennsylvania) fell and the garrison was massacred, Fort Presqu'ile (Erie, Pennsylvania) was also destroyed that month. In the fall, British columns were attempting to recover lost ground. As a measure of appeasement toward the English, Governor Nicolas-Antoine Coulon de Villiers sent a messenger from Fort de Chartres to Detroit with letters for Pontiac, the French settlers, and the British officer in command, Major Henry Gladwin. Villiers made it clear that Pontiac was fighting a losing battle now that France was living in peace with England. While disowning the rash actions of his former fellow countrymen, he also wanted to preserve the interests of the fur trade on both sides of the Upper Mississippi. Once Pontiac and his French allies had given up fighting, they were convinced by Villiers to move across the Mississippi to escape possible retaliation, which infuriated General Thomas Gage, commander in chief of the British forces.[19]

The royal proclamation issued by Britain in 1763 threw open the fur trade to all who were interested. From the number of trade licenses granted in Quebec, it appears that many French Canadians were spurred on by the prospect of reaching west for Michilimackinac, Detroit, Fort de Chartres, the Great Lakes, and even far beyond if fur loads were to meet expectations despite the high risks. In the early spring of 1764 Pontiac went west with Ottawa tribes and French settler families. On his way he stopped at Fort Vincennes where a few hundred pioneers lived, then at Fort de Chartres where he was met by Villiers when Saint-Ange de Bellerive was just about to take command. Pontiac could obtain no support from the representatives of a government that had definitely renounced its possessions along the Mississippi. Canada's military authorities eventually took control of the Illinois in their haste to gain a monopoly over the fur trade in the West.

In June 1764, Bellerive kept only forty men at Fort de Chartres, some of whom were assigned to Sainte Geneviève. While the garrison was waiting for the arrival of the British troops, Pontiac turned up with Charlot Kaské, the half-breed chief of the Shawnees, whose father was German. Both received unofficial support from settlers who offered them supplies to engage in new campaigns, but all their efforts to rekindle uprisings were in vain.

In London, there were fierce debates over the control of western territories, few politicians being aware that several thousand French inhabitants living in the Indian country of the Illinois now came under direct rule of the Canadian military government. By the end of December 1764, Thomas Gage, commander in chief of the forces of his majesty in America, let it be known to the inhabitants of the Illinois that they were granted the freedom to practice the Catholic faith. They were also allowed to go wherever they wanted in full safety depending, however, on the will of the Spanish occupants in Louisiana. Those who chose to stay on their lands and become British subjects were requested to take the oath of fidelity and obedience to the Crown. While British troops were gradually taking control of the region, they met with open Indian hostility. The French settlers along the Mississippi were no longer in a mood to resist after they had seen the last soldiers packing and leaving behind empty warehouses. It was now time for a new generation to take over.[20]

THE WITHERED FLEUR-DE-LIS: FORMER FRENCH SUBJECTS UNDER FOREIGN RULE

It took a year for British troops to make their way to Fort de Chartres. Seneca, Delaware, and Shawnee bands had earlier stopped Captain Thomas Morris and his detachment before Fort Miami. On October 10, 1765, the day after Captain Stirling had reached Fort de Chartres, Bellerive handed the place over to the new occupants and embarked with his troops in boats for Saint Louis. In Kaskaskia the French soon protested against the demand to decide on the short notice whether they were loyal to the British crown or not. Pragmatically, Stirling allowed them to delay their answer until March 1766. The French were now determined to use obstructive tactics against the new authorities. Stirling appointed Lagrange, a local judge, to settle disputes according to French common law. Under the Union Jack, age-old legal and administrative procedures continued. Traders carried on business as usual with the Indians. But there were clues about creeping resistance. Farmers hindered any measure to facilitate food sales to the British residents, and instead sent food clandestinely across the Mississippi. Lacking competent interpreters, the commanders took exception to the friendly relations between the French population and the local Indians, always suspecting some conspiracy. After Major Farmar had taken over from Stirling at the head of Illinois, one of his officers, Lieutenant Fraser, openly complained that the French were mostly transported convicts given over to drunkenness, and hastily likened them to their allegedly deceitful, slovenly Indian accomplices. Aside from such judgments based on age-old prejudice, there was a great deal of misunderstanding between the British and the French, because of the language barrier. The former had little knowledge about life in the Illinois communities for want of competent agents, and could not establish a reliable system of intelligence.

Successive commandants of Illinois in the following years were still faced with threats of Indian insurrection. In 1768, Lieutenant–Commander Wilkins antagonized the French by granting lands to English merchants, yet the presence of a majority of Irish Catholics in his regiment eased relations with the inhabitants. The British had expected that the Illinois habitants would help the fur trade to develop on the left bank of the Upper Mississippi along the routes leading to the East. But since 1763 it had been constantly on the decline, whereas French traders were still happily paddling on the Illinois and the Ohio before carrying their peltries to Sainte Genevieve and Saint Louis. The English merchants' reluctance to leave their settlements and seek friendly tribes was aggravated by their bargaining methods based on the offer of cheap whiskey, double dealings, and arrogant distrust of Indian discourse. Facing French resentment, colonial policies lacked coherence. Although General Gage would not respond to the claims for a French civil government of Illinois, the integrity of the French character of the region was maintained by the crown. At last, by the Quebec Act of June 1774, French law applied to civil litigations. Since the inhabitants of the Illinois were mostly French, the territory was also incorporated into the province of Quebec. No wonder English-speaking settlers hoping to extend their claims as far as the east bank of the Mississippi were revolted by the Quebec Act, by which the British openly favored Catholics and savages at the expense of the New England Protestants. The French trading companies dissolved, after having become the first business to operate on a continental scale. Their vast holdings, by right of possession, were administered by an elaborate code of conduct, being a blend of monopolistic and native free-trade arrangements.[21]

The Mississippi River now constituted the great dividing line between two alienated French communities now subject to naturalization. The family pact sealed by the French and Spanish Bourbons against England, their hereditary enemy, had failed in 1763. Spain had lost much by the Treaty of Paris, especially Florida. But in 1762 the Catholic alliance found a new strength with the secret agreement signed on November 13, 1762 in Fontainebleau, after talks between the Duc de Choiseul and the Spanish ambassador, the Marquis de Grimaldi, by which Louis XV committed himself to cede Louisiana to His Catholic Majesty. It was an immense territory with a potential already foreseen by fur traders at its westernmost bounds.[22]

The legends surrounding the genesis of Saint Louis evoke the background of Mark Twain's tales about French nobility.[23] Its founder, Pierre de Laclède Liguest, who was from Guyenne, challenged the imaginations of his contemporaries. They believed he had been a page at the court of Louis XV, then a *mousquetaire* before he fell out of favor with Madame de Pompadour and was accordingly given a choice between the Bastille jail and exile in Louisiana. Laclède was, in fact, ordered to America with a special mission to inquire into the condition of things in that distant colony. He happened to be neither a gentleman adventurer nor a colonizer for the greater glory of France. Like many others he started as an officer and turned to commerce to acquire wealth. In New Orleans Gilbert Antoine Maxent and his associate Laclède were granted exclusive Indian trade rights for the Upper Mississippi and the Lower Missouri River in June 1763 by Jean Jacques Blaise d'Abbadie, the last French governor of the province. Laclède took with him his thirteen-year-old stepson, Auguste Chouteau, and reached Kaskaskia in November on a vessel laden with goods. Looking for an appropriate site for a trading post, he chose a location south of the fork of the Missouri and Mississippi rivers, across from Cahokia. He named it Saint Louis in 1764 to honor Louis XV, before the cession of Louisiana was known to the population in western Illinois. Laclède, Chouteau, and thirty laborers felled the first trees on the site by mid-February 1764. Among the remaining French settlers of the Mississippi Valley, they symbolized a new spirit of enterprise, open to the commercial opportunities offered by the presence of the British on the east bank. Those who had not left for New Orleans with Villiers were induced to come across the river with their belongings. The village next to Fort de Chartres became a ghost town. The thousand inhabitants of Kaskaskia, equally divided between whites and black slaves, lost seventy families who settled in Sainte Geneviève.[24]

If Laclède was the founding father of Saint Louis, Auguste and his younger brother Pierre were destined to be unrivalled godfathers for decades. For traders, Saint Louis was an ideal location between Montreal and New Orleans. The Chouteaus proved to be empire builders under Spanish rule after 1763. Of the French in and around Saint Louis who engaged in the fur trade the more prominent were of Canadian stock, such as François Vallé, Charles Sanguinet, and Joseph Robidoux, all from the province of Quebec. Many inhabitants of the newly conquered territories in the French West were the peasants of the former seigneuries, long acquainted with Indian culture and adapted to the harsh conditions of the wilderness.

Meanwhile the majority of the inhabitants of Saint Louis were committed to the fur trade and relied on the fields across the river for food products. In 1766 Don Antonio Ulloa became the first Spanish governor in New Orleans, and a year later he sent a detachment led by Captain Don Francisco Riu to establish posts at the junction of the Missouri and the Mississippi. The captain proved to be a petty tyrant by restricting French trade in Saint Louis. To avoid fierce opposition, in 1768 Ulloa replaced him with Don Pedro Piernas who, having no sooner reached Saint Louis, had to rush back to

New Orleans where French merchants had overthrown the governor. Ulloa's efforts to regulate commerce, end smuggling, and interrupt the wine trade with France were ruined when amid shouts of "*Vive le Roi, vive le bon vin de Bordeaux*" [Long live the king, long live the fine Bordeaux wine] the rebels forced him to retreat. The appeal to France to regain its sovereignty over Louisiana went unheard. The colony remained uncontrolled until the new governor General Alejandro O'Reilly, arrived in New Orleans with two thousand troops in August 1769. O'Reilly also raised Spain's banner over Sainte Genevieve and Saint Louis and followed the king's instructions to punish the participants in the uprising. A dozen ringleaders were found guilty, five of whom were executed by a firing squad. Although French historians later called the governor "Bloody O'Reilly" there is no proof that he retaliated savagely. Most rioters were, in fact, pardoned.[25]

Drastic measures, however, were taken in Louisiana by the Spanish colonial government. French laws were nullified and Spanish became the official language. Within a dozen years exclusive commerce with Spain brought prosperity, but opened the region to immigrant traders and smugglers. Despite their oath of allegiance the French-speaking inhabitants of the colony were not hispanicized because they blatantly outnumbered Spanish settlers. Immigrants from the Canary Islands, Andalucia, and the Caribbean islands remained a minority in comparison to the French population that numbered 5,700 in 1766. In the following decades French immigration resumed, with an influx from Nova Scotia Acadians, Illinois residents fleeing from British rule, and émigré aristocrats during the French Revolution.

In Upper Louisiana the French were spared the turmoil of resistance under the Ulloa régime in New Orleans. The appeal to natural rights to justify a revolt against a despot was not heard in Saint Louis, perhaps because there were fewer heavy wine drinkers and more pragmatic traders. Saint Ange de Bellerive and Philippe Rastel de Rocheblave, a time-serving aristocrat, were able to preserve civil peace. Rocheblave had previously fought the British. He had been under Aubry's command in 1759, and escaped from the trap laid by General William Johnson and his Iroquois allies near Fort Niagara. He had been trained by Charles-Michel de Langlade and "developed a knack for dealing with Indians and a skill in the guer[r]illa style warfare of the American frontier."[26] Rocheblave retired in New Orleans in 1763. In 1765 this dashing gentleman served as commanding officer at Sainte Genevieve under Spanish rule. At the time Bellerive and Rocheblave relied on the influence of François Vallé who was captain of the Sainte Genevieve militia.[27] When Don Pedro Piernas became lieutenant-governor of Illinois in 1770, Rocheblave was replaced by Louis Dubreuil Villars, another French officer in the service of Spain, who had married one of François Vallé's daughters. The increase of population in Sainte Genevieve was welcomed by the Spanish rulers who resented the influx of British traders across the Mississippi. Actually, French voyageurs were often hired by both sides as guides to explore the wilderness in western Louisiana.

François Vallé's zeal in the militia under the Spanish régime was rewarded by the title of *Lieutenant particulier et juge* [special lieutenant and judge], meaning that he was the major judicial officer in the town of Sainte Genevieve. As a mediator, he discreetly covered up the illicit practices of the French Creoles in Spanish Illinois. For example, they took advantage of the presence of British troops on the east side of the Mississippi by selling them liquor bought in New Orleans.

Vallé's interpretation of Spanish culture also revealed his opportunism, for instance in cases of adultery. It was not a criminal act under French law but O'Reilly, who was an Irish hard-liner, wanted the cuckolded husband to have the power of life and death over the fornicating couple. The ban on fornication had been abrogated under the new Spanish law which, however, prescribed banishment for the adulterous partner, while the offending wife was publicly whipped and sent to a convent. Vallé seldom enforced the law on adultery. The representatives of His Catholic Majesty were faced with a permissive society in which adulterous sexual gratification was more commonly condoned than in Spain. Vallé died in 1783. No one in Upper Louisiana ever held power for as long a period of time as he did. The Spanish authorities all over Louisiana were aware of his experience in financial and political affairs aside from his role as chief magistrate. Vallé made a fortune as a trader, but also as a slave owner. In 1777 he was accused of unduly selling an African family after seizing the property of a debtor. But he skillfully flaunted the Code Noir promulgated at Versailles in 1685 to exonerate himself from the accusation. In addition, Vallé acted as banker to the Spanish troops in Upper Louisiana, being involved in the shipping and the distribution of specie. He regularly informed Governor General Unzaga about the financial operations involved. In 1772, when Piernas heard that the Osages were planning to attack Sainte Genevieve to monopolize the fur trade for themselves, he wanted to launch a campaign to destabilize the native populations. Vallé was shrewd enough to advise the Spanish official against such a rash initiative. Francisco Cruzat, another Frenchman, replaced Piernas as Spanish commandant of Upper Louisiana in April 1775, and served until 1778 as lieutenant-governor in Saint Louis. His close connection with Vallé was due especially to their common interest in the slave trade.[28]

In 1772 Jean-Marie Ducharme and a group of Canadians from Montreal went up the Missouri unnoticed by Spanish soldiers in their outpost of Fort Don Carlos along the river. Ducharme traded with the Osages before he was chased by Pierre Laclède's own party. Ducharme was able to escape but his pelts were confiscated.[29] Permanent unrest among the communities of Illinois was plaguing French-British relations. Such discontent was also imparted to Indian tribes, especially after Pontiac was murdered in Cahokia in 1769 by a Peoria agent of British merchants. The event led to harsh conflicts between native tribes. Facing each other across the Mississippi, French-speaking settlers and traders were separated by their newly imposed nationalities. Migration westward toward Saint Genevieve and Saint Louis was intensifying by the time the British troops moved back east in the 1770s to contain the insurgents of the looming American Revolution.

The cession of the French provinces of Canada to the British crown had bred resentment in the French-Canadian communities against the mother country. But ethnic unity was preserved around the Catholic Church. Britain remained preoccupied with the fate of the western lands still in the scope of French boatmen, merchants, and voyageurs. Illinois was placed under the military government residing in Quebec to preserve the region from encroachments by neighboring colonists increasingly tempted to sever ties with the crown. The Quebec Act passed by the British Parliament on June 22, 1774, infuriated the pioneers who protested against the preservation of French civil law from the Ohio to Lake Erie and the Mississippi. The settlers attracted to the West were crowding into Pittsburgh where boats took them down the Ohio River. It was now clear that the status of the territories seized from France was to bear on the decisions made by the Continental Congress when the War for Independence broke out.[30]

The Burning Issue of Allegiance: The French and the American Revolution in the West

In the four years preceding the War of Independence the responsibilities of command in the Illinois country were assumed by Captain Hugh Lord. In the spring of 1776 the British commander in chief decided to gather all the isolated garrisons of the West. Lord appointed as his successor Philippe Rastel de Rocheblave, who had returned to Illinois in 1776 to marry a young lady whose father was a prominent member of the French community in Kaskaskia. As acting lieutenant-governor, Rocheblave counted on some French bourgeois to counteract the British officials defecting to the American side. George Morgan, the Commissioner for Indian Affairs who corresponded with agents in Kaskaskia, was one of his secret agents. Rocheblave could also count on pro-English Frenchmen like Gabriel Cerré, Louis Viviat, and Nicolas Lachance, but the few British residents living in the area supported the American insurgents. The British commander of the West stationed in Detroit never responded to Rocheblave's requests for military reinforcement in Illinois, even after Rocheblave had written that the population was on the eve of seeing a numerous band of brigands intending to establish a chain of communication that would not be easy to break, once formed.[31]

Rocheblave arrested Thomas Bentley, a Kaskaskia resident who had married into a wealthy French family. He had informed the American patriots about the lack of defense of the French settlements along the Mississippi, which endangered the garrison of Vincennes and eventually Detroit. George Rogers Clark, the elder brother of William, had earned a reputation in the colonization of Kentucky as major of its militia. In January 1778, Virginia decided to launch an operation to protect the state against Indian raids and commissioned Clark to muster Rangers for a military expedition. Clark's mission soon extended to the occupation of Illinois. In February, France declared war on Britain, thus letting Americans hope for an upheaval of the French under British rule. Clark learned about the French decision when he was on his march toward his destination. Although he knew about French-Canadian hostility to the Anglo-Americans he nevertheless intended to rally the former to the American cause. Rocheblave had already weathered many local storms before he was informed that American Rangers were closing in.

On July 4, 1778 Clark and his 175 Long Knives stalked Kaskaskia until dark before they took the town. Rocheblave was made prisoner and sent under escort to Virginia. The Americans thought that a man who had already served two masters might be safely employed by a third one. But Rocheblave turned down the offer of an appointment as governor of Illinois in behalf of Virginia, and returned to Canada in 1782, still determined to reconquer the territory. Father Pierre Gibault found himself to be the natural leader of the

Kaskaskia French community. After Clark had reassured him, the priest, who was also Vicar General of the Bishop of Quebec, wielded enough power among his parishioners to vindicate the new allegiance to the American victors. Two dozen Frenchmen were enlisted immediately to accompany the Rangers of Captain Joseph Bowman to take over Cahokia. When Father Gibault was escorted by Clark's envoy, Captain Leonard Helm, to visit Vincennes, the population was not long to abide by his advice to accept the American presence. Vincennes had been the largest French town west of Detroit. Its 621 inhabitants wanted to retreat to Spanish Illinois because they now had to comply with American regulations.[32]

Clark reorganized the Illinois territory and enforced American law and order. Law courts were empowered to handle civil and criminal justice with elected judges. The records had to be written in English, which was the first step toward acculturation. By the end of 1778, it was obvious that the Virginia constitution had also become the supreme law of Illinois. Yet Clark remained isolated in a French enclave with fewer than two hundred men.

Up north at Michilimackinac, Métis Charles Langlade was voicing the feelings of a majority of the French population apprehensive of ethnic disintegration under the pressure of American land hunger. Along the Ohio, Clark's Kentuckians had shown no concern for the treaties protecting tribal interests. Indians had turned in despair to the British for help with arms and ammunitions. Henry Hamilton, governor of Detroit, organized an expedition of 250 men to launch an attack and reoccupy Vincennes, hastily deserted by American forces. With the financial assistance of French traders, Clark mobilized 172 men and departed from Kaskaskia in February 1779. After walking waist-deep across rivers and suffering from cold and hunger, they finally reached Fort Vincennes, which they stormed at the end of the month, compelling Hamilton to surrender.

On his return to Illinois, Clark was angered at the brutal manners of the Kentuckian occupants toward the French population. They stole goods, killed the cattle of local farmers, and considered the Catholics as enemies, especially when they saw them live on friendly terms with the Indians. Although flaunting their ethnic pride against the Americans, the French were not immune to corruption. Presumed above suspicion, Father Gibault secretly sold twelve thousand acres that belonged to missionaries to speculators until the government in Philadelphia canceled the deal.[33] In 1779, Clark planned an expedition against Detroit with a contingent of French minutemen under the leadership of Godefroy de Linctot. But news of the preparations was leaked to British intelligence. From Michilimackinac English regulars accompanied by sixty Frenchmen and two hundred Indians made for Saint Joseph to intercept Linctot's group. On the way the corps arrested Jean Baptiste Du Sable, a trader in the pay of the Americans.[34]

As the American Revolution was creeping ever closer to the Spanish boundary line, Anglo-Spanish rivalry intensified. Spain was already supporting the American insurgents when the lieutenant-governor of Spanish Illinois, Don Fernando de Leyba, arrived in Upper Louisiana in 1778. He regularly conferred with George Rogers Clark after 1776, thus testifying to the connivance between American insurgents and Spaniards.

When Spain allied with the French against the British, Richard Lemoult, the acting commander at Detroit after Hamilton's term, remained on the alert, in expectation of Clark's offensive. Meanwhile Charles Langlade was given the task of blockading trade between the Spanish colonists and the American patriots in the Mississippi Valley. Heading for Saint Louis and Cahokia in 1780, he gathered a force of a thousand Frenchmen, Menominee, and Winnebago warriors at Prairie du Chien, planning to attack Saint Louis. Spain had then declared war on the British, siding with the American patriots and France. The French inhabitants had no interest in supporting the American cause but they were eager to defend Spanish Illinois.

In early May 1780, while De Leyba was on his deathbed, a huge force of Indians, Englishmen, and Canadians was swooping down the Mississippi to Upper Louisiana. The lieutenant-governor could only muster the garrison at Sainte Geneviève and a few hundred militiamen, among whom were the three sons of François Vallé.[35] On May 9, 1780, from behind the stockade three hundred heroic defenders repelled an attack of the Redcoats with well-concentrated fire from five cannons. The British onslaught on Saint-Louis was ultimately unsuccessful. Not all of Spanish Illinois remained unscathed however. Peoria was burnt by an Indian contingent mustered at Michilimackinac, under the command of Charles–Gauthier Verville. Vallé's loyalty to the Spanish monarchy was rewarded by a personal letter from Governor Bernardo de Galvez, who extolled the virtues of a man who had begun his life as an illiterate French Canadian peasant and was now conferred the title of Don Francisco.[36] In the French-speaking population the political issues remained divisive, as shown by Jean-Marie Ducharme's new commitment in 1780. He was one of the leaders of the British expedition against Saint Louis. He also crossed the Mississippi to attack Cahokia but his raid was repulsed. Lieutenant-Governor Patrick Sinclair, who masterminded the operation from Michilimackinac, accused Ducharme of treachery and threatened to put him under arrest when he heard that he had let two French prisoners escape. But the lifelong adventurer managed to get out of the scrape once again. He returned to Lachine and in 1796, became an honorable member of the Quebec assembly in Montreal.

Francisco Cruzat returned to Saint Louis as lieutenant-governor after the sudden death of De Leyba, and appointed trader Auguste Chouteau captain of the militia. Having extended their influence over the Osages, the Chouteaus had a monopoly over the fur trade southwest of Saint Louis toward the Arkansas. In January 1781 Cruzat sent a group of sixty-five militiamen and Indian allies under the command of Eugène Beausoleil Pourée to retaliate for the British offensive against Saint Louis. They arrived at Fort Saint Joseph, located in British territory, in the spring. They stormed the place held by few French Canadians, Métis, and Indians. Pourée hoisted the red-and-gold Spanish flag in triumph.[37]

Much depended on the economy to maintain Spanish sovereignty over Upper Louisiana. Feeding Indians, especially the Osages, was an urgent issue in the early 1780s if the allegiance of local tribes was to be preserved. Saint Louis was a grain storehouse and a trade gateway to the breadbasket. If it had fallen to the British the supply of food to the tribes would have been cut off. Fortunately the Osages had not defected to the enemy.

Meanwhile Cahokia and Saint Genevieve were rife with a fratricidal war. Clark's efforts to neutralize the Shawnees were ruined by French informers at Vincennes who warned their longtime Indian friends. A raid was organized in February 1781 by Cahokia inhabitants against Saint Joseph to revenge the onslaught on Saint Louis. It involved Spaniards dispatched by Cruzat as well as Indians. Among the forty Frenchmen of Saint Joseph was Lieutenant Guillaume-François Dagneau Douville de Quindre who commanded the British garrison.[38] He was away at the time and could not prevent the occupation of the fort which lasted only one day. Needless to say the victors were acclaimed on their return to Cahokia.

In late September 1780 Colonel Mottin de La Balme was dispatched by De la Luzerne, then French Plenipotentiary Minister in Philadelphia, to rally the inhabitants of Kaskaskia. He made fiery speeches against the British but was aware of the local anti-American sentiment. The population was especially angered at the aggressiveness of Captain Richard Macarty, who commanded the American garrison. La Balme raised a party of volunteers to capture Detroit, still in British hands. When the expedition left Cahokia on October

3, 1780, he asserted he could count on Indian allies. His first objective was the warehouse at Wea Town (near present-day Lafayette, Indiana) that was owned by two Detroit traders, Beaubien and La Fontaine. At Fort Miami, La Balme's group destroyed the cattle and plundered the store, but was soon overpowered by Indian warriors led by Little Turtle, who had been after them for several days. La Balme was killed with thirty of his men. His role remained mysterious. In 1777, he had been appointed general in the United States cavalry, but had resigned to go into private business. It seems he was in correspondence with George Washington and engaged in a secret mission when he went to Illinois. On the other hand he openly found fault with the Virginians' Indian policy. Was he involved in French espionage? In any event La Balme overreached himself.[39]

In August 1782, Simon Girty, a white who had joined the Shawnees, and British agent Alexander McKee, led an Indian army that ambushed two hundred Kentuckians at the battle of Blue Licks. The Ohio Valley was blighted by merciless warfare. The Virginia government ordered Clark to build defensive forts along the Ohio. He was supported by a fleet of keelboats equipped with artillery. In November, Clark and a thousand men rode up the Great Miami River and burnt Shawnee villages, destroyed their crops, and laid waste the region. A detachment looted a post kept by Louis Lorimier, a French Canadian trader, and stole his peltries. Lorimier was a squaw man whose wife was a Shawnee. Almost two decades later, in the fall of 1803, Meriwether Lewis met him and his Métis daughter Agatha at Cape Girardeau, when he was on his way to Saint Louis to prepare the voyage of discovery. William Clark was ill at the time and did not visit Lorimier, who undoubtedly remembered what his elder brother had done to him.[40]

After five years of military occupation, the French population of Illinois was exhausted and bewildered. Once peace restored after the Treaty of Paris in 1783, American settlers brought their families south of Cahokia and established a community against the will of the French, who were now regarded as aliens on American soil.

Among the most prominent members of the French colony in the Cahokia neighborhood was Pierre Ménard, a French Canadian born in 1766. He first settled in Vincennes on the banks of the Wabash River in the 1780s. His achievements as merchant and businessman made him a popular personality. He worked for Francisco Vigo, an acquaintance of George Washington, who invited them to discuss the future of the American frontier. Ménard then saw the potential of the Saint Louis environment and opened a store at Kaskaskia in 1789. His French background gave him easy access to the trading community especially at Sainte Genevieve where he entered into partnership with François Vallé. In 1795 Ménard was appointed major in the Randolph County militia and rose to the rank of colonel. Meanwhile he remained active in the Indian fur trade at Kaskaskia.[41]

Indian agent John Dodge was instrumental in depriving the French habitants of administrative and judicial powers, their community being now surrounded by the settlements of avid Americans. The territory northwest of the Ohio was officially organized by an ordinance of July 13, 1787. As slavery was banned, French slave owners, particularly the Kaskaskia families, chose to leave for the opposite bank of the Mississippi. By 1789, the news of the storming of the Bastille was received by an awestruck French population. Traditionally attached to the ancien régime despite the plight of the French Canadians decades before, the Saint Louis bourgeois colony resented the revolutionaries' hostility to the Catholic Church and persecution of the aristocracy. French émigré noblemen and their families reached a site south of Sainte Geneviève to plant New Bourbon. The new governor of the Northwest territory, Arthur Saint Clair, had little time to devote to the Cahokia or Kaskaskia inmates. The seat of his government was the town of Marietta on the Ohio. After severe defeats from well-prepared Miami warriors in 1790, Saint Clair was discharged by president George Washington and replaced by General "Mad Anthony" Wayne, an American revolutionary hero and experienced officer, who later marched west to fight two thousand Miamis led by Chief Little Turtle accompanied by French militiamen. On August 20, 1794, Wayne fought a decisive battle at Fallen Timbers near the western shore of Lake Erie. His troops put Indian villages and crops to the torch, sending a strong signal throughout the old northwest. A junior officer, William Clark, learned a lot from French guerrilla warfare under Wayne's command.[42]

FRENCH TRADERS IN THE AFTERMATH

In 1760 the Compagnie des Indes had been eliminated from the fur trade. The Hudson's Bay Company, which had been in existence since 1670, expanded its outposts in the West. But traders who had settled in Montreal and Quebec did not tarry to become serious competitors. Fierce conflicts between trading interests, sometimes ending in murder, were threatening to weaken the fur trade in the confrontation with the nascent United States.

In 1779, Paul de Chomedey de Maisonneuve and a group of three dozen Montreal merchants agreed to form a new partnership called the North West Company whose single-word motto was "perseverance." The company, however, did not start operating until 1784.The capital was divided into sixteen shares held by nine different partners—Charles Paterson, Isaac Todd, John McGill, Simon McTavish, George McBeath, Benjamin Frobisher, Joseph Frobisher, John Ross, and Peter Pond. Later Duncan McGillivray and Alexander Henry the Older entered into partnership. Traders from Michilimackinac had joined forces with them and placed their goods in a general store. Formerly they had been ruined by the frauds of Robert Roger, appointed commandant of the post in 1765 by the British. In contrast, the North West Company was a remarkable combination of energy and business acumen. It soon extended its operations along the Missouri, which was to be come a highly strategic area.[43]

Travelers between the Great Lakes and Upper Louisiana used French Canadian voyageurs to paddle their canoes, lead their packhorses, and choose their routes. Topographical features, birds, fish, and reptiles encountered by the wayfarer had received French names borrowed from native terms. Such words were then translated into English when they were significant landmarks, such as *Portage des épinettes* [Pine Portage], *Portage des haliers* [Thicket Portage], *Rapide de l'équerre* [Angle Rapid], *La Grande île des épinettes* [Great Balsam Fir Island], *Deschutes* [Falls]. Place names formerly ascribed by voyageurs either remained in their original form or were distorted, such as *Platte, Grand Portage, Lac qui parle, Prairie du chien, Presqu'île, Detroit, Rivière du canot* [Cannon River], *La Rivière qui pleure* [Water-which-cries]. It was the difficulty of transportation that explained *Travers* or *Portage*.[44] The French West was to leave useful landmarks for American explorers.

6

French Culture in Transition

THE COMMON GROUND: FROM ISOLATION
TO THE SENSE OF BELONGING

EVER SINCE THE BEGINNING OF THE WESTWARD MOVEMENT IN NEW France, chronicles had pointed to the influence of the environment on colonial minds. Far removed from their youthful neighborhoods, priests, officers, and trappers readily confessed to their mixed feelings of fear and exhilaration. Confronted with combined natural forces, they constantly reminded their listeners or readers of impenetrable forests and scathing thorns, of benumbing cold and stifling heat. The accounts were not necessarily intended to turn the protagonists into heroes when they evoked frozen limbs, sickness, and hunger. Such ordeals often appeared as inevitable hardships that inspired no sense of fatality or invited romantic meditations on utter loneliness. Isolation resulted from the scarcity of trails, the distances to cover in an inhospitable climate and the perils of encounters with Indian predators who would outnumber white drifters. In the summer of 1715, Louis de Maunoir de Ramezay, an officer on duty, lost his way when trying to meet with Miami tribes near Chicago. He found himself in the middle of nowhere with a few men now deprived of canoes. Another officer, Dadoncour, remembered he had to walk 130 leagues, living on dried meat and scant water while suffering from fever. The sense of estrangement was also due to the lack of news from France. Reaching Fort Saint Louis in September 1687, Joutel, a former companion of La Salle, learned about the eradication of Calvinism with the abolition of the Edict of Nantes in August 1684. In the garrisons along the Mississippi men found comfort within their small communities, which did not exclude tension and quarrels. Most of those expatriates took to liquor and the missionaries themselves admitted soldiers might sometimes drink the altar wine before Mass. Winter was always associated with penury and suffering before the thaw came, allowing paddling on rivers and leaving winter quarters for new adventures.[1]

While the glorious ceremony celebrating the appropriation of Louisiana on April 9, 1682 involved hymns to Louis XIV, the Te Deum, and a military pageant, French trappers were starving along the Mississippi. Soldiers stationed at Michilimackinac received fish and corn in small quantities for an entire year while they kept dreaming of bread, meat, and wine. The chronicler of La Salle's journey down the Mississippi, Father Louis Hennepin, also held that not only was bread sacred food, but salt and spices constituted indispensable ingredients in French habits. Priests could hardly dispense with wafers and wine in their religious services. In 1679 the Récollets had even made wine from grapes grown on the shores of *Lac des Illinois* [Lake Michigan]. It was often Indian hospitality that enabled the French to live in the West. But the assistance afforded by the natives involved at least a tacit agreement allowing the latter to benefit from such indebtedness.[2]

The French colonists who were first likened to deities by the Indians would fall from their supernatural status whenever they showed themselves in dire straits. When Tonty and his five companions tried to reach Michilimackinac after leaving Fort Crèvecoeur they found refuge in a deserted Potawatomi village, expecting to die in a hut warmed by logs. Father Zenobe Membré said later that they looked like skeletons. They were eventually rescued by a band of Kiskakons who took them to their village only five miles away. After a month's starvation they wintered among the Indians who gladly shared their food. In some instances, the French were often reluctant to reveal their weaknesses before finally giving way to their dismay and imploring pity.[3] In 1688, the men of the Niagara garrison, hard-pressed by Iroquois warriors and dying of scurvy, at first denied entrance to a band of eighty friendly Miami hunters for fear that the natives might witness their despair. Finally a dozen French survivors let the Miamis in, enabling the starving soldiers to feed on the venison and fowl that were available at last.[4]

The French usually counted on tribes for food supplies. La Salle rewarded the Loups with a hundred beaver skins for the buck meat they had supplied. Along his route he constantly relied on tribes for corn. Sometimes woodrunners were sent to enroll Indian hunters while purveying them with cheap gunpowder. However, the French did not want to depend entirely on tribal trade. They would catch fish with nets to show their partners that they were able to do without them, which in fact tended to lower prices. Nevertheless, Tonty felt so much indebted to Indian cooperation that when he published the roster of his expedition in 1684, he included the names of natives who had participated, listing such members as Amabanso,

Sénéché and Chouakost. But he transcribed merely the tribal identity of the women who, incidentally, were mostly Huron or Abenaki.[5]

The relationships between Indians and soldiers in the outposts of the West were generally watched over by Jesuits who feared the whites might lapse into savagery. Indians were screened before entering forts and ritually offered a pipe and tobacco. Later the guest might come back with pelts to demonstrate his goodwill. Most often trading took place outside forts to avoid rampage if bargains were celebrated with firewater. At Fort Saint Louis, Illinois and Miamis were given a shelter behind the gates to protect them from Iroquois assaults. Over the decades, forts and villages focused their cooperation on vital matters such as military defense, medicine and construction. Each Frenchman had his own circle of Indian friends with whom he had been acquainted for some time by common work such as repairing tools, hunting together, or sharing meals. On both sides nicknames were also commonly given, such as "Jean le Blanc" or "Le baron." Brawls often occurred between rivals for an Indian girl. Racial prejudice was also the cause of conflicts.

Louis-Armand de Lom d'Arce, Baron de Lahontan, was in command of Fort Saint Joseph in 1687–88. His experience as hunter and traveler appeared invaluable when he wrote his exploration narratives. An early pioneer in native American ethnology, he deliberately contrasted the inhibitions of the French aristocrats with the permissiveness of the Noble Savage. In terms of comparative status he drew attention to social norms that could disconcert good-mannered French subjects. He pointedly recalled a man named Deliette who had become the laughingstock of his Illinois hosts after he had fled from a buffalo herd.[6]

European and native cultures came together in the face of common obstacles, whether natural or social. Yet the estrangement from colonial settlements and the loosening of social ties could determine deviant social behavior in such remote places as the Great Lakes. New trends in cross-cultural attitudes were already emerging from the Louisiana environment when Lamothe Cadillac landed in 1713. His unmitigated castigation of the rabble linked miscegenation to degeneracy. Lahontan himself was less peremptory when he dismissed the haunting fears that interracial relations would inexorably transmute woodrunners into savages.[7] To what extent was the model of the *honnête homme*—the civilized Frenchman in the shade of the Sun King—compatible with the immersion into the pagan backwoods? The Enlightenment would later partially help to reconcile nature with culture, nobility with the wilderness, and make the taste of the forbidden fruit intellectually fascinating.

By the early eighteenth century the settlements of New France represented a welcome replica of French social structures. The Pays d'en Haut polarized the dangers of anarchy by harboring the evils threatening body and soul. Soldiers scattered in forts along the Mississippi seemed to experiment with libertine precepts, allowing promiscuity at the expense of piety and discipline. The existence of the backwoodsman was a challenge to social norms. He conformed to the image of a trickster who shared the benefits of two different worlds. He enjoyed sexual freedom in the wilderness and the comfort of home when he was back from his peregrinations. Woodrunners seemed to epitomize all the transgressions undermining authority in the ancien régime.[8]

It also became obvious that there was no hope left to convert Indians into French subjects of His Majesty. Le Sueur noted that French squaw men fought with their new kin against their compatriots living in enemy tribes. For the most pessimistic of observers Indians had not only imparted idleness and immorality to the colonists but adopted their worst habits like drunkenness. Denonville was well aware of the constraints of close alliances with the natives. For him the *Pax Gallica* now depended on the efforts to emulate the natives with a view toward gaining their confidence. Trappers were not slow to join communities gathered for Dionysian celebrations involving lascivious dances, drinking, and masquerading. Indians even borrowed fancy garments imported from France to dress up on festive occasions.[9]

Co-existence with the Native Americans was on a day-to-day basis and implied phases of merciless conflict and peaceful negotiation, both sides having to find a middle ground to regain or keep the peace. For centuries the Illinois had waged war against the Iroquois, harassed the Winnebagos, and made slaves of Pawnee captives. Before La Salle arrived the Illinois had been threatened by the Dakota Sioux, the Sauks, the Foxes, and the Kickapoos, and even worse— decimated by epidemics. By 1735 the Illinois population was still recovering from the Iroquois and Fox wars. Among the surviving hundreds half were seeking French protection at Fort de Chartres. The land lying between Lake Michigan and the Mississippi River was also home of the Potawatomis, the Menominees, and the Shawnees. To escape from Iroquois raids Potawatomi refugees had settled near a Jesuit mission near Green Bay. In 1720 they lived in villages near French outposts at Saint Joseph and Detroit.

In 1744, Father Charlevoix meticulously described tribal mores. Aside from his deploration of promiscuity, thievery, and alcoholism, he observed that Indian mothers suckled their babies sometimes for years, as opposed to French housewives of the bourgeoisie who readily left their newborn children to the care of wet nurses. Sexual relations being banned among the Indians during nursing time, Charlevoix believed that this native taboo encouraged the permissiveness allowed with unmarried girls acting as surrogate wives when young mothers were unavailable. Charlevoix also noted the acute mental capacities of the Illinois who enjoyed a quasi-photographic memory, which may also explain Sacagawea's immediate recognition of sites like Beaverhead in Montana when the Lewis and Clark expedition reached her native Shoshone grounds.[10]

A large number of the Illinois tribes rejected the Christian faith, which prohibited polygamy. In fact, the multiplication of French-Indian unions was not delayed by banns and solemn wedding ceremonies. The coureurs des bois might well have several wives à la façon du pays scattered along his route. When they married in a church, their Christianized spouses became French, as legally determined under Louis XIV. It was the exotic image of unrestrained erotism that the French libertines vicariously enjoyed in the shade of the Jardin du Luxembourg in Paris.

Throughout the Seven Years' War, officers from France discovered in the alleged half-savage Canadian the brave fighters of the Pays d'en Haut. The coureur des bois was frequently enlisted to fight side-by-side with the friendly savages. Some would be hired as guides, hunters, and interpreters. Many of them were the sons of former exiles and squaws. The native allies of the English were apprehensive of the undaunted half-breeds, who provided intelligence to the regulars after infiltrating enemy territory.

The fur traders had their meeting place at Michilimackinac, a privileged site between lakes with a relatively mild climate and abundant fish. Wintering was also attractive in the Indian villages of Cahokia and Kaskaskia. Up the river woodrunners would also find plentiful buffalo and game. Smugglers could be found around the outposts at the furthermost parts of those regions. Some French-Indian couples chose to settle down in isolated places to grow corn and breed pigs. But they still traded furs down the Mississippi. By the mid-eighteenth century Michel Chartier de Lotbinière met half-breed derelicts stubbornly averse to farming, and given over to swapping cheap pelts for food from time to time.[11] In the same years a missionary saw two hundred rivermen, trappers, hunters, and squaws living in log cabins at Sainte Geneviève. They sailed up the Mississippi for seven hundred miles toward the end of the summer, then hunted buffalo, salted the meat, made oil from bear grease, and returned home in the spring. Along the Mississippi half-breeds began to form small communities but remained outsiders, and never associated with traders. Still the governor of Louisiana spared them. Sparse though they were on the frontier they served as a bulwark against undesirable newcomers.

Between 1756 and 1763 the Seven Years' War harmed the fur trade along the Mississippi and the Missouri. Indians were running short of firearms, and pelts remained piled up in camps. The most friendly tribes felt the French defeat bitterly and feared reprisals. General Thomas Gage pointed to hundreds of woodrunners fomenting trouble against the Iroquois. When Pontiac's coalition attempted to drive away the English from the Ohio Valley, bands of coureur des bois were on their side and even duped their enemies into believing that a French army was on its way to support them. Although the number of casualties was never known among the French allies of Pontiac, the survivors presumably took flight in the West.

Despite the efforts of Governor Antonio de Ulloa, fur traders often remained prone to trafficking and smuggling in New Spain, especially in areas where no firm control could be enforced on Métis communities. According to an Upper Louisiana census of 1772 there were about two hundred people of French origin, one hundred fifty of them being hunters or voyageurs. There was no count of Métis at the time.[12]

In the last decades of the eighteenth century the French presence was predominant west of the Mississippi. The powerful Sioux relied on smugglers for liquor and firearms. The Osages and Omahas also took advantage of the arms trade. Abandoned by the French crown the descendants of the early coureurs des bois had no choice but stay in the Spanish colony. Joseph Garreau married an Arikara girl and lived in the tribe in 1790. Increasing numbers of French traders of Saint Louis often visited the Arikaras, the Pawnees, and the Mandans.[13]

In the course of the eighteenth century the broader gap between the Canadians living in Quebec and the backwoodsmen who went west substantiates Frederick Turner's frontier thesis. A new French Canadian identity emerged from a process of adaptation to the wilderness. The nomadic voyageur was always far ahead of the sedentary habitant in terms of economic and social change. Not only was he a trailblazer but also an observer of native mentalities who learned how to deal with local beliefs, taboos, and value systems. The eagerness shown by Indians to acquire *commodités* [goods] met the French demands for furs. But it was by no means a market on equal terms, for the former were unaware of the wealth they owned. Indians craved tobacco, firewater, and trinkets, which they were happy to get by gladly surrendering invaluable pelts. La Salle had skillfully made allies of the Indians by transforming them into subdued partners enslaved to new needs. Thomas Jefferson's Indian policy was identical in 1804. It was intended to exploit native dependence on the amenities of Euro-American civilization. As early as 1670, Nicolas Perrot had persuaded the Miamis that French knives were incomparably more suitable than stones to cut meat.[14] The colonists thus relied on native fascination with foreign modes of life. But axes, stoves, and guns did not preclude the use of ancestral tools and weapons that retained their ritual functions. The French traders preferred to offer fabrics or tobacco instead of durable products like axes or pans. The market made it clear that they could thus set a high price on objects constantly in demand.

Among Indians, rifles never totally superseded bows and tomahawks. Until the beginning of the eighteenth century the Illinois hunted buffalo with bow and arrow. They would run after the animal, shoot arrows, and then draw them out from the sides before using them again several times. They would also spare guns when hunting for small game. Loud reports were also detrimental to stalking bears. The animal was far more dangerous when hurt by a bullet. The grease of a bear staunches the blood, and stains can seldom be seen by hunters on its track, which makes the search particularly hazardous. Yet the use of lead and gunpowder was bound to spread in the long run and become a major source of profits for traders.

The French immersion into the New World environment still left room for a lingering nostalgia when news came from the homeland. But being removed from their surroundings, many exiles hardly understood the pros and cons of domestic policies. Some measures, however, determined the future of the colonies. The repeal of the Edict of Nantes by Louis XIV altered the status of the Protestants who had been protected by Henry IV since 1598. For the Huguenots it now meant either exile or relocation in specific French regions. In the West, the voyageurs and engagés sensed they could have no part to play in French politics, isolated as they remained from the civilized world. They were actually more concerned with survival.

Lahontan noted that he was going to be deprived of the joys of life when he left his friends at Niagara to spend two years in the West.[15] The misfortunes experienced in the Indian country soon damped the spirits of the would-be swashbucklers of the wilderness, eager to emulate the famous musketeers serving the king. When La Salle was claiming half of the American territory by putting up the Holy Cross down south in the name of Louis XIV on April 9, 1682, his men were exhausted and despondent. The exaltation of power, ambition and glory had long faded out.

For the French around the Great Lakes and along the Mississippi, full priority was not given to the *Pax Gallica* but to food. In Ojibwa legends the first explorers had eaten their clothes and blankets before being rescued by hunters. The dearth of bread and salt was felt as a painful renunciation of a time-honored way of life. Penury was humiliating when the French had to rely on Indian assistance. Native support was by no means free of cost in the West. Food and transportation were often provided by tribes under contract. Father Marest left Kaskaskia for Michilimackinac in 1711 with his crucifix and breviary. Three Indian scouts accompanied him on his long journey. Suspicious though he might remain, he had to trust them in order to survive. As he was suffering from sores on his feet he was apprehensive of their attitudes when he compared their agility with his handicap, in case enemy attacks would frighten them away. He first imagined himself dying alone in the deep woods, but soon realized his native companions were determined to take great care of him. They carried him on their shoulders while fording creeks and even built rafts with logs when the water was too deep for fording streams.[16] Voyageurs and Jesuits also hired Miami boatmen to go down the Wisconsin to the Mississippi. In 1687 Joutel offered a gun, bracelets, two axes, gunpowder, and bullets to the Arkansas who led him to Fort des Illinois.[17]

THE FRANCO-INDIAN MODUS VIVENDI

When Joutel was hunting buffalo on the banks of the Mississippi in 1687, Indians marveled at the holes of the bullets in the bones of the prey. They would readily forsake their bows and arrows for the rifle to acquire a supernatural power to kill. Joutel observed that they interpreted gun reports as the flapping of wings by a mythical thunderbird. The capacity to light a fire with pistols, gunpowder, and dry grass evoked magic practices and the smoking gun was likened to the ritual use of tobacco to celebrate the Spirits. Despite Nicolas Jeremie's assertion that Indians had thrown away their bows for firearms by the early eighteenth century, tribes still depended for armament on French traders whose intermittent presence in the backwoods made supplies scarce and delivery irregular.[18] Pierre Charles Deliette, who was in command of several forts in La Salle's times, nevertheless mentioned the Illinois' preference of bows to hunt buffalo, considering they could shoot their rifles only once before reloading. Yet the use of new firearms in wartime enabled chiefs to display their power of destruction that enemy tribes were at pains to evaluate.[19]

The commodities that Indians received from the French were granted new ritual functions that were a far cry from their former use. The Illinois buried stoves and knives with the deceased in anticipation of a long journey. Handles were added to swords and transformed into spears or harpoons to become prestigious weapons to catch beaver, moose, and trout. European clothes were also adopted, as shown in the case of an Iroquois who donned the garb of a Jesuit to gain power before fighting the Illinois. The sale of alcoholic beverages to tribes was prohibited but Indian addiction to firewater was such that regulations were bypassed. Various French observers were eyewitnesses of Indian mores. François Clairambault d'Aigremont recognized that in Detroit native trappers spent all their profits on liquor and could no longer afford to buy gunpowder and lead. In command of Michilimackinac, Louis de La Porte de Louvigny likened the place to Hell in 1715.[20] Forty barrels of brandy had been made available to Indians who did not drink for the taste of the beverage but to become intoxicated collectively. Excess was part and parcel of their willingness to demonstrate their respect for the supernatural force of the animal spirits. Drunkenness seemed to allow rights usually denied by tribal law, including the privilege to shed the blood of an enemy. When Lahontan objected one day to allied Indians who were torturing a prisoner, he was threatened by them until his friends declared he was drunk, which exonerated him of evil intentions.[21] In the Illinois, brandy was not just a commodity but a token of spiritual affiliation, which facilitated commercial relations when the natives implored the French to take their beaver.

The fur trade dramatically changed the tribal mode of life over the years in the Illinois. Known as the "people of the prairies," the Miamis had long lived off the fat of the land as sedentary peasants never threatened with starvation. Until the end of the seventeenth century they split their time between hunting and agriculture. After wintering in the woods for bear and deer, they returned home to grow corn, watermelons, and pumpkins. By July the whole community would track buffalo herds for three weeks. Although the first horses reached the Illinois by 1690, hunters still chased their prey after setting fire to the dry grass of the prairies to drive the buffalo toward stalking hunters with their bows. The fur trade soon proved detrimental to the stability of the beaver and deer population in the territories given over to hectic exploitation. The military presence around Detroit also hastened the decimation of bucks and wild birds in the area. In the West, the natives were not concerned with the conservation of natural resources until they realized there was a shortage of peltries.

Traditionally, Indians waged war against wild animals, sometimes charging them with murder or spreading diseases. While tribes were badly in need of meat to survive, their taboos did not mean that they feared the vanishing of species, convinced as they were that the herds disappeared underground before emerging again the following hunting season. Their spiritual relationship to animals was intended to avoid offending whatever game might otherwise desert the hunting grounds. Hennepin mentioned that the Sioux would kill forty buffalo to eat only the tongues.[22]

Faced with men and women sharing cultural values unknown to them, many Frenchmen were enjoying the freedom offered in exile, far from family ties and indifferent to the observance of rules dictated by religion or imposed by decorum. They proudly felt they were judged at their true worth. In 1774 Matthew Cocking, an Englishman who was also a bigamist, observed with astonishment that sixty-two-year-old François LeBlanc took no precautions even at night against the Indians who gathered in great numbers around the fort at Michilimackinac.[23] Unlike the English, the French Canadians welcomed the savages to their tables, entertained them in their posts, and offered them lodgings as they would to one of their own people. They never worried about the consequences that might follow if an Indian got drunk, nor did they take offense at his indiscretions. The English haughtily disapproved of such attitudes but secretly envied the privileges of the French among the natives.[24]

FROM ETHNOCENTRISM TO INDIANIZATION

The Catholic Church had a hard time rallying infrequent attendees. Isolation was naturally detrimental to the observance of Christian rites. Furthermore, missionaries complained that soldiers and trappers ignored both confession and communion. Blasphemy and indecency prevailed not only in the wilderness but in villages, especially in Louisiana where the Canadian exiles spurned the sacraments when estranged from zealots. Despite the insistence of priests, congregations numbered more women than men. Whenever Jesuits and Sulpicians were present in settlements and forts they celebrated a religious service every week. Psalms were sung in French and Huron or Illinois languages, officers being more regular in their church attendance than the rank and file. But the clergy had the power to ban a libertine or refuse spiritual succor to a sacrilegious individual whatever his status might be. Backwoodsmen had retained ancient superstitions conveyed through generations in France and abroad. To ward off the perils of navigation, traders prayed to Saint Francis. On Lake Michigan, the spirit of Father Marquette was said to accomplish miracles. The meaning of Catholic rituals was, however, dubious when the French shared their prayers with Indians. Missionaries resented the influence of the Great Manitu on simple Christian souls. With their tattooed faces woodrunners who bore the marks of their propensity to paganism devised syncretic ceremonies to curry favor with the natives. Agents and officers belonging to the upper classes sneered at those bumpkins whom they often likened to barbarians. Transplanted in the New World, the underclass of exiles had retained the folk beliefs of their native Normandy or Saintonge. They were naturally attracted to Indian witchcraft and sought the company of shamans and jugglers who could heal wounds and foretell the future.

When Nicolas Perrot endeavored to establish a *Pax Gallica* he was confronted by the Sioux. To frighten them he levied an army including Miamis, Foxes, and Illinois, but the Sioux soon made clear that their medicine men had already located the enemy some three days' distance away. They declared themselves capable of withstanding the French onslaught. Perrot had to recognize the truth of this but readily attributed the shamans' vision to satanic powers.[25]

The colonization of New France was constantly interpreted as a war between Christianity and paganism by the Jesuits who considered themselves as the soldiers of Jesus. All over Europe, Louis XIV was known as the King of War, an egomaniac whose ambition always remained to gain glory through victories on the battlefield. But against the barbarians of the New World, the elaborate tactics displayed by worthy generals proved ineffective. The standard rules of European warfare could not be enforced in the wilderness where the French had still to learn from the Indians' guerrilla strategy.

In his book published in 1653, *Histoire de l'Amérique septentrionale*, officer Claude Charles Leroy Baqueville de la Potherie drew on the lessons of his campaigns around the Great Lakes, thereby acknowledging the necessity to adapt military movements to the natural environment of deep forests, hazardous waterways and rapids. Indian warfare implied few frontal assaults but, rather, numerous skirmishes. Soldiers had to wade through creeks and jump from rocks, handicapped by heavy equipment. Indians valued heroic deeds, expecting to see French officers fight at close quarters. Yet commanders were not prepared to renounce age-old traditions. During his campaign against the Onondagas in 1696, Cadillac was carried in a sedan chair. He hoisted his flag on his canoes when tracked down by the Miamis in 1708, making his exhausted troops visible from the banks, whereas he should have sought refuge in the woods.[25]

The French commanders of necessity gradually borrowed Indian ways, such as the habit of lying in ambush for the enemy. Topography became an asset instead of an impediment and mobility allowed surprise attacks. The French soon capitalized on their new skills to harass the British troops. At Beauport in 1690, the Redcoats unfortunately remained in closed order when surrounded by ubiquitous Canadians whose elusiveness made them immune to volleys fired from British ranks. The French were so familiar with Indian culture that they participated in war dances, thus singing and howling like the savages. They struck a pole with their tomahawks while reciting their own exploits, and in combat uttered war cries that were intended to frighten the enemy. This habit had long been banned in the French armies as damaging the sense of discipline but nobody cared about etiquette in the backwoods.[26]

In many cases the French scalped their Indian foes, as happened in 1682 after La Salle's men killed two Quinipisas and before they decapitated them, after which they stuck their heads on spears.[27] Torture and public executions were already a habit of Europeans, whether in the police or the military but now the modus operandi was somewhat harsher. The Thirty Years' War accounted for horrors on both the battlefield and among civilian populations in Europe. Even as the palace of Versailles was displaying the luxury of the Grand Siècle, terror was part and parcel of war culture. Even though observers like Lahontan objected to such treatments, governors and commanders applied brutal methods to enforce law and order. Torture had become mere routine around the Great Lakes where in 1660 Radisson and Des Groseilliers captured Iroquois and tore off their fingernails one after another. In 1688 Deliette had six Iroquois burnt alive at Fort Saint Louis. The following year Tonty submitted eighty Iroquois prisoners brought by friendly Illinois to the same punishment. Cadillac noted in 1695 that Hurons had come back to Michilimackinac with fifty Iroquois scalps. To their French allies they also gave away prisoners who were "grilled," in Cadillac's own words.[28]

To support alliances Lahontan conceded that French emissaries to the tribes felt obliged to attend cruel treatments. During the expedition against the Onondagas in 1696, an old man was held captive for treachery. Allied Indians wanted to inflict ritual wounds on him first, but the French insisted on having him executed immediately.[29] Cadillac admitted that torture often horrified his compatriots, but leniency being equated to cowardice by his Indian partners, he sometimes wished to outdo them in cruelty to appear reliable. In 1698 Iroquois captured by Huron warriors were kept as slaves, but one offered to Tonty was burnt alive to demonstrate the ruthlessness of the French troops. At Michilimackinac around 1693, the Hurons spared prisoners except for an Iroquois chief who was handed over to commander Louvigny. Ottawas were invited to "drink the broth of the Iroquois" after he was put to death. The man was tied to a pole, his limbs burnt by red-hot iron rods. Then they set fire to gunpowder inserted into a gash in his body while he was chanting a death song. Once scalped, he was untied and forced to run westward, to the land of the Spirits. The Iroquois was finally quartered and pounds of his flesh were distributed to his captors.[30] The scene of cannibalism was not only accepted but encouraged by the French who delighted in watching the Hurons drink the warm blood of an enemy. Ironically, such inhuman behavior was condemned in the abstract by civilized Europeans, but on the French frontier guns, stoves, and iron tools were used by the natives to refine violent rituals. Even Montaigne vindicated cannibalism as a religious act in contrast to gratuitous cruelty.

French indianization on the frontier of Le Pays d'en Haut paralleled the adoption of new weapons by Indian allies, although tomahawks, bows, and arrows were still in use. In 1677, Allouez already noted that the Illinois found guns too cumbersome. At times they would fire two shots, forget about reloading, and strike down their adversaries with their tomahawks before capturing them alive. In the seventeenth century the Iroquois launched massive attacks against the Hurons in the east. But later they were at great pains to enlist troops in decimated communities. Indians chiefs were mostly concerned with avoiding casualties. Despite their self-proclaimed respect for innocent lives, it was not uncommon to see Illinois, Potawatomi, and Mascouten braves loot huts, burn corn, and profane sepultures under the eyes of the French officers and men. Yet It seems that in the early decades of the eighteenth century, the Illinois gradually learnt from the Jesuits how to spare prisoners and raise captive children without harsh treatments. They developed a prosperous slave trade that the woodrunners patronized on the Missouri. According to Margry, the foremost chronicler of early New France life, Pénicault, who traveled through the Illinois around 1700, discovered that the French settlers at Kaskaskia encouraged nations to war with each other to collect slaves in the aftermath.[31]

It is not the least paradox of colonization to see aristocrats and

drifters alike stoop to conquer the minds of so-called savages by emulating them. To what extent were the French representatives earnest in their impersonation of wise sachems when dealing with
native tribes? Their eagerness to get the most from an alliance with
Indians may have been an incentive to self-delusion. Jesuit Pierre-
François Xavier de Charlevoix relates that Frontenac disguised himself to address western Indians in Montreal in the summer of 1690.
The bewigged, powdered governor held up a tomahawk and sang a
war song to energize fierce allies to go and fight the Iroquois. As
Frontenac's yelling added to the bacchanalian frenzy, his hosts responded with rounds of applause.[32] When ascending the Mississippi
in 1700, Le Sueur spent days performing the smoking pipe ceremony while attending drum dances before he was carried in triumph on deerskins. Father Saint-Cosme confessed to being
uncomfortable in the same situation with the Arkansas in 1698. As a
priest sent to convert heathens he had to submit to their pagan rituals so as not to appear condescending.[33] Marquette and La Salle had
to be spoon-fed by obliging Miamis, and Lahontan spent three days
eating with Menominees and Potawatomis, having to swallow food
without recess. Was it sheer demagogy or self-sacrificial masquerading? Perhaps an ingrained sense of exotic gratification that has always pervaded French culture was then a welcome escape from the
hardships of discipline in a despotic monarchy.

Nurtured on the culture of the king's court, French diplomats
were used to rhetoric and dramatic art in a world of make-believe
that Benjamin Franklin learnt to practice at ironic distance in the
last quarter of the eighteenth century. The openness of the French
colonists has often been contrasted to the stilted attitudes of their
English adversaries. It is true that the Enlightenment trained French
intellects to dissociate traditional ethics from modern rationaliza-
tion, self-defeating though their attitudes might be. The libertine
aristocrats who advocated radical changes in government loved that
kind of role-playing until they were led to the guillotine by fanatic
compatriots. On the western frontier the wilderness was a stage for
diplomats. They imagined anticipating the intentions of their Indian partners by pretending to adopt their manners. The shift from
the Versailles ballroom to the Buffalo Dance may have been facilitated by the adaptable skills of courtiers sent across the Atlantic. Yet
Indians expected more than the spectacular show of warm feelings
from their occupiers. At any rate they were clever enough to exploit
the vanity and gullibility of the French. Frontenac and Charlevoix
were both enraptured by the eloquence of sachems whom they compared to the orators of ancient Greece. Imaginative chroniclers im-

parted a thrill to their narratives about outlandish peoples in whom they paradoxically sensed a common view of the sublime. By acting out their claims, Indians impressed French observers whose inborn arrogance generally snubbed the Natural Man in the age of classicism. Facing narcissistic colonists who sought recognition, the mimetic natives also wore long hair, sometimes powdered wigs, like the Fox chief Miskouenza who, in 1701, was unaware of ridicule in front of Charlevoix. The Jesuit never dared to make fun of him in public and remained impassive.[34]

Interpreters had key roles in diplomacy by conveying the meanings of natives whose speech was rife with far-fetched hyperboles and elaborate similes. Officials learned appropriate metaphors from sometimes uncouth woodrunners, and applied them to address tribes. French negotiators had to deal with the studied pause, or the nerve racking silence, as opposed to outright refusal or objection. The never-ending discussions taxed the patience of the French and unfortunately incited them to conclude talks with little or no benefit to themselves. The treaties with the Iroquois in 1700 were drafted in spoken language, recording harangues delivered at random during previous debates. Presents were usually more meaningful than signatures and wampums more significant than seals as La Salle soon observed. Most of the documents signed at the turn of the eighteenth century reflected tribal identity with beaver, deer, or otter icons. Totems such as the thunderbird could stand for symbols of pacts with whites.

In 1759 Antoine Louis Descomp-Labadie had gained the trust and respect of the Ottawas in their territory by his honesty in his dealings with them. His grandson, Captain Charles Labadie, possessed a collection of archives about talks between his grandfather and various Ottawa chiefs, especially the famous Pontiac. One document records an agreement signed by him with the assent of all his nation, in the presence of George Croughan, superintendent of Indian affairs. The signature of Pontiac consists of hieroglyphics with signs resembling the figure nine. The majority of the titles are in French and some are written on small sheets of paper using symbols, each representing eight chiefs, like bear, stag, cow, fox, and fish.[35]

Aristocrats painstakingly adapted the language of the Grand Siècle to savage expressiveness. Refined French calligraphy transcribed principles and clauses, whereas Indian pictograms represented what was allowed or prohibited. Emblems on animal or human skin, cork or even rock bore the marks of victory to substantiate oral history.

No impartial observer could have easily perceived the dividing line between artful theatricals and deeply felt religious practice in such dramatic performances. In fact, what was conceived as an elaborate strategic device for the French turned out to be a self-defeating process. To display tolerance and sympathy and enlist the support of the natives, the colonial agents overreached themselves, and instead of manipulating their partners eventually found themselves under their spell.

7

The Métis

THE WHITE INDIAN

GENERATIONS OF HALF-BREEDS GRADUALLY EMERGED IN THE REGIONS extending from the Great Lakes to the Illinois. It was at the time of La Vérendrye's expedition that the figures increased in the hinterland. In 1743 the Montreal register of trading permits, with which every trader wishing to enter the West had to conform, recorded the departure of fifty-three employees. The highest point was attained in 1791 with ninety-three entries for the Grand Portage and the Western Sea. There were also unidentified woodrunners going West from the Saint Lawrence Valley from the nearer base of Michilimackinac. Before 1763 about two hundred scattered Canadians lived permanently in the West. Afterwards, the Canadians spread among the native peoples. Where the British of the Hudson's Bay Company settled in groups of ten to twenty, the French Canadian was often on his own. After the North West Company was organized, the population from Lake Superior to Illinois was about 1,600, especially along the waterways.[1] The voyageurs, those wintering agents of the companies, and independent coureurs des bois reached their wintering places, provided themselves with trade goods, and lived among the Indians. The *coureur de drouine* became the essential cogwheel in a trading post. Many of the Canadians lived in their tents indifferent to the uncomfortable quarters. The officers of the Hudson's Bay Company had the impression of a veritable swarm of Canadians among the native tribes. The seigneurial system and the self-righteous values of bourgeois families could no longer forestall a transmutation of cultural values. New France was seeking its center of gravity outside the densely settled areas.

The colony had first received a majority of well-chosen immigrants, Colbert being averse to letting in poor workers lacking in religious zeal. But the turbulent rural population resisted constraints and was attracted to a native environment where the instinct of liberty seemed to have free rein. This new frame of mind, which seemed to foreshadow the peasants' revolt of the Revolution, found an outlet in the wilderness. There emerged a semi-nomadic way of life that was likened to that of the Indians. Some historians have seen in the French Normands' constant wandering a reflection of their Viking heritage.[2] The settlement of New France had first developed along the curves of the Saint Lawrence and against the dark line of the woods. The river culture now ingrained in the inhabitants encouraged dreams of exile.[3]

Champlain had promised the Hurons that the French would marry their daughters. Louis XIV had instituted the king's gift, a pecuniary subsidy for mixed marriages.[4] But the Jesuits, who had themselves initially supported legal miscegenation, finally renounced their policy of assimilation. The clergy separated the natives from the whites and strove to pen the former in missions. But in the wilderness neither isolation nor the ideal of sanctified fusion was possible.

The Canadians drew a distinction between sedentary and nomadic tribes to guard themselves against depredation, but spontaneous intimacy was the principal strength of the Quebec traders. In contrast, the Hudson's Bay Company's forts were enclosed with palisades, preventing the natives from coming and going freely, which was a violation of their habits.[5]

In the second half of the eighteenth century the voyageurs were almost savages in appearance, simply dressed in capotes of coarse wool, trousers of leather without stockings, a shirt of striped cotton with long sleeves, a vest of wool drawn in at the waist by a belt, and moccasins. The rigid attitude of Alexander Henry the Younger in the service of the North West Company after long contact with Indians could be contrasted with the ease Charles Chaboillez showed among the Hidatsas. Henry felt revulsion and Chaboillez behaved like the Indians, seated familiarly in their midst and smoking the pipe that circulated from mouth to mouth. The French Canadian was known as a white Indian, a Franco-Indian, or a half-French naturalized Indian.[6]

The Squaw man

Regular marriages were at first exceptional, for the Indian women would not readily lend themselves to form unions that might imply a denial of inborn values. Conversely, free unions seemed to leave more autonomy to the female companion. Most of the children were absorbed into the mother's tribe and remained outside the French Canadian population. Half-breeds, who were often interpreters, knew how to mobilize the braves of the allied tribes and intervene as mediators. Captured Canadians depended on families to decide their fate. The resentment of the clan for the loss of a warrior might be assuaged either by the captive's death or by his adoption by the grieving relatives or parents.

Either willingly or by force the French inmate adopted the Indian way of life, like avoiding the look of a stranger or using sign language. The white Indian emerged in an environment where Christian concepts were alien if not ridiculed. Philippe Chabert de Joncaire, an officer serving Governor Comte de Frontenac, who was captured by the Iroquois and adopted by the Senecas, took a wife in the tribe, and then acted as a mediator between whites and natives.[7] The coureurs des bois became the essential moving force of cultural interpenetration. Young people with no vocational training, young noblemen unaccustomed to the plough, the mattock, and the axe chose a nomadic life. Living with Indian women proved to be invaluable in local trading relations.

The settling of New France was Malthusian compared to English territorial expansion in colonial America. The region extending from Michilimackinac to Illinois suffered from the scarcity of white women. Until 1700 there were only fifteen of them around the Great Lakes, all married. When Marguerite Le Sueur accompanied her husband on the Mississippi, she aroused the admiration of the Illinois, who crowded around her. She was even invited to spend two days outside a fort to gratify the curiosity of the locals. Three Métis sisters—Marguerite, Madeleine, and Isabelle Couc, who lived in the Pays d'en Haut by the early eighteenth century—were from the Trois Rivières region. Their father Pierre Couc, alias La Fleur (1624–90) was from Cognac, France. He had been wounded by the Iroquois in 1652 during the siege of Fort Trois Rivières. Pierre married Miteouamegoukoue, an Algonquian girl, at Trois Rivières in 1657. She was the widow of Assababich, an Algonquian who had been captured and killed with their two children by the Iroquois in 1652. Madeleine Couc had wed the interpreter Maurice Ménard at Michilimackinac in 1692 but soon had to return to the Saint Lawrence region. In 1713 Father Chardon, a missionary, pleaded to let Ménard's wife come back to Michilimackinac after years of separation. Her sister Isabelle moved to Detroit with her husband, also a fur trader. Marguerite had four children from Jean Fafard, another interpreter at Michilimackinac. The three Couc sisters had a brother, Louis, who adopted the name of Montour, a village close to Cognac, probably in remembrance of his father's hometown.[8]

In the same years, Amiot Villeneuve, a woodrunner, lived with Domitilde Oukabé, an Ottawa native.[9] She taught her language to Father Chardon upon the request of Marest, the influential Jesuit, who thought of her as a model of wisdom for both French and Indian communities. Few wives came from France to live with their husbands in western garrisons. Madame de Tonty and Madame de Lamothe Cadillac rejoined their husbands in Detroit during the fall of 1701. Iroquois women celebrated their arrival, kissed their hands, and wept with joy for the noble wives who had consented to live among savages.[10] In 1704 there were fewer than a dozen French women in the fort of Detroit. In a letter to his minister in October 1713 Lamothe Cadillac recognized that colonists preferred Indian women to the French.[11] To avoid the extension of debauchery, in 1709 La Salle had recommended the transportation of French women, provided they were good-looking, otherwise he thought the men would prefer Indian girls. The higher-ups like Tonty used to blame the young soldiers for their lack of restraint, which to him regrettably gave an outlet to *la sève d'Adam* [Adam's sap]. Deliette openly judged Indian women ugly. Was it a devious way to conceal his preferences under the veneer of disdain, or was it the attitude of nobles and bourgeois idealizing the European woman to avoid the pitfalls of temptation in the wilderness?[12] Lamothe Cadillac himself found the Menominees pretty. The West was indeed more hospitable to native paramours than the banks of the Saint Lawrence. For the religious authorities back in Quebec, abstinence should have been the rule on a land where the most lofty aim was to evangelize Indians. Young men had, however, no sense of guilt when they could find women whose ethics were dictated by tribal codes incompatible with the Biblical recognition of man's sinful nature. Among the Hurons, ritual orgies consisted of public copulation to cure the sick.[13] As witnessed by the men of Meriwether Lewis's Corps of Discovery in the winter of 1804, the Mandans organized the Buffalo Dance to improve the skills of the hunters by offering their young wives to experienced old men. In Michilimackinac, Father Carheil accused the soldiers at Fort Buade of transforming Indian villages into the Sodom of impurity.[14] In the West, the French became experts in terms of native sexual relations, adultery, and marriage. In their early twenties, unmarried Indian women enjoyed many partners who were above jealousy as Radisson noticed after spending a night with a girl he had found *gracieuse* [graceful]. Lamothe Cadillac considered such habits as a welcome probation before marriage. Travelers observed the frequency of separation and divorce. The French trappers and voyageurs were advised not to seek sex with married women in the Miami, Illinois and Sioux tribes because unfaithful wives were severely punished, sometimes by mutilation. Or they could be surrendered to a group of tribesmen who raped them. Such punishments were so severe for adulterous women that French suitors refrained from putting them in jeopardy by making conspicuous passes at them.

For fear of retaliation from husbands many Frenchmen staying in Illinois chose to live with women still free from the bonds of marriage before they became their legal wives. Others might take slaves captured by allied tribes on the Missouri. A slave woman was permitted to marry into the tribe. In case of adultery she returned to the former status of potential enemy for the whole band, which often meant retribution by gang rape.

French trappers were naturally attracted to easy young girls who enjoyed unexpected freedom, even though their siblings might have their say about their affairs. But the cult of virginity prevailing in Europe was unknown to Indians in the French West. On the other hand, the inferior status of Indian women forced to carry heavy loads, mend clothing, and build canoes, prompted them to seek the company of those strangers who would display their gallantry to court them. Frenchmen were also proud to gain recognition at little cost, while believing that they both emancipated Indian girls and easily took their pleasure with them.

The French might also take a fancy to single women who were widowed or repudiated. Some of them—called Ickoue ne Kiossa among the Hurons—entertained hunters rather than bind themselves to a husband. Many of those fancy-free women accompanied their companion in their canoes. The coureur des bois could find his way more easily with his Indian mate and ensure his safety when she acted as a guide in the backwoods or on the rapids. Moreover she carried materials, cooked, picked up fruit, gathered firewood, killed small game, and selected medicinal herbs.[15]

The reputation of French lovers was high compared to the relative chastity ascribed to natives. Another cause of French popularity was the scarcity of men in villages. Wars decimated them. A great number of captives thus increased the female population and thus the birthrate. The squaw was prompted by a dual impulse. Being a Frenchman's companion enabled her to escape from her harsh life and also to live more comfortably with a status previously denied her. Her paramour also availed himself of tools and utensils, making her daily life easier.

Sexual relations were used by Indians to keep peace with the French. Lahontan noted that the Sioux offered their women to soldiers. Many chiefs believed that interracial unions would further alliances. Entire communities took advantage of such matings to gain military support, food supplies and most of all, additional spiritual force. In some cases traders received gifts after spending nights with young women in exchange for the powers thus imparted to them. The half-breed born of these short-lived love affairs was considered as a full member of the clan or tribe.

Michel Accault was one of La Salle's men in 1680. Later he worked with Henry de Tonty at Fort Saint Louis. He convinced Rouensa, chief of the Kaskaskia natives, to let him take his young daughter Marie for wife, but well-informed about Accault's loose morality she at first refused his offer. It was not until a Jesuit missionary, Father Gravier, had planned a true marriage for her that she finally submitted. A devout Catholic, she turned her husband away from sin by her prayers. She had two sons, was widowed, then married the captain of the militia in Kaskaskia. Within twenty years of the existence of the village, the parish registered many baptisms of Indian wives and children. Among the class of administrators and military officers, Indian blood was no obstacle to unions even with noblemen, as happened in the case of Pierre Groton de Saint-Ange and François Bissot de Vincennes, who married Métis girls. But the official view of mixed marriages was altered in 1735 when an order prohibited priests from celebrating them without the formal consent of the Church.[16]

Civil authorities held that the sons and daughters of Indian women were ill-adjusted to the requirements of a civilized life. In fact, the New Orleans Creoles felt that the standards of Upper Louisiana and the Illinois had to be raised. As unruly young Métis seemed to antagonize colonial law and order, their rebellious attitudes were hastily attributed to the bad example given by the coureurs des bois. Prior to her death in 1725 Marie Rouensa had anticipated the new restrictions. After her second son by Michel Accault had returned to live with his grandfather's Indian family, she disinherited him unless he returned to live among the French. But the measures against miscegenation did not deter the French from looking for mates as far as the regions well beyond the Mississippi, among the Osages and the Pawnees. Thus the number of illegitimate children was bound to grow in the Illinois villages.

The upper class usually thought that half-breeds were threatened with degeneracy. In 1706 Governor Vaudreuil asked Lamothe Cadillac, then in command of Detroit, to prohibit marriages with Indian women. The Intendant Raudot's firm approval was confirmed by his statement that the offspring of such degrading unions were lazy, licentious, and brutish. He was equally convinced that the tribal chiefs were aware of these disastrous consequences. It also occurred that a Métis turned against his father and defected to the British as happened with Louis Montour, who was later assassinated by Joncaire upon Vaudreuil's order. Louis Couc, alias Montour, was a Métis like his three younger sisters. Born in 1659, at 20 he spoke French, Huron, Algonquin, and Sioux, and was in the fur trade by 1677. He married an Abenaki girl, Sacokie, alias Madeleine, who bore him two children. In 1688, he married Quiquetigoukoue, Jeanne, an Algonquin, by whom he had four children. The same year Louis was hired by a trader, Boisgillot, and went to La Baie des Puants (now Green Bay). He then felt that his future was no longer within New France and probably made contact with commissioners of Indian affairs at Albany where he left part of his family, to serve as a covert British agent among the Great Lakes Indians. He was murdered in 1709 after guiding sachems to British territory. Then his family took the name of Montour to honor his memory.[17] Such an episode in the history of New France made the authorities even more wary of miscegenation. In the case of officers, their superiors dissuaded them from marrying natives although many had concubines in Indian villages in addition to their legitimate wives left behind in France. Around Saint Louis the presence of both Africans and Indians was also bound to stimulate interracial sex. By 1735 intermarriages were banned by a royal edict, unless the governor gave his consent in particular cases.

Such debates on interracial relations shed light on the contradictions undermining the French empire in America. The conquest of the territory was deemed inseparable from staunch alliances with tribes. Whereas the French government found an outlet to social tension between the natives and the colonists by mixing bloods, most governors still dreamed of preserving racial purity. Was the western terra incognita destined to be a royal province or a Franco-Indian empire? History was soon to put an end to such questions.

Derived from the Spanish word *mestizo*, the term *Métis* first appeared in Louisiana in the mid-eighteenth century. It was seldom used elsewhere until a century later. Even though the population of half-breeds was significant, the children born of French fathers and their squaws remained undistinguished natives in European eyes. Sometimes the offspring of interracial couples had fair hair and blue eyes, as noted by puzzled travelers in the Sioux country. In 1751, Bossu met an Arkansas Métis who told him he was the son of a Breton sailor involved in La Salle's expedition of 1685. [18] The land of the Illinois was uncontrollable in the early decades of the eighteenth century when dozens of woodrunners had unlawfully withdrawn in the wilderness despite the restrictive measures taken by the authorities to restrain the westward migration of unidentified individuals. A missionary in Kaskaskia in 1711, Father Marest numbered several Canadian traders whose debauchery with Indian wives and daughters was for him an affront to colonial morality. [19] In 1715, nearly fifty Frenchmen lived in Cahokia off the fat of the land, after capturing black slaves on the Missouri to till their cornfields. Their Indian mates had bred many mixed bloods who looked so happy that traders extolled their Arcadian mode of life, although they were lost to Christianity. [20]

In forts along the Mississippi, soldiers stationed for long periods of time felt so isolated that they would seek company in the backcountry, and eventually lived part of their time with squaws in villages. Such was the case in Sainte Geneviève. Officers were horrified at the thought of regulars deserting their posts to vanish among natives. When compelled to remain on watch, soldiers would manage to have Indian girls come over and spend days with them. They kept them in separate houses outside the forts, as happened in Michilimackinac. In 1706, commander Deliette (in charge of Fort Pimitoui) had to face the recriminations of an Illinois chief whose wife had an affair with the French cook. When the two lovers were caught in the act, the betrayed husband submitted the unfaithful woman to a ritual gang rape by a score of young men inside the fort. Within the precincts of the colonial authority, the tribe thus enforced traditional laws. The cook was spared a trial upon the request of the commander who relied on him to feed the company. [21]

Most officers wished to offer the best image of their behavior overseas. To preserve their reputation they very seldom revealed their affairs with Indian women. But living away from their families they had casual sexual experiences with the natives. At Fort Saint Louis, Father Gravier complained that the tolerance shown by Tonty and Deliette toward high-ranking regulars jeopardized his efforts to convert Indians. Throughout the eighteenth century, Fort Saint Louis was peopled with Métis fathered by Frenchmen who had lived there for many years. Whether obtained from her family with lavish presents or bought when she was a slave, a squaw was considered as a precarious concubine unless she married according to Catholic rituals. To encourage her belated chastity, she was baptized, although she might still be tempted to have her children return to the so-called savage state. The Christian ceremony was also apt to enhance the status of the Indian wife and bestow spiritual gifts on her tribe. It fell to discharged soldiers to adopt staid behavior by founding a family in the west. Besides, the religious devotion of Indian wives was such that many were known to induce their husbands to return to church after a dissolute life in the wilderness.

Jesuits and officers joined efforts to track down woodrunners who seduced young Indians before taking it on the lam. Meanwhile mixed marriages were frequent in Kaskaskia. Reversing French habits, the native customs excluded dowries from parents, whereas the suitor had to offer gifts to the bride's brother who vouched for her. The marriage was celebrated at church and duly registered before French and Indian guests who shared their tastes for carousing.

Many half-breeds emerged from tribal communities to play a role in French-Indian relations. At Michilimackinac, Isabelle, Madeleine Fafard's sister, married a trader, Joachim Germano, from Confolens in southern France, who had come to the Saint Lawrence Valley in 1665 as a soldier in Carignan's regiment. They were married in 1684, and Joachim died in 1695 in an unknown place. After his premature death while serving as an interpreter in Detroit around 1704, Isabelle married Outoutagan, alias Jean Le Blanc, an Ottawa chief; then, according to Lamothe Cadillac, Pierre Téchenet, a Frenchman born in 1671, became her husband. A year after the murder of her brother Louis Montour, she wanted to avenge his death. The hate of the French colonial government prompted her to defect to the Iroquois and stir up tribes around the Great Lakes. She probably had an affair with Lamothe Cadillac who, out of spite, denounced her as a spy to defend himself when he was jailed in Quebec for corruption. Later she married Sachem Carundawana, an Oneida chief from the southeast of Lake Ontario, who was killed in 1730. She had a son, Andrew, before moving to Pennsylvania. Andrew was an interpreter for William Johnson and George Washington in the French and Indian War. Isabelle Couc, alias Elizabeth Montour, died in 1749.[22]

How the Métis Went West

In the mid-eighteenth century French-Indian couples were already instrumental in the westward movement.[23] In 1750, La Jonquière sent Chevalier de Repentigny to re-occupy Sault Sainte Marie, abandoned since 1689. The outpost was to be a hereditary seigneurial domain, should a new fort be built. Repentigny found a Frenchman named Jean-Baptiste Cadotte who was living with a native woman in an Ojibwa village. He hired him to take some land, and farm it while he directed the construction of the fort. Cadotte (1723–1803) became Repentigny's vassal settler there with two native slaves purchased from the Ojibwas. He served as both interpreter and general contractor. He later married Quessway, a Métis who gave him two sons, Jean Baptiste Junior and Michel.[24] Louis Le Gardeur and other coureurs des bois temporarily depended on Cadotte in the Lakes trading system. In the 1750s Paul Martin helped the Dakotas and Ojibwas negotiate winter hunting grounds along the Sainte Croix and Chippewa Rivers. In 1753 Joseph La Verendrye, the French commander of Fort Lapointe, who took over from Martin, encouraged trappers to advance on the Dakota territory to obtain furs.

To the south, Father Vivier provided an early view of the colony's demography. He saw three classes of inhabitants between the Mississippi and Kaskaskia Rivers: French, Blacks, and Sauvages. He did not include the half-breeds, born of one or the other, as a rule, against the Laws of God, as the saying went. According to Vivier's evaluation, there were 1,100 white people, three hundred black slaves, and sixty native slaves around and among the local tribes.[25]

The Assiniboia Métis were located on a territory that extended from Lake Winnepeg south to the divide between the Red River and the Mississippi Basin, from the Lake of the Woods on the east to the Assiniboine River on the west. Nearly half of the Métis population was residing within the limits of what are now Minnesota and North Dakota. The Red River settlement later known as Pembina was rapidly becoming the hub of the fur trade on the northwestern territories. Farming there consisted primarily of wild rice, corn, maple syrup, and especially pemmican for the fur traders. Métis, Crees, and Ojibwas were culturally mixed. The Crees considered the Métis as children as having superior physical attributes that made them bolder hunters and warriors. The fact that half-breeds had great affinity with Indian tribes explains why their settlement in the northwest did not entail violent resistance as happened later on the American frontier.[26]

The Métis had the option of trading with the Hudson's Bay Company to the north or with the French to the southeast. The Hudson's Bay Company had for eighty years slept at the edge of the Great Lakes, showing no desire to explore any further. As a result, the Assiniboia Métis preferred to trade with the more adventurous French who traveled hundreds of miles overland from Canada to the heads of rivers in the Hudson Bay.

A short distance from Fort de Chartres was the Métis settlement of Cahokia. Its inmates were everywhere collecting furs far beyond the ability of the French government to control them. There was a deepening culture gap between English and Métis traders. In the mid-1750s, five members of the Hudson's Bay Company were executed because they had taken two Cree women as concubines. In June 1754, Anthony Henday, an agent of the company, set out from York Factory with Conawapa and Attickosish, two Cree guides, They traveled over a hundred days through Blackfeet territory, and reached Fort Paskoyac, also called Basque. It was an impressive building for the time: twenty-six-feet long, twelve feet wide and nine feet tall. Henday had a narrow escape when the Métis living in the fort tried to capture him.[27]

Throughout the 1750s the Métis population was expanding from Michilimackinac to Detroit, Chicago, Peoria, Green Bay, and Prairie du Chien (Wisconsin). Travelers saw French half-breeds everywhere. They baked bread for the passing voyageurs in improvised ovens, operated country stores, while also trading horses and maple sugar.

Alexander Henry the Elder, born in 1739, belonged to a generation of Englishmen destined to penetrate into the remote regions of the French West during and after the Seven Years' War. [28] Henry left Albany to follow General Gage's army to Canadian territory. He was in charge of three loaded supply boats bound for Montreal. At Les Cèdres he met fur trader Jean-Baptiste Leduc, who informed him about the opportunities offered at Michilimackinac and around Lake Superior. In September 1761, after securing a fur trade pass, Henry followed the Ottawa River-Lake Nipissing-French River route to Michilimackinac with his guide Étienne-Charles Campion. Henry wanted to conceal his identity in a place where the inhabitants were hostile to the British. He disguised himself as a French trader but was unmasked by Ojibwa Chief Minweweh and his warriors who threatened to scalp him. When the British forces took over Michilimackinac from Langlade, the Ojibwas became more friendly with the new occupants. Chief Wawatam helped Henry with finding outlets in the fur trade. While living in an Ojibwa village for a year, he met Jean-Baptiste Cadotte at Sault Sainte Marie and learned a great deal about the Métis. Later, Henry, Cadotte, and Frobisher led a flotilla of sixteen canoes to challenge the Hudson's Bay Company to the northwest of Lake Superior. They set up a trading post on Beaver Lake (Amisk Lake) before Henry went to the Great Plains. He came upon a large Cree village when reaching Lake Winnipeg (otherwise known as Lac Christinaux, from the name given by the Crees). He realized that the French had established close relations with the tribes in regions that were isolated from Lower Canada.

The fusion of races they had developed facilitated their assimilation with the natives. Such affinities fostered solidarity between the two groups. The British were prone to see unrestrained duplicity in the French-Indian alliance. Henry could not fail to understand the power of such familiarity when Joseph, a white Indian living at La Pointe, was murdered by his French engagé, who also killed his Ojibwa wife and their two children. The Ojibwas eventually put the Frenchman to death at Saint Mary's Falls for his crimes.

When the Métis became Canadians subjects after the Treaty of Paris they easily survived what was a trauma in the East, being more attracted to the woods and prairies than repelled by the British presence in Quebec. The loss of their legal French identity drew them closer to the West and their trade. Many of the earlier Michilimackinac inhabitants moved to the junction of the Red River and Assiniboine River to trade with the Assiniboines. Having severed relations with the East they now referred to themselves as *Les Gens Libres* [the Free People].

Southwest of Lake Superior Jean Baptiste Cadotte had settled at Sault Sainte Marie with his Chippewa wife Anastasie Nipissing among fifty-five Chippewas and Métis. Alexander Henry visited him there, noting that the natives were engaged in large-scale commercial netting of fish. Cadotte served as an interpreter for the small garrison, fluent as he was in Ojibwa and Chippewa.

In 1772, a Chippewyan guide enabled Samuel Hearne (1745–92) to go from Hudson's Bay to the Coppermine River. Two years later, Hearne and five men set up the first trading post for the Hudson's Bay Company sixty miles beyond the Pas at Oine Island Lake, just north of the Saskatchewan. Over a hundred Montreal traders surrounded them. They were accompanied by Métis who held the *Potties* [English] in contempt, patronized the French, loved the natives, especially the women, and considered the northwestern territory as their domain.[29]

At the outbreak of the War of Independence, the French Métis felt they had no stake in the conflict. They had gone West by choice to adopt a new culture and their relations with the British remained limited to the fur trade. From Montreal new traders such as Charles Chaboillez and Benjamin Frobisher gained access to western tribes. In 1778, Métis John Langlade, related to the famous Charles Langlade, wintered at Red Lake, Minnesota, then on the north shore of Lake Superior, and at Sturgeon Lake, where he traded with hundreds of Indians for dried meat, oats, bear grease, and beaver.

In the 1780s a new class of *hommes libres* [free men] arose in the ethnic environment of the French West. Aside from the ties of blood, they were now closely linked to the Indian country by their way of life and Métis loyalty. Isolated individuals, of whom the trader Louis Primeau served as an example, found their place among the native peoples. [30] A fair number of former voyageurs lost the memory of their homeland, sometimes regressed into illiteracy, and could no longer understand messages from their families. They were reluctant to return to their previous homes, and fearful of the disapproval they would incur for their bonds with native spouses. Some had deserted their past managers—the bourgeois—after a breach of contract. The free men arranged their lives as it pleased them, sometimes entering a new temporary arrangement with their former boss and at other times preferring to hunt big game on their own. They usually gathered rich stores of furs that they would take to exchange in the forts. The custom spread of consigning to the freemen the task of supplying the trading posts with goods needed for their existence.

Some of the free men cleverly assisted the caravans that passed through the country. They prepared slabs of bark and resin with which the voyageurs could repair the rents in their canoes. They traded the horses which they had raised or bought from the Indians, and in exchange received merchandise that would allow them to get furs they could sell at the nearest post. Before their tents they built a wooden scaffold on which they accumulated the meat of the slaughtered animals.. The French spoken by a Métis was somewhat outdated, full of sacrilegious oaths. As an interpreter he spoke the language of the natives, which was actually his mother's idiom. Interracial relations in the French West differed considerably from British practices. The Scottish voyager most often used the native women as concubines, selling them upon their departure or simply abandoning them and their children to their own fate. The French were more inclined to form permanent relationships based on the sense of family.

In the 1790s a significant influx of coureurs de bois and voyageurs wintered in the northwest, especially in a Red River settlement occupied by a majority of Métis. Jean Baptiste and Michel Cadotte, sons of Jean Baptiste Cadotte Sr., were then offered to take the Leech Lake band of Ojibwas into the valley of the Red River to catch beaver. They left their women and children at Fond du Lac, deeming the expedition too dangerous for them. In 1792, with sixty men they traded along the headwaters of the Mississippi and wintered at the mouth of the Leaf River, met the Dakota Indians and returned by way of Winnipeg Lake to Grande Portage, loaded with furs. As a result of this expedition the North West Company opened up the

Fond du Lac outpost where the Cadotte brothers served for the next two years. At that time Michel Cadotte frequently wintered in the region. The Ojibwas called him "Kichemashane" [Great Michel] after he married Madeleine Equay-say-way, daughter of Waubijejauk, a Chipewyan Chief. He then moved to La Pointe (Wisconsin) where he made his home until his death. After 1790, the Cadotte family of Sault Sainte Marie ruled at La Pointe Wisconsin, in addition to posts along lakes in northern Wisconsin.[31]

In the last decade of the eighteenth century, Charles Chaboillez received an assignment to the Red River settlement by the North West Company. His father was Charles Jean Baptiste Chaboillez (1736–1808), the storekeeper for the British Indian Department at Saint Joseph Island from 1802 to 1807, before he retired to Montreal. By 1800 the Hudson's Bay Company contended that some North West Company Canadian employees followed the example of Simon McTavish, one of its owners, and perverted the Indian custom of taking female slaves as wives, turning some of them into trade items to settle debts with the company. Alexander Henry the Younger mentioned transactions in which women were traded off as commodities for wages. Traders and engagés sometimes bargained over squaws when the terms of a contract were unclear regarding the requirement of specific duties.[32]

This gloomy picture of French Canadian perversion was at least partly an argument against a powerful commercial rival. Generally, most traders considered that native wives were a necessity to the trade, had excellent manners, and loved to sing and dance. Uncommitted observers usually dismissed the idea of rampant prostitution being organized by French pimps on the frontier with the approval and support of the North West Company.

THE MÉTIS AND INDIAN CULTURE

The Canadian Métis developed a sense of resignation, stoicism, and fatalism, frequently misidentified as slovenliness by bourgeois observers. He was said to be capable of vigorous efforts in navigating canoes but liable to idleness. He seemed to be immune to discouragement and vexation, and his exhaustion vanished in jesting, dancing, and tall talk. Voyageurs who were attached to their Métis families no longer dared to return to Lower Canada or Saint Louis where their behavior would arouse strong reprobation. The half-breed, often an outcast back east, was considered obedient but not faithful. Stereotypes abounded in a nascent mythology: the Métis abused the credulity of Indians by disparaging rival traders. He could be vindictive, but his excitability did not involve the pugnacity with which the Indian would nurse his resentment until the fitting moment for revenge. He was outspoken and quarrelsome, yet respected the terms of contracts.

When William Tomison undertook his first journey into the hinterland in 1767 he described François, a Métis traveling with his squaw and his child in a canoe. His account substantiated many previous observations. For example, imitating the gestures and the appearance of the natives, the half-breed seemed to impose himself on everybody around him. He totally relied on his native spouse, who carried out tasks for which white men were not trained. The squaw had been used to those chores since childhood. She was an expert at seasonal occupations: in the summer she picked berries to feed the canoe brigades, in spring she extracted the sap from the maple trees, and she dressed buffalo skins. In trading posts she wore a white woman's clothes to please her French companion.[33]

As late as the turn of the nineteenth century the Métis had to comply with norms that would have offended a European. When natives offered women a refusal was considered as an insult, and it was known, for instance, that the Assiniboines exchanged wives for minimal gains. The Hidatsas gave their women to Europeans for a few inches of tobacco. The Mandans were particularly lax, as experienced by the men of the Lewis and Clark expedition in 1804. The Crees would rent their women to passing voyageurs. The Métis was himself incorporated into an environment to which his way of life had drawn him. Alliances with Indian girls aged ten to fourteen were usual in the northwest. A modified type of polygamy developed if a French man was a bourgeois. The natives regarded it as an honor if he accepted a second or third wife. The squaw man Charbonneau, who acted as interpreter with his Shoshone wife Sacagawea, was ranked highly among the Hidatsas. Voyageurs gained the approbation of the tribes by acquiring a companion with a few presents and trade goods. The alliance was concluded without the formal approval of the Indian girl. Bids could be high. The Canadian who was unable to put up the sum needed to buy a squaw would not hesitate to give up his freedom by binding himself for an indefinite term to the service of a bourgeois who would advance whatever asset was needed. A woman could be acquired for one or two horses. The Métis was naturally attracted to Indian women after living among his mother's clan. He had no special privilege in that case. In many tribes it was a time-honored belief that a marriage could not outlast a reciprocal disagreement. Anyway, an Indian mother showed the same affection toward her native and Métis children.

The most scathing castigation of the Métis mentality was written by the nephew of Alexander Henry, who kept a journal begun in 1799 which was published posthumously. Alexander Henry the younger (1764–1814) wrote one of the most vivid records from the early nineteenth century of the fur trade in the vast area from Lake Superior to the mouth of the Columbia River. He began trading among the Ojibwas in 1791 and wintered in Manitoba a decade later. In August 1800 he met Ojibwas at the mouth of the Assiniboine River to trade rum for buffalo meat. Henry observed that little progress had been made in civilizing the natives. He ascribed their degeneracy to their relations with the whites who shamelessly supplied them with liquor. Henry's attitude was full of paradoxes. Not only did he himself sell firewater, but in 1801 he took an Indian wife, daughter of an Ojibwa chief, and became a squaw man, allegedly against his will.[34]

When Henry arrived at Red River, he saw Métis who had borrowed habits of marauding from the Indians. In those truculent, shifty, and often arrogant half-breeds, he perceived neither honor nor honesty, and derisively called them "meadow gentry." Many of them had broken their links with the trading companies after several years of life shared with the natives. Henry ironically stated that they had done more harm in the prairies than the Blackfeet.[34] Worse, the Métis were accused of selling the favors of their squaws to Hudson's Bay Company's agents for supplies of meat.[35]

It was not until the early 1800s that the North West Company, whose affairs had begun to decline, became troubled by the excessive costs to its posts because of the presence of women and children. Contamination by venereal diseases was also spreading, especially among the Missouri Indians like the Hidatsas and the Mandans. Meanwhile, Canadian iconography had now portrayed a legendary northwest trader in the image of the Nor'wester.

THE MYTH OF THE NOR'WESTER

In the years preceding the Louisiana Purchase, greater numbers of the Nor'westers were Métis, emerging from decades of intermarriages between French Canadians and native women. Newcomers to the trade were most likely to throw in their lot with these Métis people and find their own native women mostly in Ojibwa, Cree, Mandan, and Hidatsa villages.

The Nor'westers were pranksters, bold and provocative—in short, the French forefathers of the frontier demigods Mike Fink and Timothy Flint. They gloried in persuading natives not to trade food with an opponent. They fell huge trees across narrow streams, slashed tents or destroyed trading goods and canoes, and rejoiced in their eccentric swaggering. The Nor'westers were hard-drinking and heavy-smoking men. They spent their time paddling through the woodland streams, crossing the most distant lakes, and entertaining the natives. The Métis mapped the labyrinthine waterways and the hills of Upper Missouri by using French names for new sites. Lewis and Clark were often disconcerted by the toponymy ascribed to coureurs des bois. During the merrymaking at the forts, the dances included the French jig and the Ojibwa step. Singing involved salacious French songs and romantic ballads, but the natives and Métis preferred the former. Their fathers had rejoiced in sin and they were often themselves the unexpected offspring of casual sex. But there were no longer any "black robes" in sight to try and redeem them. They had gladly elected the path of hell and damnation for personal reasons: the Ojibwa and Mandan women were appreciated for temporary favors, and described as having a softness and delicacy not found in the French belles. Most often, the attempt to resolve the conflict between loyalty to their Indian stock and the impulse to identify with the whites was not made rationally by the Métis people. They honored their mothers as well as their fathers and did not concern themselves about the ratio of French to Indian blood in their veins.

The Métis were naturally involved in the conflicts dividing Indian tribes. The delivery of muskets by traders could only aggravate dissensions. The squaw man was identified with a particular clan and had to commit himself when the hatchet was unearthed. When he was in charge of a trading post in the West, Alexander Henry the Younger supported the natives who wanted to avenge the death of a member of his Indian wife's community. As time passed, interracial marriages, either official or countrywise, offered a more stable status to the Métis child who grew in a bicultural environment. After the Louisiana Purchase, the Métis assumed epic tasks in the saga of the American West. To blaze the trail to the Pacific in 1804 Lewis and Clark relied on a group that Alexander Henry might have called the "French Dirty Half Dozen."

8

French America Seen from France

The American Savage

In the early days of the colony, the French outlook on New France was nurtured on paradoxes. Derogatory and racist though the term "savage" may seem today, it was used by the Jesuits with a strictly religious meaning within their mission to convert the pagans. Louis XV would say with great solemnity that he had given hospitality to a king of the savages. Yet the transit of population from New France to Upper Louisiana bred conflicting views of Native Americans. Enlightenment idealists put them on an equal footing with the demigods of ancient Greece. The cult of the Noble Savage challenged the privileges of aristocrats by vindicating the image of a pastoral society based on equality and fraternity. By implicitly referring to a prelapsarian universe devoid of sin, such icons reflected a utopian vision in a closed despotic realm.

Lahontan addressed the issue in so-called curious dialogues between himself and a sensible savage in a book about his voyages to America, published in 1703.[1] It was an imaginary conversation abundant in circumstantial evidence about the customs and attitudes of barbarians on a new continent. It involved the narrator and Adario, a distinguished, proud Huron, in a text with satiric overtones that offered an insight into the mind of a savage in the style of Montesquieu's *Les Lettres Persanes*.[2] The character of Adario was inspired by a real Huron named Kondiaronk, known in New France as Le Rat, who had approved of the breach of a peace treaty between Denonville's forces and the Iroquois by revealing that the truce was a French trick to lull their defenses. Kondiaronk's betrayal resulted in an Iroquois attack that wreaked havoc in Montreal in 1689. Yet he was pardoned and reinstated in the French–Huron alliance. At his death in 1701 during a French-Iroquois conference, he was buried with great pomp.

In the *Dialogues*, Adario makes it clear that he is master of his body, fears no man, and depends only upon the Great Spirit. Through ironic reversal the Enlightenment philosophy is therefore substantiated by the statements of a savage. Averse to violent passion, Adario advocates sexual freedom, therefore safeguarding the Indian woman 's right to choose her partner. As seen by Lahontan, the blissful destiny of native couples is dramatically set in contrast with the bleak condition of transported French girls literally stockpiled in houses where colonists came to single out their brides just as a butcher does a ewe.[3]

As a Jesuit missionary, Joseph-François Lafitau (1681–1746), was a privileged observer on both sides of the Atlantic. Shifting from Sault Saint Louis to Paris and back, he concentrated on Indian manners and beliefs in minute studies foreshadowing modern anthropological works. Beneath the crust of barbarity, Lafitau discovered native fortitude concealed in reticence and an inborn scorn of death strengthened by a harsh life in the wilderness. His idealization of the American Indian went beyond primitivism to seek evidence of God's revelation in savages seen as a chosen people. Lafitau condoned the use of torture among the Iroquois, while considering that the French were more barbarous than the Indians.[4] In 1721 Delisle de la Drevetière wrote a play, *L'Arlequin sauvage,* in which a native wonders at the necessity of laws to become good and implores his masters to be shipped back to his forests so that he may forget about the rich and the poor in European society.[5] It means that the Indian cannot adapt to the Paris environment as is the case with Persians and Turks.

Over the years the brutal facts of colonization dampened the Jesuits' enthusiasm. Although the mirage of a Golden Age was subsiding, the natives remained a model of wisdom for the Old World. Yet their innocence was no longer enhanced by their exposure to sin and virtuous resistance to it. The main factor was their indifference to private property. Philosophy transformed the lost paradise and rationalized it to coin the concept of *état de nature* [natural state]. Jean-Jacques Rousseau published *Le Discours sur l'Origine et les Fondements de l'inégalité* in 1755. It was a pamphlet denouncing inequalities in modern society in an idyllic vision of primitive communities. But Jean-Jacques went too far for the French wits of the eighteenth century. Voltaire derided the idealization of the savage in *L'Ingénu,* and Charles André Helvetius as well as Charles Pinot Duclos pointed to the frequency of crime in primitive societies. Despite those negative evaluations, the theme of the Noble Savage was used by Diderot in *Supplément au Voyage de Bougainville* to condemn the moral inhibitions of an arrogant French society. Abbé Prévost's novel, *La Véritable histoire du Chevalier Desgrieux et de Manon Lescaut,* evoked in 1731 the chaotic passions of two libertines when the regency constituted a period of decadence after the death of Louis XIV in 1715. Like Defoe's Moll Flanders, Manon gives free play to her sensuality and becomes a prostitute while leading her romantic lover Desgrieux into debauchery. She is put under arrest after betraying a rich old man and transported to Louisiana. Desgrieux manages to find a passage on the ship and temporarily benefits from the goodwill of the governor to live in peace with Manon. But they cannot escape their fate in the New World, which proves to be a mere extension of the French evils. The governor's nephew is attracted by Manon's beauty and proposes to her. Desgrieux kills him in a duel before the doomed couple escapes to the desert where Manon meets her death. For Prévost, Louisiana could not be the Promised Land.[6]

AMERICA AND THE ENLIGHTENMENT

The emergence of America as a civilized world for the poor and the persecuted perturbed the French intellectuals who could not imagine living in a world different from their own fantasies. The crux of the matter was the state of a remote country in which nature was said to be deviant and almost moribund. Buffon, Voltaire, Cornelius de Pauw, and Abbé Raynal joined efforts to expose the flaws of the New World.[7] The process was at first scientific, enlisting natural history, but it turned out to be ethical and political in the 1780s. Their statements were based on book knowledge. None of them had ever crossed the Atlantic. Their demonstrations thus ignored hard facts. Instead of describing indigenous flora and fauna they arbitrarily sorted out elements apt to substantiate their hypotheses. It was the cold prevailing in Canada that was for them the cause for the deficiencies of the nourishing earth. Lafitau's and Charlevoix's reports on the variety of climates, racial diversity and physical types no longer had the favor of Parisian thinkers who emphasized the uniformity of America. It was the vast necropolis of things of a past that had no chance to come to life again. De Pauw insisted on leaving in peace savage survivors already plagued by an innate backwardness. Montesquieu thought that the laws of nature dictated that one live in one's native country. It was likewise essential for De Pauw to discourage massive emigration to such unfortunate lands. The injunction had a dual benefit. It saved Indians from extermination and in the nascent Industrial Revolution it stopped workers from deserting French cities.

The Enlightenment did not improve French minds in terms of racial attitudes. The libertines and other intellectuals habitually biting the hand that fed them at the court of Louis XV would relentlessly question the power of aristocrats. Yet they shared with them the same scorn of the people. They trampled Jean-Jacques Rousseau's philosophy of the Noble Savage, as illustrated in sentimental plays like Chamfort's *La Jeune Indienne* performed in 1764 at the Comédie française.[8]

By the mid-eighteenth century Buffon had warned against the irremediable degeneracy affecting Europeans transplanted to the New World. A tragic fate awaited colonists suspected of being cannibals by necessity. From Diderot to Montesquieu the idea prevailed that on the new continent natives and colonists were doomed to perish. In 1770 Cornelius De Pauw went a step further in his anti-American crusade. The fourth part of his book *Recherches philosophiques sur les Américains* was entitled "Du génie abruti des Américains" [The innate character of brutish Americans].[9] In a wilderness that seemed to suffer more than ancient Egypt from the seven plagues, viscous humours thickened the blood of both colonists and natives. Undermined by genetic weaknesses, the Indian male had become next to impotent. His alleged resistance to torture was derived from his atrophied sensitivity, his lack of vitality being thus unduly sublimated into heroism by poets. The future of the Indian was uncertain. Whereas the male was "antiphysical"—that is, prone to feminization—the female's notorious lasciviousness toward the white man led to moral disorder rather than prolific procreation. The French hosts of tribes were confronted with the debauchery of Sodom and Gomorrah. In short, De Pauw held that from the very beginning America had been doomed to putrefaction. And to discredit Lafitau, he was trenchant: "America is not the Canaan of the Patriarchs described by enraptured missionaries."[10] In *L'Histoire des deux Indes* by Abbé Raynal Creoles were said to be feebleminded, aside from becoming sterile after a few generations.[11] Epitomizing all the vices of the two races, half-breeds were bound to regress from the human to the brute. The lack of energy and courage perceived in the inhabitants of the English settlements allowed the author to foresee the defeat of any uprising against the colonial power.

In the years following the Treaty of Paris, Choiseul, the French foreign minister, concentrated his efforts on the West Indies, purchased Corsica from the republic of Genoa, and left Louisiana very much on its own. Only French merchants continued to trade with New Orleans after it became known that the colony was no longer French. The Louisianans were reluctant Spanish subjects. When

Governor Ulloa antagonized the population with a decree allowing no ship in Louisiana unless it was built in Spain, French-born leaders demonstrated their faithfulness to France by forcibly removing him from New Orleans in 1768. Five rebels were condemned to death and executed a year later. Choiseul's only efforts consisted of pleas to reduce the prison sentences of the others. His cautious handling of Spain was linked to his plan for retaliation against England. This explains the lack of reaction of the French public opinion to the executions. The French government knew that the British wanted Louisiana for themselves and were overjoyed with the opportunity the 1768 uprising gave them. Jean-Baptiste, Comte d'Estaing, was among the few Frenchmen who thought of plans to establish Louisiana as a republic. He believed the new state would serve as a model for the American colonies by generously granting what the English Parliament refused. D'Estaing was not heard, and a few years later eagerly supported the cause of freedom in America. To save the family compact with Spain, Louis XV and Choiseul were impervious to the demands of the Louisianans. Less than a decade later, Louis XVI and Vergennes still saw the loss of Canada and the cession of Louisiana as a fait accompli.

Before Benjamin Franklin's arrival in the fall of 1776, the court of Versailles was echoing with rumors about precocious Americans who literally collapsed physically and mentally at middle age. Franklin delighted in refuting such notions about premature senility in his country. Mistaken for a Quaker, he was first likened to the type of anchorite courtiers loved to exhibit in their households as a token of their open-mindedness and exotic leanings. The image of wildness was equally thrilling in sophisticated *salons littéraires*. On the battlefield, Lafayette and Washington amply showed the strength of the New Adam depicted in the *Letters from an American Farmer* by Crèvecoeur.

Once Franklin invited Abbé Raynal to dinner with an equal number of Frenchmen and Americans. The priest eloquently developed his theory of the degeneracy of men and animals in America. Meanwhile Franklin noticed that the Americans were sitting on one side of the table, and the French on the other. He playfully asked his guests to stand up to see on which side nature had degenerated. It happened that the Americans were particularly tall and the French very short. Raynal himself, who was "a mere shrimp" in Jefferson's own words, readily admitted exceptions, which allowed him to remain seated by Franklin, another American six-footer.[12] (Bonaparte was about a foot shorter than Jefferson.) Abbé Raynal progressively qualified his negative statements, but still insisted on the appalling expanse of badlands, rebellious sand dunes, turbid swamps, and forbidding craggy rocks to be encountered in barbarian America. It remained for Jefferson to dispel these stereotypes and clean the Augean stables.

American insurgents were popular, as exemplified by songs and hairdresses, Revolutionary style, despite judgments uttered by skeptics on the inevitable advent of local tyrants and rogue states in an immature republic. In the 1780s Jefferson was prone to retort that it was not reasonable to depict the combatants at Valley Forge as a band of degenerates. His gift of a Vermont moose to Buffon belied the notion of a dwarfish America. But soaked in spurious concepts Buffon's, Raynal's, and De Pauw's theories of the *homo americanus* were not easily dismissed by Jefferson's factual evidence. America was back in 1790 when France decreed three days of mourning after the death of Franklin, only a year after the storming of the Bastille. Relations were strained in the following years. The Jay Treaty angered Bonaparte's Directoire and the revolutionaries jailed Thomas Paine during the Terror. The so-called "Undeclared War" involved the French corsairs in the pursuit of American ships.

THE ARISTOCRAT AND THE BACKWOODSMAN

At the turn of the nineteenth century, aristocratic French emigrants to the United States who had returned home published disillusioned accounts about uncouth, vulgar, and miserly Americans given over to profit-making, swapping, and swindling. In 1794 all the French visitors François de La Rochefoucauld-Liancourt met in his travels found fault with American philistines unsuccessfully trying to emulate British models, and impervious to good taste.[13] Other statements were not so negative. Jean-Pierre Brissot de Warville spent nine months in the United States in 1788. A great admirer of American pragmatism, he linked egalitarianism to utilitarian thinking, while ranking the pursuit of happiness higher than the obsession with age-old monuments.[14]

Charles Maurice de Talleyrand-Périgord was the essence of the metamorphic talent inherent in French aristocracy. The so-called *Diable boiteux* [lame devil], born in 1754 was not fit for armed service. He first made a career in the clergy, being the bishop of Autun, before becoming a delegate of the States General in 1789. He participated in the reforms of the Church by drafting the civil constitution of the clergy. He was condemned by the Pope, and deprived of his ecclesiastical title for his involvement in the Revolution. He spent the rest of his life serving successive régimes. Napoleon called him *une merde dans un bas de soie* [shit in a silk stocking] to define his devious ways as a diplomat. Talleyrand landed in Philadelphia in 1794 to avoid the guillotine during the Terror. He first found Americans close to Perfidious Albion in spirit and language. He castigated the diversity of religious sects and disowned his earlier interest in the agrarian myth borrowed from Jefferson. In his *Mémoire sur les Relations commerciales des Etats-Unis avec l'Angleterre* published in 1799, he summed up his experience in rural America.[15]

For him the frontiersman was subhuman, the exact opposite of Crèvecoeur's image of the New American. Talleyrand discovered in the wilderness sluggish woodcutters and bumpkins who looked like savages, and whose vices were aggravated by ignorance. Worse, insensitive and deprived of imagination, they were unable to appreciate natural beauty. Talleyrand's journey into the American heart of darkness was meant to evaluate the extent of biological regression. In the Native American, he found a look of sullenness and decrepitude as if Nature had left on him the mark of racial decline.

After the years of revolutionary terror, Joseph de Maistre castigated the *homo democraticus* in his book *Considérations sur la France*, also finding fault with the New Republic in the United States.[16] Rousseau's Noble Savage was not the primitive man but the product of sophistry, a derelict drifting away from common sense and dignity. The origins of the Native American could be traced back to no recorded past, only to some unidentified original sin. He was a degraded human, perhaps a fallen Adam whose fate was to be alienated from civilization. De Maistre detected a similar syndrome among mimetic Europeans immersed in the wilderness.

François-René, vicomte de Chateaubriand, born in 1768, who earned his reputation as forefather of French romanticism through *Le Génie du Christianisme* (1802), renewed the myth of the Noble Savage, whom he linked to the sublime in nature. His military career had been interrupted by the Revolution after his refusal to take the oath of allegiance to the Constitution. In 1791 he met Christian-Guillaume de Malesherbes, a former minister of Louis XVI and protector of the *Encyclopédistes*. Malesherbes advised Chateaubriand to visit the United States, and to make his journey useful, suggested he seek information on the Northwest Passage. The objective thus set was in fact more a pretext to go abroad than a true incentive to reach the Pacific. Chateaubriand left Saint Malo in April 1791, visited Niagara Falls, then went south to Tennessee and returned to France the following January. Like many aristocrats he soon fled the country and rallied the Prussian troops with other émigrés. After the

Battle of Valmy in September 1792, he went to England where he lived seven years in exile, and wrote extensively about Christianity, revolutions, and the Natchez Indians. In 1799, Bonaparte moved toward national reconciliation by granting a pardon to the émigrés, which caused Chateaubriand to leave London for Paris in 1800. During his years in exile he wrote two novels, *Atala ou les amours de deux sauvages dans le désert*, and *René*, which were published in 1801 and 1802, respectively. They then appeared together under the title *Les Natchez*.[17]

In *Atala* a Frenchman named René arrives in Louisiana around 1725. The Natchez Indians give him hospitality along the *Meschacébé* [Mississippi]. Settlers are living along the banks of the river close to Fort Rosalie. To depict Indian life, Chateaubriand was indebted to the accounts of Jean-Bernard Bossu, the naval officer who traveled along the Mississippi in the mid-eighteenth century. Bossu collected information on the tragic events that took place in the 1720s when the commander of Fort Rosalie wanted the Natchez to surrender their lands. But the elders met in council; and decided to withstand the threats. In 1729, the Natchez sacked the fort, and killed or captured hundreds of settlers. The French enlisted their Choctaw allies to retaliate. Etienne Boucher de Périer, who had taken over from Lemoyne de Bienville as governor, involved his troops in a genocide. By 1731 the Natchez population was reduced to a hundred warriors, two dozen old men, and a few women. Against this background of colonial warfare, and fratricidal conflicts among Indians, Chateaubriand imagined the life story of an old sachem named Chactas. At the beginning of the eighteenth century he was involved in wars against the Seminoles and the Muskogee tribes who belonged to the Creek nation. A romantic character, René has chosen exile to heal a secret wound that has haunted him for years. He is adopted by the wise sachem who tells him the history of the Natchez. Chactas was once torn away from his native forests and held prisoner by French troops, then was removed to Paris and later introduced to Louis XIV. He attended the court at the Palace of Versailles, met Fénelon, listened to Bossuet's sermons, and watched Racine's tragedies. In *René*, the eponymous character marries Chactas's daughter Celuta. He is then initiated into Indian rituals on his way to the Ohio to trap beaver.

Chactas confides his inconsolable passion for Atala to René. As a young warrior who had stayed among the Sioux, he fought the Muskogees and was captured. Threatened with torture and death, he was saved by Atala, a beautiful girl belonging to the enemy tribe, who risked her life and escaped with him. Neoplatonic love at first sight between Chactas, an idolatrous pagan, and Atala, a Métis converted to Christianity, is, however, doomed from the start. They were born of the same father, Lopez, a Spanish adventurer. To avert the risk of incest, Atala has promised her mother she would remain a virgin. But she soon falls sick and suffers the long agony of death. At her bedside, Father Aubry, a Jesuit who combats sin in the wilderness, has Chactas eventually share his faith in the Christian God as a way of coping with his misfortune. The fate of the Natchez reminds Father Aubry of the book of Genesis, in which sisters and brothers were doomed to become wives and husbands. The Jesuit's reference to the Bible exemplifies Chateaubriand's vision of America as a primeval forest, evoking the times after the Fall, when incest was inevitable under the spell of Original Sin.

Strikingly, René's plight in the New World duplicates Chactas's past experience. During his stay, he is mistakenly responsible for the war that breaks out between the Natchez and the Illinois, who eventually capture him. He is saved from torture by his friend Outougamiz, the brother of Celuta, the squaw René has married. When set free René faces the hatred of Ondouré, a rival who conspires to arouse the Natchez against the French, and who also wants to discredit him in the eyes of the governor. After running away from the tribe, René returns, still weighed down by a sense of guilt. Later he confesses to Chactas the incestuous love that binds him to his sister Amélie. When Chactas dies, Ondouré seizes power, only to wreak havoc among his kin. He murders René and rapes Celuta, who then jumps to her death in a cascade. Half a century later a traveler meets a young couple rocking a dead infant. He is the great-grandson of René and Celuta, the last of the Natchez.

Much of Chateaubriand's thinking about the New World was included in *Le Génie du Christianisme*, the sum total of his ideas on Christianity. In Atala Father Aubry, who lives among the Natchez, embodies the Jesuits' dedication to evangelize the natives. Chactas tolerates the priest for his competence in medicine and agriculture, but at times resents his God who disregards the supernatural powers immanent in nature. The wilderness expresses lethal violence in the chiaroscuro surrounding the surviving tribes, while the tumultuous waters of the Mississippi carry corpses and engulf joyful expectations. As Chateaubriand transforms history into myth, the wilderness first evokes Eden, when René first sees peaceful bears intoxicated with grape juice, but Nature is soon polluted by both Indian and French hunters. Bent on the graves of a vanishing nation, Chateaubriand removes the Native American from history by sublimating him into the archetype of a lost paradise. The ending of *Atala* is thus meant as a funeral celebration of Indian destiny and retrospectively appears as a premature elegy. In his preface to the first edition of the novel, Chateaubriand contended that he was aware of the excess of tearful evocations, but believed that the tragedy of the American Indian was more heartrending than the *Aeneid*. In *Atala*, the religious fervor of the Indian converts is recaptured with passionate eloquence. Their sufferings implicitly refer to the martyrdom of the early Christians. Chateaubriand was inspired by the holy life of Kateri Tekakwitha (1656–80), the first Native North American proposed for sainthood. In his Christian epic of the New World, he offered a romantic solution to the issues of the French empire in America when Bonaparte was losing his grip on historical realities. His transfigured Indian was a dead Indian, and his fate condemned René, the French squaw man, to wander in solitude, for ever estranged from the American dream.[18]

THE LOUISIANA PURCHASE

In the turmoil of the French Revolution, the most contradictory attitudes had access to the rostrum. Gouverneur Morris, the United States ambassador to Paris, remarked that orators substituted their genius for reason and preferred the thunderbolt to pure daylight. Washington's proclaimed neutrality was jeopardized by Jay's Treaty of 1794, which provided that American ships carrying French property that were captured by the British should be taken to ports and their property removed. The French fiercely contended that the treaty was inconsistent with the American principle that free ships made free goods. Peace was also gravely endangered by the incredible awkwardness of Edmond Genet, the French ambassador to the United States in 1793. Instead of landing at Philadelphia to present his credentials to Washington, this brash radical aristocrat meddled with domestic policies, hoping to enlist American public opinion against the English crown. Not only did he create democratic societies soon dubbed the Genet Clubs, but also plotted to outfit French warships in American ports, and issued letters of marque authorizing American shipowners to serve as French privateers. On a tour of the interior, Genet appealed to pro-French crowds against Washington's orders while embarrassing all but the most francophile republicans.

On the eve of the Revolution Saint Domingue was the most productive colony in the French overseas empire. The production of coffee, sugar, indigo, and cotton made of the island "the pearl of the Antilles." Thirty thousand whites ruled over half a million black slaves. The thirty thousand free mulattoes constituted an underclass. The colony was administered by the Ministry of the Marine, which held exclusive authority over international trade. The *Grands Blancs* [planter aristocracy] who claimed independence after the storming of the Bastille, were staunch supporters of the rights of men but desperately clung to slave property. In 1791, they overthrew the governor and seized power while excluding the black population from their revolution. The immediate uprising of the mulattoes under the leadership of Boukman revealed the vulnerability of colonists concerned only with their status.[19] Port-au-Prince, the capital, and then the whole island were put to fire and the sword. England and Spain stepped in. Planters fled to Louisiana by the hundreds. As a measure of appeasement, slavery was abolished by French envoys from Paris in August 1793, and confirmed by the Convention in 1794. Commander in chief of the troops in 1796, Toussaint-Louverture, a free black slave owner, drove back the British forces and drafted a constitution that made him governor general of the island.

Revolutionary France had dreamed of an empire extending from the Caribbean Sea to the Gulf of Mexico. While French colonists were losing ground in Guadeloupe, the United States was taking steps down the path of national expansion. The success of a westward movement depended on the number of common citizens who would stake their claim to the land and thereby promote the interests of the whole nation. For Washington, one of the most obvious obstacles to expansion was the claims of France, Spain and England on North America. Diplomacy or warmaking were the alternatives for Washington and his successors.

In 1793, Jefferson proposed an expedition led by André Michaux, a brilliant French scientist with an interest in American fauna and flora. The enterprise had been initiated by the American Philosophical Society before receiving the full support of the government. The chief objective was to find the best route to the Pacific as indicated by Jefferson's instructions, which suggested crossing from the Mississippi to the Missouri, well above Spanish outposts and within temperate latitudes. To challenge the French theories of American degeneracy, Jefferson wanted Michaux to search for evidence of mammoths.[20]

Meanwhile, brazenly violating the Neutrality Act, Genet commissioned George Rogers Clark to undertake an overland expedition against Spanish possessions when Spain was an ally of Britain against France. On September 17, 1793, Michaux visited Clark at Mulberry Hill, his home near Louisville. He gave him a letter from Genet to confirm his appointment by the French Republic as commander of the Revolutionary and Independent Legion of the Mississippi.[21] It was thus Clark's task to foment rebellion among Americans living between the Mississippi and the Alleghenies, and ultimately free Louisiana from Spanish rule. Michaux's duplicity was evident. After a stay in Canada, he had first asked the American Philosophical Society to commission him to discover the transcontinental water route before the British did so. Being now entangled in Genet's plot, he allowed the expedition to serve as a decoy for a raid into New Spain. When Washington learned of the conspiracy he demanded that the French government recall the ambassador. But Genet's Girondin party was then out of control and the hard-line Jacobins in power. It would not have been safe for Genet to return to France. Washington generously agreed to grant him political asylum in the United States, and he settled down to live to a ripe old age with his American wife on a Long Island farm.

When John Adams was elected president, the Directoire was ending the Terror. A new government in Paris held that according to Jay's Treaty, American vessels were under British control. Meanwhile the French were aware that freedom of navigation on the Mississippi was an absolute necessity for the United States. Spain had allowed such freedom in addition to a storehouse in New Orleans. The first objective of the Directoire was to purchase Louisiana back from Spain to control the Mississippi River but negotiations failed. Although it was good news for Americans, French corsairs gave them a hard time between the Caribbean and the Gulf of Mexico where three hundreds of their ships were seized. France and the United States were now engaged in an *quasi guerre* [undeclared war]. In Paris Foreign Minister Talleyrand unsuccessfully attempted to bribe Adams's emissaries before finally reaching a peace agreement. No one could imagine Bonaparte leaving Egypt to sail across the Atlantic and fight Washington who had nearly been called back from retirement.[22]

Bonaparte seized power as First Consul on November 10, 1799, a month before Washington died. Grandiose ceremonies dedicated to the American president ostentatiously overshadowed the past crisis. The Federalists who disliked Bonaparte resented his renewed hostility toward Austria and Britain. His victory at Marengo in June 1800 encouraged him to rivalry with the hereditary enemy overseas. At his mansion of Mortefontaine Joseph Bonaparte welcomed French and American delegates who signed a pact to avert new conflicts. Gorgeous receptions entailed theatricals and fireworks around the illuminated ponds.

Bonaparte was sensitive to Abbé Raynal's preference for colonies in a warm climate, implicitly in keeping with Voltaire's abhorrence of Canada's acres of snow. But the Spanish crown was soon torn by internecine rivalries. Three months after the Mortefontaine meeting, the secret Treaty of Ildefonso was signed with Spain to return Louisiana to France.[23] Lucien Bonaparte ratified it in March 1801 at Aranjuez, the summer residence of the Spanish sovereigns. Jefferson was inaugurated president at the same time.

Bonaparte was preparing an expedition to the Caribbean island of Saint Domingue with the intention of using it as a base to prepare troops for the occupation of Louisiana. In fact the 20,000 men sent in December 1801 were primarily committed to crushing Toussaint-Louverture's rebellion. General Leclerc, the husband of Bonaparte's sister Pauline, was in command. He landed at Cap Français in February 1802. In the following weeks there were heavy casualties on both sides before the French victory, despite the heroic resistance of chief Dessalines at La Crête-Pierrot in March. Toussaint-Louverture surrendered in June. While Bonaparte's army was still confronted with guerrilla warfare, yellow fever decimated thousands of his men. He had dreamed of acquiring a strategic stronghold in Louisiana to fight British hegemony. The outcome of the expedition turned out to be disastrous.[24]

The tragedy made the First Consul aware of the pitfalls of his imperial policy. He also realized that Louisiana would remain a bone of contention between France and the United States if territorial expansion was stopped at the boundary line of a French Mississippi. Barbé-Marbois, minister of the treasury and Decrès, minister of the navy, were summoned by Bonaparte in April 1803 to learn that he had abandoned all thought of occupying Louisiana. For him the territory would be in better hands if ceded to the United States so as to facilitate diplomatic and trade relations with France. Barbé-Marbois agreed, also adding that Britain was still in a position to take possession of Louisiana by attacking from the Great Lakes. Decrès disagreed on the grounds that France could wage war with Britain in northern Europe and thus compel the Redcoats to rush back from America to European shores. He was deeply convinced that Louisiana remained the gateway to the West with its fabulous natural resources. Negotiations were opened with Livingstone in Paris. Monroe made an offer to Talleyrand who, upon Bonaparte's instructions, replied that the whole territory was for sale. The First Consul had evaluated the cost at fifty million francs, but Barbé-Marbois raised the sum to eighty million. Bonaparte was crowned Emperor

Napoleon I in 1804, the year when Lewis and Clark set out from Saint Louis. He won a supreme title but lost an empire overseas.[25]

The First Consul had a merely geopolitical vision of the United States while weighing the pros and cons of a return of Louisiana to France. But as emperor, he never ceased to be interested in the geography of America. For instance, he pondered over the possibility of having vineyards along the Mississippi despite the fog and rain near the riverbanks. The country always imposed itself on his imagination by the sheer mirage of a prolific nature. After the defeat at Waterloo in 1815, he rallied at the Island of Aix, off La Rochelle, wanting to board a ship and find refuge in the United States, studying the flora and fauna in company with famous scientist Gaspard Monge. Accordingly, he spent a fortune on scientific instruments. Banker Jacques Lafitte transferred three million francs to the United States, General Bertrand shipped books, china, guns, and furniture. But former minister of the interior Fouché, and Talleyrand, then close to Louis XVIII, betrayed the fallen emperor by surrendering him when he was on board the frigate *La Salle*. He was escorted to the Island of Sainte Hélène where he died in 1821.[26]

9

The French Background of the
Lewis and Clark Expedition

FRENCH CANADIANS AND FRENCH SPANIARDS
IN A STATE OF UNCERTAINTY

IN 1799 THE HUDSON'S BAY COMPANY STILL ONLY HAD 498 MEN IN NORTH America, whereas the North West Company had 1,276. Frustrated with the authoritarian style of his co-managers, Alexander Mackenzie Sr. had resigned. The company was now in the hands of Simon McTavish and Joseph Frobisher. Some believed this was the beginning of the company's decline and fall. To add to the problems, the United States government had discovered that Grand Portage was on American soil and so started charging tariff on all goods passing through the territory. Sault Sainte Marie was made a port of entry, thereby ensuring American control over the waterways.

A growing number of retired Canadian North West employees were choosing to remain in the field with their country wives and children, leading the Métis to regard themselves as a new nation with the Red River colony as the capital, and Red Lake and Sault Sainte Marie as its primary territory. In reality, the Métis occupied the Great Lakes, down the Mississippi and up the Missouri as well as the Red Lake area, the Red River of the North, and Saskatchewan River systems. Alexander Henry the Younger, who reported on the North West Company's fifteen districts in Indian country, announced a total white fur trade population of 1,090 men, 368 women, and 569 children.

With one thousand country wives and Métis children dependent on the forts, a new regulation was passed by a majority vote that prohibited employees from marrying native women, subject to a £100 fine. Arguments in favor of the prohibition claimed that it would reduce the dependence of abandoned wives on the posts.[1]

By the end of the eighteenth century the west of Upper Louisiana appeared on most Spanish maps, but His Catholic Majesty's subjects

147

living in Ylinoa—that is, in the upper Mississippi Basin—knew little about the measures taken by their government to counter Russian, British, French Canadian, and American activities. Reports about the upper Missouri made officials apprehensive that it stemmed from tributaries close to other streams leading to the Rio Grande and the Colorado. Their concern about foreign intrusion was substantiated in 1789 by the Spanish Minister to the United States, Diego de Gardoqui, who mentioned an explorer who had reached the mountains from which rivers flowed into the Pacific. He suggested that the wealth of furs in the territory revealed by Cook's expedition in the 1790s be opened up for exploitation, hence the necessity to explore the country westward. The maximum penetration toward the northwest occurred in 1790 when a Frenchman, Jacques d'Eglise, [Santiago de la Iglesia], met the Mandans in present-day North Dakota and reported that British traders from the Hudson's Bay Company were among them. He later lived with the Missouris until 1792.[2]

Would the British challenge Spanish claims in territories further south? To make alliances with Indian nations and attract immigrants to colonize underpopulated areas, Baron de Carondelet (of French descent) replaced Esteban Miro as governor of Louisiana. He instituted a vigorous frontier policy to counteract American penetration, strengthening Spanish control over the Upper Missouri as well as attempting to discover an overland route to the Pacific and establish a chain of outposts all the way to the small Nootka settlement on present-day Vancouver Island.[3] In 1793, the French Convention declared war on Spain. Governor Carondelet was hard put to stem French agitators demonstrating support for the Revolution. They sang "La Marseillaise," danced "La Carmagnole." "Ah, ça ira" was a subversive tune tentatively ascribed to Benjamin Franklin.[4] Meanwhile, the society of the Jacobins circulated pamphlets pressing the French to rebel against a government that allegedly treated them like cattle.

In the last decade of the eighteenth century Spain was unable to supply its French-speaking adventurers with the trade goods necessary for holding the Indians to New Spain. British traders had captured control of the Indian trade on both sides of the Mississippi north of Saint Louis. The Chouteau brothers—the major traders in Upper Louisiana—still fared better than their rivals, but conflicts between nations were soon to disrupt commercial relations. The Chouteaus found themselves forced to choose between conflicting national loyalties. They were Frenchmen by birth, language, and culture, but Spanish subjects and imperial agents closely linked to British suppliers and fur dealers in Canada and England. At the outbreak of the Revolution they usually sent their furs north to agents at Michilimackinac. When they heard that Britain had joined the war against France in 1793 they wished to preserve their alliances with British manufacturers who provided the Indian trade goods. As the disruption of the continental markets was reducing the demands for furs in England, Auguste Chouteau strove hard to maintain his trade with the North West Company. Carondelet devoted much attention to planning for the defense of the region against possible British incursions from the north. The Spaniards worried about the influence of revolutionary ideas while doubting the loyalty of the French-born subjects. But Chouteau reassured them by heartily welcoming the governor of Natchez, Manuel Gayoso de Lemos, in 1795. He convinced him of the French allegiance to His Majesty the very year that Spain decided to come to terms with France.[5] In the 1790s Lieutenant Governor Trudeau, in charge of Upper Louisiana, and Baron Carondelet, the governor in New Orleans, launched a campaign to revitalize the fur trade in Saint Louis and to counter British intrusions into Spanish territory. They named Jacques Clamorgan trade syndic.[6] He was a dashing young man whose swaggering gestures dazzled the Spaniards. The Chouteaus feared for their quasi-monopoly because the decision to distribute the Missouri trade equally among the region's licensed traders would force them to drastically limit their operations. While the Chouteaus concentrated on the Osage trade they nervously eyed Clamorgan's newly formed Company of Explorers of the Upper Missouri, which sent out three expeditions in 1794 and 1795.

By 1800, fluctuating prices in the erratic fur trade had made it more vulnerable to the demands of Canadian and British merchants. The Chouteaus' faithfulness to the Spanish government earned them the esteem of the new lieutenant-governor, Charles Dehault Delassus, an officer who had left his native Flanders after the outbreak of the French Revolution.[7] The Chouteaus were also instrumental in appeasing the restless Osages who had remained hostile to the Spanish presence in Upper Louisiana.

The monopoly of the Chouteaus was disputed by a young enterprising Spaniard, Manuel Lisa, who joined efforts with local bourgeois like Joseph Robidoux, Charles Sanguinet, and Jacques Chauvin.[8] The assault on their closed trading system rankled the Chouteaus and their allies. When Lisa failed to make headway in Saint Louis, he traveled down the Mississippi in 1801 with a petition bearing thirty signatures supporting his campaign for free trade. Although Lieutenant Governor Delassus labeled his conduct impudent and seditious Lisa succeeded in gaining the Osage trade with the support of Governor Salcedo. It was a blow to Auguste Chouteau who, in 1803, reacted violently by pressing friendly Osage tribes to ruin his competitors with legal action to collect debt from Lisa and his associates. The former was even jailed by Delassus. Auguste Chouteau was then confident that the retrocession of Louisiana to France would facilitate his operations. In 1798 the United States had taken possession of the Natchez country and part of the region along the Mississippi. Baron de Carondelet had been replaced first by Manuel Gayoso de Lemos, then by Casa Calvo. Reports from Spanish Louisiana by Xavier Delfau de Pontalba, a colonel in the militia, made it clear, however, that Americans were averse to a return of the colony to France. The weakened king of Spain, Carlos IV, ceded Louisiana against the guarantee that his son-in-law would be Duke of Parma and possibly king of Etruria.[9] Like many French-speaking inhabitants of Saint Louis the Chouteaus were now faced with the prospect of French citizenship. But what did the Revolution mean to them?

A former governor of Guadeloupe, General Victor Collot, came to Saint Louis in 1796, probably inspired by Genet's former plans regarding George Rogers Clark's designs in the Southwest.[10] The warm welcome extended by the populace to the radical conspirator had aroused fears in the bourgeois population. Spain was equally suspicious of the projects of Collot. Governor Zenon Trudeau had been naive enough to respond favorably to his request to visit Upper Louisiana. When tension mounted, suspected French revolutionaries were deported to New Orleans, while Auguste and Pierre made donations to form militia companies in Upper Louisiana to fend off agitators.

Collot resented the British for his own failure to rouse the masses in the West Indies, and shared the feelings of the French government toward Washington and the Federalists, especially in relation to the XYZ affair. Collot scornfully observed the French settlements in Illinois, deploring the fact that the inhabitants were mostly occupied with hunting and fur trading, and disregarded farming although the land was exceptionally fertile. He found them utterly ignorant, stupid, ugly, and miserable. To him it seemed the consequence of extreme poverty. It had blunted their sensibility and destroyed their intellectual powers. Their lack of education also precluded any possibility of self-improvement. The offspring of the French colonists of the ancien régime were degenerates.[11]

Collot went up to the River of the Great Osages, met some traders, and relied on Jean Baptiste Truteau for copies of his own accounts summed up in a volume later published and entitled *Description of the Upper Missouri*. While in Saint Louis, Collot initiated the French inhabitants into the subtleties of revolutionary thinking, thus enlisting them to challenge Spanish domination in the spirit of the "sansculottes" who had stormed the Bastille. Carondelet soon cast doubts on Collot's goodwill and brought his plans to an end. He had him put under arrest and his papers confiscated. Humiliated and depressed, the would-be liberator of Louisiana went back to New Orleans, abandoning the hopes of converting the New World to the ideals of the French Revolution. Upon his return to Philadelphia in December 1796, Collot wrote to Carondelet's successor Gayoso to suggest means for the defense of Saint Louis. He had previously discussed the matter with the Spanish minister in Saint Louis, Casa Irujo. The chameleon French agitator recommended Nicolas de Finiels, an émigré who had fled the revolutionary régime, to build the proposed fortifications. Finiels settled in Sainte Geneviève with his family in 1797 but was not considered equal to the task by the military commander of Upper Louisiana, Lieutenant-Colonel Carlos Howard. Finiels was ordered out of Upper Louisiana in May 1798. But Gayoso utilized the Frenchman's services to draw maps of the lower Mississippi region. In the following decade Finiels served the Spanish crown faithfully, and directed fortifications at Mobile and Pensacola.[12]

On October 15, 1803, three years after the Treaty of Ildefonso and just months following the Louisiana Purchase, Prefect Laussat landed in New Orleans. Governor Salcedo did not resign his authority until November, when he finally returned the keys of Fort Saint Charles and Saint Louis to Laussat, and authorized the Spanish subjects to pledge allegiance to France. On November 30, Laussat announced peace and happiness to the new French citizens now administered by Bonaparte's Consulate. The same day he informed Pichon, the chargé d'affaires in Washington, that Louisiana was ready to be turned over to the United States.[13] On December 4, 1803, a Te Deum was celebrated at the cathedral of New Orleans where the clergy sang *Domine salvan fac republican* and *Domine salvos fac consules*. The interim regime under Laussat's authority lasted twenty days, during which there were no incidents. The French flag flew over the governor's palace, then was replaced by the Stars and Stripes on December 20. On that day a ceremony was followed by a banquet involving Laussat and the American representatives Claiborne and Wilkinson. Four toasts were offered: Madeira wine to Jefferson, Malaga to Carlos IV, champagne to Bonaparte, and the fourth to the everlasting happiness of Louisiana.

On December 26 Laussat wrote to Barbé-Marbois that the French were shedding tears in Louisiana, and insisted that France should not give the impression of having sold her sons and daughters. The wounds inflicted by Louis XV in 1763 on his abandoned subjects in New France had never healed.[14]

How French were the inhabitants of Upper Louisiana in 1803? Forty years had elapsed since they had abandoned their identities as subjects of His Majesty Louis XV. They had pondered what their fate might be under the authority of the French First Consul. Over the generations the very concept of republic had not yet been understood or accepted by people so estranged from the land of their ancestors. Although French minds were naturally prone to delight in subversive attitudes in the abstract, the uncertainties born of changing régimes could distress them. The inhabitants of Upper Louisiana spoke the rural French of the seventeenth century, whereas the snobs of the Directoire, the "Incoyables and Meveilleuses" of the Paris high life dropped the peasant "r" consonant, which sounded too vulgar. Having little in common with the sons and daughters of the Revolution the Louisiana French were now fully aware that their future was nowhere else than in their country of birth. In those crucial days, Prefect Laussat reassured the Chouteaus about their future dealings with the Americans.[15]

Meriwether Lewis arrived in Saint Louis in December 1803 before the transfer of sovereignty.[16] He was denied permission by governor Pierre Charles Dehault de Lassus de Luzières to ascend the Missouri under the pretext that he had no passport in the name of the King of Spain. Lewis replied that when he left Philadelphia in the summer of 1803 he was persuaded that the French would already be in Saint Louis before Louisiana became American.[17] How could it be possible that several years after the retrocession no official from the sovereign state had yet set foot in the territory?

The Three Flags Ceremony took two days. On March 9, 1804, the Spanish flag was lowered and the French tricolor hoisted. American colonel Stoddard received Upper Louisiana in Saint Louis in behalf of France from Dehault Delassus, a landed aristocrat from Flanders who was an émigré during the Revolution. He had been appointed lieutenant-governor of Upper Louisiana in 1799. Acting in the name of Spain, he gave the region of Upper Louisiana to Amos Stoddard who received it in the name of France the following day. A salute was then fired.[18]

French settlers in Saint Louis petitioned Laussat to oppose the humiliating loss of their homeland. They claimed to stand by their fundamental rights to form an independent state, keep their mother language in all official acts, preserve their slaves from Guinea and the Caribbean islands, and have an exclusive privilege to buy new ones and reject those that would be imposed on them.

The Chouteaus insisted on being privileged informants when William Clark rallied the city to organize the expedition. Lewis was a guest at Pierre Chouteau's and a great admirer of his wife.[19] It made things easier when he had to borrow money from the Chouteaus' bank. The almighty brothers also procured seven engagés, knowing how much they could gain from government supply contracts. Lewis also purchased gunpowder, bullets, and blankets from the Chouteaus' stores. In the following years, Pierre's visit to Washington with Osage delegates entitled him to the function as an Indian agent. Auguste was designated a justice of the peace. During the expedition, they forwarded to Jefferson many items collected on the way by Lewis and Clark, such as mineral specimens, prairie dogs, and buffalo robes. They hosted Lewis and Clark on their return in September 1806.

The Chouteaus were hoping to keep their rights, privileges and property claims, including their black slaves. They were men of the ancien régime, impervious to the ideals of the Enlightenment. American territorial expansion equally ran counter to their interests. But they were clever enough to swallow their grievances. They did not obtain everything that they wanted, but at least their land claims were partially settled. They had now taken the first steps toward Americanization while doing minimal damage to their concerns.

Americans knew little about western tribal customs. Pierre's appointment to the Indian agency was a personal triumph for the family. He thought that this would enable him to retain his influence in the Indian country. Pierre's trip to Washington with an Osage delegation in the summer of 1804 was the first visit of a trans-Mississippi Indian group to Washington. He was accompanied by Osage Chief White Hair who wore a wig he had picked up on the battlefield in 1791 when Little Turtle and the Miami Indians had defeated General Arthur Saint-Clair.[20] The Chouteaus did not share Jefferson's idealism. They were traders and entertained no hope that tribesmen could transcend the savage state. However, in Washington, White Hair pledged allegiance to the Great Father, thanks to Pierre Chouteau's mediation.

While Pierre was Jefferson's guest, Auguste and the Upper Louisiana mercantile elite were already fighting with the administration of the territory to defend the privileges enjoyed under the Spanish régime. In later negotiations Pierre Chouteau steadily demonstrated his eagerness to have exclusive trading rights with the Osages and other nations. In the long run, he infuriated Secretary of the Treasury Albert Gallatin with his demands. In the summer of 1805, Pierre suffered a rebuff when his planned visit to Washington with another Indian delegation was cancelled.

Yet in October 1806 Pierre Chouteau, the Osages, and Mandan chief Sheheke accompanied Lewis and Clark from Saint Louis to Washington before they split up. The delegation arrived earlier than Lewis, who had gone through Charlottesville. Chouteau eagerly tried to repair his strained relations with the administration, but he was no longer a French potentate pulling strings in an age-old decadent monarchy. Although he still tried to make himself indispensable to the American government, Jefferson chose William Clark to replace him as Indian agent after the "Voyage of Discovery."

THE FUR TRADE IN TRANSITION

Aside from men like the Chouteaus and François Vallé of Sainte Geneviève, there were many former French subjects who in the last decades of the eighteenth century served the King of Spain loyally even though they resented a transfer of power not of their own choosing. The Spaniards were eager to exploit the most attractive natural resources of the time, hence their determination to prevent any encroachment upon the territory of Louisiana by first the British, then the Americans, following the War of Independence. The turn of the century saw a revival of the spirit of the Renaissance conquistadores who had won His Catholic Majesty a worldwide empire. It was lingering in the minds of Spanish colonists laying claims far up the Pacific northwest at Nootka. It was with the British traders that the Spanish forces expected to clash more violently, especially on the Missouri among the Mandans in the north, and down south with the French Canadians in the Osage country. The major goals assigned to the governors of Louisiana were determining the British from infiltrating the interior regions, gaining a monopoly over the fur trade, and finding a transcontinental route to Mexico and California. In 1792, Jacques d'Eglise was the first Spanish subject to ascend the Missouri. He returned with many observations about the natives living along its banks and their partners, the British fur traders. In 1796 Spain approved the foundation of the "Compagnie du commerce pour la découverte des nations du Haut Missouri," otherwise known as the Missouri Company. Well before the official authorization of Baron de Carondelet, the governor general of Louisiana, the company sent out its first expedition in 1794 under the leadership of Jean Baptiste Truteau, a distant relative of Lieutenant Governor Zenon Trudeau, who had first conceived the basic strategy about thorough explorations. D'Eglise declined the offer to join him. For reasons less scientific than commercial he had already made a second trip up the Missouri only to encounter the hostility of the Arikaras and the Sioux. The company organized two other expeditions, one with Lécuyer, a Frenchman, which was ill fated at the Poncas after the Indians retaliated for the corrupt practices of the whites. In 1796 Lécuyer was determined to head for the Pacific, though he unfortunately had no instructions making it easier for him to secure his discoveries for the Spanish government. How far he penetrated on his trek has never been ascertained but he did survive the effort as years later he visited Santa Fe.[21]

In 1795 John T. Evans, a Welshman of the Missouri Company, and James Mackay led an expedition up the Missouri river and established Fort Charles [Carlos] in what is now northeastern Nebraska. Evans had come to America to seek the Welsh Indians, descendants of Prince Madoc who, he believed, discovered America in 1170. Mackay sent him with a small party to Mandan villages in September 1796. The Welshman made a detailed map that Lewis and Clark would later use. The Mandans had generally turned down the costly Spanish trade goods and preferred to deal with Michilimackinac and Prairie du Chien Canadians. Evans spent the winter there, leaving on May 9, 1797 and returning to Saint Louis a little later. It was the most important expedition up the Missouri before Lewis and Clark. On his arrival at the mouth of the Knife River, Evans confiscated a post built by the North West Company. His expedition resulted in international rivalry for control of the fur trade on the Upper Missouri. He brazenly sent copies of a proclamation by Mackay to the Canadian posts along the Assiniboine, which prohibited trade along the Missouri by British Canadian interests.[22]

Pierre-Antoine Tabeau was born at Lachine in 1755. His great-uncle Jean had gone as far as Detroit. His father was a riverman and his brother a voyageur. First schooled at the seminary in Quebec, he studied rhetoric for two years until 1773. He went west as an engagé in his brother's canoe around 1776. In 1783, he was a trader at Michilimackinac in a joint venture with his brother. Four years later he formed a partnership with Etienne Campion and from then on both were linked to the North West Company. A notorious Indian fighter, Campion was arrested in 1792 for the murder of a native. In 1787 Pierre Antoine obtained a trader's license for Michilimackinac, but sometimes resided at Cahokia where he had pledged allegiance to the United States in 1785. Being a militiaman in the district of Kaskaskia earned him a grant of one hundred acres of land. By 1790 Illinois was in a chaotic state. The Ordinance of 1787 had banned slavery in the Northwest and accordingly threatened the property of French slave owners who were attracted to the opposite bank of the Mississippi where the colony of New Madrid seemed hospitable. Tabeau's overweening ambition led him to the inner circle of Clamorgan's relations, as well as involvement in the expedition of the Missouri Company led by Lécuyer. Whatever damage his self-serving attitudes might have caused, his own intellectual background was bound to give him a sense of superiority likely to offend his uncouth companions in the fur trade.[23]

Tabeau had been previously employed at Red River by the North West Company. As a member of the Lécuyer expedition he was admonished by James Mackay, who called him an infamous rascal and a white renegade. Tabeau was accused of squandering the property of the company to buy the favors of Indian women. Lewis and Clark never called him those names when he met them along the Missouri in October 1804. They entertained him at breakfast and were satisfied with the information he supplied whenever they sought his advice.[24]

Meanwhile Jacques Clamorgan was at the head of the new Missouri company. Born in Guadeloupe of Welsh and French African descent, he was a self-made man, respected in New Orleans and Saint Louis. He enjoyed a monopoly of whatever profits he could make from his expeditions. Other Saint Louis traders stood aloof from his company, which had only a few shareholders. Chouteau, for example, was not a member, being too busy trading with the Osages. Clamorgan extended some of his privileges to Andrew Todd, an Irish merchant who had been trading for several years at Michilimackinac. Because he had once outfitted Mackay's expedition he was also rewarded with the exclusive trade in Sac and Fox countries.[25]

While consolidating his fur empire Andrew Todd died within a few days of an illness caught in New Orleans. The executor of Todd's will discovered that a huge amount of money was owed to the deceased. The largest sum was against the firm of Clamorgan, Loisel and Company, a part of which Todd had assumed for Jean Baptiste Vallé of Sainte Geneviève. Todd had the greatest number of shares in the Missouri Company and paid eight thousand dollars in goods to trade with the Indians. If his heirs, creditors, and companions should demand the payment, the company would go bankrupt. The firm Clamorgan, Loisel and Company was, in fact, to begin its operations when Todd died. Pending the settlement of his estate, Clamorgan appropriated the privileges bestowed on the Irishman. Carondelet raised no objection when he petitioned for a ten year monopoly of the Upper Missouri commerce. The Spanish authorities acquiesced all the more willingly as Clamorgan was shrewd enough to flaunt his capacities to ward off foreign influence and provide intelligence on intruders.

The French traders of Saint Louis did not share such confidence. Their distrust of Clamorgan was blatantly expressed in a petition that, ignoring the shareholders of the Missouri Company, was addressed to Carondelet through Joseph Robidoux, the veteran trader. The disgruntled merchants had hoped to have Clamorgan's privileges withdrawn, but the reverse happened. Clamorgan, Loisel and Company emerged from the transformation of the original enterprise and took over the Missouri Company.

Régis Loisel's date of birth is not known but he was baptized in the Parish of l'Assomption in Montreal. His parents were married in 1772 and he arrived in Saint Louis in 1793 when he was probably just out of his teens. He must have gone through Illinois when the French were struggling under British rule. On his mother's side Régis was connected with the Vallé family, which was already powerful in Sainte Geneviève. As soon as he entered into partnership with Clamorgan, he was used as a screen to cover the misappropriation of the Missouri Company funds. Loisel went to Des Moines to make acquaintance with the Sioux. After the Missouri Company came under the aegis of Clamorgan in 1798, Loisel remained a close partner, although his newly acquired status as a competent trader allowed him more independence. In 1800 Loisel married Hélène Chauvin, whose father Jacques was an influential merchant. Considering that he had made too many sacrifices in the Missouri Company, he petitioned for the right to form an establishment in Upper Missouri and build a fort. Almost simultaneously Clamorgan made a similar request to trade with the Otos and Poncas. He also offered to support a hundred militiamen to protect the selected concession from the incursion of the British and their allies, the Mandans. The dual projects sounded the toll for the Missouri Company, while strengthening the control of each former partner over the Missouri. In 1800, Loisel went up the river, allegedly to build the fort, the building of which was confirmed by a statement of Auguste Chouteau. The following year he struck a deal with Hugh Heney, a Montreal storekeeper who had year after year applied for a license to sell liquor armed with the warm recommendation of a priest from the parish of Lachine, until he could finally open a public alehouse.

Heney was presumably robbed of goods he was transporting along the Missouri in the opening expedition. According to the trade agreement signed with the latter in 1801, the alliance was to last two consecutive years, thus ending in July 1803. At the expiration of the contract, it had to be liquidated by the partners. In the event of the death of one of the parties before the complete sale of all the merchandise asked and bought in behalf of the company, the survivor had to close by turning it into a profit-and-loss account. He was also under an obligation to render account to the heirs of the deceased.

Loisel was expected to remain two years upstream on a site named *Ile aux Cèdres* [Cedar Island] to trade with the Teton Bois Brûlés. He stayed only a few months because of the presence of threatening Sioux. Chouteau had been deluded into believing that the fort was in existence. In fact, it took two more years for its erection between Old Englishman's Island and Little Missouri River, on Ile aux Cèdres, 1,226 miles up the Missouri as Clark stated in his field notes. The island was one of a group above the Great Bend of the Missouri and below the Little Missouri that was named Teton (Bad River) by the Corps of Discovery in 1804.[26]

Loisel collected alarming information for Delassus on impending British intrusions. In the spring of 1803, he was commissioned to engage in an investigation which took him up upstream once again. In the late summer, together with Pierre Antoine Tabeau and a few men, he went first to Cedar Island, then proceeded over one hundred sixty miles upriver before returning to winter in the fort. The restive Teton hindered explorations of the local potentialities in the fur trade, and he was left with a great deal of goods in want of outlets. He decided to return to Saint Louis a year sooner than he had expected and left behind Tabeau, who chose to live among the Arikaras.[27]

10

Across the Great Ethnic Divide: The French in the Lewis and Clark Expedition

A MULTICULTURAL ENTERPRISE

THE MULTICULTURAL ACHIEVEMENTS OF THE CORPS OF DISCOVERY IN THE trailblazing Lewis and Clark expedition of 1804–6 reflected the interaction between nature and culture against a background of economic, ethnic, and political conflicts. William Clark had an innate talent for exploration as riverman and engineer. Meriwether Lewis was the zoologist and botanist of the corps. With them were regular Army men, Kentucky hunters, French-speaking trappers, and rivermen—some of them Métis, including an Indian woman and her newborn. This heterogeneous group progressively achieved unity while sailing up the Missouri, trekking over the Rockies, and going down the Columbia River to reach the Pacific coast.

William Clark was no newcomer to Upper Louisiana. His brother George Rogers had prompted him to visit Kaskaskia, Sainte Genevieve, and Saint Louis in 1787. He already knew prominent figures such as Zenon Trudeau, François Vallé, and the Chouteaus. He had discovered French dancing at a ball, and marveled at the way gentlemen dared to put their arms around ladies' waists in a prudish Spanish environment.

In the fall of 1803, while Auguste Chouteau was taking the utmost care of Lewis in Saint Louis, Clark stayed some time at Cahokia with Charles Gratiot, Chouteau's brother-in-law. Born in Switzerland, Gratiot had come to Montreal in 1769, and belonged to George Rogers Clark's entourage during the War of Independence. He engaged in the fur trade, established a store at Cahokia in 1777, and later became Chouteau's agent at Michilimackinac until he got into trouble with the Canadians traders. To ingratiate himself with the captains, Gratiot offered them horses.[1] On March 10, the ceremony of transfer of Upper Louisiana to the United States took place on the portico of his home.[2] On March 21, Auguste Chouteau, Gratiot,

Lewis, and Clark went to Portage des Sioux to negotiate with a war party of a hundred Kickapoos, who were intending to attack Osage villages.[3] Two days later a messenger brought a letter from François Saucier, commander of Portage des Sioux, informing them that the Kickapoos had left.[4] The four partners were united again during the farewell party at Saint Charles on May 20.

Such timely demonstrations of loyalty to the Americans minimized the former subjection of the French-speaking population to His Catholic Majesty. The mood changed in the spring of 1804, when rumors reached Saint Louis that the federal government was planning basic alterations in the administration of Upper Louisiana. Spanish land grants issued after 1800 were to be nullified, the institution of slavery might be in jeopardy, and eastern Indian tribes were to be relocated in the territory. A committee of the ciy's leading citizens including Auguste Chouteau, Charles Gratiot, and Louis Labeaume convened a meeting to register the community's opposition to the proposed measures. A convention of French delegates met with Governor Harrison on September 14. It was presided over by Charles Gratiot. In Sainte Genevieve, an assembly of American settlers accused them of attempting to maintain privileges obtained under Spanish auspices. In October Auguste Chouteau welcomed Governor Harrison to Saint Louis and tried to convince him that the French residents were moved by a spirit of cooperation. In March 1805, Congress granted the Territory of Louisiana its own government, in keeping with the principles outlined in the Northwest Ordinance of 1787. At least the French could keep their slaves.[5]

The wilderness was by no means a no-man's-land awaiting the benefits of civilization. The Indians met along the way were aware that they could take advantage of conflicting interests among the British, the Spaniards, and the Americans by enlisting the support of the scattered Frenchmen remaining east of the "Stony Mountains." For Jefferson's agents, clarifying the new situation involved time-serving alliances as well as agonizing reappraisals. Within a short span of time, the hunters, trappers, scouts, and traders of the West had switched back and forth under French and Spanish rule before the deal ultimately struck between Napoleon and Jefferson in 1803. Shoshones, Blackfeet, Mandans, and Sioux had long been familiar with French coureurs des bois and Spanish explorers. Drifting from Canada, the descendants of the New France colonists were by turns collecting pelts and furs, acting as emissaries among Indian tribes, spying for the Spanish authorities, and serving as interpreters for wealthy French residents in Saint Louis.

Several of the daredevil guides and boatmen who went along with

Lewis and Clark were white Indians, who as backwoods runners had *ni foi, ni Roi, ni loi* [neither faith, nor king, nor law]. The escort of Lewis and Clark nevertheless proved invaluable to overcome the manifold obstacles encountered on the way. No doubt the leaders of the expedition enlisted half-breeds for their hard-won skills, regardless of their sometimes notorious reputation.

Jefferson was interested in the scientific aspects of the enterprise, but economic penetration was a major objective. According to his instructions, the mission was intended to explore the Missouri River and its tributaries, then find practicable water communication with the Pacific coast. The portage between the headwaters of the Missouri and those of the Columbia turned out to be over two hundred miles of rugged mountain country. Another purpose was to acquaint the Indian tribes with the American flag. The Spanish government, after all, maintained that the Louisiana Purchase did not extend beyond the Platte River. Jefferson also had in mind to discredit French slander on the fatal decay of flora and fauna in America.

Leaving from Saint Charles in May 1804, the expedition made its way up the Missouri in a huge keelboat and three pirogues. Close to the mouth of the Bad River, the flotilla met the Sioux. Of all the Indians east of the mountains, it was the formidable Sioux nation that the president had singled out for the explorers' attention. He was impressed with their military power and economic potential with the fur trade. Diplomatic efforts were thus made by Lewis to lure the Sioux away from their close alliance with the British North West Company. In September, a meeting with Teton Brûlé chief Black Buffalo revealed that serious trouble was in store as the warriors were expecting more gifts than the expedition could afford. The culture gap was such that it could not easily be bridged by gestures of goodwill. The interpreter Pierre Cruzatte gathered intelligence from Omaha prisoners of the Sioux, information that put the expedition even more on its guard. Violence was brewing and escaping the dangers of the Sioux encounter was no easy task.[6] The expedition then turned its attention to the Arikaras, who were first spotted in October in fortified villages on the banks of the Missouri. The captains misunderstood the connection between the sedentary Arikaras and the nomadic Sioux, considering the former as victims of oppression, even though an enduring pact between the tribes had so far benefited the Arikaras, thus providing them with manufactured products and firearms in exchange for corn and horses. The Cheyennes were certainly more friendly to the Arikaras than the allegedly lawless and rapacious Sioux. Cheyenne horses were essential to fill out herds and preserve the livestock for trading with the Sioux.

If relations were to be severed with the Sioux upon the request of the United States government, the Arikaras had no guarantee of safety against retaliation by the dominant nation in the Great Plains. Anyway, the young men of the expedition had intimate encounters with Arikara women that proved beneficial to peacemaking.[7] After the tense days with the Sioux, the hospitality of the Arikaras was a welcome recess. The Canadian squaw men were naturally instrumental in arranging love affairs with uninhibited fancy-free Indian girls.

The Corps reached the Mandan and Hidatsa villages near the Great Bend of the river at the end of October 1804. In the great council that soon brought together Mandan, Hidatsa, Arikara, and the United States representatives, Lewis and Clark announced American sovereignty over the lands of the purchase and maintained that the Great Father in Washington kept an eye on his dutiful children of the Northwest. Assuming that domination and business enterprise had to be closely associated, the captains outlined a plan to form an alliance of sedentary tribes against the bellicose nomads of the plains. The Arikaras had to make peace with their Mandan and Hidatsa neighbors after years of harsh conflicts. To show their goodwill the Americans handed out medals, coats, hats, and even silver dollar coins to the natives. On the last day of October Clark was welcomed with impressive decorum. Mandan chief Black Cat put a fine buffalo robe over his shoulders, before smoking the peace pipe with several old leaders. In his speech he declared that the end of violence would enable the tribes to hunt without fear or work in the fields at no risk, thereby responding to the captains' move.[8] In the following months, Jefferson's emissaries realized that the new *pax americana* was hard to enforce. Skirmishes involving Sioux and Arikara hunters against Mandan villagers induced the captains to use military action. They organized a large armed party to restore order. But white outsiders were at pains to alter native realities. Even the Mandan chiefs found the American display of military power irrelevant in the cold season.

All through the winter Fort Mandan remained a showcase of American lifestyles. Quadrants, thermometers, and paper were on display to attract Indian visitors to what they likened to Great Medicines. The Mandans themselves had some interesting rituals to entertain the bearded strangers. Their buffalo-calling ceremony exemplified the belief that sexual intercourse was a means of transferring spiritual power from one partner to another. Women who had sex with elderly men were assigned the task to learn their skills. The French guides, especially René Jusseaume, who was a squaw man among the Mandans, were persuasive enough to let Mandan women swap partners and choose young strangers to transmit their expertise on to their mates. Interethnic sexual intercourse was therefore a pleasurable way to appropriate the tremendous power ascribed to the white race.[9]

The men were still sturdy enough to build dugout canoes which were to be used further upriver. From those Indians who lived in earth lodges, the corps learned much about the Rockies. The hunters raided westward in territories unknown by other tribes, and knew about the habits of the Shoshones, who gathered salmon from the mountain streams in the summer and moved east to the plains to find buffalo in winter. The ideal link between the Mandans and the Shoshones was to be Sacagawea a Shoshone girl captured by the Hidatsa, then sold to Toussaint Charbonneau.

Leaving Fort Mandan in April 1804 the corps reached the three Forks of the Missouri in July after a lengthy portage, and thanks to Sacagawea found horses among Shoshone tribes. At the end of a tortuous nine-day trip the exhausted men rested in a Nez Percé village before journeying down the Snake and Columbia Rivers to the coast. The Indians of the Columbia had been corrupted by two decades of contact with the British traders of the Hudson's Bay Company, operating along the Oregon shore. Lewis and Clark spent the winter of 1805–6 at Fort Clatsop, built on a tributary of the Columbia. On the Pacific slope, the Nez Percé offered geographical information but hastened to steal knives and other objects at hand when the Americans were busy elsewhere. The linguistic barrier was such that communication appeared much less rewarding than at Fort Mandan. At Fort Clatsop the restrictions on hospitality limited the number of Chinookan visitors, but the lure of furs and firearms was a strong incentive to maintain private ties between Indians and Americans. On the return journey in the spring the two captains split their party to blaze new trails. Clark followed the Yellowstone River down to the Missouri. On his way Lewis encountered Blackfeet, the most dangerous Indians of the northern plains. In a fight two natives were killed, which caused an enduring hostility toward the Americans. The party reunited in August and was back to Saint Louis in September. Lewis and Clark had traveled six thousand miles in twenty-eight months, and come across a dozen Indian tribes. Aside from the information collected on flora and fauna, they noted the abundance of beaver and otter, which brought great numbers of mountain men to the Northwest. The explorers also added hundreds of words to the American language to name the trees and plants, sometimes after Indian terms. In the first winter, it was the high season at the Mandan villages, actually the time of the traditional rendez-vous attracting mountain men from distant regions. The friendly Indians, already plagued with smallpox, had so far established their winter camp as the hub of the western trade. Ironically, the epic discovery of the West by Lewis and Clark, at first followed routes already familiar to the wild bunch of French-speaking trappers and traders.

The seemingly boundless living space of what Zebulon Pike and Stephen Long called the Great American Desert was in fact a new Tower of Babel. French, Spanish, and British explorers had much earlier discovered different tribes of Native Americans. Ancient Greece and Rome had their barbarians, but neither Homer nor Virgil ever mentioned the existence of wild people. The Voyage of Discovery also constituted a return journey to prehistoric times, when the struggle for life and the survival of the fittest were exemplified in daily occurrences. In this respect, the expedition inherited invaluable knowledge and practices from the age-old coureur des bois generations.

The French trader Jean Baptiste Truteau from Saint Louis had made fairly accurate skin maps after an earlier exploration. They proved useful for the first leg of the expedition. Having no compass at hand the French woodrunners had always measured distances by the number of days spent in canoes or by walking from dawn to dusk. Anomalies, skirmishes, encounters with grizzlies or wolves were memorized through place names, elements of a primitive toponymy. Needless to say such empirical landmarks were useful in designing the routes followed by Lewis and Clark.[10]

Yet to what extent were the backwoodsmen who served as guides reliable? Several were half-breeds, indeed nomads with a divided allegiance, partly to their Native American kin, and partly to the Spanish and British traders who employed them. They often struck secret compromises at the expense of the merchants' interests. Usually likened to vagabonds, they had been a matter of great concern to colonial governments until the military realized how useful they could be in guerrilla warfare. Some had abandoned civilized space and no one knew how far west some of them had gone. Others made a career in American society. A French voyageur temporarily involved in the expedition, Pierre Ménard, had settled in Upper Missouri in 1777 and spent fourteen years with the Mandans. In 1789, he guided trading parties for Spanish companies. In 1792 he settled down in Illinois, was appointed colonel in the Randolph County militia, then judge of the Court of Common Pleas by Governor Harrison. He was a representative in the Indiana Territorial Legislature, but resigned in 1804 in protest against the rough politics rife on the territory. He lost his wife and did not mourn long before marrying Angélique Saucier, a descendant of the famous engineer, also related to the Chouteau family. A prosperous trader, Ménard formed a partnership with Manuel Lisa with whom he launched new trapping expeditions.[11]

There is no clear proof that the guides enlisted by Lewis and Clark were undercover agents for either the fur companies or the Indians. At least their loyalty to the corps was never openly questioned. It is true that during the expedition the Hidatsas sought to prevent Manuel Lisa and his French partners from opening trade with the Crows. The writings of Meriwether Lewis sometimes bear witness to such double-dealings.[12] In addition, the "gun frontier" had reached the Shoshone and Blackfeet territories well before 1804. This means for instance that the Nez Percés were in great demand for arms and ammunitions at the time, which explains some interferences with the expedition. The Blackfeet entertained friendly relations with the Hudson's Bay Company and the North West Company while expanding their territory to the south and west. Armed with guns they received through the fur trade the Blackfeet had begun a long period of conflict in western Montana. By 1800 the Nez Percés had known about a very powerful people to the east. They heartily welcomed Lewis and Clark, hoping to receive arms in the future. It was in the interest of British and Canadian traders to set the western tribes against the expedition. The Spanish government had put a ban on the arms trade with Indians, which hit the Shoshones who exchanged goods with New Spain. No wonder England and Spain dreamed of infiltrating the expedition with French agents.

The Native Americans then living in the West did not feel the need to learn French or English since they were happy with their own sign language to communicate with tribes whose native idiom was not undertood. Sometimes, to amuse their French visitors, they simply repeated oaths uttered by angered backwoodsmen. A Métis translator had an instinctive understanding born of intimacy and direct contact with the tribes on his mother's side. Yet some who claimed to be interpreters only knew a hodgepodge of phrases. The French interpreters of Lewis and Clark wielded great influence for they could have their own way by manipulating words and subtly shaping the direction that negotiations took. Elaborate queries about chiefdom and warfare, uttered by the captains, might also boil down to questions about personal rivalries, casualties, and captives through interpretive oversimplifications.

All through the expedition, Lewis and Clark tried to read a for-

eign text on native lips, including the symbolic implications of giving and receiving, but most of the time they had to rely on French
Métis *truchement,* which could not be exact translation. Interpreters
were well aware that Indian language tended to be oracular, emphasizing eloquence, as was mostly the case with oral culture. Meetings
were at times highly ceremonial and participants seemed to enact a
drama in the wilderness.

Lewis and Clark appreciated the French flair demonstrated by the
white Indians who undoubtedly initiated an early pattern of ethnic
relationships, if not an advanced model for the melting pot. A major
task assigned by Jefferson was diplomatic. All tribes were informed
that the Great Father of the whites wanted peace with and among
the tribes. If they met his requirements, he would facilitate all kinds
of trade, including guns and ammunition. As the Blackfeet and Hidatsas were already supplied with muskets by British merchants, the
Shoshones and Flatheads, still deprived of firearms, were eager to
respond to Jefferson's offer. The technological achievements displayed by the expedition were obviously major assets in the diplomatic venture. An ultimate example of the American spirit of
enterprise was offered to Mandan Chief Sheheke who accompanied
the corps back to Saint Louis. On September 23, 1806 Clark escorted
him to a country store at Fort Bellefontaine along the Missouri. The
Indian rummaged through fancy shirts and handkerchiefs for his
family and himself. Within a few months Sheheke had gone all the
way from the wilderness to the Industrial Revolution. He was now in
the hands of politicians, officeholders, and agents and hardly realized that the Lewis and Clark expedition had changed his world for
the best and the worst. Within a few weeks he had learned more
about white society than in decades spent with French-Canadian
voyageurs.[13]

THE FRENCH-SPEAKING MEMBERS OF
THE CORPS OF DISCOVERY

Aside from the functions ascribed to the members of the expedition as indicated by the roster, the object of innumerable analyses,
it may be instructive to suggest a typology of the French participa-
tion with reference to the ethnic identities and archetypes that have
informed values, myths, and folk culture in American history since
frontier times.

Saint Charles was the logical place to seek qualified boatmen, especially because the village had more trappers and traders than

other settlements in the Mississippi Valley. The journals of the expedition did not always retain the spelling used by the French-born priest who ministered to these men and their families. Hence the necessity for present historians to trace such names back to the church records of baptisms and marriages. Only men with ties to the tribes out west, especially the Missouris, Arikaras, and Crows, were hired as engagés. These men were also chosen for their close relations with at least one other member of the expedition.[14] Saint Charles was founded in 1769 by French Canadian hunter Louis Blanchette who had married an Osage or Pawnee woman. The settlement was known as Les Petites Côtes until 1791 when the village was renamed to honor King Charles IV. In 1798 Father Leander Lusson took over as priest and remained in Saint Charles until 1804. He was the only minister in the area. There were under five hundred residents but few could read or write. In 1804 most able-bodied men still went upriver in the warm months to trade furs among the tribes. Unions with Indian women were common, hence the number of squaw men and Métis in the area. François Duquette was among the civic leaders. He lived with his wife on a hill overlooking the Missouri. On May 16, 1804 Clark joined the couple for dinner.[15]

Little is known about the boatman Jean-Baptiste Deschamps. He was recruited at Kaskaskia and accompanied the Corps from Camp Dubois to Fort Mandan. He was probably related to the wife of Commandant Joseph Tayon, a prominent member of the community. The Deschamps family was one of the earliest in the area, probably dating back to 1766. Jean Baptiste was the son of Marie Pinot, who might be related to the Pineau family, given the haphazard spelling of illiterate people at the time. Jean Baptiste lived with a local woman, Marie Anne Baguette Langevin. They had several children. Deschamps, who was illiterate, usually made a cross-shaped mark on registers. He was not a member of the permanent party that traveled to the Pacific and back. On May 14, 1804, he was appointed "patron" of the French watermen on the expedition. He commanded nine oarsmen in the red pirogue, companion vessel of the smaller white pirogue, in the three-boat flotilla that was led by the captains' flagship, the keelboat. As leader of the French-speaking boatmen, he had a full-time job that excused him from guard duty. Deschamps was among the men who, on April 7, 1805, navigated the keelboat downriver to Saint Louis. Corporal Richard Warfington was in charge of the crew.

The captains encountered privates François Labiche and Pierre Cruzatte when they reached Kaskaskia on November 28, 1803. The officers, however, apparently did not learn until later that the two men were experienced boatmen and frontier traders, and that both knew several lower Missouri Indian languages. Labiche was also fluent in both English and French, which would prove to be vital in the involved chain of interpreters later needed to communicate with the Shoshone Indians. Clark enlisted the two men as part of the permanent party on May 16, 1804 at Saint Charles, where they were eagerly seeking the explorers in hopes of joining the Pacific-bound expedition. In a Detachment Order dated May 26, 1804, both men were given assignments on the keelboat. As Lewis wrote: "Labiche and Crusatte will man the larboard bow oar alternately, and one not engaged at the oar will attend as the Bows-man, and when the attention of both these persons is necessary at the bow, their oar is to be manned by an idle hand on board."[16]

On August 6, 1804, Labiche was called upon to interpret during a council with the Oto Indians. Chief Petit Voleur (Little Thief), who apparently had known Labiche during his former trading days, said, "I want . . . Mr. La bi[e]che to make a piece [sic] with the Panis Loups Skiri Pawnees . . . he can Speake english & will doe well."[17] On August 7, Labiche and four others were assigned by Clark to bring Moses Reed, a deserter, back into camp with the order to kill him if he did not surrender. Reed confessed that he had deserted, and the captains only sentenced him to run the gauntlet four times. Labiche obviously had a position of trust in the expedition. Because of his language skills, he often played key roles in establishing relations with the various Indian tribes that the Corps encountered. In September 1804, Labiche and Cruzatte served as interpreters during talks with the Bois Brûlé Teton Sioux to gain access to the Upper Missouri. This was especially critical when the Sioux captured one of the Corps' pirogues, demanding that the Americans either trade with them exclusively or surrender the pirogue as a tribute. Cruzatte's translations, along with donations of useful gifts, were crucial in helping the Americans recover the pirogue and gain peaceful entry to the upper Missouri. Upon arrival at the friendly Shoshone villages that were home to Sacagawea in August 1805, Labiche again played a critical role as a translator when Meriwether Lewis was able to communicate with Chief Cameahwait of the Lemhi Shoshone band. Lewis would speak English to Labiche, who would speak French to Toussaint Charbonneau, who would speak Hidatsa to Sacagawea, who would speak Shoshone to Chief Cameahwait. Then, Cameahwait's reply would move along the language chain back to Lewis. This activity would have allowed a linguist to step into the shoes of each translator in the chain and decode the language, if the successive utterances had been transcribed. But in Native American language there could be no equivalent of the Rosetta Stone discovered in Egypt only five years earlier. Later, on the expedition's return home from the Pacific in September 1806, Labiche's and Cruzatte's translations would again prove invaluable in helping the Corps sneak through Sioux territory.

In late November 1805 near the mouth of the Columbia River, while the Corps tried to decide on a suitable winter camp location, Lewis, accompanied by Labiche and a few others, explored the coast of what is now Young's Bay. It was during this trek that the crew discovered an inlet to the Neteul River (now the Lewis and Clark River). After the survey of the river's inland was complete, they determined that the area, with its abundant wild life and vegetation, would be a good place to set up camp. Within the next week and a half, the entire Corps returned, building what would become Fort Clatsop, their winter camp among the Indians of the Pacific Coast.

In October 1806, after returning to Saint Louis, Labiche and Sergeant Ordway were placed in charge of a pack train that was bound for the East and loaded with the plants, seeds, bird skins, animal skeletons, and furs that they had saved from their caches. The Washington-bound party included Lewis and Clark, Mandan Indians, and Osage Indians.

Charles Pineau was the natural son of a Missouri Indian woman and the deceased Joseph Pineau, who had acknowledged paternity of Charles before he died. He was born in the backwoods about 1776 and baptized by Father Lusson in Saint Louis as late as 1790 probably because he belatedly sought to be cleansed of original sin before returning to the wilderness. He was listed on May 26, 1804 as a member of the party and started with the expedition. Pineau had a close tie with Deschamps with whom he was sent back to Saint Louis in April 1805.

Charles Hebert was a native of Prairie de la Madeleine in Canada. As engagé, he had spent much of his life in Saint Charles and Portage des Sioux, a village that attracted fur traders as well as farmers because of the easy access to the Missouri and Mississippi. He was in his thirties at the time of the expedition. He had been married since 1792. His wife's name was Julie Hubert dite La Croix. They had one son and two daughters baptized at Saint Charles or Portage des Sioux. While staying in Saint Louis after the expedition he may have discovered undeclared Métis offspring who were baptized later.

Jean Baptiste Lajeunesse was the son of Ambrose and Marie Boyer La Jeunesse of Sainte Rose, Quebec. He was married in 1797 to Elisabeth Malboeuf, the daughter of a Canadian and Mandan woman. Etienne Malboeuf, another member of the expedition, also from

Saint Charles, was his brother-in-law. Jean Baptiste died at about age 45 and was buried on May 4, 1807. His son was also named Jean Baptiste. Born in 1807, he made his living upriver in the following decades. It was probably his nephew Basil, born on June 25, 1814, who accompanied Frémont on his first and second expeditions to the West. La Jeunesse was discharged and likely paid off at the Mandan villages in the fall of 1804. He left the expedition with Paul Primeau to paddle downriver in a canoe on November 6. He may have stopped later at an Arikara village and stayed there for wintering.

Etienne Malboeuf was born about 1775 at Lac de Sable, Canada. François, his father, had married a Crow woman, either Josephe de Bel Homme of the Mountain Crow nation or Josephe Beau Sauvage. The Mountain Crows lived in south central Montana on the outskirts of the territories known to the whites. François Malboeuf had fathered at least seven children by two or three Indian women. Elisabeth, his daughter by Angélique, a Mandan woman, was baptized at Saint Charles in 1797, and married Jean Baptiste La Jeunesse in July 1797. Etienne's father died at the age of 72 in the home of his son-in-law, La Jeunesse. Etienne was christened at Saint Charles on December 1792, but no age is transcribed in the parish register. By 1804 he was living in Kaskaskia where he was hired for the expedition. He returned from Fort Mandan in the spring of 1805.

Pierre Roy might have been the son of a Sainte Genevieve resident who had come from Green Bay. He was probably related to Joseph Roy (LeRoy) (1744–1825) and Marguerite Oskinanotame (1760–1835), the daughter of Ahkenepaweh Akeeneebaway (Standing Earth), a Menominee. Pierre Roy married Marie Louise Vallé, daughter of Jean Baptiste Vallé and Thérèse, an Arikara resident of the parish. The bride may have been the daughter of the trader Jean Vallé who had been upriver for about a year when he encountered Lewis and Clark in October 1804 and gave information about the Cheyennes and the Arikaras. Malboeuf and Lajeunesse were witnesses at the wedding of Pierre Roy. The captain's choice of men from the same surroundings was intended to strengthen the cohesion of the French party. On the other hand the language barrier and their location in one pirogue did not facilitate contacts with the English-speaking members of the trip. It was only by facing the same ordeals that all the men were inevitably brought together.

FREEMEN AND SQUAW MEN IN THE AMERICAN EPIC

Throughout the long journey, Lewis and Clark thus relied on resourceful Frenchmen whose long immersion in the wilderness had given them invaluable experience. Some of them played a modest part, others were more often in the foreground, and left their marks in the journals.

Paul Primeau was from Chateauguay, Canada, the son of Louis Primeau, a legend among the voyageurs, who worked for the Hudson's Bay Company in 1764–65, and wintered many times at Pine Island Lake with Frobisher. Paul married Pelagie Bissonet in 1799 in Saint Louis and may have had a family of ten children. He left the expedition with La Jeunesse for the Arikara nation where he probably wintered.

Joseph Collin was born in 1770 of Joseph and Marie Collin from Sainte Geneviève de Montreal in Canada. He formerly belonged to the North West Company. He was listed as a member of the expedition in May 1804 as a hired boatman. There is no record of Collin being on Lewis's payroll. He may have been discharged at an Arikara or Mandan village and paid in cash. When Lewis and Clark returned from the Pacific they again met Collin among the Arikaras on August 21, 1806 and, as he wished to return to Saint Louis, he was taken along. It has been suggested that Collin was confused with La Liberté in several records because the latter had assumed a false identity, but no evidence of this has been given.

Joseph Barter ("La Liberté") was probably born in 1777. He may have drifted down the Missouri from Fort Gage, Canada, and lived among the Oto Indians a year or two before joining Lewis and Clark. He does not appear under this name in the list of engagés in the detachment order of May 26, 1804. He was hired later, perhaps picked up from some group of traders along the Missouri. The list of July 4, 1804 gives "J. Le bartee" who was assigned first to a pirogue then to the keelboat.

La Liberté was sent by Lewis in July 1804 to the Oto Indians in northeastern Nebraska to invite them to confer with the captains but he took this chance to desert the party and eluded attempts to catch up with him, and could never be identified thereafter. La Liberté spoke the Oto language, suggesting that he had probably lived a long time with them.

Jean Baptiste Lepage was a French Canadian fur trader who was living among the Hidatsa and Mandan Indians near present-day Bismarck, North Dakota, when the explorers arrived there on October 27, 1804. Enlisted at Fort Mandan on November 2, 1804 as a substitute in the permanent party, he went all the way to the Pacific Ocean and back to Saint Louis, where he was discharged. He must have been a conscientious but discreet member who had no outstanding performance in his record.[18]

Probably the best-known of the Frenchmen, Toussaint Charbonneau, was born of Jean Baptiste Charbonneau and Marguerite Deniau at Boucherville, Canada, on March 2, 1767.[19] There is no proof that he was a Métis as often indicated by historians. He went west to Lake of the Woods and the Assiniboine River in 1793 for the North West Company. Coues considered him as a laggard, a coward, and a womanizer. In early 1795 at Fort Esperance on the Qu'Appelle River, a tributary of the Assininoine, Charbonneau was stabbed by a native woman who declared she had caught him raping her daughter.[20] He then lived among the Hidatsas, above the mouth of the Knife River, and in 1796 stayed with the Mandans a few miles below, sometimes with Ménard and Jusseaume, two other squaw men.

Hired as an interpreter at the Mandan village in the fall of 1804, Charbonneau became a very controversial figure, a man of no peculiar merit for Lewis and useful only as an interpreter. But toward the end of the expedition on August 20, 1806, Clark wrote him to acknowledge that he had conducted himself in such a manner as to gain his friendship. He offered him an allotment of horses, cows, and hogs if he wanted to settle down in the West. Clark added that he would cover his expenses should he want to visit his relatives in Montreal. Most of all, Clark was concerned with the future of Jean-Baptiste ("Pomp"), the child of Charbonneau and Sacagawea whom he offered to take care of. The mediocre figure of Charbonneau is often set off against the aura of Sacagawea in American iconography, as if he was the ignoble Frenchman escorting the Noble Sauvagesse. But the squaw man probably never realized that he was participating in an epoch-making expedition. Considering how rebellious, unreliable, and shifty his peers could be in the backwoods, it is miraculous that Clark won obedience and integrity from a nomadic freeman who was instinctively averse to authority. In October 1804, when the expedition arrived at the Upper Missouri villages, Charbonneau was already working as an independent trader among the Hidatsas near present-day Bismarck, North Dakota.

Lewis and Clark settled at Fort Mandan in the fall of 1804. The two captains hoped to acquire useful information from the Indians and to accustom their fellow explorers to living in Indian country. What the expedition needed most were Indian interpreters, especially any who were familiar with the western terrain. Clark wrote on November 4: "A french man by Name Chabonah . . . visit us, he wished to hire & informed us his 2 squars (squaws) were Snake [Shoshone] Indians."[21]

Having been told that Sacagawea's Shoshone tribe lived at the headwaters of the Missouri and was well-equipped with horses, Lewis and Clark foresaw that Charbonneau and Sacagawea's interpreting skills would be instrumental when the expedition reached the mountains. On March 19, 1805, Clark wrote that Toussaint was to be enlisted as an interpreter through his wife, notwithstanding that Sacagawea's child was two months old at the time.[22] Charbonneau knew how indispensable Sacagawea would be to Lewis and Clark when dealing with the Shoshones, so he attempted to dictate the terms of his employment. When the captains told him he would have to perform the duties of enlisted men and stand regular guard, Charbonneau flatly rejected their offer. As Lewis recorded, Charbonneau replied that he wanted to have at his disposal as many provisions as he could carry. At first, Charbonneau was reluctant to be committed to serve the group. He would not be bound to Lewis and Clark if one day he felt like returning to the Mandans. Impatient with his demands, the captains told him to move out of the fort with his family, and then promptly hired another freeman, Joseph Gravelines, as an interpreter. Four days later, for whatever reason, Charbonneau offered his apologies and the captains signed him on. He was one of only few people on the expedition who were not in the military. In fact, he and George Drouillard were the only two official interpreters of the Corps, and was paid twice as much as the private soldiers.

Unlike his fellow traders, Charbonneau was not a jack-of-all-trades. A poor boatman, he could not swim. His lack of boating skills created two near disasters on the river. On April 13, just a few days after leaving Fort Mandan, Charbonneau was at the helm of one of the pirogues. When a sudden wind hit and rocked the boat, the French Canadian panicked and instead of bringing the boat into the wind, he laid her broadside to it, almost oversetting the pirogue. Drouillard had to take the helm to correct the situation. Despite this near disaster, only a month later, as the Corps moved upriver from the Yellowstone, Charbonneau was again temporarily relieving Drouillard at the helm of the white pirogue. The boat contained papers, books, instruments, medicines, and many of the trade goods. Again, a sudden squall hit the boat obliquely and turned it. Charbonneau swung the rudder around so as to bring the full force of the wind against the square sail. The sail rope flew out of the hand of the person holding it, the pirogue turned over on its side, and the water began pouring in. By the time the crew took in the sail and righted the boat, it was filled with water to within an inch of the gunnels. Cruzatte, a shipmate, threatened to shoot Charbonneau immediately if he did not take up the rudder and regain control. Sacagawea, who was in the back of the boat, remained calm and recovered most of the light articles as they floated past. The next two days were spent unpacking, drying and repacking the soaked supplies, papers, and medicine. Losses included some medicine, gunpowder, garden seeds, and culinary articles. Afterward, Lewis did not overly fault Charbonneau's inept steersmanship. He was too much in need of the couple to antagonize the squaw man.

Charbonneau seldom carried a gun and once cowered before a grizzly. As a cook for the Corps of Discovery, he took advantage of the abundance of buffalo. He specialized in boudin blanc, a white pudding of chopped buffalo meat and kidneys stuffed into an intestine. Charbonneau was also requested by Clark to keep blacksmith tools to educate the Mandans.

On August 14, 1806, the Corps arrived back at the Mandan villages. Charbonneau was given a voucher in the sum of $500.33, his payment for his interpreter duties and "public services," plus the price of a horse and lodge. Charbonneau had vainly tried hard to persuade the Hidatsa chiefs to join the Indian delegation and accompany Lewis and Clark to Saint Louis before going to Washington. On August, 17, Clark offered to take Charbonneau to Illinois but he declined to proceed, observing that he had no acquaintances or prospects of making a living there. Clark bluntly recorded that Charbonneau's services were no longer of use to the United States, thus barring his way to the White House.

Charbonneau resided among the Hidatsa and Mandans from 1806 until late fall of 1809. Then, he, Sacagawea, and Pomp boarded a Missouri Fur Company barge and traveled to St. Louis, where he cashed in his voucher, and he, together with all of the enlisted men, were granted land warrants, each amounting to 320 acres.[23]

Charbonneau was not suited to tilling the soil and moreover, both he and Sacagawea longed to return to their former lives on the Upper Missouri. Selling his land to Clark for $100, Charbonneau ended his visit in the spring of 1811. Charbonneau took employment with the Missouri Fur Company. With Sacagawea he departed up the river, again aboard a company barge, leaving his son Baptiste in the care of Clark, who would see to the boy's education. Charbonneau was stationed at Fort Manuel (South Dakota), a company trading post, where Sacagawea would die on December 20, 1812 after the birth of a daughter, Lisette. The two Charbonneau children, Jean Baptiste and Lisette, were formally entrusted to Clark's care under a guardianship appointment from a Saint Louis Orphan's Court proceeding on August 11, 1813.[24]

Outliving Sacagawea by about twenty-eight years, Charbonneau's principal place of residence was among the Mandans and Hidatsas.

Clark, then Superintendent of Indian Affairs, employed him as an interpreter for government officials, explorers, artists, and visiting dignitaries. In 1833–34, Charbonneau provided interpreter services for Prince Maximilien of Germany, who wintered on the Upper Missouri.

In 1839, the year after Clark's death, Charbonneau visited Saint Louis to collect back pay owed to him. The next year, he vanished from recorded history, probably en route to his Upper Missouri home. His estate was settled in 1843 by his son, Jean Baptiste Charbonneau.[25]

Toussaint was a product of the rough-and-tumble life of a fur trader. He was maligned by virtually every writer of the expedition, in both fiction and non-fiction alike. Considering the context of time, place, and social values under which he lived, his unseemly traits have been accentuated in those writings, influenced by behavioral standards socially illuminated two centuries after the expedition. He was not the Pistol of a Shakespearian historic drama in the New World saga of Lewis and Clark. He could have been a traitor when François Larocque, an emissary of the North West Company, came to the Mandan village to bribe him in the winter of 1804–5. Perhaps Charbonneau did not find the bid high enough.

At Clatsop, the couple lived in a cabin close to Lewis and Clark, who acted almost as guardians protecting their short-term wards. Perhaps too Charbonneau thought it more comfortable to stay with the Americans. At least he fostered a genuine frontiersman in Jean Baptiste, whose dual American and German education promoted a French Métis to a higher status in the Westward movement after having been America's youngest explorer.

How French was Sacagawea?

Sacagawea, with the infant Jean Baptiste, was the only woman to accompany the members of the permanent party to the Pacific Ocean and back.[26] Jean Baptiste, whom Captain Clark affectionately named "Pomp" or "Pompy" for his "little dancing boy" frolicking, rode with Sacagawea in the boats and on her back when they traveled on horseback.[27] Her activities as a member of the Corps included digging for roots, collecting edible plants, and picking berries; all of these were used as food and, sometimes, as medicine.

On August 12, 1805, Captain Lewis and three men scouted seventy miles ahead of the expedition's main party, crossing the Continental Divide at today's Lemhi Pass. The next day, they found a group of Shoshones. Not only did they prove to be Sacagawea's band, but their leader, Chief Cameahwait, turned out to be none other than her brother. On August 17, after five years of separation, Sacagawea and Cameahwait had an emotional reunion. Then, through their interpreting chain of the captains—Labiche, Charbonneau, and Sacagawea—the expedition was able to purchase the horses it needed. She must have impressed her kinsmen with her linguistic skill. At least Charbonneau had made her aware of the significance of the French language. She may also have memorized her lord and master's frequent oaths, as was the case with many freemen's squaws.

Sacagawea turned out to be incredibly valuable to the Corps as it traveled westward through the territories of many new tribes. Some of these Indians, prepared to defend their lands, had never seen white men before. If they had, they would have probably been French. As Clark noted on October 19, 1805, the Indians were inclined to believe that the whites were friendly when they saw Sacagawea. During council meetings between Indian chiefs and the Corps where Shoshone was spoken, Sacagawea was always highly valued as an interpreter. But what kind of meaning could she convey to Charbonneau? How could he understand native cosmogony if it was related to political strategy? French toponymy had already invaded the American West. It made it easier for Charbonneau to locate sites indicated by Indian speakers in their language. Jefferson believed that the knowledge of the Indian lexicon would facilitate trade and interracial relations. At least Sacagawea easily substantiated the idea that some words had necessarily their rough equivalents in any language, whether white or native. Jefferson had prepared a list of words that could not fail to bring the interpreters to the heart of the matter in all dialogues. They were, for instance, yesterday/today, day/month/ year, man/woman, smoke/ fire/earth/air, sky/wind, sun/moon, light/star/darkness, father/mother, brother/sister, son/daughter, head/body, joy/sadness, tobacco/berry. The combination or opposition of idioms without syntactic structures multiplied meanings, from denotation to connotation.[28] On the other hand, Sacagawea could easily bridge any gap between Shoshone and Hidatsa because she had lived through many experiences with both peoples. She was not concerned with geopolitics, but simply eager to survive as wife and mother. The transit of words from Indian to spoken French was vital to her. Both Charbonneau and Sacagawea were bilingual. She spoke Shoshone and Hidatsa. Toussaint spoke Hidatsa and French. It fell to François Labiche to translate from French into English for the captains. The process probably gave her a sense of relativity. She understood that Hidatsa was as significant as French and realized that the powerful Americans were dependent on a backwoods squaw man. In November 1805, when the expedition reached the place where the Columbia River emptied into the Pacific Ocean, the captains held a vote among all the members to decide where to settle for the winter. Sacagawea's vote, as well as the vote of Clark's man-servant York, were counted equally with those of the captains and the men. As a result of the election, the Corps stayed at a site near present-day Astoria, Oregon, in Fort Clatsop, which they constructed and inhabited during the winter of 1805–6.

Charbonneau never taught Sacagawea the French *Déclaration des Droits de l'Homme et du Citoyen,* the founding document of the Révolution française. He could not care less about what had happened to the Bastille on July 14, 1789. But along the Missouri, Sacagawea could perceive even through casual attitudes what the Declaration of Independence meant to the captains in terms of equality and freedom. Although a battered woman, ironically, she owed her democratic experience to being Charbonneau's wife.

While at Fort Clatsop, local Indians told the expedition of a whale that had been stranded on a beach some miles to the south. Clark gathered a group of men to find the whale and possibly obtain some oil and blubber, which could be used to feed the Corps. Sacagawea had yet to see the ocean, and after willfully asking Clark, she was allowed to accompany the group to the sea. Captain Lewis recorded her argument as she observed that she had traveled a long way to watch the big waters and a monstrous fish. She concluded it would be unfair if she was not be permitted to see either. This was stated in the captain's words, but Sacagawea's oral phraseology could not be transcribed. Perhaps she had learned from Charbonneau to be outspoken after having cringed for so long. One cannot imagine that among the Hidatsas she would have shown such obstinateness to gratify her desire for the unknown. Again, Charbonneau had been a useful escort, if not a liberator.

During the expedition's return journey, as they passed through her homeland, Sacagawea proved a valuable guide. She remembered Shoshone trails from her childhood, and Clark praised her as his pilot. The most important trail she recalled, which Clark described as "a large road passing through a gap in the mountain," led to the Yellowstone River.[29] Today, it is known as Bozeman Pass, Montana. The Corps returned to the Hidatsa-Mandan villages on August 14, 1806, marking the end of the trip for Sacagawea, Charbonneau, and their boy, Jean Baptiste. She received nothing but praise. Had she been French she would have vehemently protested for being deprived of financial compensation.

Six years after the expedition, Sacagawea gave birth to her daughter Lisette. On December 22, 1812, the Shoshone woman died at age 25 due to what later medical researchers believed was a serious illness she had suffered most of her adult life. Her condition may have been aggravated by Lisette's birth. At the time of her death, Sacagawea was with her husband at Fort Manuel, a Missouri Fur Company trading post in present-day South Dakota. Eight months after her death, Clark legally adopted Sacagawea's two children. Baptiste was educated by Clark in Saint Louis, and then, at age eighteen, was sent to Europe with Prince Maximilien. It is not known whether Lisette survived past infancy.[30]

What did Sacagawea really learn from Charbonneau? Like all other Indian women living with squaw men, Sacagawea pounded Indian corn, prepared sagamite, dressed the furs Charbonneau collected, cut out from skins the moccasins he used in traveling over the frozen soil, and repaired his canoes. She intervened personally in relations and transactions with the Indians. And if need arose she warded off the plots that threatened him. Although the French Canadian freeman incurred Clark's blame for his brutality, she was likely to see a promotion in a French companion who retained even a semblance of European manners. She carried her child while Charbonneau was taking care of the bundle of moss serving as diapers, which was considered beneath the dignity of a Hidatsa.[31] Nobody knows if he ever taught her how to cook boudin or whisper French cradle songs to Pomp. Travelers had heard oaths or sayings uttered by Indian women such as *pas d'argent, pas de Suisse* [don't expect any task without wages].[32] At least Sacagawea grew confident and took initiatives along the way. Her presence was staggering to Indians who had never seen a woman with her baby in a war party. On the Great Divide she found herself promoted to the status of Chief Cameahwait's sister. The Great Father in Washington was unknown to her, and she was unable to evaluate the significance of the expedition, but Charbonneau had unwittingly enabled her to sight a whale on a Pacific shore even though Jefferson remained a myth. Perhaps Sacagawea was "tormented by an everlasting itch for things remote," and haunted by "the overwhelming idea of the great whale himself. "Such a portentous and mysterious monster," as Ishmael says in *Moby Dick*,[33] Charbonneau was not in a position to teach her the Christian faith, human rights, and Rousseau's conception of the Noble Savage. Both would have been at great pains to find themselves in the images of America conveyed by Chateaubriand's premature elegy. Sacagawea did not belong to the same world as Atala. They were as opposed as fiction to reality, and as Thanatos to Eros.

FRENCH-AMERICAN FRONTIERSMEN

The most entertaining and unpredictable member of the Corps happened to be another freeman. Private Pierre Cruzatte, who was of French and Omaha Indian extraction, enlisted with Lewis and Clark on May 16, 1804, at Saint Charles.[34] He had been a trader on the Missouri for the Chouteaus. He could speak Omaha and was skilled in sign language, so he proved to be of valuable assistance to the captains at the Indian councils and encounters with the tribes on the Lower Missouri. He was short, wiry, and one-eyed. He had spent several winters trading up the Missouri as far as the Platte River. In the Corps, he held the function of bowman in the keelboat for his ability to navigate upstream. In early June 1805, he was one of six men selected to accompany Lewis on an exploration of the north fork of the Missouri River. Over a year later, in August 1806, while elk hunting, Cruzatte accidentally shot Lewis in the left thigh without identifying himself immediately after the accident. The Corps found no evidence of Blackfeet presence so that he finally confessed that the shooting was his fault, which Lewis forgave magnanimously. Cruzatte often entertained the explorers with his exuberant fiddle-playing, keeping spirits high. On New Year's Day 1805, he and seven other Corps members carried a fiddle, a tambourine, and a sound horn in tin, with a brass reed, across the river to the Mandan village, amusing the villagers with their singing, dancing, and frolicking.

Cruzatte often played key roles with the various Indian tribes that the Corps encountered. In September 1804, he served as an interpreter with Labiche during talks with the Bois Brûlé Teton Sioux to gain access to the Upper Missouri. His translations, together with the gifts he made to his hosts, were instrumental in helping the Americans gain peaceful entry to that part of the river.

Another key member of the expedition was George Drouillard, the twenty-nine-year-old son of a French Canadian father and Shawnee Indian mother.[35] His father, Pierre Drouillard, born in 1746, belonged to a large family of the Detroit region. In 1776 he married Angelica Descomps-Labadie, born in 1760. He long served as an official Huron interpreter for the British. After the cession of Detroit he fell in disfavor with the British, moved to Ohio, and was an interpreter for the Americans. He was famous for having saved a captive,

Simon Kenton, in Sandusky when Daniel Boone was active in the region. Before marrying he lived with Asoundechris Flat Head, a Shawnee, and had two sons, Peter, born in 1773 and George, born in 1775. He also had seven children with Angelica.

In his youth George migrated with his mother's family south of Saint Louis, below Kaskaskia, in a thriving Spanish area east of the Shawnee country. On his father's side he was related to Louis Lorimer, commander of the Spanish garrison at Cape Girardeau. Then on his own George made his residence at Fort Massac on the Ohio. He was recruited by Captain Meriwether Lewis upon his arrival at Fort Massac in November 1803. Captain Daniel Bissell, who had been ordered by the War Department to recruit volunteers for the Corps of Discovery, recommended Drouillard as an excellent hunter with a good knowledge of the Indians' character and sign language.

In his job as civilian interpreter, Drouillard was offered a salary of $25 a month. He also received a $30 advance from Lewis for transporting eight volunteers from South West Point, Tennessee, to Fort Massac to join the Corps. Drouillard and York, Clark's servant, were the only non-military members of the Corps on the expedition from Camp Dubois to the Pacific and back. Drouillard generally accompanied Lewis on scouting missions. He was superior in hazardous situations when nerve, endurance, and cool judgment were needed. Lewis praised him highly as the most skilled hunter among the men.

Because of his working knowledge of sign language, Drouillard often played a key role in establishing relations with the various Indian tribes that the Corps encountered. In late July 1804, just north of the Platte River's entrance into the Missouri River, he and Cruzatte were sent by the captains to scout out the villages of the Oto and the Missouri Indians. After several days, Drouillard came into contact with one Missouri and two Otoes, with whom Lewis and Clark sought to have council. In early August 1804, Drouillard was one of four men named to a search party charged with locating La Liberté, who had deserted the Corps while on his way to the Oto tribe.

During the winter of 1804–5, Drouillard was key in establishing friendly relations with the Mandan Indians, with whom the Corps survived an incredibly cold winter. He was often assigned to small hunting groups to collect meat to feed the Corps and to trade with the Mandans for other foodstuffs. In February 1805, after recovering from pleurisy, Drouillard and three other men were called upon to transport some buffalo meat that had been cached downriver. The team headed down the river on the ice with two sleighs, three horses, and a colt to where the hunting party had stored the meat in log cribs, safe from predators. One evening during this trip, the team was attacked by more than one hundred Sioux Indians, who stole the two sleigh horses and some of the team's weapons. Upon Drouillard's advice, the team held their fire to keep the Indians at a distance. He and his companions were safe, but returned to Fort Mandan without the needed meat.

After departing Fort Mandan on April 7, 1805, the Corps reached the mouth of the Yellowstone River. Lewis and Clark decided to examine and map the area. Lewis led a team that included Drouillard to climb to the top of the Missouri's southern bluffs where they were amazed at the amount of wildlife. On June 11, 1805, Drouillard accompanied Lewis and a party to locate the Great Falls. On June 13, upon sighting the falls, the captain found them a sublime spectacle. Drouillard shared his feelings. Balzac said that James Fenimore Cooper's Natty Bumppo was a magnificent moral hermaphrodite born between the savage and the civilized state of man.[36] In Drouillard's case, was the romantic *beau idéal* no longer a poetic fantasy but the end result of cross-breeding? An episode seems to shed another light on the character of the Métis. On June 14, 1804, when the expedition passed a sandbar, Drouillard told the captains about a huge snake living in a lake nearby. The monster gobbled like a turkey and could be heard from a distance of several miles. Perhaps Drouillard shared native folk beliefs. This anticlimactic episode may also evoke frontier tall tales. Tartarin de Tarascon, a comic demigod from Provence, was the French counterpart of Davy Crockett in the nineteenth century. Also a hunter, he was so blissfully engrossed in his storytelling that he finally believed in his own lies. The Canadian's calculated extravagance was possibly due to a multicultural heritage.

Drouillard provided vital interpreter services to Lewis. In August 1805, he helped the captain with sign language when they were confronted with the first Shoshones while Sacagawea was away with Clark's party. Sign language was for the French trappers a kind of lingua franca, understood by all the natives in the West. Nurtured on meaningful gestures and motions, Drouillard's culture of communication made familiar what would have been outlandish when awkwardly expressed in words. Making a circle above the forehead with a finger indicated craziness, two index fingers cocked at each side of the head meant buffalo. Sometimes conversations and narratives were carried on without the utterance of a single word. Such nonverbal language was imperfect and liable to error, but it conveyed essential meanings on the spur of the moment and performed preliminary peace-making rituals, weapons not being at arm's length.

In early July 1806, Lewis and Clark divided the Corps into two groups at Traveler's Rest, near present-day Missoula, Montana. Lewis would head northward to determine the upper limit of the Marias River; in turn, his exploration would help determine the northern extent of the Louisiana Purchase Territory. Clark would lead a detachment to explore the Yellowstone. Drouillard, as well as Joseph and Reuben Field accompanied Lewis into the northern country, where they skirmished with some roving Piegans, a band of the Blackfeet tribe, on July 27. Attempting to steal the weapons and horses of the white men, two Piegans perished. Lewis was nearly shot by one of the Indians. The explorers escaped, managing to reclaim their horses, together with taking several of the Indians' horses. Lewis, Drouillard, and the Field brothers rode away as fast as possible because they believed that Indians were trying to catch up with them. They decided that if they were attacked they would tie the horses together, and they would stand and defend themselves desperately. Thereby, Drouillard demonstrated his esprit de corps and loyalty in combat, as an Americanized French Métis. In this respect, Skarsten contends that Drouillard served Lewis not merely as a hunter, scout, outdoorsman, interpreter, and ambassador to the Indians, but as a companion and a friend.[37]

When the Corps safely reached Saint Louis on September 23, 1806, Lewis entrusted Drouillard with the delivery of the first letters containing reports of the expedition to the postmaster in Cahokia. These letters were then sent on to President Jefferson. According to Clark, in 1808 Paul Primeau belatedly paid off a debt of $300 owed to George Drouillard and Manuel Lisa. Later, after the Corps was disbanded, Drouillard returned to the Three Forks region of the Upper Missouri as a member of Manuel Lisa's fur trading party. He was accompanied by John Colter, another participant in the expedition, It was there that Indians killed Drouillard, horribly mutilating him. He had been one of the early members of a new community of adventurers, the mountainmen whose figureheads were later Jim Bridger and Kit Carson.

The biographical data collected on Pierre Dorion contribute to make him the archetype of the French squaw man.[38] He was born to Jean Marie Dorion and Marie Thérèse Lenormand on January 17, 1740, in Canada. He moved to Cahokia after the Treaty of Paris, and in 1773 was granted 240 acres of land in Saint Louis by the Spanish government. He later chose to live as a freeman among the Sioux and in 1780 took a Yankton woman (Holy Rainbow). Their son,

Pierre Dorion was born in 1782 in the Dakotas and died in 1814. Dorion the elder also married Marie Laguivoise (Wi-hmunke-wakan), an Iowa Indian. She was known as Marie Aioe Dorion Venier Toupin. It is difficult to trace Dorion's itinerary in the last decades of the eighteenth century between the Des Moines and James Rivers. In any case, he became notorious as a polygamist and had numerous offspring among whom were Charles (1781), Pierre (1782), Antoine (1785), Thomas (1787), Joseph (1789), Perchie (1789), Ellen (1796), and Margaret (1800).

Pierre Dorion was first involved with Pierre Chouteau before working independently.[39] He was hired by the captains as an interpreter in July 1804 just prior to an August confrontation with the Teton Sioux Indians. Considered a shrewd, hard-bitten, semiliterate half-breed, Dorion had lived intermittently with the Yankton Sioux Indians for twenty years prior to the arrival of the explorers. In dire need of an interpreter, the Americans paid Dorion not only a good salary, but also purchased from him three hundred pounds of buffalo grease that was used to repel insects. Dorion retained the motivation of a voyageur. He was thus in a position to energize the Indian communities in which he had settled and show them the advantages to be derived from mutual trust.

Although Dorion lived a secluded existence with his Métis families, he had spent so many decades along the routes of the fur traders' convoys that he could facilitate contacts with the posts and the natives. In August 29, 1804, Pierre Dorion Jr. and a large band of seventy Yankton men and boys met the Lewis and Clark expedition on the Missouri, just above the mouth of the James River. When the captains called the Sioux to council at Calumet Bluff on August 30, 1804, the elder Dorion, whose son also resided with the Yankton Sioux, proved indispensable. He contributed reliable information about Indian culture, and urged the Yanktons to make peace with neighboring tribes such as the Bois Brûlé Tetons. Dorion's skills also helped to ease relations between the warring Omahas and their Sioux enemies. Accordingly, Clark persuaded the latter to release forty-eight prisoners of war by turning them over to Dorion, who lived in Yankton villages.

As the Corps progressed up the Missouri River, Dorion was commissioned to collect and transport selected chiefs from the Yankton Sioux, Omaha, Oto, and Missouri tribes downstream to visit Saint Louis and Washington. These diplomatic moves were critical in helping Jefferson cement and formalize relations with the tribes. Pierre Dorion Sr. survived the expedition and died among the Yankton Sioux in 1810. As in the case of Charbonneau and Drouillard,

Dorion was too immersed in the wilderness ever to become a pioneer in settled areas.

It seems legitimate to vindicate the choice of René Jusseaume as the most representative of the saga that led freemen, Métis, and squaw men to participate in the conquest of the American West.[40] He was probably the most American of the Frenchmen encountered in the Lewis and Clark expedition. For a long time Jusseaume had served as a mediator between the Canadian posts and the native tribes of the Missouri. Supplied with trade goods that he obtained from the forts, he went to villages, buying horses, buffalo robes, and pelts, which he afterwards bartered at the trading posts, earning a profit that enabled him to increase his stock of merchandise. After a long residence among the sedentary Mandans, Jusseaume carried on a regular traffic between the posts of the North West Company and the villages of his host tribe on the Missouri.

Throughout the 1790s contacts with both Canadian and Saint Louis traders increased as men like Jacques d'Eglise, René Jusseaume, and John Evans waged economic war to gain control of the Mandan-Hidatsa trade. In October 1794, Jusseaume, Ménard, and five associates packed five horses with guns, powder, and merchandise at Knife River to trade with the Mandans and Hidatsas of North Dakota. Jusseaume and his Indian wife had been living with the Indians for fourteen years. He had a small fort and a hut built between the two nations. Meanwhile, Jacques Clamorgan and other Saint Louis merchants were organizing the Missouri Company to establish trade with the Mandans and keep the British out. In 1795 Jusseaume returned to Fort La Souris with peltries, leaving four men behind to keep watch.[41]

In 1797 John Evans, the Welsh trader dispatched by Clamorgan's Missouri Company, took possession of the fort built by Jusseaume and his former associates. When the Canadian voyageurs came back later Jusseaume tried to kill Evans but was prevented from doing so by the natives. In July 1797, David Thompson, a young British trader, arrived at Grand Portage and hired Jusseaume as a guide and interpreter.[42] They departed for the interior in August. In 1797 David Thompson had just left the Hudson's Bay Company for the North West Company. His first trip for his new employer was a visit to the Mandans during which he surveyed the area La Vérendrye had explored sixty years before.[43] David Thompson often complained that Jusseaume led them out of their way. On December 23, 1797, he wrote in his journal that Jusseaume was by no means reliable. On January 9, 1798, Thompson recorded a list of furs obtained from his French mentor at the Mandan-Hidatsa villages in exchange for horses sometimes at an extravagant price. In fact, Jusseaume's reputation as a con man was growing fast. The oligarchy of fur traders was well aware that French Canadians had the mastery of native languages. Many freemen were poorly educated, if not illiterate, but their insight into Indian arrogant willpower, resilience, and whims was precious. Through this acquired language of daily experience a man like Jusseaume could arouse superstitious terrors while making the most of native confidence and fear. For example, he displayed his talent as a conjuror to pretend he worked miracles.

Charles Mckenzie participated in four trips to the Missouri for the North West Company. The first was headed by François Larocque when Lewis and Clark were wintering at Fort Mandan in 1804–5.[44] He attended ceremonies performed by Jusseaume among the Cheyennes. The French Métis subdued them by acting like the Father of all the white people, after which he cynically justified his antics by telling Mckenzie: "il faut faire comme cela pour être considéré par les sauvages" [this is the way to be respected by the savages] and "il faut hurler avec les loups" [to follow the pack].[45] A born demagogue, Jusseaume publicly implored the god of the Cheyennes in words such as: "Hoo-ho-hou ! Smoke thou, bright son of the East and thou great being who disposeth of the white people's life at thy pleasure."[46] Mckenzie recognized that he had recorded Jusseaume's harangue to show how a civilized man lapsed into "savage life" and commit "absurdities in words and deeds."[47] Was he fully aware that Jusseaume was a trickster? As an interpreter Jusseaume often came in for harsh criticism. The reason may be that he disconcerted the whites by participating fully in the antics of his Indian hosts. On October 26, 1804, the captains walked from their camp to Mitutanka, the Mandan village close the mouth of the Knife River. They met with Chief Sheheke, Little Raven the second chief, and Jusseaume. They were impressed with his fluency in the Mandan language. He told Clark he had been a spy for his elder brother in the Illinois during the Revolutionary war.[48] For a controversial figure like him, there was no better way to ingratiate himself with the captains. Few whites could actually match his experience on the Upper Missouri, but many traders disliked him. Alexander Henry the Younger called Jusseaume "that old sneaking cheat" and described him as a man who was a disgrace to the Métis.[49] Lewis was eager to hire him as an interpreter and informant on Upper Missouri life, whereas Clark described him as cunning, artful, and insolent. Despite his unsavory reputation, Jusseaume had firsthand information that Lewis and Clark needed. Some of the most valuable comments in the journals about Mandan beliefs and intertribal relations came from him.

Lewis and Clark often struggled to record a Hidatsa vocabulary, in which each word had to pass along a cumbersome translation chain stretching from a native speaker through Sacagawea, Charbonneau, Jusseaume, and other members of the Corps. Heated arguments among the various translators were frequent, slowing the process and worrying the Indians. The way Mackenzie remembered it, the Indians were aware that their words were recorded, and concluded that the Americans had a wicked design.

Jusseaume was to become one of the best-known freemen along the Missouri. He lived in the Mandan village known as the Deapolis site but often left his Métis children on the care of their Indian mother. On October 29, 1804 he served as interpreter for Black Cat and Hidatsa chief Caltarcota. Lewis's speech stressed American sovereignty and intertribal peace through trade. This displeased Caltarcota who had ties with British traders. Jusseaume was probably able to eavesdrop on conversations between the Arikaras and the Hidatsas, and could later outwit them. On November 25 Lewis, Jusseaume, and Charbonneau rode from Fort Mandan to the Hidatsa villages. The destination was Menatarra, the largest Hidatsa settlement upriver. But Mackenzie had dissuaded the Hidatsas from contacts with Americans. Meanwhile Clark had no interpreter at Fort Mandan to entertain Hidatsa visitors such as Waukeressara. He contented himself with handing out gifts such as a handkerchiefs, which was insufficient. When Jusseaume brought his family into the American compound he thus allowed immediate access to his interpreting skills.

On the way back from the Pacific, Clark carried on negotiations with the Mandan and Hidatsa leaders on August 14, 1806. Charbonneau called on Hidatsa chiefs, while Drouillard was sent to Sheheke's village to hire René Jusseaume as council interpreter. When Jusseaume arrived at the expedition's camp, just above the village of the Mitutanka tribe, the talks began. Black Cat was a privileged negotiator. Clark reiterated to Jusseaume his offer to send delegations to Washington. Indians would see for themselves the wealth of the nation. Le Borgne, the Hidatsa chief, was not impressed. Black Cat admitted that risk of Sioux ambushes made it impossible for anyone to accompany the expedition. Later the same day Jusseaume brought some startling news. He claimed that Little Raven, second Chief of Mitutanka, had expressed the desire to go down to Washington to meet the Great Father. Clark needed a major diplomatic success, which was still hard to achieve.

Charbonneau was just back from a short visit at Metaharta, a Hidatsa village on the Knife River, where he and Sacagawea had lived before joining the corps. He had learnt that several Hidatsa war parties had gone out to raid the Lemhi Shoshones and the Grand River Arikaras. Continued Hidatsa attacks against the Shoshones and other potential American allies could jeopardize American efforts to establish peace among the Indian nations. Le Borgne received a swivel cannon as a gift, but allowed Chief Caltarcota to state that the Hidatsas would never make peace with the Arikaras nor with the Tetons. Raids were part of their strategy and culture. On the other hand, Little Raven recanted his former acceptance of the trip to Washington, under the pressure of Sheheke who was probably jealous of the prestige he would gain by a visit to the Great Father's White House. This was what Lewis heard from Jusseaume. Clark asked him to use his influence to enlist Sheheke in the expedition. Jusseaume, who was a born manipulator, always eager for a bargain, asked if the captains would provide transportation and rations for both Sheheke and the Jusseaume families. Clark grudgingly agreed and Sheheke went to Washington.

On August 30, 1806 near Yankton, South Dakota, Clark and his group came across the Bois Brûlés of Black Buffalo's band.[50] Clark then had Jusseaume tell the Tetons that future traders would be sufficiently strong to whip any party who dared to oppose them. He also shouted across the river that the Sioux were bad people. Then Clark notified the Sioux that they had given guns and a cannon to the Hidatsas and the Mandans, weapons that would surely be turned against raiders. Several warriors remained on a hill jeering and proclaiming their readiness to kill the Americans. A nasty verbal exchange pitted Jusseaume and Clark against Black Buffalo. The alliance between a French scoundrel and the representative of the American presidency was thus sealed for urgent diplomatic purposes. For Marcel Giraud the example of Jusseaume, sharing the life and the superstitions of the Mandans, reveals the extent of the regression which the Canadians underwent if they were limited to the company of the natives[51] He finally sums up the slurs aimed at the French half-breeds by referring to the judgment William Joseph Snelling made of the freemen: "Ten civilized men degenerate into barbarism where one savage is reclaimed from it. Metaphysicians may speculate upon such a propensity as long and as much as they please but the fact is thus and it is believed, always will be."[52]

But Jusseaume could not be merely identified with the marauders and horse rustlers who threatened the outposts. He kept up sustained relations with traders without ever declining to the level of primitive violence. He was close to the type that Jefferson had in mind in 1824, when he recalled the evolution of Western society:

"Then succeed our own semi-barbarous citizens, the pioneers of the advance of civilization."[53] Jusseaume already embodied the true grit West of the mountainmen. His shifty, cynical attitudes foreshadowed the rise of the backwoodsmen who became the demigods of the frontier. During the attempted return of Sheheke in 1807, which was stopped by the Arikaras, Jusseaume suffered a crippling wound and petitioned Jefferson for a pension. He apprenticed his thirteen-year-old son to Lewis in 1809 to provide for the boy's education. He was still alive when Prince Maximilien visited the Mandans in 1833–34 before taking Jean Baptiste with him back to Germany.

11

The French Around and
Against the Expedition

DOUBLE-DEALERS

AROUND THE TIME OF THE LEWIS AND CLARK EXPEDITION, MANY observers of French extraction waited cautiously to see what would come out of Jefferson's long-term project. They did not fully realize the implications of the acquisition of Louisiana, nor conceived of themselves as French Americans. But they could not imagine they were outsiders lacking a capacity to alter the course of history. Entangled alliances and fragile compromises ran across ethnic loyalties. Régis Loisel was a French Canadian working for the Spanish colonists but leaning toward the powerful American explorers. Pierre-Antoine Tabeau was also torn between his loyalty to this employers and his future in the fur trade. Lewis and Clark had to deal with time-servers who used devious means to know more about Jefferson's plans. But the main danger for the expedition might come from angered Spaniards, resentful of apparently boundless American expansion.

On his way down the Missouri on May 25, 1804 Loisel encountered Lewis and Clark, who had left Saint Charles only a few days before and from whom he learned about the change of government in Louisiana. Lewis and Clark had expected to meet him way up the river. Louis Labeaume, who belonged to the Chouteaus' entourage, had told them that should they see Tabeau. He might be very informative about the Indian country.[1]

In his report to Delassus, in accordance with his instructions of April 15, 1803, Loisel gave a general survey of the situation.[2] He mentioned large assemblies of tribes organizing resistance against Spanish rule. Indians realized they were dispossessed of their rich furs by means of cheap gifts. The Sioux were blocking the access to the Upper Missouri, and the unexpected change of government was aggravating the situation. To maintain a presence along the river, Tabeau and seven men had remained on Cedar Island.

Loisel had gathered information concerning a possible link between Hudson Bay and Santa Fe. It involved a short portage to get across the isthmus from the James (Dakota) River to the Cheyenne (Red) River. He believed that the tribes south of the Platte would resist in case of American invasion. He was especially concerned with their vulnerability to bribes by a new people of whom they knew nothing more than the name. Loisel insisted on the necessity of taking greater care of native needs. Turning to the Black Hills, three hundred miles above the mouth of the Platte, he also reported on the existence of hidden precious minerals found in nuggets under the earth. After listing the nations between the Missouri and New Mexico, Loisel's alarmist discourse was rounded off by an injunction to define the boundaries of colonial Mexico. For him, the United States government considered that American territory extended to the sources of the rivers emptying into the Mississippi. Americans were enterprising and ambitious. They would avail themselves of any opportunity to convince Indians of their goodwill and discredit Spanish authorities. The enormous expenditures consented to by his majesty to make peace with the natives would be forgotten if Americans mustered them to achieve their ambitious designs. To conclude, Loisel wished to capitalize on his contribution and placed himself readily under his excellency's banner. He therefore offered his services as an agent among the tribes along the Missouri to dissuade them from heeding American propaganda.

The Marquis of Casa Calvo responded to Loisel's report in a letter to Don Pedro Ceballo, dated September 30, 1804.[3] He recognized American ambitions to reach the Rio Grande across from New Mexico. He knew Jefferson had planned to send troops to the headwaters of the Missouri. Other expeditions were to explore avenues to New Mexico. One was equipped by William Morrison, a wealthy American living in Kaskaskia who had enrolled two traders, Jeannot Metoyer and Baptiste Lalande, to be later joined by Joseph Gervais. They left Saint Louis in July 1804.[4] Jacques d'Eglise was not yet back from Upper Missouri. Casa Calvo also referred to Stoddard, the American captain of Illinois who was himself accused of inciting unrest among the Osages and looting the Spanish silver convoys. He vowed not to cede one single foot of the west bank of the Mississippi even at the cost of bloodshed. Calvo praised Loisel for his youthful energy, loyalty, insight, and linguistic talents, aside from the fact that he knew practically thirteen hundred miles of the course of the Missouri. Calvo's aim was to disrupt any American plan to rouse the native nations against Spain. As late as the early fall of 1804, Calvo's wishful thinking let him still imagine the Mississippi as the natural borderline between the United States and Spain.

The New Orleans fever was as fatal to Loisel as it had been to Todd. He met his death in October 1805 at the age of thirty-one.[5] His report did not receive the same attention in the upper circles that it had received from Calvo. He had disclosed no more than Truteau, Mackay, and D'Eglise, but had hinted of special intelligence that his trusted agent Tabeau was in a position to reveal, disreputable though he might be after Mackay's derogatory judgments about him.

When Loisel parted with him to go to Saint Louis, Tabeau went to live in an Arikara village on an island about three miles long, until 1805. He was the guest of Chief Kakawita who, in Tabeau's own words, was the only one to make himself respected by other nations through bravery and pretended magic.[6] According to Tabeau, even though he led one of the weakest bands, Kakawita's ferocity and his medicines were deemed awe-inspiring. There was no slyness in him nor did he lower himself to begging for articles of clothing and other items.

Joseph Gravelines was one of the seven men Loisel left under the order of Tabeau, his agent and man of affairs, when he returned to Saint Louis. Gravelines was famous for having spent more than twenty years of his life with the Arikaras. On Cedar Island he had taken over from Joseph Garreau, who had lived with the Arikaras since 1790.

On October 10, 1804, Lewis and Clark saw Tabeau arrive at their camp in company with Gravelines, whom they had met two days before when they had first caught sight of the island. After holding a council with the Arikaras, the Americans went to the Mandan villages to winter.

The following day Gravelines visited their camp with Tabeau and breakfasted with the captains. So impressed were Lewis and Clark with Gravelines's fluency that they hired him in March 1805 when they suspected Toussaint Charbonneau of double-crossing them in service to Larocque, who had employed Charbonneau as an interpreter upon his arrival on the Upper Missouri. Charbonneau finally kept his prior commitment, and Gravelines, also a good boatman, was put in charge of the barge descending to Saint Louis, on which Tabeau was only a passenger. Gravelines accompanied the Arikara chiefs to Washington. He had the misfortune to see one of them die in Richmond but was rewarded with a commission to teach agriculture to the Arikaras.[7]

In April 1805, as Lewis and Clark were preparing to proceed on their journey upstream, Arikara Chief Kakawita returned to the camp with three tribesmen. He was given a certificate of good conduct, a medal, a carrot of tobacco, and a wampum. He also delivered a letter from Tabeau explaining the chief's desire to visit the Great Father in Washington and board the barge that was to transport more than a dozen men to Saint Louis. Tabeau, nicknamed Anty (for Antoine) by the Americans, was also invited to embark with his peltry. Did he know about Loisel's death, which had occurred in October? Tabeau's long absence from Saint Louis might recall Rip Van Winkle's sleep, should it be taken for granted that the French trader was deprived of contacts. He had left a place still under provisional Spanish rule and now returned to see the Stars and Stripes flying over the governor's mansion. But in the meantime voyageurs and coureurs des bois along the river were conveying pieces of news which, distorted as they might be, certainly referred to the scope of the Lewis and Clark expedition.

The trade partnership with Loisel, which should have come to an end in June 1803, was extended beyond the deadline. When Loisel left Cedar Island in the spring of 1804, Tabeau was still cooperating with Heney, who at the same time was staying with the Teton Sioux. Tabeau resented being merely Loisel's agent but owed had no grudge against Heney. The latter was received at Fort Mandan as a representative of the North West Company on the Assiniboine. He introduced himself on December 16, 1804 with a letter from Charles Chaboillez, with whom he was the preceding month. In his journal Patrick Gass suggests that Heney's object in crossing over to the Missouri was to gain information with respect to the change of government.[8] Heney not only brought with him credentials from Chaboillez but probably forged some to impress Lewis and Clark. They thought Heney, now related to the North West Company, could convince a Teton chief to visit Washington. They sensibly deemed Tabeau, who proclaimed himself French American, closer to the Arikaras. Years later Heney deserted the North West Company at Red River and joined its rival the Hudson's Bay Company.

A year passed before Tabeau reappeared in public in August 1806, when he gave evidence as an adversarial witness in court re Loisel's property rights on Cedar Island. A month later he was among those who gave an enthusiastic welcome to Lewis and Clark at Saint Charles.

The report that Tabeau had drafted while staying with the Arikaras was meant to supplement Loisel's own official account presented to the Spanish governor. He probably saw no point in turning the document over to the American authorities. Thus it remained unnoticed until Jean Nicollet discovered it in his topographical data intended for the United States War Department. Never contenting himself with answering questions, Tabeau had given Lewis and Clark some precious personal material. But the time was up for adventures in the West. Back to Canada, he retired on a farm at Lachine where he died on March 10, 1820.

TABEAU'S PERSONAL VISION OF THE AMERICAN WEST

Tabeau recorded his unique western experience in a manuscript reflecting both his accuracy and outspoken cynicism. His unflinching attitude about the American Indians may sometimes evoke Mark Twain's satire in *Roughing It*. Writing was for him the equivalent of laudanum. It appeased him while living in an Arikara lodge, surrounded by four families and by a crowd of "admiring imbeciles disturbed every moment to dispute over a buffalo robe."[9] No doubt Tabeau's advice was precious to the captains. He knew that the rapidity of the water over a muddy bottom made navigation perilous as the great rises of the water could sweep away islands. On May 19, 1804, Tabeau suddenly discovered that a bank was gradually crumbling away. He had time to embark but could not keep fifty pounds of powder dry.

Tabeau's narrative is not devoid of wry humor as opposed to the strict daily reports in the expedition journals. For instance, he states that old bulls were called "coast guards" because they lacked the strength to go far inland. The Indians even said that the bisons exposed themselves to view to invite the hunters to free them from life. In November 1804 the Bois Brûlés and other Sioux tribes either around Cedar Island or with Hugh Heney at the fork of the Cheyenne River, some forty miles upstream, were reduced to the last extremity. The women surrounded the fur traders when they ate their meals and offered their favors for a few mouthfuls. The husbands who seemed to pardon the union paid no attention, being sufficiently occupied in fighting over the soup. Tabeau's keen observations of the fauna were concomitant with the ordeal of the Corps of Discovery in the Missouri wilderness. He noted that the gray and white wolves of the woods would follow the buffalo herds and attack anything they met. Like sly warriors they sneaked through huts at dawn as happened to Jean Vallé and Joseph Calvé, an engagé, on April 24, 1804. The former was bitten by the animal before he could seize its lower jaw and hit its head with the butt of his rifle. Vallé's thumb was so badly lacerated that his hand was useless for weeks. Fortunately, Heney applied the chewed root of the white wood of the prairie on the wound. Lewis and Clark knew of this episode when Heney visited them in December 1804 at Fort Mandan. They found him a very intelligent man, articulate enough to share his expert knowledge of Sioux habits. He came back to the fort in February 1805 to get skins to make shoes. In exchange, he sent two messengers in early March who, upon the captains' request, brought "the root and top of a plant" with instructions as to how cures might be effected.[10]

On the subject of the beaver, Tabeau recalled the expedition equipped by Loisel when ten French Canadians with more than fifty traps competed from spring to fall 1803 to take almost all the beaver to be found between Cedar Island and the Arikaras. In October, they went up the Fork River towards its source in the Black Hills, to trap until it was ice blocked. Tabeau also mentions that a man named Guenneville left the Arikara village on August 1, 1804, followed the Cheyennes toward the northwest and assured Tabeau on his return the following April that he had seldom seen beaver. It was the first time the Cheyennes had met a trader and they had surpassed themselves in the hunt. Tabeau believed that the beaver could not become the object of the fur trade with the Sioux and the Arikaras at least from River qui Court up to the Mandans, who themselves could hardly supply the British Hudson's Bay and the North West Companies.

The classification of the tribes gathered in the journals of the Lewis and Clark expedition is similar to Tabeau's. For instance, the Sioux bands were so numerous and so widespread that even traders dealing with them could never estimate the whole population. Tabeau resorted to the method of naming the groups in terms of habitat or geographical situations, such as *Le Peuple des lacs* [People of the Lakes].The listings transcribed by the captains of the expedition for December 27, 1804 at Fort Mandan were likely contributed by Hugh Heney ten days before and were directly indebted to Tabeau's previous work.

Having observed the aggressiveness of the Teton Sioux, Tabeau deplored the quarrels that perpetuated hatred through generations. He ascribed such disunion to the multiplicity of chiefs but acknowledged the legitimate ascendancy of Matowinkay, a Yankton of the north, at the head of five hundred men whose reputation and power gave him an exceptional influence upon other nations such as the Arikaras. A trader under Matowinkay's protection was safe so far as the trader gave him tokens worthy of his rank. Tabeau ultimately regretted that Lewis had been too diffident to make him a trustworthy ally. Tabeau was obviously eager to reveal his willingness to cooperate with the American explorers.

When Gravelines arrived at Fort Mandan on February 28, 1805, as a messenger from Tabeau, he mentioned to Lewis and Clark the Teton chief Black Buffalo and also his friendly attitude toward them. He also warned against Torto-hongar, the Partisan, whose inquisitive habits and devious ways had been noted by Clark after a meeting on September 25, 1804. The chief had simulated drunkenness "as a cloak for his vilenous [sic] intentions"[11] to try and stay on board the boat. On the 28th he was equally obnoxious, and the following day offered to trade women for tobacco. A fellow chief stigmatized him as double-faced, prurient, and grumpy. Clark reluctantly gave the Partisan some tobacco to get him to calm him down. Tabeau and Loisel had long been in the habit of negotiating with the Tetons, who frequently intercepted loaded pirogues. The French traders were at pains to explain that other nations would not fail to take revenge for the damage caused by stopping and sometimes pillaging the merchandize destined for them. It happened once that a warrior who had been humiliated by Loisel's refusal to marry his daughter had threatened to trade the peltries with other partners.

Having pelts in excess, the Bois Brûlés sold them at a low price, arousing the anger of other tribes and inducing them to pillage the pirogues on their way back to Saint Louis. Tabeau hoped to be as successful with the Tetons as he was with the Arikaras, and trusted that the new government, without being "the tyrant of the Savages"[12] would not also be their slaves. He thereby implicitly blamed the Spaniards for their inefficiency and anticipated the enforcement of law and order on the Sioux. He acknowledged the beneficial influence of Black Bull, Untongasabaw, in the journals of the Lewis and Clark expedition but doubted his ability to oppose Torto-Hongar who had first established links with Loisel as early as 1802, and according to Sioux customs had claimed to be his exclusive protector.

When Loisel was still at Cedar Island on September 5, 1803 the Poncas and the Bois Brûlés convened to negotiate peace, leaving aside the band of warriors Partisan had sent off to Black Bull's camp the night before the meeting. They stole six horses and the Bois Brûlés' chief mistakenly swore vengeance on the Poncas as planned by the Partisan. Tabeau called him an Indian Proteus but the analogy was more ironic than laudatory. Whatever power he could snatch from the white intruders likened him more to a trickster. Tabeau went further with an in-depth analysis of his character. Erratic and self-seeking, the Partisan also lacked patience and courage. In August and September 1803, several incidents alarmed Loisel, who had refused to take sides and therefore declined the Partisan's support. Shortly after, one of his engagés narrowly escaped death after two shots were fired at him before fifty natives rushed to the fort to hunt the French. The Partisan was encouraged to set higher prices on furs and scare the French traders so as to receive the best possible treatment because of the arrival of tribesmen on September 17, 1803, from Rivière Saint Pierre, where the British traders had lavished goods on their Indian partners while defaming the French and inducing the Indians to betray them. This explains why the Partisan blackmailed Loisel by suggesting he might well reserve his pelts for Rivière Saint Pierre.

Tabeau was particularly suspicious of the so-called soldiers who were appointed by the Partisan's tribal council to enforce law and order. They were empowered to punish delinquents arbitrarily in any way they deemed appropriate. Those in charge of the stores of Cedar Island did not care much about the interests of the French trader. In exchange for his protection, the Partisan required valuable gifts. When unruly tribesmen assaulted traders, his soldiers' leniency bordered on complicity.

On October 8, 1804, Lewis came back from a trip with several Frenchmen, including Gravelines the interpreter, and on the following day three chiefs appeared: "Kakawissassa" [Lighting Crow], "Pocasse" [Hay], and "Piaheto" [Eagle's Feather]. The following year, on April 7, 1805, the Arikara War chief "Kakawita" [Brave Raven] came to Fort Mandan, bringing a letter from Tabeau, who had listed all these names with additional comments. His added translations into French were at times more faithful to the original Indian meaning. Kakawissassa was *le corbeau au repos* [the crow at rest], Piaheto, *la plume* [the feather], Kakawita, *le corbeau mâle* [the male crow]. Tabeau transcribed ten names altogether, adding the Chief Robe, the White Kiliou, the Chief Crow, the Rattle, the Chief Dog, and Great Wolf. [13]

For Tabeau, the Loups and all the different Pawnees on the river Platte originally made, with the Arikaras, a single nation that was progressively divided. The language also evolved into so many dialects that no one could claim to be fluent among all the tribes. At Fort Mandan Lewis and Clark found that the Mandans usually referred to the Arikaras as Pawnees, and reported that the Arikara speech was Pania with a different accent and a number of peculiar words.[14]

On August 31, 1804, the Arikaras accepted an offer of peace from the Mandans, whom Tabeau considered a peaceful nation. One of the abandoned Arikara villages Lewis and Clark discovered was named as "La hoo catt" and had been occupied since 1797 according to their information. Nine Arikara bands decided to ally themselves to the Mandans to annihilate Lakota Sioux parties guilty of raiding villages to steal horses. With a delegation of Arikaras, Tabeau himself went to the Lakotas, who welcomed them heartily. But he learnt after that the Lakotas were also expecting Mandan envoys, plotting to murder them upon their arrival. But the wary Mandans canceled their visit.

For Tabeau, Lewis had aroused mixed feelings among the Arikaras, who realized that peace with the Mandans had become indispensable to escape the slavery of the Sioux. In the fall of 1804, Chief Kakawita prepared to carry the skin of a white buffalo to the Mandans as a token of goodwill. But other chiefs feared he had received too many marks of honor from Lewis and Clark. Meanwhile the Sioux continued their incursions in the guise of Arikara warriors. On February 15, they rustled two horses from the expedition and then ambushed the Americans who were chasing them. Tabeau thought fit to warn Lewis, sending off Gravelines and Roi on February 28, 1805 with a message exonerating the Arikaras from the robbery and deterring the Mandans from launching a war party. Tabeau reassured the captains of the peaceful intentions of the Arikaras toward the Mandans, whom they wished to visit before settling close to them and allying against their common enemy the Sioux. Gravelines also announced to Lewis that the Tetons and the Yanktons were on the warpath, not only to fight their hereditary enemies but also to kill every white they found.[15] Obviously, Tabeau's assistance to Lewis and Clark, self-seeking though it was, nevertheless reveals that he always responded to the requests of the American explorers in the interest of peace. When he returned to Saint Louis, they rewarded him with transportation on the barge that set out from Fort Mandan down the Missouri on April 7, 1805. Tabeau joined it at the Arikara village with Lewis's approval.

A few days before Tabeau's departure Kakawita carried the peace pipe to the Mandans. On April 6, 1805, some of them told Lewis that the Arikaras were coming to their villages to stay with them. He sent Toussaint Charbonneau and two other Frenchmen to check. The day after, the interpreter came back with four Arikaras, including two chiefs who announced that their group comprised only ten members. They produced a letter from Tabeau with the news that three Sioux chiefs would board the barge on their way to the Great Father.

Tabeau judged the Sioux nation as a formidable power that held the Arikaras in slavery, bound to cultivate for them, and as they said derisively, having a status as low as women. Yet both nations were permanently at war. The Arikaras could not let their horses out of sight and had to tie them to their lodges at night. When the Sioux came loaded with meat and other merchandise, they fixed their prices very high and obtained large quantities of corn and tobacco in exchange. Their hegemony allowed them to keep buffalo far away from the villages of other nations, which gave them a monopoly over meat and skins. For Tabeau, the Arikaras were stupid, cowardly, and unable to offer much resistance, apart from occasionally assassinating an isolated Sioux, as happened when Kakawita treacherously killed the brother of Black Bull, a Bois Brûlé who was visiting him after concluding a treaty. Plagued by vanity, indolence, and self-pity, the Arikaras most often proved, according to Tabeau, incapable of taking his advice to regain their dignity.

In August 1804, Tabeau's interpreter Joseph Gravelines also upbraided the Arikaras on their poor performance as hunters and trappers. The most rebellious of them responded by blaming the French Canadians for displaying tantalizing commodities that they could not afford. Pocosse, otherwise *La Paille* [the straw] inveighed against Tabeau and Gravelines, pressing them to go back to their Mandan friends, which would have permitted the looting of the store in their absence.

Tabeau's protection was naturally appreciated on several occasions by French Canadians, as shown in the case of Joseph Garreau. He was a Métis voyageur with the North West Company. His father had married a captive Dakota girl after buying her from the Ojibwas. In 1795 Joseph went up the Assiniboine River to trade in the Rivière La Souris with the Assiniboines, Hidatsas, Crees, and some Mandans and Blackfeet who ventured into the region. On his way back he stayed in the lodge of Foutreau, a squaw man whose daughter he coveted. Garreau gave him a one-gallon keg of rum. When the single keg was not enough to get Foutreau's daughter, as he had expected, he pierced the keg of spirits he had and gave it, plus six large knives, to the Indians. Thanks to Foutreau's son-in-law, Garreau made a narrow escape when dead-drunk inmates of the lodge became aggressive. Known as a libertine in Saint Louis, Joseph Garreau had escaped from creditors and settled with the Arikaras. But having grown averse to him, the tribe prevented him from trading with Tabeau and Garreau had to return articles he had bartered for fear they should be stolen.[16]

As death threats proliferated, Tabeau decided to summon an assembly and employ Garreau as an interpreter. He displayed gunpowder, balls, knives, and hardware to be bargained at a reasonable price but also explained that he had run out of supplies because he gave gifts but got nothing in return. Tabeau closed his speech by suggesting that the change of government in Saint Louis would be in their favor if they behaved well. Kakawissassa, the chief of the village, backed him up, stressing the fact that they had the exclusive privilege of trading with Tabeau. [17]

Since life with the Arikaras had nothing to offer in the winter months, Tabeau was depressed by the end of February 1805. He ought to have been relieved in March by another trader but as no one turned up he was again under fire. Kakawissassa's demands became more and more threatening. He threw a buffalo robe at him and required the price of two. Tabeau understood more from his glance than through ceremonious speech. This was only the beginning of a conspiracy intended to kill Tabeau as Garreau told him, being able to understand covert messages in the Arikara language.

Tired of native harassment and insults, Tabeau found refuge in a separate section of Kakawita's lodge, behind a partition of upright stakes where he no longer shared his food with the dozen inmates. By the spring he loathed his surroundings and hoped future traders would at last realize that they had to build a house of their own to achieve their independence. Since Tabeau was no squaw man or Métis, he deplored Loisel's negligence of his agents' well being. He could have let him settle in the fort, instead of living in a lodge, being deprived of the sight of the sun and wallowing in the dirt. The rain leaked through the roof made of willowmats covered with a layer of straw. As time passed Tabeau's abhorrence was vented through his castigation of the "inhuman monsters" who reduced women to slavery. The squaws were conscious of their bondage and often told him that if enough whites came, the Arikaras would no longer have women.[32] To prop up his argument against the area, Tabeau pointed to frequent raids of the Crows as happened on June 15, 1804, when six women and their children were captured and their husbands killed. Tabeau's companions were then with Jean Vallé making pirogues a few miles away. They would have been killed if the Crows had not promptly retreated after the onslaught.[18] This new mishap made Tabeau determined to leave with no intention of return. The French Canadian's adventure in the West came to a close when Lewis and Clark arrived in the cause of freedom.

Several French Canadians connected with the Lewis and Clark Expedition crossed Tabeau's path. François Rivet was born near Montreal in 1757. He came to the Mississippi Valley at an early age and engaged in hunting and trading in Upper Louisiana for the North West Company. He was hired by Lewis and Clark as an engagé for the first leg of the voyage. With Malboeuf and Deschamps he was discharged at Fort Mandan. They built a hut and remained there under the protection of the expedition during the winter of 1804–1805.[19]

On October 18, 1804, Lewis and Clark came to the mouth of the Cannon Ball River. They met Philippe Degie and Joseph Grenier who were descending the Missouri in a canoe.[20] Both were employed by Gravelines and they had had their traps, furs, and other articles stolen by Mandan warriors, despite the peace treaty signed by local tribes. Degie and Grenier turned back and followed the expedition with the expectation of obtaining redress. Upon the captains' insistence the Mandans eventually returned the stolen goods, except for the beaver skins that had already been traded.

It seems possible that Francis Fleury dit Grenier was the hunter met by the Corps of Discovery. There was, however, a Joseph Grenier of the parish of Pointe au Tremblay, who stayed at Fort Mandan at different times during the winter of 1804–5. [20] Although no longer a member of the Corps, Rivet was unwittingly helpful to Lewis and Clark in the fall, during a period of mounting tension in November. Lewis had just returned from the Hidatsa villages with two chiefs. He wanted to convince them of his peaceful intentions after the Mandans had told them how the expedition intended to join the Sioux and blockade the Mandan villages for the winter. Lewis and Clark discovered that two North West Company traders, François Larocque and Baptiste LaFrance, had, in fact, spread the rumor and alarmed the Mandans to discredit the Americans. The captains organized a meeting with the Indians on November 27. It was a cheerful gathering with dances in the evening. Rivet had gained some celebrity for his histrionics and was well-known for his capers. He danced on his head and upside down on his hands that night. The Hidatsa and Mandan chiefs were delighted at the fun and had a better impression of the Americans.

In the spring of 1805, Rivet and Degie built a canoe of their own and on April 7, 1805, they accompanied Warfington's return party to Saint Louis as far as the Arikara villages. Gravelines was the pilot of the keelboat and among the passengers were Tabeau, La Jeunesse, Deschamps, Primeau, and Malboeuf.

Rivet and Grenier spent most of their time in the following months between Mandan and Arikara villages. On August 21, 1806 Lewis and Clark met them south of the mouth of the Cannon Ball River. Rivet and Grenier told them they were going to the Mandans for their traps. They added that seven hundred Sioux had passed the Arikara country on their way to war with the Mandans and the Hidatsas. Running short on powder and lead, the two trappers were grateful to receive a horn of powder and some balls from the expedition. Lewis and Clark also learned from them that the Arikara chief had died on his return journey from Washington.

Rivet went west again after the expedition, as far as the upper Columbia River country a few years later. In 1810, he was sent to the Flathead country by Manuel Lisa and stayed there until 1824 as trapper and interpreter. He later worked there for the North West Company and the Hudson's Bay Company at Fort Colville. He ended up in the Willamette Valley, Oregon, where he was a blacksmith. He died in September 1852.[21]

Tabeau's debunking of the Noble Savage

Tabeau's observations of Indian life were a dependable source of information for Lewis and Clark. He felt that, except for spreading venereal diseases, the natives had so far enjoyed good health in the Upper Missouri and Dakota regions. Former farmers, the Cheyennes had turned nomads and wandered away from their Missouri abodes to escape persecutions from the Sioux. They had also suffered heavy losses in their fights with the Crows [Corbeaux], the best warriors in the north according to Charles Mckenzie.[22] In the long run they had been able to oppose the aggressiveness of their age-old enemies. The Cheyennes were now supplied with corn, pumpkins, and tobacco by the Arikaras in exchange for buffalo meat and robes.

Tabeau knew how to comply with Indian protocol. Whenever a stranger wished to trade peacefully he was not expected to raise the least doubt on the way business was conducted. When Cheyenne and Sioux traders came to the Arikara villages, they did not usually antagonize white residents and ignored the differences between their nationalities. Their inclination to worship the white man had to be encouraged, according to Tabeau, who warned newcomers against familiarity. Should they step down from their superior status, they shattered Indian beliefs in their supernatural powers.

Tabeau's tendency to lend his views a historical perspective even allowed him to describe the ups and downs of Indian-white relations in rhetorical terms. His own version of mythology in the American West was compulsive. After the first meeting had opened a Golden Age, then came the Iron Age of disillusion when the natives gained a clearer insight into the white man's motivation. The Brass Age was

the mature period when common experience and conciliatory attitudes smoothed out difficulties, making each indispensable to the
other. Referring to the yearly rendezvous in the Black Hills, Tabeau
also drew attention to the sign language used by tribes. The codified
gestures enabled the participants to communicate with each other
to make up for the disparity of idioms west of the Mississippi. Incidentally, it was not until they reached the Shoshones on the Great
Divide that Lewis and Clark mentioned the use of sign language,
although George Drouillard had long been an expert at it. Tabeau
made it clear in his comments that though unintelligible to the lay-
man those gesticulations could be meaningful with even a short
training period. Such a broad picture of the annual rendezvous on
Sioux hallowed grounds was obviously useful to the captains who
could figure out ahead of time the intricacies of Indian relations
over a territory extending from the Platte to the Yellowstone. Tabeau's own denominations differed from the records of native nations in the journals of the expedition, but he had reliable
geopolitical views emphasizing the causes of conflict between the
Canninanbiches (Arapahao), the Cayowa (Kiowa), the Nimonssines
(Comanches), the Ski-hi-tanes (Snakes) and the Pelés (Paloos).[23]
They all went as far south as Santa Fe to get horses from the Spaniards who did not care much about furs. They rather welcomed ante-
lope skins and moccasins but offered only cheap hardware in
exchange. Tabeau was ready to trust Lewis and Clark for their evaluation of the peaceful Mandans, aware as he was that the Arikaras
were in the habits of disparaging their neighbors. When calling the
Mandans cowards Kakawita's people appeared superior in their own
eyes and avenged themselves on the evils inflicted by the scornful
Sioux. Whether Tabeau's information was trustworthy or not when
Lewis and Clark met him is a moot point. Alexander Henry had previously noted their barbarous behavior to the whites and their atavis-
tic lasciviousness. Tabeau's superior knowledge of the region
resulted in fine distinctions between nations, which was beyond the
grasps of transient observers. Even though Tabeau had never traveled further west to the Black Feet country, he had come across
many tribes at the rendezvous with the Mandans where they traded
horses for rifles and ammunition. Participants in those annual meetings were the Gros Ventres of the Prairie, mostly farmers who lived
west of the Assiniboines and east of the Black Feet, almost two hundred miles from the Arikaras, and shared their language with the
Crows south of them. The latter were nomads who roamed along
the tributaries of the Yellowstone where they usually met the Shoshones. The Assiniboines, the Flatheads, and the Pawnees hunted as

far as the Upper Missouri and the Yellowstone. They supplied the best peltries to the North West and Hudson's Bay Companies. Tabeau was therefore in a privileged position to remind Lewis and Clark that their headquarters among the Mandans was the crossroads for Indian crowds paddling down the Missouri from the Yellowstone.

Sixteen hundred Indians gathered at the rendezvous of August 1804. The preceding fall, Loisel had received encouraging news from the Cheyennes at Cedar Island. But the promise to send their people to the Fork, the Arikara, and Mandan villages with peltries was kept by none of the nations present. As nomads they did not stay long enough at locations where beaver was abundant, nor were they good trappers. Tabeau blamed their failure on slovenly habits. Besides, the most destitute tribes were merely interested in iron tools, still using bows and arrows when hunting buffalo or bears. He saw the future of the fur trade near the sources of the Missouri just east of the Great Divide. He thought a company could make a fortune if the government of the United States freed the trade from the shackles of the Spanish authorities. The merchandise to be traded would be transported from Europe to New Orleans then shipped up the Mississippi and the Missouri. The North West Company and the Hudson's Bay Company would no longer retain their monopoly. Tabeau further suggested that an outpost built in the Mandan country would attract at least twenty nations from the west and induce the Arikaras to join efforts with them. The same venture on the Yellowstone would also spare the Crows and the Shoshones the hazards of transportation over long distances. For Tabeau, detachments had to be stationed near villages where white men stayed with natives. If commerce was the basis of civilization, Indians would have to be instructed in making iron traps to improve their output of beaver skins. War parties often followed each other in periods of conflicts between tribes and no white man was spared in case of attacks. For instance, Jacques d'Eglise had received information on the Mandans from Ménard, who had lived thirty years among the Mandans before he was murdered by the Assiniboines whom he also knew well. [24]

Tabeau was in favor of attracting the Yankton Sioux to the Fork, owing to the low price and good quality of buffalo and beaver skins. The only impediment was the cost of merchandise to be offered by the whites. Tabeau was equally concerned by their meanness toward the natives. The "Rule for the Illinois Trade" enacted by the Spanish colonial Government on October 15, 1793 in Saint Louis was too often ignored by traders who exploited Indian credulity, debauched their women, and incited drunkenness.[25] Tabeau went as far as advocating a law requiring both traders and engagés to pledge to respect native dignity. He perceptibly discriminated between articles to exchange with reference to the various demands of tribes. Glass beads, brass wire, hardware, and framed mirrors were fit items for fox skins, knives, and spears for buffalo robes.

The Arikaras disliked firewater and admonished anyone for providing them with any alcoholic beverage. To those who offered them liquor they replied that since the whites wished to laugh at their expense, they ought to pay them for their antics once they were intoxicated. However, Tabeau recognized that the Assiniboines did not have such qualms about drinking and were more easily swindled. Living through the age of the Noble Savage, Loisel's so-called man of affairs held that poetic license had distorted the figure of the Arikara and Sioux braves. Such idealized pictures stood in sharp contrast to reality. Did instinctive discrimination blur firsthand experience to produce stereotypes? Tabeau's unmitigated denunciation of Tetons was corroborated by Lewis himself who held them as the vilest miscreants of the savage race. Patrick Gass found the Mandans great pilferers, but like Lewis thought Arikara people clever, active, and humane. They had a great reputation as runners and could walk hundreds of miles in any season. But this did not impress Tabeau who upbraided them as stupid, superstitious, and treacherous, but always cowardly when faced with men of equal strength. He shared Lewis's judgment on their slovenliness and, as a libertine, became sarcastic when evoking their penchant for elaborate costumes. A husband had once decked himself out in a Parisian garb that the Ursuline nuns had presented to his bride and would strut pompously about, unaware of the ridicule in the eyes of a French observer. A notorious womanizer, Tabeau confessed to no personal sexual involvement in the communities. In seemingly objective terms he repeatedly pointed to a native woman's freedom insofar as her husband stood witness to adultery. He felt dishonored only when adulterous sex was concealed from him. He would then kill his wife on the slightest suspicion. If the sin was less he could scalp her, mutilate her arms or cut her shoulder blade with a knife. On the other hand, he was ready to prostitute her for a small reward. Fornication with a white man was more easily accepted, for the Indian male did not see him as a rival. But it was mainly the nature and quality of the gifts that determined if a squaw would have sex with the whites. Since a woman was bought her male owner was welcome to lend her. Tabeau recalled an episode of his life among the Arikaras, when a husband killed his wife, dismembered her, and gave her to the Frenchman who had seduced her because he disapproved of the secret relationship. The clan system also made it advisable for a young husband to sleep with his bride's sisters. Promiscuity took a heavy toll among tribes. Venereal diseases ravaged the tribe savagely, all the more so since Indians did not use purgative roots.

To Tabeau, the medicine man was a charlatan, more foolish than his patient and the dupe of his professed knowledge. If a disease persisted after his incantations he was convinced or at least feigned to be convinced that sorcery opposed his cure of magic feathers and other paraphernalia. The shaman would also apply his mouth to the skin and draw from the body of the sick person all kinds of shells, and pieces of horn, which he declared were the source of the evil. Tabeau thought that all the medicine men were not stupid enough to believe in this nonsense. His host Kakawita he gleefully labeled a trickster, who prided himself on scattering epidemics with a powder from the head of a woodpecker. Magic entered into the strategy of the Arikaras who wanted to get rid of engagés around Tabeau. Once they took offense at the departure of one of them while smoking. Anyone could accuse an isolated French Canadian of transgression when he was unfamiliar with rituals. Although far removed from his familiar surroundings, Tabeau was still indebted to the legacy of the Enlightenment in his critique of Indian religion. He never marveled at visions and prophecies, deeming irrational and obscurantist what nascent romanticism extolled. When warriors inflicted torture on themselves to ward off terror, he never lapsed into a lyrical flow of primitivistic emotions. His ethnological comments were derived from everyday life.[26] They might stem from a smug sense of superiority but rarely distorted scenes of native celebrations. In the winter of 1804–5, the Corps of Discovery was confronted with the Buffalo Dance in the Mandan village. The ritual exemplified the significance of the bison in native culture, especially white buffalo skin which was worth ten horses. Superstitions were numerous regarding the means of attracting cows, and blame for failing to attract them was laid on the wickedness of tribes, internecine conflicts, and sometimes even the presence of whites. Before the celebration, buffalo heads were set up around the camp to attract a cow. In what Tabeau called a senseless ceremony old men assembled in the medicine lodge and announced that she was close by. Lewis and Clark witnessed the performance, waiting for the sacrifices the braves were expected to make in her honor. They had already been instructed by Jusseaume in native sexual ritualism. Tabeau said that the men brought their wives to the altar of Paphos, evoking a nature worship of the Phoenician Astarte.[27] The women in a row wore a single garment. The nude old men touched them while mimicking the buffalo, bellowing, pawing the earth, and charging like the bull chasing a heifer. The women then came to the medicine lodge to perfume themselves with an odoriferous herb without observing decency. Afterwards, they walked in front of young men seated in a row. Each husband put a stick in the hand of one he had singled out. When the wife passed before the elected paramour, she seized the red-painted stick she had identified and dragged the young man out of the lodge. Many couples formed and scattered in the prairie while the old men kept at a distance, expressing their sorrowful frustration. The ceremony lasted all night as partners were swapped at each new parade. The husband who had made the selections hastened to show how proud and grateful he was about the young man's performance. Usually the ceremony lasted up to fifteen days but the Mandans rejoiced that the buffalo herds had arrived three days after the Lewis and Clark Expedition participated in the rituals. The men of the Corps of Discovery had been judged exceptionally instrumental in the enterprise owing to their zeal to please husbands. Among the members of the party, York was transfigured into a demigod because in the eyes of the Arikara and Mandans he looked, spoke, and acted like a bear.[28]

Tabeau's uncompromising evaluation of native weaknesses stressed the credulity of savages. He acknowledged that cunning was often concealed under the garb of naïveté. His thinking preceded Auguste Comte's positivism, by a few decades. In Comte's history of ideas superstition belonged to a primitive state that was followed by the era of ideas and concepts verified by experience. Tabeau deemed absurd whatever Indian belief had no ground in everyday life. Yet he was always tempted to spin yarns about the most outlandish interpretations of the universe by the Arikaras. One day Kakawita, whom he held as one of the most perceptive of them, told him in earnest that, after Lewis and Clark had left the area, the expedition had encountered insuperable obstacles. The Arikara chief had visions of fantastic creatures surrounding the captains. One was without a mouth and was nourished only by breathing the smoke of the meat through his nose. The creature gained weight in the spring and fall by its victories over the swans and bustards that were stubbornly at war with it. The other vision was about a troop of Amazons who killed their male children, pulverized their genitals, and conceived again by the injection of the powder. When born, the girls were put in a cradle and hung on a tree where the air nourished them. Kakawita's supernatural visions bore witness to the lasting impression produced on the natives by the presence of the captains at Fort Mandan. Tabeau thus casually acknowledged the absence of a

Noble Savage in the West. He also recalled that the Arikaras had first deified the French who, unhappily, made them lose their illusions by their conduct. Thus the former rulers had passed from one extreme to the other and were now "nothing in their eyes."[29]

Was Tabeau carried off by his own phraseology? His anecdote verged on the tall tale as the narrator claims to borrow a story from Kakawita whose mythopoetic imagination could hardly cross over to the culture of ancient Greece to follow the paths of the Amazons. Probably more useful to Lewis and Clark was the intelligence on objects of worship conveyed by Tabeau. Since the first settlements of New France, Native Americans had transmuted manufactured products from Europe into magic artifacts. The journals of the Voyage of Discovery record that Indian communities celebrated the keelboat with offerings and sacrifices. Aside from sundry vehicles, Tabeau himself listed the objects considered as great medicine, namely quadrants and magnets. The supernatural power attributed to the whites could also be detrimental, as happened to Tabeau and his engagés when staying with the Bois Brûlés. It was then rumored that the Frenchmen had in a casket the spirit of a medicine man named Bateur de Chaudière who had been killed by the natives, and whose limbs had been scattered on the prairie a decade before.[30] The deceased had terrorized his community and asked his mother to dismember him after his death, if he was murdered, and throw his limbs into the Missouri. He expected his body to come together again in Illinois. He would then return to wreak vengeance on his assassins. But the mother had found the task too harrowing to be fulfilled. The chiefs of the village kept harassing Tabeau to force him to admit that he was under the spell of Bateur. A Bois Brûlé named Tongue of the Hind who had lost two sons within a short period of time ascribed their death to the witchcraft of two French hunters who had left some time before because he had stolen their property. The father had entrusted a fellow man with the bow and arrows of his eldest son, who was then allegedly followed by a French shade. Tabeau learned that the Indian wanted to blackmail him, but he remained firm and eventually the cause of the sons' death was discovered. Tabeau also mentioned that along the Missouri, no Indian tribe enjoyed perfect security as war was necessary to solve conflicts. A young man who had never fought could claim no right to answer the insults of a seasoned warrior. However sensible he might be, a father could not see his son in such a shameful position and he encouraged him to steal horses even at the risk of reprisals. Father and son always had in mind that heroic deeds gave access to privileges. War parties were generally small to ambush the enemy.

The French had long been used to this kind of guerrilla warfare. No doubt Lewis and Clark remembered the surprise attacks against Braddock and Washington during the French and Indian War. When a warrior was missing the leader or partisan was held responsible since the loss of a fighter could further endanger an already decimated community. Prisoners were held in slavery to substitute for missing hands. Tabeau remarked that in his time captives were no longer burnt alive but only jeered at before they were sent to a lodge of grace where those in power disposed of them. One day, a funeral, otherwise a ceremony for assuaging grief, was attended by Loisel, Dorion, and Tabeau, which was a unusual honor.[31] The gathering in a lodge was composed of a priest, the relatives of the dead and guests Accompanied by chants and music, the priest addressed the gods and the deceased whose clothes and hair were distributed among his family. Eating and smoking were also part of the ritual. Those last details in Tabeau's account reveal that the Frenchman retained the scathing, provocative wit of his ancestors. His narrative technique seems to reverse the angle of vision that the journals of the expedition provide. Undoubtedly too self-conscious, analytical, and skeptical, Tabeau had become unfit for epic adventures out West. He was a French Canadian from Montreal who had settled at Cahokia, then taken the oath of loyalty to the United States government in 1785 and finally worked for a fur company under Spanish control.[32] He certainly exemplified the paradoxes of shifting identities when he used the term "French" for himself.

FRENCH DOUBLE TROUBLE FROM NORTH AND SOUTH

Born at L'Assomption, Quebec, in 1784 François Antoine Larocque went to school in Montreal and learned English in the United States after 1792. His father was a merchant and a politician. At the age of eighteen François was hired in 1801 by the XY Fur Company and sent to the Assiniboine region.[33] He left Canada for the West in April 1801 and arrived at Grand Portage in June. In 1802 he entered Simon McTavish's North West Company. Many traders considered McTavish arrogant and tyrannical, and he was disliked by the majority of his wintering partners who called him the Premier, or Marquis. He was also known for appointing his relatives and friends to key positions. Charles Chaboillez became superintendent of the Métis Red River settlement for the North West Company in 1804. He still liked to tour the country and winter among Indians. His Métis daughter Marguerite married McTavish in his old age. To supply goods to traders and above all protect the interests of the company, Chaboillez sent Larocque, interpreter Jean-Baptiste LaFrance, Charles McKenzie, and four voyageurs to the Missouri when Lewis and Clark were wintering with the Mandans.[34] The Louisiana Purchase had opened dark perspectives on the Canadian fur trade in the border regions. It was therefore necessary for the North West Company to maintain a presence in the Upper Missouri. The party left discreetly on November 11, 1804, not telling the Assiniboine Indians who were at war with Southern tribes. After fifteen days they reached the "Mississsouri," in McKenzie's own words. Upon arriving at the Mandan camp, they received help from Lewis and Clark whose men protected their horses and repaired their harnesses. Clark was particularly warm. Lewis's anti-British sentiment made contacts less easy. Larocque had known about the American expedition to explore the Pacific in the spring. He now learned how the Corps of Discovery was dealing with the Mandans, especially their repeated counciling. The Hidatsas told him that the captains gave out presents in return for their obedience to their Great Father in Washington. Larocque was pleased to hear that they refused such gifts because they were inferior to those of the Mandans. It was, of course, a covert invitation to the North West Company to be generous with them. Fearing a conspiracy, Lewis decided to investigate. He went to the Hidatsas with a party and soon discovered that their chief, Horned Weasel, refused to receive him, not having been officially notified about the visit. The Hidatsas whom Lewis met paid lip service to his offers. Later, Lewis accused LaFrance of speaking unfavorably of their intentions and warned Larocque against giving medals, flags, and liquor to the Mandans thinking to further the interests of the company. However, the French Canadian visitors were told that the trade would be as free to foreigners as to Americans, but the boundary with Canada passed the Red River between the entrance of the Assiniboine and Lake Winnipeg and no permanent British establishment would be allowed on the Missouri.[35]

On November 25th Larocque met Lewis with Jusseaume and Charbonneau and spoke to them for a quarter of an hour. They were friendly and invited him to their homes.[36] He even settled with Jusseaume for some skins. Lewis showed his goodwill by letting Charbonneau interpret for the North Company emissaries. Yet they were deceptively amiable. They welcomed the news from the Mandans that the Americans often fired their rifles for drilling and did not give ammunition to the natives. The Hidatsa chiefs told them that the white warriors would easily be defeated on the Great Plains, just like the Loup enemies. They thought that, isolated as they would be, Lewis and Clark ran great dangers from the Sioux. Larocque himself believed that, whatever the risks, the prospects were better for Indian nomads relying on the buffalo for a living, than the poverty-stricken Arikaras and Mandan, but it was for the North West Company to decide. Larocque offered to accompany the captains on their way west from Fort Mandan but they declined the offer. When he was back in Montreal, his report must have been well received since he was commissioned to return to the Mandans with Charles McKenzie in February 1805. The French Canadians were at the Indian rendezvous with their pack train of goods. When the Mandans learned from Larocque that he was planning to go west after the trading was done, they warned him that, over there, the tribes would become dangerous if they obtained more guns. Pierre Ménard, who had stayed with the Hidatsas for several years, had been not only waylaid, robbed of his arms and clothing, but also deprived of his two captive women and nine horses. Larocque's journal ends abruptly on February 28. He leaves no record of his activities for the next three and one-half months. His next account began on June 2, 1805.[37] He was then on his way to the Missouri, having in essence received orders from Chaboillez to visit the Rocky Mountains and evaluate the beaver population. The account is recorded in his Yellowstone journal. By mid-June 1805, when Lewis and Clark were camped in the red bluff region of the Missouri near Portage Creek in the mountainous Indian country, two thousand Snakes, Crows, and Hidatsas were gathered nearby at their annual rendezvous. Some of the Hidatsas had robbed and killed whites and were celebrating their triumphant campaigns. Larocque and Mackenzie had come at the invitation of Le Borgne, the Hidatsa chief, to meet Red Calf, his adopted son. The latter spoke favorably of the North West Company and disparaged the Lewis and Clark expedition that Crows and Blackfeet had seen pass by. Larocque had a large collection of gifts, including a Canadian flag he gave to Red Calf. As he was waiting for Crows to guide them to the Rockies, Mackenzie accepted beaver furs from them though they were damaged. Both Hidatsas and Crows were hostile to Larocque's plan to meet Rocky Mountain Indians farther west. They became so aggressive that Le Borgne had to protect his white guests.[38] The Indians' deep-rooted motivation was the desire to have the North West Company keep exclusive trade agreements with the tribes along the Missouri and avoid extensive armed conflicts. But the young Canadian was determined to reach the Powder River, which was more promising with its many beaver dams, grizzly bears, and buffaloes. He and his party traveled with some Crows on horseback. His exploration lasted till early October. Up the Powder River he went to the Big Horn Mountains and skirted the Black Hills. In September, ten months before Clark, he reached the Yellowstone River, which he followed to its mouth, a site that Lewis and Clark had left in early spring, six months before, bound for the Great Falls. On his way, Larocque met a party of Arapaho Gros Ventres who had traded with the Hudson's Bay Company the winter before. As Larocque and Mackenzie were approaching the big Hidatsa camp on the Knife River, they heard that fourteen small boats of American traders were below the Five Villages. It was one of the first waves of the westward movement up the Missouri.[39]

Larocque's project actually misfired because he had overrated his capacity to rival Lewis and Clark. He lacked curiosity and writing skill. As DeVoto puts it, he thus missed or forgot to record the kind of item that would have taken pages in the journals of the Lewis and Clark expedition.[40] Erratic errands in the West by an inexperienced young man from Quebec could not match the magnitude of Jefferson's vision and the meticulous preparation of the Corps of Discovery.

On December 20, 1803, upon Jefferson's request, James Wilkinson shared with the first American governor of Louisiana the honor of taking possession of the new territory. By early March, Wilkinson submitted to Spanish authorities a secret report suggesting how they could protect their colonies in "El Norte" from American encroachment. [41] He revealed the objectives of the Lewis and Clark expedition to the Spanish colonial governor the Marquis of Casa Calvo. The regional governor of New Mexico, Fernando de Chacon, and Nimesio Salcedo, the commander in chief of the provinces of the Southwest (based in Chihuahua), organized three raids to intercept the expedition. Calvo waited a month before sending a message to Madrid via Pedro Cevallos, commandant general of the interior provinces, making it clear that the Americans had entered Spanish territory.[42] On behalf of His Catholic Majesty, New Spain formally denied that the area along the Missouri belonged to the United States. To capture "capitan Mery," Pierre Vial, a Frenchman from Lyon, otherwise known as Pedro Vial, was appointed mastermind of the operation. Vial was on the Missouri River before the Revolutionary War but he first appeared actively on the scene in the Southwest in 1786 to open a trail between San Antonio and Santa Fe.[43] He had followed the Red River and lived with the Comanches for twenty years before he made a total journey of 2,377 miles in 1788–89. In 1792 he had discovered a way from Santa Fe to San Luis de Illinueces, the future Santa Fe trail. He had been captured by a Kansas war party, tortured and held naked for six weeks. Vial would have been slaughtered had he not been recognized by a warrior as a friend in previous years. The French explorer/guide had acquired extensive knowledge of the uppermost Missouri before. He prided himself on being able to cover the distance between Santa Fe and Saint Louis in twenty-five days, which made the Spaniards aware of the proximity of the American presence. Sent to make peace with the Pawnees in 1795, Vial met traders who were only ten days from Saint Louis by canoe.[44] Spain thus realized that the desert was no longer a barrier against foreign penetration. In 1797 he sought refuge in Upper Louisiana because of the repressive measures taken against the inhabitants of French origin as a result of the threats of the French Revolution to European monarchies.[45] He then lived at Portage des Sioux, north of Saint Louis. He was back to Santa Fe in 1803 after an abortive attempt to exploit lead mines around Sainte Geneviève where he was in close contact with François Vallé.

Salcedo ordered Chacon to capture "capitan Mery" after receiving instructions from Salcedo only a week before Lewis and Clark departed from Saint Charles.[46] June and July passed before Vial left from Santa Fe with a column of soldiers on August 1, 1804. A dozen inhabitants of Taos joined them as well as two dozen Indians. The company followed the Platte River to a Pawnee village in Nebraska. They learned from French squaw men that Americans had taken over in Saint Louis. Along the Missouri, Indian chiefs had been induced to surrender medals and patents in their possession given by the Spanish government. French traders told them that the American expedition had reached the mouth of the Niobrarra, between present-day Nebraska and South Dakota, on September 4. It was obviously too late to catch up with Lewis and Clark who were now well upriver. When back in Santa Fe, Vial informed Chacon that Americans had sent an expedition to attract to their side all the heathen nations they might encounter. The Spanish officials then hurried to lavish gifts on the Pawnees to ensure their allegiance. It was around this time that Loisel also proved a double dealer, first providing Lewis with valuable information but then, upon his arrival in Saint Louis, drafting his memorial to Dehault-Delassus.

In 1805, Chacon was replaced as governor by Joaquin del Real Alencaster. With the advance of Lewis and Clark toward the south bend of the Missouri, it became even more apparent that its tributaries, including the Platte, were close to the sources of the Colorado and the Rio Grande. Salcedo wanted to infuse the Arapahos, Pawnees, and Utes with a horror of the British and Americans. He counted on an Indian upheaval when the expedition returned to

Saint Louis. Vial was only second in command of a party led by a man named Jarvet to stir up Indian hostility. The Pawnee were strangely absent from such preparations. Vial was ordered to infiltrate tribes near the Missouri and examine the progress of the Corps of Discovery. A long-term strategy consisted of preparing them to ambush the Corps of Discovery on their return from the Pacific, and robbing them of their material and documents. Salcedo ordered from Mexico City two dozen silver medals bearing royal portraits on one side. Vial's party left from Santa Fe on October 14, 1805 with forty-eight soldiers, traders Baptiste Lalande and Laurent Durocher, and three other French coureurs des bois. Meanwhile French-speaking secret agents were sent to spy on the Saint Charles community. Fifty militiamen were seconded to join the column at Taos. But on November 5 they were attacked by Loup Pawnees, lost their baggage, and had to turn back. Alencaster failed to rally the Kiowas and the Comanches, and enlisted the Cheyennes to resist American intrusion. He also learned from his emissary Juan Lucero north of Taos that the mercenary Frenchmen under Vial's command had disparaged Spanish chances of competing with the Americans. To make matters worse they claimed that "Captain Meri" paid interpreters and guides twice as much as the Spanish government. While the Corps of Discovery was spending the winter on the Pacific shore, the Spanish governor recommended the use of interpreters to live among friendly tribes, build a fort on the Arkansas River as suggested by Vial, and renew alliances with the Pawnees.[47] In April 1806 it was decided to outfit a third of three hundred men expedition to be led north by Vial, but within a month militiamen and Indians had deserted. Salcedo had never agreed on the project. Most deserters were brought to trial and Vial's reputation as a trailblazer did not survive the disaster.[48]

Conclusion

IN NEW FRANCE, IT HAD BEEN THE LIFELONG DREAM OF MANY ARISTOCRATS to become the overlords of admiring, faithful, and permissive savages, far removed from the vulgar herd of dull bourgeois and unruly peasants in the home country. On the other hand, disgruntled exiles dreamed of emulating the seigneurs by holding a fief among native tribes. Whether noble or not the Indians never fully conformed to such wishful thinking. The hatred of their British rivals in the new world could temporarily reconcile conflicting aims and foster union in adversity among the migrants, pushed or pulled to New France. But the seeds of destruction were within French society at home and abroad. The Frenchman often considered himself as a temporary resident, who always kept in mind the possibility of returning home, especially if he was a bachelor. Many officers hoped to receive a seigneurie when back from military campaigns overseas; administrators longed for a peaceful retirement on their estates in Anjou or Normandy. It did not take a generation for the French Canadian settlers to feel estranged from the mother country, sometimes betrayed by the government. Explorers, Jesuits, and coureurs des bois were adventurers, prompted by the call of the wild, by their spirituality, or by their hedonistic leanings. Most French colonists had little in common with the gritty English yeoman. In Acadia, the salt meadows reminded the farmer of the Norman coast. Along the Illinois the transplanted Canadian strove to recapture the mood of the Loire Valley hamlets.

In February 1784 Benjamin Franklin published "Information to Those Who Would Remove to America" at Passy. It was intended for noblemen who expected much from expatriation. The American ambassador discouraged office seekers who thought their ranks and titles would naturally qualify them for prestigious positions. "A mere man of Quality," he said, "will be despised and disregarded." It must have seemed a cruel reminder to the few retired dignitaries of Canada and Louisiana still alive in Douce France. On the other hand, Franklin stated that a poor man could have his own property if he worked hard. America was no Pays de Cocagne where "the fowls fly about ready roasted."[1] But the French reader also learned from Franklin that the ignorance of every gainful skill compelled the youth to become soldiers, servants, or thieves, which was roughly what happened in feudal New France.

At the turn of the nineteenth century, anti-American rearguard action in the post-colonial environment had become a losing battle. Yet, confronted with the acquisitive spirit of the American pioneers, the descendants of New France still recalled pictures of pastoral bliss in Illinois or icons of daredevil explorers in the wilderness. Even the most remote French coureurs des bois had heard about the "Grand Siècle" in the decades before, although the images of the Versailles Palace were blurred in transatlantic memories. Nostalgia also affected the bourgeois communities of New Orleans and Saint Louis when the United States government enforced the prohibition of whiskey in Indian trade. Some of the forts in Upper Missouri far from the reach of government inspection had their own stills and produced alcohol in volume. Franco-American moonshining was definitely in operation. The exiled French Canadians still had a sense of belonging to an idealized belle province but Native Americans sometimes gave the fur traders difficulty. By 1810 the upriver trip on the Missouri was dangerous, for the Arikaras wanted to control all passage upstream and imposed a toll on transit. As early as 1802 Congress had forbidden whites to trap in Indian lands and made it mandatory to get a license for bartering.[2]

Although the West was changing, the French in the Mississippi Valley still worked and lived as if in the remote past, unmindful of the American settlers engulfing the lands around them. The French lacked the bustle and energy of the small-propertied frontiersmen, and were considered as suspect hedonists by sneering Americans who resented their levity. Mobility was uncommon among the former Canadian colonists who preferred to gather around churches and remained clannish. They tilled long fields as in manorial France while keeping farm implements that were those of their ancestors. If French methods were labeled inadequate for the painstaking tasks relevant to a frontier environment, at least the coureurs des bois had shown the way to the new mountainmen now scattered throughout the Rockies. Jeremiah Johnson and Jedediah Smith owed something to Drouillard and Jusseaume. In *Letters from an American Farmer*, Crèvecoeur's outlook epitomized many of the contradictions of New France. Born into French aristocracy, he left Normandy for Canada at the outbreak of the Seven Years' War. He served as a militiaman for the French. Then he went to New York and assumed a new identity: Michel-Guillaume-Jean became J. Hector St. John. He traveled and reached the Great Lakes, was adopted by the Oneidas as Cahio-Harra. He became a naturalized citizen of New York, got married, and settled down to farm in the Hudson Valley. He went to France and returned at the end of the War of Independence to find his farm burned by Indians, his wife dead, and his children gone. He was appointed consul by Louis XVI and belonged to the American Philosophical Society. Crèvecoeur was read by the Abbé Raynal and Jefferson.[3] He was both fascinated and repulsed by frontiersmen. He thought they had moved westward by necessity, most of them being degenerate, no better than carnivorous animals. Hunting made them derelicts, half-civilized, half-savage. The French American was a Janus figure, and Crèvecoeur was at pains to discover a new man in him.

Constantin-François de Chasseboeuf, Count of Volney was another French eyewitness observer of the West in the late eighteenth century. A member of the Convention, he had been jailed during the Terror in 1793. He regained power under the Thermidor Revolution and as an emissary of the government went to the United States in 1795. He was already acquainted with Jefferson, who gave him letters of recommendation. In Ohio he met a colony of five hundred émigrés who had turned to agriculture after decades of city life in Paris. They complained to him of their degraded status. Many French families had deserted in Prairie du Rocher and Cahokia. He soon realized that the French community could not survive among the crowds of gritty American pioneers.[4]

The account of François-Marie Perrin du Lac's visit to the French West in 1801–3 was probably borrowed from Truteau's journal.[5] But in a crucial period of colonial history, he revealed the extent of the opportunities offered by the retrocession of Louisiana to France. Born in Chaux-de-Fonds, Switzerland in 1766 Perrin du Lac entered the administration in 1789. As an agent of the treasury at Saint Dominque he faced the slave revolt of 1791, and fought under Colonel Mauduit-Duplessis, a royalist who was assassinated by the insurgents. Perrin was one of the delegates sent to the United States to seek the support of Congress against the rebels *Pompons rouges* [Red Tassels]. Although he remained in exile during the Terror his name was erased from the list of the émigrés thanks to an influential member of his family. He explored Ohio, Illinois, and Louisiana. On May 18, 1802 he left Saint Louis to ascend the Missouri as far as the White River. After a voyage of four months he realized that the Spanish fur trade was no match for the Canadians, who would challenge the French on their hunting grounds. Perrin returned to France at the close of 1803, after the Louisiana Purchase. France was thus never confronted by such competitors. The Americans still employed a few French voyageurs like Drouillard or Rivet. After the War of 1812, Congress excluded foreigners from the fur trade in the United States. Yet the hiring of French Canadian voyageurs was deemed essential, owing to their experience with the natives.

In the long run the French community of the West was absorbed into the nation. The process of Americanization altered the national character even though the French language and folk culture survived in enclaves like Sainte Genevieve. The former subjects of Louis XV had never become citizens of Bonaparte's First Consulate after bypassing the Terror, just as Rip Van Winkle had slept through the American Revolution. In Upper Louisiana they had seen the effects of the War of Independence before the storming of the Bastille was represented in French iconography. They had become the subjects of His Catholic Majesty, although many of them preserved their anticlerical leanings owing to the small number of Spaniards in Upper Louisiana.

As early as the seventeenth century, the class structure was reflected in the organization of the seignorial system in New France. The coureurs des bois appeared as lusty outlaws indebted to Robin Hood, while the transplanted noblemen shifted their loyalties according to the prestige they could preserve by serving a foreign power. As usual, merchants and traders believed in profit making. They feared poverty and were thus ready to cooperate with the winners who distributed the spoils. As time passed heirlooms were still carefully kept in the French households but the sense of alienation gradually subsided into the pursuit of happiness, a bigger challenge than practicing joie de vivre.

Strikingly, New France had launched voyages of discovery that in many aspects were more daring than the Lewis and Clark expedition. La Vérendrye would have marveled at American logistics in 1804. None of the French explorers, including Tonty and La Salle, had the support that the captains received from Jefferson. It was not a lack of courage that doomed the French West, but erratic ventures triggered by unrealistic ambitions. In the last three centuries, monarchs, presidents, and emperors vainly endeavored to recapture the aura of Louis XIV, the Sun King, for their own glory. All failed in the New World, from Louis XV in Canada to Napoleon I in Saint Domingue and Louisiana, and Napoleon III in Mexico. The power of castes, whether feudal or republican, hampered efforts toward an acceptance of sacrifices while faced with the prospect of reaping the fruit of self-denial. Through Lewis and Clark, Jefferson Americanized the French West. Jusseaume rose from backwoods scoundrel to delegate in Washington, Charbonneau was unwittingly the promoter of Sacagawea, an American icon comparable to Pocahontas. In the American West, French names still reveal the extent of the colonial fur trade, especially in Native American communities. *L'étoile du nord* [The North Star] appears today on the flag of the State of Minnesota. The lasting presence of such names in the American West was hardly expected in 1804. For example, the language barrier between the English-speaking and French-speaking members of the Corps of Discovery was evident in the misspelling of French names by Patrick Gass in his journal. Prarow was his attempt at *blaireau* [badger], *Gros Ventres* became Grossventers. He also misunderstood *chien* for prairie dog, and *Rivière de la Roche jaune* [Yellowstone River] was shortened to the Jaune.[6]

In their journals, Lewis and Clark did not care about the accuracy of spelling, as exemplified in *Drewyer* [Drouillard], *Grienyea* [Grenier], *Chaubonée* [Charbonneau] and *Taboe* [Tabeau]. The culture gap between the Americans and the French engagés probably resulted in exchanges of ethnic slurs before they united to face the wilderness. Patrick Gass was an outspoken member of the Corps of Discovery who voiced his feelings about the French character by resorting to stereotypes. Talking about the "fair sex of the Missouri," he ascribed Indian debauchery to notions inculcated by the French. The calculated understatement was intended to titillate the readers, as Gary Moulton states.[7] Gass targeted the French libertines but also suggested that the symptoms of the so-called "French disease" had spread among the tribes. Gass could, however, be fair and perceptive. As the expedition reached the junction of the Clearwater and the Snake rivers on October 9, 1805, he was surprised to see that the Frenchmen preferred dog flesh to salmon. But two days later, he seemed to relish dog meat.[8] As with Charbonneau's use of offal in his *boudin blanc,* Gass thus realized that the best of French cuisine was based on the innovative recipe, not on the basic elements of the dish. Like Gass, Lewis and Clark and their men were able to put generally accepted ideas to the test of experience. They established in the West the ascendancy over the Indians that both French aristocrats and coureurs des bois had long sought. But it lasted only a few decades before the waves of immigrants and migrants trampled Jefferson's ideal garden of the New World. Yet the West has both French and American heroes in common among the coureurs des bois and mountainmen. They offer an image of raw vitality and endurance against a background of undulating grasslands and great shining mountains.

Notes

CHAPTER 1. THE "PAYS D'EN HAUT"

1. Major sources on Cartier in this volume are *The Voyages of Jacques Cartier, 1534–42*, ed. H. P. Biggar (Ottawa: F. A. Acland, 1924); Cartier, *Voyages en Nouvelle-France* (Collection Documents d'histoire, Montréal: Éditions Hurtubise, 1977); Cartier, *Relations,* ed. Michel Bideaux (Montréal: Presses Universitaires de Montréal, 1986); Camille Laverdière, *le Sieur de Roberval: Jean-François de Larocque* (Chicoutimi, Québec: Editions JCL, 2005); Marcel Trudel, *Initiation à la Nouvelle France; 1558–1628* (Montreal/ Toronto: Holt, Rinehart and Winston, 1968); Philippe Jacquin, *Les Indiens Blancs. Français et Indiens en Amérique du Nord, XVIIe–XVIIIe siècles* (Paris: Payot, 1987).

2. Théodore de Bry, *Grands Voyages,* 23 vols. (Frankfurt, 1590–1634); Michel de Montaigne, *Essais* (Paris: 1582). Repr., "Des Cannibales" in *Essais,* 3 vols. (Paris: Garnier, 1958), 3:110.

3. Du Gua de Monts was in Acadia between 1600 and 1606. In 1603 he was appointed lieutenant general of New France to organize settlements and spread the Christian faith. Until 1611, Jean de Poutrincourt evangelized the Indians with Abbé Fléché in Acadia, but failed to obtain the expected support of Queen Marie de Medicis, widow of King Henrl IV, assassinated in 1610. She was more interested in missions to Brazil. Gilles Havard and Cécile Vidal, *Histoire de l'Amérique française* (Paris: Flammarion, 2003), 41–55. The case of La Jeunesse is dealt with in Marc Lescarbot, *Histoire de la Nouvelle France* (Paris: Jean Milot, 1609), 563; see also *The Works of Samuel de Champlain,* ed. H. P. Biggar (Ottawa: F. A. Acland, 1924); *Les Voyages de Champlain,* ed. Hubert Deschamps (Paris: Presses universitaires de France,1951).

4. Gabriel Sagard-Théodat, *Grand voyage,* 49; also in Philippe Jacquin, *Indiens blancs,* 40–41.

5. Deschamps, *Voyages de Champlain,* 119–66; Philippe Jacquin, *Les Indiens Blancs,* 40–41.

6. Deschamps, *Voyages de Champlain,* 171–75. Vert Galant = womanizer.

7. *Voyages of Peter-Esprit Radisson,* ed. Gideon Scull (Princeton, NJ: Prince Society Publications,1885), 149. Unless otherwise noted, all translations in this book are my own.

8. See Bruce Trigger, *Natives and Newcomers: Canada's Heroic Age Reconsidered* (Kingston and Montreal: McGill-Queen's University Press, 1985); Trigger, *The Children of Aataentsic: A History of the Huron People to 1660* (Montreal: McGill-Queen's University Press, 1976); Gordon M. Sayre, *Les Sauvages américains, Representations of Native Americans in French and English Colonial Literature* (Chapel Hill: University of North Carolina Press, 1997).

9. Marcel Trudel, *Histoire de la Nouvelle France* (Montreal: Fidès, 1979) Appendix E, 3:485–500, contains the list of men who wintered between 1605 and 1629.

10. Robert Mandrou, "Les Français hors de France aux XVIe et XVIIe siècles," Paris: *Les Annales* 5, no. 4 (1959): 662–75. Outaouais = Ottawa.

11. Reuben G. Thwaites, *The Jesuit Relations and Allied Documents—Travels and Explorations of the Jesuit Missionaries in New France, 1610–1701,* 73 vols. (Cleveland, 1904), 8:48, 10:26.

12. Trudel, *Histoire de la Nouvelle France,* 2:161.

13. Jacquin, *Indiens blancs,* 183–86.

14. Jean de Brébeuf, *La Relation de ce qui s'est passé au pays des Hurons,* ed. Théodore Besterman (Genève: Droz, 1957), 5–6, 19, 29, 83.

15. Thwaites, *Jesuit Relations,* 27:217.

16. Gustave Lanctot, *Histoire du Canada,* (Montreal: Beauchemin, 1967), 223; Trudel, *Histoire de la Nouvelle France,* 104, 366.

17. Bruce Trigger, *The Hurons: Farmers of the North* (New York: Holt, Rinehart and Winston, 1969), 325.

18. William J. Eccles, *The Canadian Frontier, 1534–1760* (Albuquerque: University of New Mexico Press, 1983), 26.

19. Sagard-Théodat, *Grand Voyage,* 135.

20. Jacquin, *Indiens blancs,* 62. Nicolas Denys described native folk beliefs about European technology in *Description Géographique et historique des côtes de l'Amérique du nord* (Paris, 1671).

21. Pierre Margry, ed. *Découvertes et établisssements des Français dans l'ouest, 1614–1754* (Paris: Jouaud, 1876–88), I:2.

22. Lescarbot, *Histoire de la Nouvelle France,* 669.

23. Jean de Brébeuf, *Relation,* 95–97.

24. La Galissonnière to Minister, October 28, 1747, ANC 11A 87:262.

25. On the subject of the right to issue orders, the clashes between the governor and the intendant were in keeping with the unstable status existing among the agents of the bureaucracy. As governor, Beauharnois had one of the longest terms of office (1726–46) In 1740–42, Intendant Gilles Hocquart was in conflict with Beauharnois over measures regulating voyageurs in the fur trade. Hocquart claimed he had jurisdiction over the Western posts when matters concerned the Montreal merchants. Beauharnois considered he was entitled to settle cases between traders in the West. Hocquart to Minister, October 14, 1742, ANC11A, 78:27. The material containing expense accounts for the Western posts is found in series ANC11A 73:117. The case is examined in depth by Norman Ward Caldwell in chapter 1 of *The French in the Mississippi Valley, 1740–1750* (Philadelphia: The Porcupine Press, 1974).

26. Jacques Lacoursière, Jean Provencher, and Denis Vaugeois, *Canada-Québec: 1534–2000* (Sillery, Québec: Septentrion, 2000), 67–70.

27. Peter Kalm, *Travels in North America; containing its Natural History in General* (Warrington, 1770–71), 3:72–74, 304–5. Marguerite Bourgeois (1620–1700) founded the Congrégation de Notre Dame in 1658. The schools admitted both French and Indian girls.

28. Henri du Breuil de Pontbriand (1709–60) was Bishop of Quebec (1741–60). He stated that from the spiritual side the trade in liquor was "absolutely contrary to Christianity." Bishop of Quebec to Minister, August 22, 1742, ANC11A 78:407–9.

29. On the Compagnie des Cent Associés "Lettres patentes de la Compagnie de la Nouvelle France," November 29, 1627, ANC11A 1:82. On the controversial subject of the wars between the Iroquois and the Hurons, George T. Hunt was a trailblazer with *The Wars of the Iroquois* (Madison: University Press of Wisconsin, 1940). Among the great number of publications also useful are Keith F. Otterbein,

"Huron vs Iroquois: A Case Study in Intertribal Warfare," *Ethnohistory* 6, no. 2 (1979): 141–52. Bruce Trigger, *Children of Aataentsic*.

30. Jean Hamelin, *Economie et société en Nouvelle France* (Québec: Presses de l'Université Laval, 1970), chapter 1.

31. Sagard-Théodat, *Grand Voyage*, 16–170.

32. Caldwell, *The French in the Mississippi Valley*, 3, 16–17.

33. Bruce Trigger, "The Jesuits and the Fur Trade," *Ethnohistory* 5, no. I (1965): 166.

34. Pierre Boucher (1622–1717) first went to Canada in 1635. His Huron wife was Marie-Madeleine Chrestienne. His book, *Histoire véritable et naturelle des moeurs et productions du pays de la Nouvelle France*, was published in Paris in 1664. It was intended as a celebration of the colony. See Sayre, *Sauvages Américains*, 141–42, 296–97.

35. Louis Dechêne, *Habitants et marchands de Montréal* (Paris: Plon, 1974),174; Havard and Vidal, *Histoire de l'Amérique française*, 83–86, 205–7, 217, 410. In 1726 King Louis XV appointed Charles de la Buache, Marquis de Beauharnois, governor of New France. The eldest of the Le Moyne brothers, Charles Le Moyne de Longueuil, was born in 1656. His candidacy was turned down because, despite his credentials, he had been a resident of Canada for too long. For the position, the monarch preferred a Frenchman with no family ties or acquaintances among the Creoles. Charles's brothers, Pierre and Jean-Baptiste, had already become famous in New France. Pierre Lemoyne d'Iberville, born in 1661, campaigned against the English troops when, in 1686, Governor Jacques-René Brisay de Denonville launched an offensive to protect the French fur trade. Pierre stormed Fort Nelson (Hudson's Bay) in 1694 and Fort Pemaquid at the mouth of the Kennebec River in 1696. In 1698 he located the mouth of the Mississippi after sailing across the Atlantic from France, and settled Ile Dauphine near the Mobile River. Jean Baptiste Le Moyne de Bienville, born in 1680, was the founder of Louisiana with his brother Pierre who was in charge of the small colony until 1707. Then Pontchartrain, minister of Marine, appointed Nicolas Daneau de Muy as governor. Bienville was disliked by politicians and clerics. He was a soldier, not a diplomat. He was blamed for corruption and debauchery but accusations were never substantiated by the new governor Lamothe Cadillac (1712). Meanwhile Louisiana had been contracted over to wealthy entrepreneur, Antoine Cruzat, Marquis de Châtel, a close councillor of Louis XIV. New Orleans was founded in 1718, To develop the colony 7000 black slaves were imported until 1735, mostly from Guinea. They constituted nearly half of the population. By 1714, Bienville came back into favor to mend Cadillac's erratic Indian policies.

36. Thwaites, *Jesuit Relations*, 25:50.

37.See Russell Bouchard, *Les Armes de la traite* (Montreal: Boreal Express, 1976) on the arms trade; on Montmagny's gift of an harquebus, Thwaites, *Jesuit Relations*, 25:26.

38. On the disasters of the wars, Lanctot, *Histoire du Canada*, 1:250–51; Thwaites, *Jesuit Relations*, 31:118–21. On the death of Jean de Brébeuf, Thwaites, *Jesuit Relations*, 34:26–29. The fate of Isaac Jogues was likened by the Catholic Church to that of a Christian martyr in ancient Rome. He was tortured during his captivity, escaped, then returned to his mission where he was killed in 1646. In Sayre, *Les Sauvages Américains*, 22–23. Gabriel Lalemant, *Relation des Hurons* (Paris, 1639), 70. Havard and Vidal, *Histoire de l'Amérique française*, 63.

39. Jacques Lacoursière, Jean Provencher, and Denis Vaugeois, *Canada-Québec*, 55–58. Informative surveys are found in Trigger, *Natives and Newcomers*.

40. Raoul Naroll, "The Cause of the Fourth Iroquois War." *Ethnohistory* 16, no. 1 (1969): 51–81. The French authorities thought they were confronted with a federal government, and hardly realized that the purpose of the Iroquois confederacy was mainly to avoid intertribal war. In *The History of the Five Indian Nations* (London, 1727, 1747) Cadwallader Colden (1688–1776) showed the significance of tribal autonomy among the Iroquois during the colonial wars in the last decades of the seventeenth century.

41. The peace treaty signed in 1666 offered a reprieve to the Iroquois, who extended their influence toward the Great Lakes. A half-century of violence resulted in heavy losses among the Indians. Hundreds of French colonists were killed or captured. Migrations and epidemics now altered the balance of power in Northeast America.

42. Antoine-Denis Raudot, "Mémoire historique à Monsieur le Comte de Pontchartrain sur le mauvais effet de la réunion du castor dans une même main" [memoir on the bad effects of merged interests in the beaver trade] February 12, 1705, ANC11A 22:363. Raudot was intendant between 1705–10. See Camille de Rochemontiex, *Relation par lettres de l'Amérique septentrionale 1709–1710* (Paris: Letouzey et Ané, 1904). He evaluated the French passion for furs and dwelt on the man's identification with the beaver in native mythologies.

43. La Rochelle was the stronghold of French protestantism before it was besieged by Richelieu's forces in 1627. The blockade prevented the inhabitants from being supplied by English ships. The city surrendered on October 28, 1628. The Huguenots were scattered all over the country and deprived of their property rights.

44. On the discharged soldiers, Dechêne, *Habitants et marchands de Montréal au XVIIe siècle*, 80–81; on underage engagés, "Mémoire de De Meulles au Ministre," November 12, 1684, ANC11A 6:401.

45. Beauharnois to Minister, September 28, 1726, ANC11A 48:155 (young men of means enlisted in Canada); Beauharnois to Minister, October 5, 1735, ANC11A 63:49 (Bouchel d'Orcival).

46. Major sources in Marcel Trudel, *La Population du Canada en 1663* (Montreal: Fides, 1973); William Bennet Munro, *The Seigniorial System in Canada: A Study in French Colonial Policy* (New York: Longmans, Green and Co., 1907); Pierre Goubert, *L'Ancien Régime* (Paris: Colin, 1969); Peter N. Moogk, "Reluctant Exiles: Emigrants from France to Canada before 1760," *William and Mary Quarterly*, Third Series, 46, no.3 (1989): 482. See also Leslie Choquet, *De Français à paysans: modernité et tradition dans le peuplement du Canada* (Sillery: Septentrion, 2001).

47. At Loudun, Jeanne des Anges, the Ursuline prioress, who had mental disorders probably due to her repressed sexuality, confessed that she and the nuns were possessed by the devil. She accused Urbain Grandier, a libertine priest from a neighboring village, of allegedly casting a spell on the community. He was sentenced to death and burnt alive.

48. Cotton Mather had long been interested in the subject of witchcraft before he wrote *The Wonders of the Invisible World* in 1693, to describe the sufferings of "A people of God in the Devil's territories," as the subtitle of the work indicates.

49. Crèvecoeur, *Letters*, ed. Warren B. Blake (London: Dent, 1912), 46, 51–52. A major comparative study of the English and French frontier environments is to be found in J. A. Leo Lemay, "The Frontiersman from Lout to Hero: Notes on the Significance of the Comparative Method and the Stage Theory in Early American Literature and Culture," *Proceedings of the American Antiquarian Society* 88, no. 2 (October 1979): 205–10. Jacques-René de Brisay de Denonville was colonel des Drag-

ons before his appointment as governor of New France in 1685. For him young Frenchmen appeared stronger and more resilient in the wilderness than in the home country. Denonville to Minister, November 23, 1685, ANC11A 7:72.

CHAPTER 2. NEW FRANCE GOES WEST

1. Lanctot, *Histoire du Canada*, 1:249.

2. *Voyages of Peter-Esprit Radisson*, 149. Pierre-Esprit Radisson (1640–1710) was from Provence. Little is known about his arrival in New France. At first a coureur des bois, he was captured by the Iroquois in 1651, escaped from torture, hunted buffalo with Indian tribes, served as an interpreter for the Dutch colonists, and returned to Europe in 1654. Returning to New France in 1658, he fooled threatening Iroquois by inducing them to drink heavily in response to his vision, which allowed Radisson and his companions to flee unharmed from captivity. In 1650, he journeyed through Sioux and Cree countries. In 1660 he and Groseilliers had their peltries taken from them for having gone west without authorization. Much of the following decades was spent in sea adventures, voyages to Hudson Bay, and shadowy dealings with English explorers as far as the mouth of the Nelson River. The founding of the Hudson's Bay Company was one of his major achievements. In 1681, Charles Aubert de la Chesnaye, a Canadian trader, hired Radisson to found a French colony on the Nelson River and dislodge the English occupants. Radisson returned triumphantly to Quebec, expecting rewards from Colbert. But he was prosecuted for tax evasion on the furs he had acquired in the West.

3. Bernard DeVoto, *The Course of Empire* (Boston: A Mariner Book Houghton Mifflin, 1998), 111–13. Colin G. Calloway, *One Vast Winter Count: The Native American West before Lewis and Clark* (Lincoln: University of Nebraska Press, 2003), 234–35.

4. Jacquin, *Indiens blancs*, 121–22.

5. Groseilliers (1618–96) was from Brie, Ile de France, south of Paris. He was hired by the Jesuits in the Huron country in 1646. With Radisson he went to Lake Huron, Detroit, Lake Michigan, and Hudson Bay. See Radisson, *Voyages of Peter-Esprit Radisson*, 123–34, 172–75, 208–18, 232. Thwaites, *Jesuit Relations*, 28:229.

6. Pierre Margry, *Découvertes et établisssements*, 1:109–11. The text includes the evidence given by La Salle in July 1669.

7. Ibid., 1:118. The text includes a statement by the abbé Gallinée on brandy.

8. Louis-Armand Lahontan, *Œuvres complètes*, 2 vols. (Montréal: Presses de l'Université de Montréal, 1990), 1:85–86,130. Louis-Armand de Lom d'Arce, Baron de Lahontan (1666–1716) was a libertine, subversive officer, prone to bite the hand that fed him. His writings often foreshadowed the satiric literature of the Enlightenment. As explorer and ethnographer he traveled in New France (1683–93), wintered with Algonquin tribes, and admired their guerrilla warfare. His observations were open-minded and provocative.

9. Dechêne, *Habitants et marchands de Montréal*, 75.

10. Lucien Campeau, *Les Cents associés et le peuplement de la Nouvelle France* (Montreal: Bellarmin, 1974), 152–53.

11. Jean Talon was intendant for a short term (1670–1675). Frontenac was governor between 1672 and 1686. Talon wielded considerable financial power in a highly centralized colonial system ruled from France by Jean Baptiste Colbert, the trusted minister of Louis XIV. Against the prevailing ideology favoring the economic development of New France within a limited space, Talon advocated expansionist policies. As early as 1670, he informed the government that adventurers were on their

way to unknown regions. Talon to Minister, October, 1670, ANC11A 5:81. A remarkable synthesis on the period is to be found in Raymonde Litalien, *Les Explorations de l'Amérique du nord* (Sillery: Septentrion, 1993).

12. On Joliet's party see Louise Phelps Kellog, *The French Régime in Wisconsin and the Northwest.* (Madison: Wisconsin: State Historical Society of Wisconsin, 1925), 114; Margry, *Découvertes et établissements,* 1: 58–72, 114); Nicolas Perrot (1644–1717), born in Burgundy, served the Jesuits, then the Sulpicians in New France (1660–66) before he formed a trading company. He wintered among the Potawatomis and the Foxes as far as the Baie des Puants (Green Bay, Wisconsin). In 1670, Intendant Talon appointed him interpreter to accompany Daumont de Saint-Lusson's expedition to Lake Superior, especially to find mines. There was some suspicion about Perrot's dealings in the fur trade. His peltries were seized in 1671 on his return from Sault Sainte Marie on Saint-Lusson's orders. Perrot was also suspected of trying to poison La Salle in 1677 but was cleared when one Perrot-Joly-cœur confessed to the attempted crimes. Governor La Barre asked Nicolas Perrot to form a coalition of western nations to fight the Iroquois in 1684. As commandant of Baie des Puants in 1685, he established peace between the Chippewas and the Foxes when he freed the daughter of a Chippewa chief, who had been held captive for a year by the Foxes. He remained active among the western Indians in the following decade to maintain peace and security against British intrusion. His efforts were not rewarded by the government, for he was heavily in debt in 1700. His *Mémoire sur les mœurs, coutumes et religion des sauvages de l'Amérique septentrionale* (Paris: Jules Tailhan, 1864), bears witness to his firsthand knowledge of Indian mentalities. He was one of the most honored Frenchmen among the Sioux, the Miamis and the Mascoutens. Margry, *Découvertes et établissements,*1:296, 389, 397; Claude Allouez, a Jesuit missionary (1622–89), preached at Rodez, France until he left for Canada. He spoke Indian languages fluently and was recognized as a major trailblazer around the Great Lakes. His prestige among the natives enabled him to convert many of them to Catholicism.

13. Jacquin, *Indiens blancs,* 135.

14. Thwaites, *Jesuit Relations,* 59:86.

15. Margry, *Découvertes et établissements,* 1:96.

16. Born at Saint-Germain-Laval, near Lyon into a family of lesser nobility, Dulhut (1639–1710) was a gendarme in the army of the prince of Condé (Le Grand Condé) that defeated William of Orange at Seneffe, Belgium, in 1674. He was in Canada in 1675, and left from Montreal, bound for the West, beyond Lake Superior, in 1678, without Frontenac's authorization, after Colbert had prohibited the Indian trade outside New France. Dulhut tried to negotiate peace between the Crees, Chippewas, and Sioux. On his return to Quebec, he was accused of being a renegade woodrunner, but was whitewashed by Frontenac. They both had private interests in the fur trade. Dulhut launched new expeditions in the 1680s to Michilimackinac and the Upper Mississippi. Aside from being an empire builder, he supported the war efforts of La Barre against the Iroquois in 1684, and had Fort Saint Joseph built in 1687. Margry, *Découvertes et établissements,* 2:5, 6. As a young discharged soldier, Pierre Le Sueur (1657–1704) was hired by the Jesuits at Sault Sainte Marie before he turned to the fur trade with the Sioux on the Upper Mississippi. He became popular among the Indians as a coureur des bois. His experience enabled him to serve Frontenac's diplomatic moves. In 1695 he returned to Quebec with Sioux and Chippewa chiefs to meet the governor and enter into an alliance. Despite the opposition of New France officials he was granted royal permission in 1700 to ascend the Mississippi. Le Sueur was linked to the Le Moyne

d'Iberville family by his marriage to Marguerite Messier. He was on his way from France to settle in Louisiana when he contracted yellow fever and died at Havana. Margry, *Découvertes et établissements*, "Journal de Pénigault," 5:375–86, 6:69–80. See also Jacquin, *Indiens blancs*, 135–36.

17. Louis Jolliet (1645–1700) was the king's cartographer. Born in Quebec, he was educated by the Jesuits and defended a thesis in philosophy. He turned to the fur trade and was at Sault Sainte Marie in 1671, then at Michilimackinac in 1673. The Jesuits strongly supported his organization of a voyage of discovery down the Mississippi. Jacques Marquette (1637–75) was born at Laon, France. A Jesuit, he spoke six Indian languages, was well-received by the natives and met many tribes from Michilimackinac to Lake Superior (1669–73). In 1674, he left the Baie des Puants (Green Bay) with Jacques Largillier and Pierre Porteret for the Illinois country. Many questions have ben raised about his credentials as a priest and his obsession with the enhancement of his image. Raymond Douville, "Jacques Largillier dit 'le castor,' coureur des bois et 'frère donné'," *Cahiers des Dix*, 29 (1964): 47–69, 50, 85; Rouxel is mentioned in the letter from Frontenac to Minister, October 29 1674, ANC11A 4:85; See Jean Delanglez, *Life and Voyages of Louis Jolliet 1645–1700* (Chicago: Institute of Jesuit History, 1948); on Jacques Marquette see Lacoursière, Provencher, and Vaugeois, *Canada-Québec*, 84–85.

18. René-Robert Cavelier de La Salle was from Rouen. He spent nine years in the Compagnie de Jésus before he was dismissed in 1667 for misconduct. He was attracted to New France by his uncle, who belonged to the Company of the Hundred Associates and by his brother, a Sulpician friar at Montreal. La Salle disliked the Jesuits, to whom had been given the spiritual guidance of New France. The Récollets returned to the colony when the Crown realized they had misused their power. Hennepin (1626–1705) was one of the five Récollet missionaries sent to New France by Louis XIV in 1675 to counterbalance the influence of the Jesuits. Derived from his *Description de la Louisiane* (Utrecht, 1697–98), Hennepin's celebrity displeased the Jesuits, who slandered him. He spent many years plotting in Holland and Rome, and remained a very controversial personality. His firm dedication to the king impelled him to denounce the Jansenists, who believed in predestination and opposed absolute monarchy. The other two Récollet fathers were Zenobe Membré and Gabriel de la Ribourde. Lake Michigan (Lac des Illinois) was renamed Lac Saint Joseph by Jesuit Father Allouez and Lac Dauphin by Father Membré. Toponymy was involved in the conflict between the two orders. Crèvecœur is the name of a medieval castle in Pays d'Auge, Normandy, his native province. For the most reliable accounts of La Salle's expeditions see Magry, *Découvertes et établissements*, vol. I; Francis Parkman, *France and England in North America: The Old Régime in Canada*. (Boston, 1884), part 4.

19. Michel Accault and Antoine Auguel, alias "Le Picard du Guay," left from Fort Crèvecoeur with Hennepin in February 1680, in a canoe loaded with goods worth a thousand piastres. They were captured by Sioux warriors on the Mississippi. The three Frenchmen were spared thanks to the gifts they made but they had to follow the Indians to their village. By July they met with Dulhut and his party and were finally freed in September.

20. Margry, *Découvertes et établissements*, 2:133.

21. Zenobe Membré (1645–89), a Récollet missionary, accompanied Cavelier de la Salle in the expedition of 1679. He lost Gabriel de la Ribourde during the journey. Despite the failure of this first trip he took part in a second venture and went down to the mouth of the Mississippi. On April 6, 1682 the cross planted by La Salle was blessed by Father Membré. After staying nearly two years in France, he

accompanied La Salle on his third expedition. They reached the Gulf of Mexico and went up as far as Fort Saint Louis where both of them died. Father Membré was killed on January 15, 1689. Membré left reports that were used by Hennepin. Membré's account was published by Chrétien Le Clerq (1641–1700) in *Premier établissement de la Foy dans la Nouvelle France contenant la publication de l'Evangile, l'histoire des colonies françaises et les fameuses découvertes de La Salle*, 2 vols. (Paris: Aimable Auroy, 1691); Sayre, *Sauvages américains*, 15,19, 90.

22. Gabriel de la Ribourde (1620–80) came to Canada in 1670. He was appointed provincial commissioner. He strove to recover the former Récollet seigneury, and restore the church of Notre Dame in Quebec. He was named spiritual leader of La Salle's expedition in 1679. In September 1680, while the men were repairing the canoe ashore, Ribourde was captured, killed, and scalped by Kickapoo warriors. See Louis Hennepin, *Description de la Louisiane* 108, 239. Le Clerq, *Premier établissement de la foy*, 2:26, 59.

23. Margry, *Découvertes et établissements* 2:150–200; Bernard Lugan, *Histoire de la Louisiane française* (Paris: Perrin, 1994), 28–34.

24. Lugan, *Histoire de la Louisiane*, 35–50.

25. La Barre (1622–88) was a controversial figure. At first Intendant of Paris during the Fronde (1648–49) (the rebellion of the city parliament against Mazarin), he was later appointed lieutenant-general in 1663, then governor of Guiana, despite Colbert's antagonism, He was in naval action as captain of a warship and sunk the *Colchester* of the British Royal Navy in the West Indies. In 1673 he commanded a ship in the fleet of Admiral d'Estrées. La Barre was appointed governor of New France in 1682 to overcome the Iroquois, and also to reform the fur trade. See Margry, *Découvertes et établissements*, 2:307–50, Havard and Vidal, *Histoire de l'Amérique française*, 72, 74, 102, 106, 184; Born into a family from Berry, France, Chevalier de Baugy came to Quebec with La Barre in 1682. The new governor commissioned Captain Morel de la Durantaye and Baugy to seize the peltries of unlicensed traders and investigate La Salle's possessions. Baugy met La Salle in 1683, then Tonty was relieved of his command at Fort Saint Louis, and La Barre's protégé took over from him. Both Tonty and Baugy, however, defended the fort against hundreds of Iroquois in 1684. Upon the arrival of Durantaye, Baugy was officially appointed commandant upon the orders of La Barre. See Margry, *Découvertes et établissements*, 5:4–7.

26. Antoine Laumet de Lamothe Cadillac (1658–1730) was from Gascony like Alexandre Dumas' three musketeers. A kind of frontier condottiere, he appeared by turns as a staid administrator and a notorious confidence man. He probably usurped his noble pedigree to gain social prestige in New France. He landed in Acadia in the 1680s and became a privateer before he married Marie-Thérèse Guion in 1687. He received a seignorial domain but preferred to enter into partnership with two traders. To escape lawsuits he went to Quebec in 1691. His experience in the navy qualified him for a mission along the coasts of New England with Jean-Baptiste Franquelin, Governor Frontenac's cartographer. Cadillac was promoted captain in October 1693, and Frontenac was appointed commandant of Michilimackinac. Despite the praise lavished on him by the western tribes, he was incapable of maintaining peace between the western tribes. Meanwhile he became a prosperous fur trader, especially by selling brandy to the Indians. In 1696, Louis XIV banned the fur trade in the Pays d'En Haut but kept the garrison at Michilimackinac. Then Cadillac proposed founding a colony at Detroit to mix a French population with western tribes and thus prevent English expansion around the Great Lakes. Despite the opposition of Minister Pontchartrain's entourage, Cadillac succeeded and arrived at Detroit in 1701. When Philippe de Rigaud de Vaudreuil,

another former musketeer, was governor of New France, he antagonized the Gascon empire builder, who wanted to be the master of the West by leaning on coureurs des bois and natives. Cadillac plotted to overthrow Vaudreuil with Claude de Ramezay, the governor of Montreal and Ruette d'Auteuil, the attorney general. By 1707, Cadillac's Indian policy proved a failure when a conflict broke out between the Hurons, Ottawas, and Miamis in Detroit. In 1708 Pontchartrain commissioned François Clairambault d'Aigremont to investigate Cadillac. The report was devastating: British interests had invested in the Detroit fur trade while corruption was rampant under Cadillac's tyrannical rule. Pontchartrain decided to get rid of Cadillac and appointed him governor of Louisiana in 1710, which was a wretched place at the time. See Marcel Giraud, *Histoire de la Louisiane française* (Paris: Presses universitaires de France, 1953), 1:122, 233, 3:153. Lugan, *Histoire de la Louisiane française*, 108–10.

27. Juchereau de Saint Denis (1676–1744) went with Le Moyne d'Iberville to Louisiana in 1699, and in 1703 commanded Fort Mississippi, close to the mouth of the river. In 1720 he was in charge of Natchitoches as lieutenant, and in 1721 entered into partnership with the Compagnie des Indes to do business with Los Adayes, the capital of Texas, although it was considered illegal by the Spanish authorities. In 1731 Juchereau defended Nachitoches against the Natchez who had captured Fort Rosalie. See Ross Phares, *Cavalier in the Wilderness, the Story of the Explorer and trader Louis Juchereau de Saint-Denis* (Baton Rouge: Louisiana State University Press, 1952).

28. Jean-Baptiste Bénard de la Harpe was commissioned by Bienville to open trade relations with New Mexico. His explorations increased the topographical knowledge of the area. In 1720 he also observed that Apaches transported *tipis* by dogs along the Red River. Back to France in 1722 he wrote his *Journal historique de l'établissement des Français en Louisiane*, which was published in Margry, *Découvertes et établissements* 6:241–306, and also in New Orleans in 1831. See "Account of the Journey of Bénard de La Harpe: Discovery Made by Him of Several Nations Situated in the West," trans. and ed. Ralph A. Smith, *Southwestern Historical Quarterly* 62 (1958–59): 75–86, 246–59, 371–85, 525–41. The authorship of the Journal has been questioned since its first publication. The account was perhaps written by Chevalier de Beaurais. See Lugan, *Histoire de la Louisiane*, 100.

29. Claude Charles du Tisné was less than twenty years old in 1719. He had been rejected from the French army as a cadet because he was too short. He had a brilliant career in the Canadian army. See Noel M. Loomis and Abraham P. Nasatir, *Pedro Vial and the Roads to Santa Fe* (Norman: University of Oklahoma Press, 1967), 43–44. Etienne Véniard de Bourgmont was from Normandy. He commanded Fort Detroit in 1706. He was a womanizer, who eloped with Madame Tichenet in 1707 and went to live in the woods with deserters. He was caught, court-martialed and acquitted. He then deserted to live in her tribe with La Charesse, a Missouri Indian girl, until 1718. He returned to France, married a rich widow, and was back to Missouri in 1723. He was then appointed commander on the Missouri River. See Henry Folmer, *Franco-Spanish Rivalry in North America, 1524–1763* (Glendale, CA: Clark, 1953); Loomis and Nasatir, *Pedro Vial*, 48–51.

30. Pierre-Antoine Mallet (1700–1751) was born in Montreal. His family moved to Detroit shortly thereafter. He then went to the Illinois country with his brother Paul, before organizing their expedition to the Southwest. Louis Denis had gone through Texas to the presidio of Piedras Negras (Mexico) in the 1720s. Traders who already supplied Spanish outposts in Texas believed that the headwaters of the Missouri were close to the Southwest. See Henry Folmer, "The Mallet Expedition

of 1739 through Nebraska, Kansas, and Colorado to Santa Fe," *Colorado Magazine* 15, no. 5 (September 1939): 163–73; Loomis and Nasatir, *Pedro Vial,* 20, 52–54.

31. Jacques LeGardeur (1701–55) was an officer with long experience among Indian tribes. In 1729, his task was to enlist the Ojibwas, the Crees, and the Sioux against the Foxes. He was in charge of Fort Beauharnois on Lake Pepin in 1734–37, but could not withstand the Sioux onslaught, and left after burning the fort. Between 1737–40 he campaigned against the Chickasaws in Louisiana and was captured. He was then the commandant at Michilimackinac (1747–49). In 1750, LeGardeur was appointed by Governor La Jonquière to lead an expedition to the Pacific, The prospect of reaping the fruit of success angered the family of La Vérendrye who had died that same year. See Margry, *Découvertes et établissements,* 6:637–52; Joseph-Boucher de Niverville (1715–1804) was a cadet in the colonial army in 1734 when he campaigned against the Foxes. He then became a fur trader at Detroit. In 1738 he went to Louisiana to secure peace among the Chickasaws, under Charles Le Moyne de Longueuil's command, and was promoted second ensign in 1743. Until 1748, he took part in many missions against New England, including raids that laid waste several settlements in Massachusetts. With Pierre-Joseph Céloron de Blainville, he was in the Ohio Valley the following year when he was captured by Shawnee warriors. In 1751, Niverville's mission was to build an outpost west of Fort Paskoyac (Le Pas, Manitoba) to be used as a base before the Rockies. Niverville fell ill and could not go any further. He left the fort two years later to return to Montreal. Niverville's long military career took him to Michilimackinac in 1755. As a lieutenant, he took part in the French and Indian Wars at the head of Abenaki bands at Lake George in 1756. After the battle of Sainte Foy, Niverville returned to France, hoping to be rewarded for his devotion to the French empire in America, But there were no spoils for the losers. It was not long before he came back to settle at Trois Rivières where his wife inherited the seignoral lands of her wealthy father. Niverville swore the oath of allegiance to the British Crown and later showed his loyalty by leading a group of Indians and Canadians to counter the American invasion during the War of Independence. But he hastily surrendered when William Thompson attacked Trois Rivières in 1776. He remained active in the local militia until 1803. See Raymond Douville, "Charles Boucher de Niverville, son ascendance et sa carrière politique," *Cahiers des Dix* 37 (1972): 87–122.

32. Louis de la Corne of Saint Luc (1711–84), a wealthy fur trader and renowned officer, explored posts around the Great Lakes, especially Kaministiquia (1742–43). He was acquainted with many Indian nations and spoke their languages fluently. During the French and Indian Wars, La Corne recruited warriors with whom he attacked the Redcoats at Lake George and Fort Clinton in 1746–47. Recommended by Duquesne, he became captain in 1755, and Governor Vaudreuil employed him as interpreter in his talks with the Senecas in 1755. In 1757 Montcalm won a decisive battle over the British at Fort George. But La Corne's Indians, who were on the left flank, massacred the members of the garrison, who had surrendered. In 1758, a few hundred Canadians and Indians under La Corne ambushed the enemy, taking dozens of prisoners and scalps. He sometimes incurred the blame of his superiors for his guerrilla warfare, although his daring was greatly admired. In 1775, La Corne who had easily adapted to British rule, conspired with the help of the Iroquois against the American troops under Ethan Allen in Montreal. He was taken prisoner and sent to Philadelphia. Shortly after his release he joined Burgoyne's forces at Saratoga in 1777. After the defeat he was denigrated by Burgoyne who blamed him for the Indians' desertion. See Guy Frégault, *Le XVIIIe siècle canadien. Etudes* (Montréal: HMH, 1968)

33. La Vérendrye (1685–1749) was not recognized as a major discoverer by early historians, who judged him uneducated, erratic, and venal. Pierre Margry established his reputation as a major figure of New France in *Découvertes et établissements,* VI. The discovery of western seas was a foremost preoccupation during the regency of the Duc d'Orléans when Louis XV was too young to reign in 1715. The cartographers in the duke's entourage hoped to build a new network of trading posts after the loss of Hudson Bay to the British in 1713. They thought the mer de l'Ouest opened on the Pacific ocean halfway between the Gulf of Mexico and the Gulf of California. La Vérendrye could have blazed many trails for Lewis and Clark had he received a firm financial support from the monarchy. He tried to maintain peace between long-time enemy tribes, but at times supported the Assiniboines and the Crees against Sioux and the Ojibwas although they were French allies. He depended on the information given by Indians, for instance a map of the western country drawn on a piece of bark. The description of the Mandans that he had obtained from a slave of the Cree chief Vieux Crapeau (Old Toad), suggested that they had fair hair and spoke French. La Vérendrye's self-proclaimed object was to carry the name and arms of His Majesty into unknown stretches of land, and enlarge New France. But Louis XV refused to fund his venture. To finance his enterprise he relied on traders who could not supply the capital needed to provision posts so far from Quebec. La Vérendrye was undoubtedely more successful in the Indian slave trade. Nevertheless, west of the Great Lakes he managed to enter into an alliance with Indian nations under the fleur-de-lys. See *Journals and Letters of Pierre Gaultier de Varennes de la Vérendrye and his Sons, with Correspondence between the Governors of Canada and the French Court, touching the search for the western sea,* edited by Lawrence J. Burpee, vol. 17. (Toronto: Publications of the Champlain Society, 1927); Martin Kavanagh, *La Vérendrye: His Life and Times* (Brandon, Manitoba: published by the author, 1967). Hubert G. Smith, *The Explorations of La Vérendrye in the Northern Plains, 1738–1743* (Lincoln: University of Nebraska Press, 1980).

CHAPTER 3. THE WILDERNESS AT STAKE

1. The correspondence of the French authorities reveals that at least six hundred individuals were counted as coureurs des bois in the last two decades of the seventeenth century. Duchesneau to Minister, November 1679, ANC11A 5:42; Denonville to Minister, August 20, 1685, ANC11A 7:58; Champigny to Minister, November 4, 1695, ANC11A 13:432. Jean Bochart de Champigny (1645–1720) was intendant of New France (1686–1702). He kept cordial relations with Governor Denonville after years of conflicts between intendants (Duchesneau, Demeulle) and governors (Frontenac, La Barre). Champigny was confronted with economic, social and military issues in a period of territorial expansion toward the Great Lakes and the Mississippi Valley. He brilliantly masterminded the capture of Iroquois at Fort Frontenac in 1687. During Governor Frontenac's second term of office, Champigny's task was less easy. As a conscientious administrator he was concerned with the welfare of the Canadian people, sometimes against the fur trade oligarchy, and always remained humane and steadfast in adversity.

2. Leo-Paul Desrosiers, "L'expédition de M. de La Barre." *Cahiers des Dix* 22 (1957): 105–35.

3. See Francis Jennings, *The Ordeal of the Longhouse. The People of the Iroquois League in the Era of European Colonization* (Chapel Hill: University of North Carolina Press, 1992).

4. Frontenac to Minister, October 12, 1679, ANC11A 5:39; Duchesneau to Minister, November 10, 1681, ANC11A 5:319–20.

5. Duchesneau to Minister, November 13, 1681, ANC11A 5:320.

6. Champigny to Minister, July 18, 1700, ANC11A 18:27. The text refers to Tonty's journey in the Assiniboine country and Le Sueur's among the Sioux.

7. Charlevoix (1682–1761), a Jesuit, was in Canada from 1705–09, then participated in an expedition to discover the *mer de l'Ouest* [western sea] in 1721–22. He had heard of a great river flowing westward and emptying in the southern sea. He went to Michilimackinac, the Illinois, and reached Kaskaskia. Then he went down the Mississippi to Natchez. He sailed back to France with a stopover in Saint Domingue (Hispaniola). He became an authority on the French West. Volume 3 of his *Histoire et description générale de la Nouvelle France* (1744) includes the journal of the expedition. See Gilbert Chinard, *L'Amérique et le rêve exotique dans la littérature française au XVIIe et XVIIIe siècles* (Paris: Hachette, 1934), 333–39.

8. Margry, *Découvertes et établissements*, 6:480–81. Fabry de la Bruyère was appointed by Governor Bienville to lead an expedition to find la mer de l'Ouest. La Bruyère was to ascend the Arkansas River but the water was too low for the pirogues. The Mallet brothers, who were with him, left the expedition to go to Santa Fe.

9. Talon to Minister, October 10, 1670, ANC11A 3:81.

10. Duchesneau to Minister, November 13, 1681, ANC11A 5:297.

11. Jacquin, *Indiens blancs*, 134–38.

12. Beauharnois to Minister, October 21, 1736, ANC11A 65:128.

13. Pierre Georges Roy, ed., *Inventaire des ordonnances des intendants de la Nouvelle France, conservées aux archives provinciales de Québec*, 3 vols. 1919: October 19, 1709 (Gai), September 26, 1719, February 27, 1727, June 4, 1727, August 10, 1727), September 8 1727 (Quenet, Fortier), October 6, 1707 (Durantaye), October 19, 1709, (Patissier).

14. Lahontan, *Oeuvres complètes*, 1:123; Chevalier de Baugy, *Journal d'une expédition contre les Iroquois au Canada en 1687*, ed. Ernest Serrigny (Paris: Ernest Leroux, 1883), 97; François-Xavier de Charlevoix, *Journal d'un voyage fait par ordre du roi dans l'Amérique septentrionale*, 2 vols. (Montreal: Presses de l'Université de Montréal, 1994): 1:515.

15. In 1685 the Duke of York ascended to the throne of England as James II. The rapprochement with another Catholic king was natural. James II fled to France when he was overthrown by the Glorious Revolution in 1688.

16. William J. Eccles, "The Fur Trade and Eighteenth Century Imperialism," *William and Mary Quarterly* 40 (July 1983):341–62.

17. Margry, *Découvertes et établissements*, 6:76 (Laplace); Beauharnois to Minister, December 29, 1745, ANC13A 29, 95 (Baudron).

18. From reports by governors. Vaudreuil to Minister May 14, 1709, ANC11 A 30:4; Denonville to Minister, November 13, 1685, ANC 11 A 8:90; See Lanctot, *Histoire du Canada*, 1:149.

19. In a memoir, Patoulet, Talon's secretary, castigated the lax morals of the woodrunners, allegedly idle, subversive and indianized, October 10, 1672, ANC11A 4:274.

20. Denonville was aware of pending dangers. Even before Quebec knew that the war had broken out between France and England, on August 5,1689, 1,500 Iroquois attacked the village of Lachine at night, set fire to houses, and killed twenty-four colonists. Although he was in the Montreal region Denonville did not give orders to chase the Iroquois warriors. In the meantime, Louis XIV had already de-

cided to appoint Frontenac as governor. See Lacoursière, Provencher, and Vaugeois, *Canada-Quebec*, 90–92.

21. Marcel Giraud, *The Métis in the Canadian West*, trans. George Woodcock (Edmonton: The University of Alberta Press, 1985), 272–77 (on Mackenzie); Honoré Riqueti, Comte de Mirabeau, advocated equal rights in the French colonies. During the debates over the abolition of slavery in Saint Domingue on July 3, 1790, he castigated the tyranny of the Creoles over the colonized people, and considered that social disunion extended to the territories overseas because the planters were themselves the new barbarians. in Aimé Césaire, *Toussaint Louverture* (Paris: Présence africaine, 1981), 42–46.

22. Crèvecoeur, *Letters*, 216–22.

23. Thwaites, *Jesuit Relations*, 21:42–45, 50.

24. Pierre Millet, *Captivity Among the Oneidas* (New York: Garland, 1978), 30–37; Radisson, *Voyages*, 50.

25. Radisson, *Voyages*, 55–56.

26. Millet, *Captivity*, 39

27. Radisson, *Voyages*, 38–39

28. La Hontan, *Nouveaux Voyages*, 1:152.

29. Frontenac to Minister, October 16, 1700, ANC11A 18:153.

30. Cadwallader Colden, *History of the Five Indian Nations Depending on the Province of New York in America* (Ithaca: Cornell University Press, 1964), 203–4.

31. François-Xavier de Charlevoix, *Journal d'un voyage fait par ordre du roi dans l'Amérique septentrionale*, ed. Pierre Berthiaume, 2 vols. (Montreal: Presses de l'Université de Montreal, 1994) 1:337; Le Clerq, *Premier établissements*, 2:178.

32. Carheil to Callières, August 30, 1702, ANC11A 19:25–28.

33. Raymond, E. Wood and Thomas D. Thiessen, *Early Fur Trade in the Northern Plains* (Norman: University of Oklahoma Press, 1985), 69.

34. Zebulon Pike, *An Account of Expeditions to the Sources of the Mississippi and through the Western Part of Louisiana* (Philadelphia: C. and A. Conrad, 1810), 118, 236.

35. Margry, *Découvertes et établissements*, 5:107.

36. Yves Zoltany, "New France in the West," *Canadian Historical Review* 46, no. 4 (1965): 301–2; Sylvie Van Kirk, *Many Tender Ties, Women in the Fur Trade Society, 1670–1870* (Winnipeg: Watson & Dwyer, 1980), 21–38; Jacquin, *Indiens blancs*, 193–98. Jean de Lamberville (1633–1714) was both a Jesuit missionary and an active diplomat among Indians.

37. Van Kirk, *Many Tender Ties*, 40.

38. Radisson, *Voyages*, 84. See Grace Nute, *Caesars of the Wilderness* (Saint Paul: Minnesota Historical Society Press, 1978) 2d ed., 2004.

39. Margry, *Découvertes et établissements*, 1:342. It is part of the "Relation de Joutel."

40. See Neal Salisbury, *Manitou and Providence* (Oxford: Oxford University Press, 1987).

41. Margry, *Découvertes et établissements*, 5:463–64.

42. The term *drouine* meant to trade with the Indians on their grounds away from the trading post. In John Francis McDermott, *A Glossary of Mississippi Valley French, 1673–1850*. Washington University Studies, New Series, Language and Literature, 12 (Saint Louis: Washington University, 1941), 66; *Courir la drouine* involved a harsh competition, sometimes with English traders. Duluth records that woodrunners were worshipped in tribes, especially when they set up a blacksmith shop to repair rifles. In Duluth to La Barre, April 5, 1679, ANC11E 16:3; see Margry, *Découvertes et établissements*, 5:281 6:59, 63.

43. In 1684 the Chevalier de Troyes under La Barre's orders launched an attack against the Iroquois, who had seized peltries despite a former agreement. In 1686 Denonville organized an expedition, again with the Knight of Troyes in command, to retaliate against the storming of Fort Bourbon by Radisson in behalf of the English two years before. In 1687, 180 woodrunners participated in the onslaught against the Tsonnontouans with 800 soldiers, 1,100 militiamen, and 400 Indians. See Lacoursière, Provencher, and Vaugeois, *Canada-Quebec*, 89–91. Guy Frégault, *Iberville le Conquérant* (Montréal: Fidès, 1968), chapter 5.

44. Jacquin, *Indiens blancs*, 226.

45. Eccles, *Canadian Frontier*, 109–10. Jacquin, *Indiens blancs*, 230–31. Giraud, *Métis in the Canadian West*, 272–77; Nicolas Jérémie. *Relation du détroit de la Baie d'Hudson* (Amsterdam: Bernard, 1720), 33–34.

CHAPTER 4. THE *PAYS DES ILLINOIS*

1. The Pays des Illinois is often referred to as Les Illinois by historians. The basic references for the period are Charles Balési, *Time of the French in the Heart of North America, 1673–1818* (Chicago: Alliance française, 1992); Norman Caldwell, *The French in the Mississippi Valley, 1740–1750.* vol. 26, (Urbana: Illinois Studies in the Social Sciences, 1941. Repr. Philadelphia: The Porcupine Press, 1974); Peter Kalm, *Travels into North America,* 3 vols. (Warrington: 1770–71); Ekberg Carl, *French Roots in the Illinois Country* (Urbana: University of Illinois Press, 1998); *François Vallé and His World* (Columbia: University of Missouri Press, 2002); John F. McDermott, ed., *The French in the Mississippi Valley* (Urbana: University of Illinois Press, 1965); John McDermott, ed., *Frenchmen and French Ways in the Mississippi Valley.* (Urbana: University of Illinois Press, 1969).

2. Natalia M. Belting, *Kaskaskia under the French Régime.* (Urbana: The University of Illinois Press, 1948).

3. See Carl J. Ekberg, *Colonial Sainte Genevieve* (Gerald, MD: The Patrice Press, 1985).

4. Norman Caldwell, *The French in the Mississippi Valley,* 17.

5. King's instructions to La Jonquière, April 30, 1749, ANB 89:49–50 (Jesuit and Récollet orders); Bishop of Quebec to Minister, August 22, 1742, ANC11A 78:407–9 (on Pontbriand's statement that the trade in liquor was absolutely contrary to Christianity); Caldwell, *The French in the Mississippi Valley,* 21 (on the Abbé de l'Isle Dieu's stance); Thwaites, *Jesuit Relations* 69:74–79 (on the Society of Jesus in New France, 1749).

6. Jean Benjamin Dumont, *Mémoires historiques sur la Louisiane,* 2 vols. (Paris: C. J. B. Bauche, 1753), 2:53–57.

7. Minister to Vaudreuil September 26, 1750, ANB 91:13.

8. De Noyan, Memoir on Louisiana, 1745, ANC13A 30:270.

9. Caldwell, *The French in the Mississippi Valley,* 39.

10. De Bertet in Ekberg, *French Roots,* 48, 69, 82; Vaudreuil in Ekberg, *French Roots,* 32, 48, 69.

11. Caldwell, *The French in the Mississippi Valley,* 45–48 (on agriculture).

12. La Galissonnière, Ekberg, *French Roots,* 14, 213, 223

13. La Galissonnière to Minister, September 1, 1748, ANC11 91:116–23. See Eccles, *Canadian Frontier,* 155.

14. Colden to Peter Collinson, December, 1743. *The Colden Papers. New York Historical Society Collection,* 3 vols. (New York: 1919) 3:42–44.

15. Minister to Hocquart April 20, 1742, ANB 74:478; Memoir of the King to Beauharnois and Hocquart, April 30, 1742, ANB 74:503–11.

16. Caldwell, *The French in the Mississippi Valley*, 55.

17. Ibid., 62–63; the marquis de La Jonquière (1685–1752) was born near Albi, the stronghold of the Albigenses in medieval France. At first a naval officer in the Mediterranean, he also participated in the removal of the Camisards, hardline protestants in the Cévennes. He was in command of several warships during campaigns against the Royal Navy, and then inspector of colonial troops in 1741. Appointed governor of New France in 1746, on his way to Canada he was involved in the abortive expedition led by the Duc d'Anville against the British near Acadia, and had to return to France as commander of the decimated squadron. In 1747, La Jonquière made for Canada again to occupy the post of governor. He was at the head of a convoy including three frigates and over thirty merchant ships. The French fleet was attacked by a British squadron with enormous firepower. La Jonquière was wounded and taken prisoner after a fiery combat. He was released two years later after the peace treaty of Aix La Chapelle. La Jonquière eventually reached Quebec in 1749, taking over from La Galissonière, who had held the appointment temporarily.

18. Colin G. Calloway, *One Vast Winter Count* (Lincoln: The University of Nebraska Press, 2003), 320.

19. Eric Hinderaker, *Elusive Empires* (Cambridge: Cambridge University Press,1997), 49.

20. David Edmunds and Joseph Peyser, *The Fox Wars* (Norman: University of Oklahoma Press, 1993), 61–85.

21. Lenville J. Stelle, "Réaume Narrative," In *Calumet and Fleur–de-Lys* ed. John Walthall and Thomas Emerson (Washington, DC: Smithsonian Institution Press, 1992), 265–307. Simon Réaume was one of the Créole traders.

22. Instructions to La Jonquière, April 1, 1746, ANB 83:78; Beauharnois to Minister, September 17, 1743, ANC11A 7:110 (on La Richardie's removal from the mission); De Noyan to Minister August 20, 1742, ANC11 78:248–54.

23. See Richard White, *The Roots of Dependency, Subsistence, Environment and Social Change among the Choctaws, Pawnees and Navajos* (Lincoln: University of Nebraska Press, 1983), chapter 5.

24. Paul Marin de La Malgue (1692–1753) served in the West most of his career as an officer. Beauharnois supported him when the minister of Marine ordered him recalled from the Sioux country in 1741 for illegal fur trading. From 1739 to 1742, La Malgue maintained between six and thirty voyageurs who supplied tribes with goods and obtained furs in exchange. It was allegedly a strategy to retain the allegiance of the western Indians and keep them away from British traders. Vaudreuil and Beauharnois established his reputation as a daredevil condottiere. He tried to keep peace among the Sioux, Fox and Sauk tribes over two decades; Memoir of the King to Beauharnois, May 13, 1740, ANB 70:359–63; Beauharnois to Minister June 30, 1739, ANC11A 71: 35; August 14, 1742, ANC11A 77: 83–48; November 2, 1742, ANC11A 75:243 (on Dazenard); September 18, 1743, ANC11A 79:115–18; October 13, 1743, ANC11A 79:126–27.

25. In 1744, Vaudreuil made a contract with Deruisseaux, banning the liquor traded in Missouri. See Memoir of Vaudreuil, August 25, 1743, ANC 13 A 28:226; Minister to Vaudreuil, April 30, 1746 ANB 83:15–16.

26. Caldwell, *The French in the Mississippi Valley*, 76–77.

27. Calloway, *One Vast Winter Count*, 320.

CHAPTER 5. SHIFTING IDENTITIES

1. Maréchal de Saxe was at the head of the French army at Fontenoy in the province of Hainaut, Belgium, against a coalition of English and Dutch troops in 1745.

2. See Eccles, *Canadian Frontier*, 140–55. The peace talks began in the spring and the treaty was signed on October 18, 1748. Louisburg was considered as the Gibraltar of New France.

3. It happened on Lake Saint Pierre, below Three Rivers. The prisoners were helped by accomplices from the shore. Being held in chains was considered by the natives as worse than death at the stake. See Caldwell, *The French in the Mississppi Valley*, 91.

4. Walter J. Sauier and Katherine W. Seineke, "François Saucier, engineer of Fort de Chartres Illinois," in McDermott, *Frenchmen and French Ways*, 199–227.

5. La Demoiselle's village, Pickawillany, was located on the Great Miami, near present-day Piqua, Ohio; Longueuil (1701–78) was a brother to Bienville and Iberville. In 1745, he informed the governor that English traders spread the rumor that the French would soon leave Canada. On the other hand, the Indians allies of New France found their war efforts against the Chickasaws unrewarding because of the shortage of goods in the western posts. Longueuil to Beauharnois, July 28, 1745, ANC11A 83:61.

6. See Andrew Gallup, *The Céloron Expedition to the Ohio Country, 1749: The Reports of Pierre-Joseph Céloron and Father Bonnecamps* (Bowie, MD: Heritage Books, 1997).

7. De Raymond was in command of the Miami post when, in 1745, he presented a memoir upon the dangers of the British trade in the region. For him, France had to fortify the Miami region instead of the Upper Ohio to stop English influence with the Indians. De Raymond also contended that the English had fomented the revolt of 1747. De Raymond to Minister, November 2, 1747, ANC11A 89:225–28. See Joseph L. Peyser, *On the Eve of Conquest: The Chevalier De Raymond's Critique of New France in 1754* (East Lansing: Michigan State University Press, 1997), 18–25.

8. Born in 1705, Barthélémy, Chevalier de Macarty, was of Irish descent. His ancestors had fled to France during Cromwell's Commonwealth. He had been a mousquetaire before taking up his appointment as a commissioned officer in New Orleans in 1732. As commandant in Illinois, he was aware that there must be a certain amount of give-and-take in the negotiations with Indians. Havard and Vidal, *Histoire de l'Amérique française*, 181.

9. Jean-Bernard Bossu, *Travels to that Part of North America Formerly Called Louisiana*. Trans. Seymour Feiler (Norman: University of Oklahoma Press, 1962), 100–130.

10. Havard and Vidal, *Histoire de l'Amérique française*, 129–30.

11. Bossu, *Travels to that Part of North America*, 131–35.

12. See Richard White, *The Middle Ground, Indians, Empires and Republics in the Great Lakes Region, 1610–1815* (Cambridge: Cambridge University Press, 1991), 228–34.

13. Paul Marin de la Malgue had turned to the fur trade in 1750, and made a fortune, while employing two hundred voyageurs. As a commander of Duquesne's forces he led a a force of Canadians and Indians into the Ohio country. He was ruthless with stragglers during his campaign. He died of exhaustion on October 29, 1753 at Fort de La Rivière au Bœuf. Calloway, *One Vast Winter Count*, 336.

14. Eccles, *Canadian Frontier,* 164. Joseph Coulon de Villiers led a party of thirty-three men sent to meet Washington's detachment and require that they retire. Washington was held responsible for the death of Jumonville by his brother, Coulon de Villiers, who asked for the honor of avenging him. He raided Fort Granville, near present-day Altoona, Pennsylvania. His captives (three women and seven children) were brought back to Fort de Chartres and held for ransom. Pécaudy de Contrecoeur was in command of Fort Duquesne; the name Monongahela came from "mal-engueulée" in colloquial French. It meant "with a bad mouth." See Marcel Trudel, "L'affaire Jumonville," *Revue d'histoire française* 6, no. 3 (1952): 331–73.

15. Havard and Vidal, *Histoire de l'Amérique française,* 425.

16. Born in 1712 in Camargue, in the Rhone delta, Montcalm died on September 12, 1759 of wounds received during the battle of the Plaines d'Abraham. He was hot-tempered and arrogant, and antagonized Vaudreuil, who was vain and erratic. To appease his starving fellow countrymen in 1757 when peasants were on the battlefields, Montcalm advocated horsemeat instead of vegetables on Canadian tables. He was himself from a region famous for horse breeding. Louis Césaire Dagneau Douville de Quindre (1704–67) was a former colonel of the Detroit militia, and owed his promotion to Céloron de Blainville in 1755. In 1763, he adjusted to British rule, and supported the Redcoats during Pontiac's revolt; François-Marie Marchand de Lignery (1703–59) served as an officer in the colonial troops. He was enlisted in a campaign against the Foxes in 1728, then fought the Chickasaws under Le Moyne de Longueuil in 1739. He was instrumental in the defeat of General Braddock at Monongahela in 1755. In 1756, as commander on the Ohio, Lignery launched many raids from Fort Duquesne against the Redcoats. His coureurs des bois and Indians became experts in guerrilla warfare, and in 1758 stopped James Grant's eight hundred Redcoats who were demoralized by such relentless harassment. See Louise Phelps Kellog, *The French Régime in Wisconsin and the Northwest* (Madison: Wisconsin State Historical Society of Wisconsin, 1925), 425–26, 434. Bougainville (1729–1811) later turned to the exploration of the Pacific, and led scientific expeditions to Tahiti and New Guinea. He published his *Voyage autour du monde* in 1771. See Bougainville, *Ecrits sur le Canada. Mémoires-Journal-Lettres* (Paris: Klincksieck, 1993), 50, 96, 253. See also *Adventure in the Wilderness: The American Journals of Louis Antoine de Bougainville 1756–1760,* ed. Edward P. Hamilton (Norman: University of Oklahoma Press, 1964).

17. For a survey of the period see Balési, *Time of the French,* 268–75.

18. Havard and Vidal, *Histoire de l'Amérique française,* 451–54.

19. Gregory Dowd, "The French King Wakes up in Detroit: Pontiac's War in Rumor and History," *Ethnohistory* 37, no. 3 (1990): 254–78; see also Dowd, *War under Heaven: Pontiac, The Indian Nations, and the British Empire* (Baltimore MD: The Johns Hopkins University Press, 2002).

20. Clarence E. Carter, *Great Britain and the Illinois Country, 1763–1774* (Washington: The American Historical Association,1910), 16–25.

21. See Balési, *Time of the French,* 280–84. Balési's minute study of the period is based on Carter, ed., *Correspondence of General Thomas Gage,* 2 vols. (New Haven: Yale University Press, 1931).

22. Alexander DeConde, *Affair of Louisiana* (New York: Charles Scribner's Sons, 1976) 22–29, 293–94; Pierre Boulle, "Some Eighteenth Century French Views on Louisiana," in McDermott, *Frenchmen and French Ways,* 26–27.

23. McDermott, "Myths and Realities Concerning the Founding of Saint Louis," in Caldwell, *The French in Mississippi Valley,* 1–15.

24. McDermott, *Frenchmen and French Ways,* 1–15 (on Auguste Chouteau). Major

sources are William E. Foley and C. David Rice, *The First Chouteaus: River Barons of Early St. Louis* (Urbana: University of Illinois Press. 1983), 1–35; Ekberg, *French Roots*, 96–108; Shirley Christian, *Before Lewis and Clark: The Story of the Chouteaus, the French Dynasty That Ruled America's Frontier* (New York: Farrar, Straus and Giroux, 2004) 25–40.

25. David I. Weber, *The Spanish Frontier in North America* (New Haven: Yale University Press,1992), 200–202 (on Ulloa); Ekberg, *Colonial Sainte Genevieve*, 26–27, 36–37 (on O'Reilly); David Ker Texada, *O'Reilly and the New Orleans Rebels* (Lafayette: University of Southwestern Louisiana, 1970), 114–25. Texada contends that O'Reilly had been unfairly judged.

26. Ekberg, *Colonial Sainte Genevieve*, 336.

27. Ekberg, *François Vallé*, 50–52, 61, 99–100, 101–2, 108, 135, 150 (on Rocheblave); 35, 88, 108–9, 111, 114–15, 135, 188, 255 (on Villars).

28. Ibid., 209–16 (on Vallé's friendship with Cruzat).

29. Jean-Marie Ducharme (1723–1807) was born at Lachine. By 1752 he was a voyageur in Illinois. A messenger in Contrecoeur's troops, he also participated in the building of Fort Duquesne in 1755. To support Pontiac's rebellion he was involved in the arms trade in Michilimackinac, and in 1764, jailed by the British in Montreal. Despite the Spanish ban on trade with the Osages, he took two canoeloads of goods into their territory in 1772. After an exchange of gunfire he fled with his Iroquois servant. His companions surrendered. In the late 1770s he was still in the fur trade in La Baye and Prairie du Chien. See Foley and Rice, *The First Chouteaus*, 18.

30. The Continental Congress drafted an address against the Quebec Act on October 21, 1774. It denied the right of the British to establish harmful religious principles to protect the Catholic Church.

31. On the period see Alvord, *Illinois Country, 1673–1818*, 2 vols. (Springfield: Centennial History of Illinois. 1920), 1:317–24; Ekberg, *French Roots*, 250–54; Balési, *Time of the French*, 294–96.

32. See Landon Y. Jones, *William Clark and the Shaping of the West* (New York: Hill and Wang, 2004), 25–48. Major sources are Frederick Palmer, *Clark of the Ohio: A Life of George Rogers Clark* (New York: Dodd, Mead and Co., 1929); Elizabeth A. Perkins, *Border Life: Experience and Memory in the Evolutionary Ohio Valley* (Chapel Hill: University of North Carolina Press, 1998); John F. Bakeless, *Background to Glory: The Life of George Rogers Clark* (Lincoln: University of Nebraska Press, 1992).

33. Ekberg, *French Roots*, 63; Ekberg, *François Vallé*, 108.

34. Balési, *Time of the French*, 301–2.

35. Foley and Rice, *First Chouteaus*, 27–28; Ekberg, *François Vallé*, 70.

36. Ekberg, *François Vallé*, 212.

37. Foley and Rice, *First Chouteaus*, 37.

38. Guillaume-François Dagneau de Quindre was the son of Louis Césaire Dagneau Douville de Quindre, who had joined Lignery to try and relieve Fort Niagara in 1759.

39. Balési, *Time of the French*, 304.

40. Jones, *William Clark*, 45, 120.

41. Hafen, *French Fur Traders, and Voyageurs in the American West* (Lincoln: University of Nebraska Press, 1997), 217–28.

42. Wiley Sword, *President Washington's Indian War: The Struggle for the Old Northwest, 1790–1795* (Norman: University of Oklahoma Press, 1985), 14–20 (on Saint Clair); Jones, *William Clark*, 64–65, 68–73, 81–93. (on Wayne).

43. On the founders of the company, see Jennifer Brown, *Strangers in Blood: Fur*

Trade Company Families in Indian Country (Vancouver: University of British Columbia Press, 1980) 39–42. See also L. R. Masson, *Bourgeois;* Robert Rumilly, *La Compagnie du Nord-Ouest, une épopée montréalaise,* 2 vols. (Montreal: Fides, 1980); Wood and Thiessen, *Early Fur Trade.*

44. In his journal of the Lewis and Clark expedition, William Gass offers many tentative translations of French place-names. As in the case of "La Rivière qui pleure," his interpretation is often correct. His attempt is less rewarding when he suggests "Cheyenne" for "chien." See *The Journal of Patrick Gass,* vol. 10, ed. Gary E. Moulton (Lincoln: University of Nebraska Press, 1996), 22. An interesting overview of French regional languages spoken in New France is offered by Marthe Faribault in "Patois et Français régionaux en Nouvelle-France," in *Mémoires de Nouvelle-France* ed. Philippe Joutard, and Thomas Wien (Rennes: Presses universitaires de Rennes, 2005), 273–92. The French spoken by colonists along the Saint Lawrence originated from three linguistic areas: Paris, Normandy, and Poitou-Charentes. In the West, the higher proportion of temporary officials and military personnel from various French provinces was instrumental in adding new vocabulary into a heterogeneous colonial idiom. Montcalm, who was from the south of France noted many peculiarities.

CHAPTER 6. FRENCH CULTURE IN TRANSITION

1. Maunoir to the acting governor of New France, Claude de Ramezay, August 28, 1715, ANC11A 35:57; Dadoncour to Longueuil, August 22, 1715, ANC11A 35:54; Henri Joutel (1643–1725) was born in Rouen, Normandy, like La Salle, whom he served faithfully during the expedition down the Mississippi. His journal was published by Margry with great accuracy. After landing on the coast of Texas, Joutel was in command of the colony near Lavaca Bay, and built the stockade at Fort Saint Louis while La Salle was exploring the local surroundings. In 1686, he demonstrated his loyalty to La Salle by destroying Father Maxime Le Clerq's journal, which held views critical of the expedition. In 1698 Joutel declined the offer to accompany Le Moyne d'Iberville along the Gulf of Mexico, but his journal was helpful to the expedition. Henri Joutel, *Joutel's Journal of La Salle's Last Voyage* (London: Lintot, 1714, Repr. New York: Franklin, 1968); Margry, *Découvertes et établissements,* 3:124, 480. See also Gilles Havard, *Empire et métissages: Indiens et Français dans le Pays d'En Haut, 1660–1715* (Sillery/ Paris: Septentrion/ Presses de l'Université Paris-Sorbonne, 2003), 518.

2. Louis Hennepin, *Description de la Louisiane,* 228.

3. Maxime Le Clerq, *Nouvelles relations,* 2:194–99; Margry, *Découvertes et établissements,* 1:589–92.

4. Louis Lahontan, *Œuvres complètes,* 2:379–80.

5. Margry, *Découvertes et établissements,* 1:593–95.

6. Lahontan, *Œuvres complètes,* 2:640.

7. Ibid., 2:673.

8. Louvigny to Minister, September 21, 1717, ANC11A 38: 198.

9. Margry, *Découvertes et établissements,* 3:342; Denonville to Minister, November 13, 1685, ANC11A 7:89–90.

10. Charlevoix, *Journal,* 239. See Bernard DeVoto, *The Course of Empire* (New York: Houghton Mifflin, 1952), 495.

11. Michel Chartier de Lotbinière (1723–98) was an officer in the colonial army. In 1749 he was sent by La Galissonière to the Pays d'En Haut to collect information

on the prospects opened by the fur trade. He then spent three years in France studing engineering. In 1757, despite the support of his cousin, Governor Vaudreuil, he did not obtain the title of chief engineer of New France as he expected. He owned two seigneuries on Lake Champlain before 1763. After much litigation he was deprived of his landed property, now in the territory of New England. He offered his services to Vergennes during the American Revolution, vainly hoping to recover his seigneuries. He was never allowed to return to Canada after 1783, and died in New York after decades of exile. See Marcel Trudel, *Louis XVI, le Congrès américain et le Canada, 1774–1789* (Québec: Les Editions du Quartier Latin, 1949).

12. Louis Houck, ed., *The Spanish Regime in Missouri,* 2 vols. (Chicago: R.R. Donnelley, 1909), 1:53–60.

13. Joseph Garreau in Pierre Antoine Tabeau, *Tabeau's Narrative of Loisel's Expedition to the Upper Missouri,* ed. Annie Heloise Abel (Norman: University of Oklahoma Press, 1939), 140–41; *The Definitive Journals of Lewis and Clark,* ed. Gary E. Moulton, 8 vols. (Lincoln: University of Nebraska Press, 1987) 3:313–14.

14. Claude-Charles Le Roy La Potherie, *Histoire de l'Amérique septentrionale* (Paris: Brocas, 1753), 2:2.

15. Lahontan, *Œuvres complètes,* 2:344, 356.

16. Thwaites, *Jesuit Relations,* 66:268, 270, 274–76.

17. Margry, *Découvertes et établissements,* 3:441, 464, 471.

18. Ibid., 3:429–30 (on Joutel).

19. Deliette was of Italian descent, and a cousin of Tonty. He commanded Fort Saint Louis in 1687, then moved to Pimitoui (Peoria) in 1692. He enjoyed friendly relations with the Illinois Indians, and accompanied them on buffalo hunts to learn their language. In 1712 he helped establish peace between the Illinois and the Miamis. Deliette, "Mémoire," in *The French Foundations 1680–1693,* eds. Thomas C Pease and Richard C. Werner, Collection of the Illinois State Historical Library, vol. 23, (Springfield, IL: 1934): 302–20.

20. Aigremont (1659–1728) was born in Burgundy. A naval commissary in Canada in 1701, he could not afford to purchase his office as decreed by Louis XIV in 1702. Beauharnois appointed him as a secretary. Aigrement was then sent by Raudot to the West to inspect trading posts, Archives de la Côte d'Or, Dijon C 2885: 307; Louvigny to Minister, October 26, 1715, ANC11A 35:224.

21. Lahontan, *Œuvres complètes,* 2:346.

22. Calvin Martin, *Keepers of the Game: Indian-Animal Relationships and the Fur Trade* (Berkeley: University of California Press, 1978) 40–65, 113, 149.

23. In 1772, Matthew Cocking was sent by the Hudson's Bay Company to the forks of the Saskatchewan, and overland to the Blackfeet to see how far the Montreal traders had trespassed on Bay territory. The only man he met was Leblanc. See Giraud, *Métis in the Canadian West,* 2:161; Mari Sandoz, *The Beaver Men* (Lincoln: University of Nebraska Press, 1964),155.

24. Havard, *Empire et métissages,* 209–10, 261–62, 443–67.

25. La Potherie, *Histoire,* 3:274, 278.

26. Marcel Giraud, *Métis in the Canadian West,* 2: 310.

27. Margry, *Découvertes et établissements,* 1:564

28. Ibid., 5:100 (on Cadillac); La Potherie, *Histoire,* 2:236–37, 298–99.

29. Thwaites, *Jesuit Relations,* 65:26.

30. La Potherie, *Histoire,* 2:299.

31. Margry, *Découvertes et établissements,* 5:492–93.

32. François-Xavier de Charlevoix, *Histoire,* 2: 60.

33. Havard, *Empire et métissages,* 753.

34. La Potherie, *Histoire* 4:247.

35. Antoine Louis Descomp-Labadie was the father of Angelica, born in 1760. In 1776, she married Pierre Drouillard, who was a bigamist. George Drouillard, who participated in the Lewis and Clark expedition, was the son of Pierre and a Shawnee woman. Francis Parkman, *The Conspiracy of Pontiac and the Indian War after the Conquest of Canada* 10th ed., 2 vols. (Boston, 1886); Gregory E. Dowd, "The French King Wakes up in Detroit: Pontiac's War in Rumor and History," *Ethnohistory* 37, no.3 (1990): 254–78; Howard Peckham, *Pontiac and the Indian Uprising of 1763* (Princeton: Princeton University Press, 1947); Richard White, *The Middle Ground, Indians, Empires, and Republics in the Great Lakes Region, 1610–1815*. Cambridge: Cambridge University Press, 1983.

CHAPTER 7. THE MÉTIS

1. Marcel Giraud, *Métis in the Canadian West*, 2:213–17.

2. Yves Landry, "Les immigrants en Nouvelle France: bilan historiographqiue et perspective de recherche." in *Mémoires de Nouvelle France*, ed. Philippe Joutard and Thomas Wien (Rennes: Presses Universitaires de Rennes, 2005), 65–80.

3. In "Le discours sur la Nouvelle France et son évolution," Gilbert Pilleul discusses the image of the New France colony in comparison with Spanish and English settlements. He suggests that the reports on the climate were not really dissuasive. In Joutard and Wien, *Mémoires de Nouvelle France*, 133–44.

4. The bonus amounted to 3000 livres (piastres) but was seldom granted. Most of the sauvagesses [savage girls] concerned had, in fact, been schooled at Ursuline institutions. See Lefevre de la Barre to Minister, November 4, 1683, ANC11A 6:140.

5. Jennifer Brown, *Strangers in Blood: Fur Trade Company Families in Indian Country* (Vancouver: University of British Columbia Press, 1980), 12–13.

6. Giraud, *Métis in the Canadian West*, 2: 252. Charles Chaboillez (1772–1812) was a Métis. In the fall of 1804, he met Lewis and Clark at the Mandan village where they wintered. His father, Charles Jean Baptiste Chaboillez (1736–1808), worked near the mouth of the Pembina River for the North West Company.

7. Chabert de Joncaire was a sergeant of the guards under Frontenac. He could use his situation to strengthen the position of France along the Great Lakes. See Giraud, *Métis in the Canadian West*, 2: 233.

8. Gilles Havard, *Empire et métissages*, 627 (on Marguerite Le Sueur). Maurice Ménard, born in 1664, was the son of Jacques Ménard, alias La Fontaine, a cartwright. As an interpreter at Michilimackinac he was on friendly terms with the local Ottawas (ANC11A 24, Letter from Vaudrot to Minister, November 3, 1706). It seems he was often involved in many legal cases either as a plaintiff or a defendant. The couple had nine children. Marguerite's husband, Jean Faffard, had served Duluth in Michigan among the Illinois in 1677. In the 1680s he was with Ménard in the fur trade. Fafard was a bigamist. His son Maconce was a Loup chief. On the Couc family see Simone Vincens, *Madame Montour et son temps* (Montreal: Québec Amérique, 1979); Thwaites, *Jesuit relations*, 37:100 (on Pierre Couc).

9. Havard, *Empire et Métissages*, 680.

10. Margry, *Découvertes et établissements*, 5:210 (on Madame de Tonty).

11. Lamothe Cadillac to Minister, October 26, 1713 ANC13A 3:13. Margry, *Découvertes*, 5:121, 464 (on Tonty and Lamothe Cadillac); Deliette, *Mémoires*, 337.

12. Gabriel Sagard-Théodat, *Le Grand voyage du Pays des Hurons*, (Paris: Troso, 1865), 195.

13. Thwaites, *Jesuit Relations*, 65, 190–97.

14. Jean-Bernard Bossu, *Nouveaux voyages en Louisiane, 1751–1762*, ed. Philippe Jacquin (Paris: Aubier-Montaigne, 1980), 88.

15. Lahontan, *Œuvres complètes*, 2: 417

16. Susan Sleeper-Smith, *Indian Women and French Men: Rethinking Cultural Encounter in the Western Great Lakes*. (Amherst: University of Massachusetts Press, 2001), 28–29 (on Accault). Chapter 2, "Marie Rouensa and the Jesuits: Conversion, Gender and Power," contends that Catholicism was a source of the Indian woman's empowerment, while Christianity was negotiated and transformed on the middle ground, 23–37.

17. Vaudreuil to Minister, November 14, 1709, ANC11A 30:81; see Havard, *Empire et métissages*, 649–50.

18. Bossu, *Nouveaux voyages*, 76–78.

19. Margry, *Découvertes* 5:488, Relation de Pénicaut.

20. Deliette, *Mémoires*, 335–36.

21. Havard, *Empire et métissages*, 658–60.

22. Ibid., 667–68.

23. Major sources are *Alexander Henry's Travels and Adventures in the Years 1760–1776*, ed. Milo M. Quaife (Chicago: Lakeside Press, 1921), 64; Jacqueline Peterson, "Many Roads to Red River, Métis Genesis in the Great Lake Region, 1680–1815, in *The New Peoples* ed. Jacqueline Peterson and Jennifer S. Brown (Winnipeg: The University of Manitoba Press, 1985), 37–72; Louis Phelps Kellog, *The French Régime in Wisconsin and the Northwest* (Madison, WI: State Historical Society of Wisconsin, 1925); Ernest Voorhis, *Historic Forts and Trading Posts of the French Régime and of the English Fur Trade Companies* (Canada: Ottawa, Ontario, 1930); Harold A. Innis, *The Fur Trade in Canada* (Toronto: University of Toronto Press, 1970).

24. Jacqueline Peterson and Jennifer S. H. Brown, *The New Peoples: Being and Becoming Métis in North America* (Winnipeg: The University of Manifoba Press, 1985), 57–60.

25. Joseph Zitomersky, "French Americans-Native Americans in Eighteenth Century Colonial Louisiana," *Studies in International History* 31 (1994), 178–220.

26. Joseph Kinsey Howard, *Strange Empire*, 1952 (Saint Paul: Minnesota Historical Society Press, 1994), 23–45.

27. The Hudson's Bay Company sent employees to winter in areas where it was possible to counter French presence. See Barbara Belyea, *A Year Inland: The Journal of a Hudson's Bay Company Winterer* (Waterloo Ontario: Wilfrid Laurier University Press, 2000), 39–40, 104–8, 180–81, 344, 370–77.

28. Alexander Henry, *Travels in Canada and the Indian Territories between the Years 1760 and 1776, by Alexander Henry, Fur Trader*, ed. James Bain (Toronto: George N. Morang, 1901. Repr.: Chicago: R. Donnelley and Sons, 1921), 34–36, 75–83.

29. Arthur J. Ray, *Indians in the Fur Trade: Their Role as Hunters, Trappers, and Middlemen in the Lands Southwest of Hudson Bay, 1660–1870* (Toronto: University of Toronto Press, 1974), 101–40.

30. Louis Primeau first belonged to the Hudson's Bay Company. He wintered in the prairies in the 1760s and visited York Factory. He was illiterate but a well-known interpreter. In 1772 several Indian tribes turned away from the Bay traders, and deserted Primeau in canoes loaded with furs when they were attracted to the Brazilian tobacco and brandy offered by competitors. He later joined the North West Company, and wintered with Joseph Frobisher near Grand Portage. Giraud suggests that Primeau left the Hudson's Bay Company because he was repelled by the excessive sufferings which the primitive life involved. Giraud, *Métis in the Canadian West*, 265.

31. Joseph Tassé, *Les Canadiens de l'Ouest*, 2 vols. (Montreal: Compagnie d'imprimerie canadienne,1882), 1:172–73; Jacqueline Peterson, "Many Roads to Red River," in *New Peoples*, 61, 124.

32. Brown, *Strangers in Blood*, 84–89.

33. Giraud, *Métis in Canadian West*, 253.

34. Elliott Coues, *New Light on the Early History of the Greater West*, 3 vols. (New York: Harper, 1897) 1:211, 225, 2:616–17.

35. Ibid., 1:228–31, 263–64, 415–16; 2:612–13.

CHAPTER 8. . . . SEEN FROM FRANCE

1. The contemporary reference for Parisian readers was Lahontan's *Nouveaux voyages dans l'Amérique septentrionale*, 3 vols. (La Haye: Les Frères Honoré,1703). English edition: *New Voyages to North America*, ed. Reuben Thwaites (Chicago: A. C. McClurg and Co., 1905). Volume 2 is titled "Supplément aux Voyages du Baron de Lahontan, où l'on trouve les dialogues curieux entre l'auteur et un sauvage de bon sens qui a voyagé [supplement to the travels of Baron de Lahontan where are found the curious dialogues between the author and a sensible, well-traveled savage].

2. Charles-Louis Secondat de Montesquieu, *Lettres Persanes* (Paris, 1721).

3. In his stimulating commentary on Lahontan's satire, Gordon Sayre contends that Adario is a synthesis of Indian culture and European radical deism, whose speeches denounce prostitution, inequitable taxation, and absolute monarchy, as well as praising the Hurons' control of their passions and disdain for the temptations of wealth, in *Sauvages Américains*, 38.

4. Joseph-François Lafitau, *Mœurs des sauvages américains comparés aux mœurs des premiers temps* (Paris: Saugrain, C.E. Hochereau, 1724), 2: 289; Sayre, *Sauvages Américains*, 303.

5. Gilbert Chinard, *Amérique et le rêve exotique*, 230–33.

6. Voltaire, *L'Ingénu* (Paris, 1767). In this picaresque short novel, a naive young Huron who has escaped from the British arrives in Paris. He is baptized by the Jesuits, received at the Court of Versailles, then jailed at the Bastille and afterwards lives as a libertine despite himself. Voltaire parodies the Jansénists and the aristocracy through a libertine evocation of the ups and down of a token savage who becomes a pawn in paternalistic high society. See *Voltaire, Oeuvres complètes* (Paris: Garnier, 1877–85); Charles André Helvetius, *Traité sur l'homme* (Paris, 1772); Charles Pinot Duclos, *Considérations sur les mœurs de ce siècle* (Paris, 1751. Repr. Cambridge: Cambridge University Press, 1939); Denis Diderot, *Supplément au Voyage de Bougainville* (Paris, 1796); Abbé Prévost. *Histoire du Chevalier Desgrieux et de Manon Lescaut* (Paris, 1731).

7. George Louis Leclerc, comte de Buffon, *Variétés dans l'espèce humaine* (Paris, 1749); Voltaire, *Essai sur les mœurs et l'esprit des nations* (Paris, 1756); Cornelius de Pauw, *Recherches philosphiques sur les Américains ou mémoires intéressant pour servir à l'histoire de l'espèce humaine* (Paris, 1768); Abbé Raynal G.T., *Histoire philosophique et politique des établissements et du commerce des Européens dans les deux Indes*, 10 vols. (Genève, 1781).

8. *La Jeune Indienne* opened at the Comédie-Française in May 1764. It was a comedy in verse dealing with an Indian girl who was under the protection of the Quakers. The lack of verisimiliude irritated the critics, who found fault with the costumes and the elaborate rhetoric of an allegedly illiterate sauvagesse.

9. De Pauw, *Recherches philosophqiues*, 2:108.

10. Ibid., 1:4–5.

11. Raynal, *Histoire des deux Indes*, 6:316.

12. On D'Estaing's project, see "Mémoire donné par Mr D'Estaing" March 10, 1769, ANC11A 125:575–77; the story about Franklin's reception was told in an 1818 letter from Thomas Jefferson to Robert Walsh. See Daniel J. Boorstin, *The Lost World of Thomas Jefferson* (Chicago University of Chicago Press,1993), 101–2.

13. François Duc de La Rochefoucauld-Liancourt, *Journal d'un Voyage en Amérique et d'un séjour à Philadelphie* (1794) (Paris: Droz,1940), 62.

14. Jean-Pierre de Warville Brissot, *Nouveau Voyage dans les Etats-Unis de l'Amérique septentrionale fait en 1788* (Paris: Buisson, 1791).

15. In Philippe Berger, *L'Ennemi américain: généalogie de l'antiaméricanisme français* (Paris: Seuil, 2002), 68–72.

16. Joseph De Maistre, *Considérations sur la France* (1797), ed. Jean-Louis Darcel (Genève: Slatkine,1980), 98, 134.

17. François-René de Chateaubriand, *Atala*, ed. A. Weil (Paris: José Corti, 1950); Chateaubriand, *Oeuvres romanesques et voyages*. Vol. 1 of *Oeuvres complètes*, edited by Maurice Regard (Paris: Gallimard, Bibliothèque de la Pléiade, 1969); *Travels in America* (Paris: 1827. Repr., trans. Richard Switzer (Lexington: University of Kentucky Press, 1969). *Les Natchez*, ed. Jean-Claude Berchet (Paris; Le Livre de poche, 1989).

18. See Bossu, *Nouveaux voyages: Travels to that Part of North America*. Born in 1656, Tekakwitha first lived in a Mohawk village hostile to the Jesuit missionaries. Her mother, a Christian Algonquin, had been captured and forced to marry a Mohawk chief. Treated as a slave, Tekakwitha suffered persecutions because of her faith in God. As Kateri, she received baptism from Father Jacques de Lamberville in 1675, and after her first Communion two years later, took a vow of virginity. A mystic, she submitted herself to severe penances for her Indian community. When she died the pockmarks left by smallpox miraculously vanished from her face. The Venerable "Genevieve of Canada" is now considered as the protectress of the former Belle Province. See Allan Greer, *Mohawk Saint: Catherine Tekakwitha and the Jesuits* (Oxford, New York: Oxford University Press, 2004).

19. See Aimé Césaire, *Toussaint-Louverture: La Révolution française et le problème colonial* (Paris: Présence africaine, 1981). Césaire shows how Toussaint-Louverture transcended the conflict between lofty principles and vested interests. He was not satisfied with the assertion of slave emancipation in the abstract, and forcefully reminded the Paris revolutionaries that the Declaration of the Rights of Man also applied to the black population in the colonies.

20. Jefferson to Michaux, April 30, 1793, in *Letters of the Lewis and Clark Expedition, with Related Documents, 1783–1854*, ed. Donald Jackson (Urbana: University of Illinois Press, 1962), 667–72.

21. "André Michaux's Travels into Kentucky, 1793–96," in *Early Western Travels, 1748–1846*, ed. Reuben G. Thwaites (Cleveland: Arthur H. Clark, 1904), 3:65–66, 89–90; Jones, *William Clark*, 90–91.

22. Michael Garnier, *Bonaparte et la Louisiane* (Paris: Kronos, 1992), 26–37.

23. Ibid., 40–46.

24. See Louis-Jaray Gabriel, *L'Empire français d'Amérique 1534–1803*, (Paris: Armand Colin, 1938).

25. Ines Murat, *Napoléon et le rêve américain* (Paris: Fayard, 1976), 11–21.

26. Ibid., 23–28.

CHAPTER 9. LEWIS AND CLARK

1. Wayne E. Stevens, *The Northwest Fur Trade, 1763–1800* (Urbana: University of Illinois Press, 1928) 89–119; Jacqueline Peterson, "Prelude to Red River: A Social Portrait of the Great Lakes Métis," *Ethnohistory* 25, no. 1 (Winter 1978): 41–67.

2. A. P. Nasatir, "Jacques D'Eglise," *Mississippi Valley Historical Review* 14 (1927): 47–71.

3. Warren Cook, *Flood Tide of Empire: Spain and the Pacific Northwest, 1543–1819* (New Haven: Yale University Press), 269, 435–36, 438.

4. Helen Marie Williams, *Souvenirs de la Révolution française* (Paris: Doudey Duprey, 1827), 12–13. When Franklin was asked about the War of Independence in Paris, he used to reply "ça ira" [things will be going well]. Composer Ladré wrote the song of the same name in July 1790. It became immensely popular. The most famous lines are: "Ah! ça ira, ça ira/ Les aristocrates à la lanterne/ Ah! Ça ira, ça ira/ Les aristocrates on les pendra/ et quand on les aura tous pendus, on leur fichera la pelle au cul." [Things will go well, let's hang aristocrats on street lamps/ Things will go well /and when they are all hanged, we'll stick up the shovel in their ass].

5. Foley and Rice, *First Chouteaus,* 79–82.

6. See A. P. Nasatir, "Jacques Clamorgan," in *French Fur Traders and Voyageurs in the American West* ed. Leroy R. Hafen (1965. Repr. Lincoln: University of Nebraska Press., 1997), 124–37.

7. Shirley Christian, *Before Lewis and Clark: The Story of the Chouteaus* (New York: Farrar, Straus and Giraux, 2004), 14–17, 101–2.

8. Richard Edward Oglesby, *Manuel Lisa and the Opening of the Missouri Fur Trade* (Norman: University of Oklahoma Press ,1963), 11–12 (on Robidoux); 23–25 (on Sanguinet); 19 (on Chauvin).

9. Michel Garnier, *Bonaparte et la Louisiane* (Paris: Kronos, 1992), 40–41.

10. Born about 1751 in France, Victor Collot served under Rochambeau in the War of Independence. As governor, he was made prisoner by the British in Guadeloupe in 1794, and sent to the United States where a merchant had filed a suit against him for confiscation of his property. Being out on bail and inactive, Collot responded to an offer of the French ambassador to the United States to explore the Ohio and Mississippi rivers. At Fort Massac, Captain Zebulon Pike threatened to put him under arrest. In Saint Louis informers told Collot that Spain was intending to abandon Upper Louisiana, and added that a British force would invade it via the Great Lakes. At Fort San Carlos in New Orleans, where he was taken after his arrest, he was searched, and evidence was found against him. His assistant, Adjutant-General Joseph Warin, a skilled draftsman, had drawn a map of every Spanish fort from Cape Girardeau to Nogales. See McDermott, *The French in Mississippi Valley,* 133–36. Collot later published a book about his exploration of the West. See Victor Collot, *Journey in North America* (Paris, 1826).

11. Collot, *Journey in North America,* 277.

12. Jean Baptiste Truteau, "The Description of the Upper Missouri," (1796), ed. Annie Heloise Abel, is printed in French and English in the *Mississippi Valley Historial Review* 8 (1921): 157–79. According to Abel, Collot simply reproduced what Truteau wrote for him about of his experiences in Missouri. See *Tabeau's Narrative of Loisel's Expedition to the Upper Missouri,* ed. Annie Heloise Abel (Norman: University of Oklahoma Press, 1939), 15–16. See Nasatir, *Before Lewis and Clark,* 376–85. On Nicolas de Finiels, see McDermott, *The French in the Mississippi Valley,*136–39; Carl

Ekberg, *An Account of Upper Louisiana by Nicolas de Finiels* (University of Missouri Press, 1989).

13. Marie-Jeanne Rossignol, "A la recherche d'une diplomatie révolutionnaire: Louis-André Pichon, chargé d'affaires à Washington, 1801–1804," in *La France et les Américains au temps de Jefferson et Miranda* ed. Marcel Dorigny and Marie-Jeanne Rossignol (Paris: Société des études robespierristes, 2001), 13–29.

14. For reports on the proceedings, see letters from Laussat to Decrès, Minister of the Marine, December 20, 1803 (An XII, 28 Frimaire), ANC13A 52:190; April 13,1804 (An XII, 23 Germinal) ANC13A 83:52–53; On the mood of the French see Garnier, *Bonaparte et la Louisiane*, 217–19. A petition sent by French-speaking Louisianans to Laussat made three major claims: 1) an independent government, 2) the recognition of the mother tongue in assemblies and courts of justice, 3) freedom of choice in the slave market, especially the exclusive right to own black slaves from Guinea.

15. Christian, *Before Lewis and Clark*, 113.

16. Moulton, *Definitive Journals*, 2: 129. Most subsequent references to the journals of the Lewis and Clark Expedition are from the *Definitive Journals* (8 vols).

17. Moulton, *Definitive Journals*, 2:128.

18. Bernard Lugan, *Histoire de la Louisiane française*, 1682–1804 (Paris: Perrin, 1994), 211.

19. Moulton, *Definitive Journals*, 2: 240.

20. See William E. Foley and C. David Rice, "A French Entrepreneur as an American Agent," in *The First Chouteaus: River Barons of Early St. Louis* (Urbana: University of Illinois Press, 1983), 105–18.

21. A. P. Nasatir, *Before Lewis and Clark*, 84–93 (on the formation of the company), 219–24 (articles of incorporation), 259–94 (on Truteau's journal).

22. Milo Quaife, ed. "Extracts of Mr. Evans' Journal" in *Proceedings of the Wisconsin State Historical Society* 63 (1915): 195–200.

23. Abel, *Tabeau's Narrative*, 32–52.

24. Moulton, *Definitive Journals*, 3: 156–57, 161, 163, 304–5.

25. A. P. Nasatir, "Jacques Clamorgan," in *French Fur Traders and Voyageurs*, ed. Leroy R. Hafen (Lincoln: University of Nebraska Press), 124–137.

26. Abel, *Tabeau's Narrative*, 19–22, 61–69, 222–31, Nasatir, *Before Lewis and Clark*, 371, 421, 690, 761, 764.

27. Abel, *Tabeau's Narrative*, 40.

CHAPTER 10. ETHNIC DIVIDE

1. Jones, *William Clark*, 96, 131–32.

2. Moulton, *Definitive Journals*, 2:139.

3. Ibid., 179–80.

4. Ibid.,180. Clark calls the place "Passage Dessous," meaning subway. Saucier had moved from French Illinois to Upper Louisiana in 1765. In 1799 the Spanish governor asked him to organize the settlement of Portage des Sioux and appointed him commander. He remained in office until the United States took official possession.

5. Foley and Rice, *First Chouteaus*, 98–101.

6. Moulton, *Definitive Journals*, 3:118–19.

7. Ibid., 163.

8. Ibid., 217.

9. Ibid., 268–69.

10. Ibid., Rivière aux cinq hommes, 2:117, Rivière aux bœufs, 2:259, Rivière du bois, 2:252, Ile du Bon Homme, 3:38–39, Rivière de la Bonne Femme Creek, 3:340–41, Rivière à la Corne de Cerf, 3:350, Rivière La Mine, 3:43.

11. Leroy R. Hafen, "Pierre Ménard," in *French Fur traders and Voyageurs*, 217–28.

12. The most criticial period was when the Corps of Discovery wintered at Fort Mandan and were confronted with visitors from the North West Company who had been sent from Montreal to spy on them and possibly hire French-speaking members of the expedition. Moulton, *Definitive Journals*, 3:158, 179, 241, 252, 257–58, 262.

13. Ibid., 8:370.

14. Sources for the background of the French members of the Corps of Discovery are: Elliott Coues, *History of the Expedition Under the Command of Lewis and Clark*, 4 vols. (New York: Harper, 1893); *Original Journals of the Lewis and Clark Expedition, 1804–1806*, ed. Reuben G. Thwaites, 8 vols. (New York: Dodd, Mead & Co., 1904–5); Nasatir, *Before Lewis and Clark;* Charles G. Clarke, *The Men of the Lewis and Clark Expedition* (Lincoln: University of Nebraska Press, 1970, Bison Books Edition, 2002).

15. Moulton, *Definitive Journals*, 2:235.

16. Ibid., 254–56.

17. Ibid., 455.

18. On Primeau, Collin, La Liberté, and Lepage, see Clarke, *Men of the Lewis and Clark Expedition*, 62–69.

19. The birth certificate is reproduced in Denis Vaugeois, *America, l'expédition de Lewis et Clark et la naissance d'une nouvelle puissance* (Sillery, Québec: Septentrion, 2002),193. Charbonneau was thirty-seven in 1804. He was considered much older by historians prone to discredit him as a dirty old man.

20. Elliott Coues, *History of the Expedition under the Command of Lewis and Clark*, 4 vols. (New York: Harper, 1893), 1:189–90.

21. Moulton, *Definitive Journals*, 3:228

22. Ibid., 291. Jean Baptiste's date of birth was February 11, 1805.

23. Ibid., 8:306–8.

24. W. Dale Nelson, *Interpreters with Lewis and Clark, The Story of Sacagawea and Toussaint Charbonneau* (Denton: University of North Texas Press, 2003), 68–79.

25. Jones, *William Clark*,144–46, 186, 194, 249, 260, 270.

26. Major sources are Grace Raymond Hebard, *Sacajawea, A guide and interpreter of the Lewis and Clark expedition with an account of the travels of Toussaint Charbonneau, and of Jean Baptiste, the expedition papoose,* (Glendale, CA: The Arthur Clarke Company, 1957); Harold P. Howard, *Sacajawea* (Norman: University of Oklahoma Press, 1971). The name is currently spelt Sacagawea by historians.

27. When reaching the Yellowstone on the way back from the Pacific Ocean, Clark named a rock Pompey's Tower to honor Jean-Baptiste. In Moulton, *Definitive Journals*, 8:225.

28. See Kim R. Stafford, "Les deux histoires du Nord-Ouest Pacifique," in *Le Mythe de l'Ouest* ed. Philippe Jacquin and Daniel Royot (Paris: Autrement, 1993), 163–77.

29. Moulton, *Definitive Journals*, 8:180.

30. Hebard, *Sacajawea*, 111.

31. L. R. Masson, ed. *Les Bourgeois de la Compagnie du Nord-Ouest: Récits de voyages . . .* (New York: Antiquarian Press, 1960), *Bourgeois*, 2:371–73.

32. Jacquin, *Indiens blancs*, 202.

33. Herman Melville, *Moby-Dick*, 1850 (New York: Norton, 1967), 16.

34. See Moulton, *Definitive Journals*, 2:516, for a brief biographical sketch.

35. The authoritative biography of George Drouillard is M. O. Skarsten, *George Drouillard, Hunter and Interpreter for Lewis and Clark and Fur Trader, 1807–1810* (Glendale, CA: The Arthur H. Clark Company, 1964). A comparative study of John Colter and George Drouillard is offered in Robert M. Utley, *A Life Wild and Perilous, Mountain Men and the Paths to the Pacific* (New York: Henry Holt and Company, 1997). A romantic evocation of Drouillard's life is to be found in James Alexander Thom, *Sign-Talker, The Adventure of George Drouillard on the Lewis and Clark Expedition* (New York: Ballantine Books, 2000).

36. Balzac's well-known appreciation of Cooper was published in the *Revue Parisienne* for July 25, 1840, in an article on the state of letters in America. The statement is discussed in Willard Thorp, "Cooper Beyond America," *New York History* 35, no. 4 (October, 1954): 522–39. The exact text is: "Leatherstocking is a statue, a magnificent moral hermaphrodite, born half-savage, half-civilized. I do not know if the extraordinary work of Walter Scott has given us any creation as magnificent as this hero of the savannahs and the forests."

37. M. O. Skarsten, *George Drouillard, Hunter and Interpreter for Lewis and Clark and Fur Trader, 1807–1810* (Glendale, CA: The Arthur H. Clark Co., 1964), 245.

38. See Nasatir, *Before Lewis and Clark*, 771; Tabeau reports on some of Dorion's misadventures with the Tetons. He escaped the tomahawk of an aggressor by drawing a pistol, was robbed of his goods, and forced to spend nights without a candle, *Tabeau's Narrative*, 118–20.

39. Foley and Rice, *First Chouteaus*, 125.

40. The most extensive references to Jusseaume are in Moulton, *Definitive Journals*, 3: 203–5 226–27, 248–49, 260, 279–80, 302; 8:298, 304–5, 331–32; Giraud, *Métis in the Canadian West*, 268; Wood and Thiessen, *Early Fur Trade*, 45–46, 50, 57, 65, 69, 96–97,100, 108, 120–22, 137, 143; on the conflict with John Evans see Nasatir, *Before Lewis and Clark*, 103–4, 106, 474–75. The name had different spellings before Moulton's editions, including Gessom by Mckenzie.

41. Fort La Souris, near the mouth of the La Souris River, was the base of the North West Company's trade with the Hidatsas and the Mandans.

42. David Thompson was born in London in 1770. He was an apprentice clerk at Fort Churchill for the Hudson's Bay Company in 1784. He became an employee of the Norh West Company in May 1797. For almost thirty years he was an explorer and a trader. Major sources are W. Raymond Wood, "David Thompson at the Mandan-Hidatsa Villages,1797–1798: The Original Journals"; *Ethnohistory* 24 no. 3 (1977): 329–42; *David Thompson's Narrative of His Explorations in Western America, 1784–1812.* (Publications of the Champlain Society, vol. 12, ed. J. B. Tyrrel. Toronto: Champlain Society, 1916, repr., New York: Green Press, 1968); *Travels in Western North America,* 1784–1812. ed. Victor G. Hopgood (Toronto: Macmillan Company of Canada, 1971).

43. La Vérendrye visited the Mandans in 1738, and left two Frenchmen with them. On their return the two Canadians reported the visit of nomadic nations from the west to the Mandan tribes. In La Vérendrye, *Journals and Letters*, 336–38.

44. Charles McKenzie was born in Scotland in 1774. His early years in the North West Company were spent in the Red River Department. He had an Indian wife and four children. His personal journals contain ethnographic information that was not recorded by other travelers. "Mr. Charles Mackenzie, The Mississouri Indians, A Narrative of Four Trading Expeditions to the Mississouri, 1804–1805–1806," in Masson, *Bourgeois*, 1:317–93.

45. Masson, *Bourgeois*, 1:372.
46. Ibid., 379.
47. Ibid., 380.
48. Moulton, *Definitive Journals*, 3:205.
49. Coues, *New Light*, 1:333, 401. See Masson, *Bourgeois*, 1:294, 303, 376.
50. Clark was accompanied by three interpreters, probably Jusseaume, Cruzatte, and Labiche. According to Ordway, Mrs. Jusseaume was with them and heard the Tetons say that they would kill them if they went across the river. See Moulton, *Definitive Journals*, 3:331–32.
51. Giraud, *Métis in the Canadian West*, 274.
52. William Joseph Snelling, *Tales of the North West* (Boston: Hilliard, Gray, Little, and Wilkins, 1830), 86.
53. Jefferson to William Ludlow, September 6, 1824, *The Writings of Thomas Jefferson*, ed. H. A. Washington (Washington: Taylor and Maury, 1854), 288.

CHAPTER 11. . . . AGAINST THE EXPEDITION

1. Foley and Rice, *Chouteaus*, 99. Louis Labeaume simultaneously belonged to the committee of the Saint Louis citizens who protested against the bill stipulating that Upper Louisiana would be governed by officials of the Indiana Territory and that Spanish land grants would be null and void.
2. "Memorial of Régis Loisel, May 28,1804, and Related Documents," in Houck, *Spanish Régime in Missouri*, 2:355–64. Delassus stayed in Saint Louis until the end of 1804, while Auguste Chouteau was supervising the removal of whatever Spanish property remained at Fort Carondelet, the governor's home.
3. The Marquis of Casa Calvo to Don Pedro Ceballo in Louis Houck, *The Spanish Régime in Missouri* (Chicago: R. R. Donnelley, 1909) 2: 356–58; also in William Morrison, who owned a farm near camp Du Bois supplied Clark with corn in December 1803.
4. In *Tabeau's Narrative*, 240–41.
5. See Nasatir, *Before Lewis and Clark*, 757.
6. *Tabeau's Narrative*, 130.
7. Thwaites, *Early Western Travels*, 4:127.
8. Gass, *Journals*, 10:66.
9. *Tabeau's Narrative*, 56.
10. Thwaites, *Original Journals*, 1:266–67.
11. Moulton, *Definitive Journals*, 3:111.
12. Ibid., 123–25 (on Clark's move to appease The Partisan); *Tabeau's Narrative*,108, for the quote about "the tyrant of the savages."
13. Coues, *Lewis and Clark*, 1:159, 252; Masson, *Bourgeois* 1:276; *Tabeau's Narrative,*, 125.
14. Coues, *Lewis and Clark*, 1:206.
15. Thwaites, *Original Journals*, 1:267.
16. Identified in journals either as a Frenchman or a Spaniard, Garreau was probably the earliest settler in present-day South Dakota. See *Letters of the Lewis and Clark Expedition with Related Documents, 1783–1854*, ed. Donald Jackson (Urbana: University of Illinois Press, 1978), 2:434, 438; Thwaites, *Early Western Travels*, 24:35, 58–61, 68–69.
17. *Tabeau's Narrative*, 141.
18. Ibid., 149–50.

19. Thwaites, *Original Journals*, 5:350.

20. There is a controversy about the identity of the two trappers. Moulton contends that they were neither Rivet nor Degie. In *Definitive Journals*, 3:183. Tabeau asserts that Grenier (spelt Greinyea by Clark) and Rivet (Reevey) were the two men, in *Tabeau's Narrative*, 168.

21. Clarke, *Men of the Lewis and Clark Expedition*, 66–67.

22. Charles McKenzie, Second Expedition, in Masson, *Bourgeois*, 1:345.

23. *Tabeau's Narrative*, 155.

24. Ibid., 159–72.

25. Articles 1–11 drawn up by Carondelet and 12–23 by Trudeau. A copy in French is in the Spanish Archives 90, Missouri Historical Society, Saint Louis. Article 12 prescribes that no intoxicating beverage is to be taken to Missouri by traders, under penalty of a fine of one hundred piastres. Article 19 prohibits the employment of negroes, half-breeds or savages free or slaves. It is intended to encourage the presence of white men in the region.

26. *Tabeau's Narrative*, 84–87.

27. Ibid., 197.

28. Ibid., 195.

29. Ibid., 200.

30. Ibid., 202.

31. Ibid., 213.

32. The following is a Court Record of Cahokia (C.W. Alvord, Illinois Historical *Collections*, 2:217): "At a Court the 19th of November, 1785, M. Pierre Antoine Tabeau made oath of fidelity to the United States of America and promised to conform to the edicts and regulations of the government of Virginia, and has signed the said day and year."

P. A. Tabeau. J. B. H. La Croix, Pres. In *Tabeau's Narrative*, 38.

33. On Larocque's biography see Masson, *Bourgeois*, 1:81–100, Tassé, *Canadiens de l'Ouest*, 2:324–25. A new French Canadian Company referred to as the "XY" Company came into existence in 1798 to challenge the North West Company and the British Hudson Bay Company. It was founded in 1798 by Montreal Scots who disagreed with Simon McTavish. The XY Company only had two hundred and fifty men in the trade, and the North West Company five times more, but its production of peltries was equal. There were harsh conflicts for a time. La Mothe, an XY man, was shot near Island Fort by James King of the North West Company while competing for Indian markets. The war came to an end after the death of McTavish in July 1804, and the XY Company merged with the North West Company. Masson, *Bourgeois*, 1:79–82.

34. Larocque's Missouri Journal is in Masson, *Bourgeois*, 1:299–402. in the text, the Hidatsas are always called *Gros Ventres* [Big Bellies].

35. Moulton, *Definitive Journals*, 3:241.

36. Ibid. 241–42.

37. The special interest of Larocque's journal is in the narrative of the first visit of white men to the country of the Crows after La Vérendrye's expedition of 1742. François-Antoine Larocque, *Journal of Larocque from the Assiniboine to the Yellowstone*, 1805, edited by Lawrence J. Burpee. Publication of the Canadian Archives, vol. 3 (Ottawa: Government Printing Bureau, 1910), 1–82.

38. Larocque, *Journal*, 17–21.

39. Ibid., 52. "Thursday october 10 I remained here all day before I proceed to the assiniboine river; among other news the indians tell me that there are 14 american crafts below the villages who are ascending to this place; the sioux have killed

8 white men last spring upon Saint Peters river and three big bellys here. Lewis and Clark had already crossed aver the Rockies."

40. Bernard DeVoto, *The Course of Empire* (New York: Mariner Books, 1980), 529

41. Isaac J. Cox, "General Wilkinson and his Later Intrigues with the Spaniards." *American Historical Review* 19 (1914): 794–812.

42. Casa Calvo to Cevallos, March 30, 1804, reference and translation in Nasatir, *Before Lewis and Clark*, 727–28.

43. The only comprehensive biography of Pedro Vial is Noel M. Loomis, and Abraham P. Nasatir, *Pedro Vial and the Roads to Santa Fe* (Norman: University of Oklahoma Press, 1967).

44. Loomis and Nasatir, *Pedro Vial*, 262–87.

45. Ibid., 408–14.

46. Warren L. Cook, *Flood Tide of Empire: Spain and the Pacific Northwest* (New Haven, CT: Yale University Press,1973), 457–58.

47. Loomis and Nasatir, *Pedro Vial*, 430–33.

48. Cook, *Flood Tide of Empire*, 470–72.

CONCLUSION

1. "Information to Those who Would Remove to America," Benjamin Franklin, *Writings*, ed. J. A. Leo Lemay (New York: The Library of America, 1987), 977, 978.

2. Jones, *William Clark*, 316.

3. J. A. Leo Lemay, "The Frontiersmen from Lout to Hero: Notes on the Significance . . . ." in *Proceedings of the American Antiquarian Society* 88, no. 2 (October 1979): 209

4. Constantin de Volney, *Œuvres complètes* (Paris: Didot, 1846). See also Gilbert Chinard, *Volney et l'Amérique* (Paris: Presses universitaires de France, 1923).

5. Perrin du Lac, *Voyage dans les deux Louisianes, et chez les nations sauvages du Missouri, par les Etats-Unis, l'Ohio, et les provinces qui le bordent, en 1801, 1802, et 1803, avec un aperçu des moeurs, des usages, du caractère et des coutumes religieuses et civiles des peuples de ces diverses contrées* (Paris, 1805).

6. William Gass, *The Journals of the Lewis and Clark Expedition*, 24, 36, 61, 36.

7. Ibid., 76.

8. Ibid., 153.

Bibliography

Manuscript Sources

The material found in the French National Archives (AN) in the sections devoted to the colonies is subdivided into several series:

B: Letters, dispatches from the King, the Minister of the Marine and the Council of State to the colonial officials.

C11A: General correspondence, letters, memoirs from Canada to the home government. The contents include expense accounts for the western posts

C11E: Correspondence related to outposts and forts.

C11G: Correspondence Raudot-Pontchartrain.

C13A: Correspondence from Louisiana officials.

Published Sources

Alvord, Clarence W. *The Illinois Country, 1673–1818, 2 vols. Springfield: Centennial History of Illinois, 1920.*

Bakeless, John E. *Background to Glory: The Life of George Rogers Clark.* Lincoln: University of Nebraska Press, 1992.

Balési, Charles J. *The Time of the French in the Heart of North America, 1673–1818.* Chicago: Alliance française, 1992.

Barclay, Donald, and James H. Maguire, Peter Wild. *Into the Wilderness Dream: Exploration Narratives of the American West, 1500–1805.* Salt Lake City: University of Utah Press, 1994.

Baudry des Lozières, Louis Narcisse. *Voyage à la Louisiane et sur le continent de l'Amérique septentrionale, fait dans les années 1794 à 1798,* Paris, 1802.

Baugy, Chevalier de. *Journal d'une expédition contre les Iroquois au Canada en 1687.* Edited by Ernest Serrigny, Paris: Ernest Leroux, 1883.

Belting, Natalia M. *Kaskaskia under the French Regime.* Urbana: The University of Illinois Press, 1948.

Belyea, Barbara. *A Year Inland: The Journal of a Hudson's Bay Company Winterer.* Waterloo, Ontario: Wilfrid Laurier University Press, 2000.

Berger, Philippe. *L'Ennemi américain: généalogie de l'antiaméricanisme français.* Paris: Seuil, 2002.

Blair, Emma H. *The Indian Tribes of the Upper Mississippi Valley and Region of the Great Lakes.* Cleveland, 1911.

Boorstin, Daniel J. *The Lost World of Thomas Jefferson.* Chicago: University of Chicago Press, 1993.

Bossu, Jean-Bernard. *Nouveaux voyages dans l'Amérique septentrionale contenant une collection de lettres écrites sur les lieuxpar l'auteur, à son ami, M. Douin, chevalier, capitaine dans les troupes du roi, ci-devant son camarade dans le Nouveau Monde.* Amsterdam: Chez Changuion, 1777.

————. *Nouveaux voyages aux Indes Occidentales: contenant une relation des différents peuples qui habitent les environs du grand fleuve Saint-Louis, appelé vulgairement le Mississippi; leur religion, leur gouvernement; leurs mœurs; leurs guerres et leur commerce. 1768. Reprint, Nouveaux voyages en Louisiane, 1751–1762.* Edited by Philippe Jacquin. Paris: Aubier-Montaigne, 1980. English edition: *Travels in the Interior of North America* (1769); *Jean-Bernard Bossu's Travels to that Part of North America Formerly Called Louisiana.* Translated and edited by Seymour Feiler. Norman: University of Oklahoma Press, 1962.

Bouchard, Russell. *Les Armes de la traite.* Montreal: Boreal Express, 1976.

Boucher, Pierre. *Histoire véritable et naturelle des mœurs et productions du pays de la Nouvelle France, vulgairement dite le Canada.* 1664. Reprint. Boucherville, Quebec: Société historique de Boucherville, 1964. English edition: *Canada in the Seventeenth Century, from the French of Pierre Boucher.* Translated by Edward L. Montizambert. Montreal: G.E. Desbarats, 1883.

Bougainville, Louis Antoine. *Adventures in the Wilderness: The American Journal of Louis Antoine de Bougainville, 1756–1760.* Translated by Edward P. Hamilton. Norman: University of Oklahoma Press, 1964.

————. *Ecrits sur le Canada. Mémoires-Journal-Lettres.* Paris: Klincksick, 1993, 50.

————. *Écrits sur le Canada.* Mémoires-Journal-Lettres, Montréal, Pélican, 1993.

Brébeuf, Jean de. *La Relation de ce qui s'est passé au pays des Hurons.* Edited by Théodore Besterman. Genève: Droz, 1957.

————. *Ecrits en Huronie* (1635–1649). Quebec: Bibliothèque Québecoise, 1996.

Brissot, Jean-Pierre de Warville. *Nouveau Voyage dans les Etats-Unis de l'Amérique septentrionale fait en 1788.* Paris: Buisson, 1791.

Brown, Jennifer. *Strangers in Blood: Fur Trade Company Families in Indian Country.* Vancouver: University of British Columbia Press, 1980.

Buffon, George Louis Leclerc, comte de. *Variétés dans l'espèce humaine.* Paris, 1749.

————. *Oeuvres complètes.* 5 vols. Paris: Imprimerie et Librairie générale de France, 1859.

Burpee, Lawrence J. *The Search for the Western Sea.* London, 1908.

Caldwell, Norman W. *The French in the Mississippi Valley, 1740–1750.* Vol 26. Urbana: Illinois Studies in the Social Sciences, 1941. Reprint, Philadelphia: The Porcupine Press, 1974.

Calloway, Colin G. *One Vast Winter Count: The Native American West before Lewis and Clark.* Lincoln: University of Nebraska Press, 2003.

Campeau, Lucien. *Les Cents associés et le peuplement de la Nouvelle France.* Montreal: Bellarmin, 1974.

Champlain, Samuel. *The Works of Samuel Champlain.* Edited by H. P. Biggar. 6 vols. Toronto: The Champlain Society, 1922–36.

Carter, Clarence E., ed. *The Correspondence of General Thomas Gage with the Secretary of State, 1763–1775,* 2 vols. New Haven: Yale University Press, 1931.

Cartier, Jacques. *The Voyages of Jacques Cartier, 1534–42.* Edited by H. P. Biggar, Ottawa: F.A. Acland, 1924.

————. *Voyages en Nouvelle-France.* The accounts of the three voyages to Canada

(1534, 1535–36, 1541–42). Texte remis en français moderne par Robert Lahaise et Marie Couturier, Collection Documents d'histoire. Montréal: Éditions Hurtubise, 1977.

———. *Relations.* Edited by Michel Bideaux,. Montréal: Presses Universitaires de Montréal, 1986.

Cavelier, Jean. *The Journal of Jean Cavelier: The Account of a Survivor of La Salle's Expedition, 1684–1688.* Translanted by Jean Delanglez. Chicago: Institute of Jesuit History, 1938.

Césaire, Aimé. *Toussaint-Louverture: La Révolution française et le problème colonial.* Paris: Présence africaine, 1981.

Champagne, Antoine. "Les La Vérendrye et le poste de l'Ouest." *Cahiers de l'Institut d'Histoire* 12. Québec: PUL, 1968.

Champlain, Samuel de. *Les Voyages de Samuel Champlain.* Edited by Hubert Deschamps. Paris: Presses universitaires de France, 1951.

———. *The Voyages of Jacques Cartier (1534–1542).* Edited by H. P. Biggar, Ottawa: F.A. Acland, 1924.

———. *Des Sauvages.* Edited by A. Beaulieu and R. Ouellet. Montréal: Typo, 1993.

———. *The Works of Samuel de Champlain.* Edited by H. P. Biggar. Toronto: The Champlain Society, 1922–1926.

Charlevoix, François-Xavier de. *Journal d'un voyage fait par ordre du roi dans l'Amérique septentrionale; où l'on trouvera la description géographique et l'histoire naturelle des pays que l'auteur a parcourus, les coutumes, le caractère, la religion, les mœurs et les traditions des peuples qui les habitent. Adressée à Madame la Duchesse de Lesdiguières (1744).* Edited by Pierre Berthiaume. 2 vols. Montreal: Presses de l'Université de Montreal, 1994. English edition: *Journal of a Voyage to North America,* 1761. Reprint, Ann Arbor: University Microfilms, 1966.

Chateaubriand, François René. *Oeuvres romanesques et voyages.* Vol. I of *Oeuvres complètes.* Paris: Gallimard, Edition de la Pléiade, 1969.

———. *Travels in America (1827).* Reprint. Translated by Richard Switzer. Lexington: University of Kentucky Press, 1969.

Chinard, Gilbert. *Volney et l'Amérique.* Paris: Presses universitaires de France, 1923.

——— *Les Réfugiés huguenots en Amérique.* Paris: Les Belles Lettres, 1925.

———. *-L'Amérique et le rêve exotique dans la littérature française aux XVIIe et XVIIIe siècles.* Paris: Hachette, 1934.

Choquet, Leslie. *De Français à paysans: modernité et tradition dans le peuplement du Canada.* Sillery, Quebec: Septentrion, 2001.

Christian, Shirley. *Before Lewis and Clark: The Story of the Chouteaus, the French Dynasty That Ruled America's Frontier.* New York: Farrar, Straus and Giroux, 2004.

Clarke, Charles G. *The Men of the Lewis and Clark Expedition.* Lincoln: University of Nebraska Press, 1970. Bison Books Edition, 2002.

Colden, Cadwallader. *The History of the Five Indian Nations Depending on the Province of New York in America.* London: 1727, 1747. Reprint. Ithaca: Cornell University Press, 1964.

———. "Colden to Peter Collinson," December, 1743. *The Colden Papers. New-York Historical Society Collection.* 3 vols. New York, 1919.

Collot, Victor. *A Journey in North America.* 2 vols. Paris: Arthur Bertrand, 1826.

Cook, Warren. *Flood Tide of Empire: Spain and the Pacific Northwest, 1543–1819.* New Haven: Yale University Press, 1973.

Coues, Elliott. *History of the Expedition under the Command of Lewis and Clark.* 4 vols. New York: Harper, 1893.

———. *New Light on the Early History of the Greater West,* 3 vols. New York: Harper, 1897.

Cox, Isaac J. "General Wilkinson and his Later Intrigues with the Spaniards." *American Historical Review* 19 (1914): 794–812.

Crèvecoeur, J. Hector St. John de. *Letters from an American farmer (1782) and Sketches of Eighteenth Century America.* Reprint. Edited by Warren Barton Blake. London: Dent, 1912. Edited by Albert Stone. Harmonsworth: Penguin, 1981.

Cronon, WIlliam, George Miles, Jay Gitlin, eds. *Under an Open Sky. Rethinking America's Western Past.* New York: W.W. Norton and Co., 1992.

De Bry, Theodore, ed. *Grands Voyages,* 23 vols. Frankfurt, 1590–1634. Nine out of the twenty-three volumes include voyages to America by Thomas Hariot, René Goulène de Laudonnière, Jean de Léry, and Sir Francis Drake. There were editions in French, German, and Latin.

Dechêne, Louise. *Habitants et marchands de Montréal au XVIIe siècle.* Paris: Plon, 1974.

DeConde, Alexander. *This Affair of Louisiana.* New York: Charles Scribner's Sons, 1976.

The Definitive Journals of Lewis and Clark. Edited by Gary E. Moulton, 8 vols. Lincoln: University of Nebraska Press, 1987.

Delanglez, Jean. *Life and Voyages of Louis Jolliet* (1645–1700). Chicago: Institute of Jesuit History, 1948.

Deliette. *Mémoires.* See Pease, Thomas.

De Maistre, Joseph. *Considérations sur la France* (1797). Edited by Jean-Louis Darcel. Genève: Slatkine, 1980.

Denys, Nicolas. *Description Géographique et historique des côtes de l'Amérique du nord.* Paris, 1671. *The Description and Natural History of the Coasts of North America (Acadia).* Champlain Society Publication. Reprint. Greenwood Press, 1968.

DePauw, Cornelius. *Recherches philosophques sur les Américains, ou mémoires intéressants pour servir à l'histoire de l'espèce humaine.* Paris: 1768. Reprint. 3 vols. Paris: Jean-François Bastien, l'an III de la république français, 1793.

Desrosiers, Leo-Paul. "L'expédition de M. de la barre." *Cahiers des Dix,* 22 (1957): 105–35.

DeVoto, Bernard. *The Course of Empire,* 1952. Boston: A Mariner Book. Houghton Mifflin, 1998.

Dickason, Olive P. *Le Mythe du sauvage.* Sillery, Quebec: Septentrion, 1984.

Diderot, Denis. *Supplément au voyage de Bougainville: Pensées philosophiques/ Lettre sur les aveugles.* Paris, 1796. Reprint edited by Antoine Adam. Paris: Garnier Flammarion, 1972.

Dorigny, Marcel, and Marie-Jeanne Rossignol, eds. *La France et les Américains au temps de Jefferson et Miranda,* Paris: Société des études robespierristes, 2001.

Douville, Raymond. "Jacques Largillier, dit le castor coureur des bois et frère donné," *Cahier des Dix* 20 (1964): 47–60, 50, 85.

———. "Charles Boucher de Niverville, son ascendance et sa carrière politique." *Cahiers des Dix* 37 (1972): 87–122.

Dowd, Gregory E. "The French King Wakes up in Detroit: Pontiac's War in Rumor and History," *Ethnohistory* 37, no.3 (1990): 254–78.

———. *War under Heaven: Pontiac, The Indian Nations, and the British Empire* . Baltimore: Johns Hopkins University Press, 2002.

Dubé, Pauline, ed. *La Nouvelle France sous Joseph-Antoine de la Barre, 1682–1685*. Siillery: Septentrion, 1993.

Dumont dit Montigny, Jean Benjamin F. *Mémoire historique sur la Louisiane contenant ce qui est arrivé de plus mémorable depuis l'année 1687 jusqu'à présent; avec l'établissement de la colonie française dans cette province de l'Amérique septentrionale sous la direction de la Compagnie des Indes : le climat, la nature et les productions de ce pays: l'origine et la religion des sauvages qui y habitent, leurs mœurs et leurs coutumes*, 2 vols. Paris: C. J. B. Bauche, 1753.

Eccles, William. *France in America*. New York: Harper and Row, 1972.

———. *The Canadian Frontier, 1534–1760*. Albuquerque: University of New Mexico Press, (1969), 1983.

———. "The Fur Trade and Eighteenth Century Imperialism." *William and Mary Quarterly* 45 (July 1983): 2:1–23.

Edmunds R. David, and Joseph L. Peyser. *The Fox Wars: The Mesquakie Challenge to New France*. Norman: University of Oklahoma Press, 1993.

Ekberg, Carl J. *Colonial Sainte Genevieve*. Gerald, Missouri: The Patrice Press, 1985.

———. *An Account of Upper Louisiana by Nicolas de Finiels*. University of Missouri Press, 1989.

———. *French Roots in the Illinois Country, The Mississippi Frontier in Colonial Times*. Urbana: The University of Illinois Press, 1998.

———. *François Vallé and His World, Upper Louisiana before Lewis and Clark*. Columbia: University of Missouri Press, 2002.

Fairchild, Hoxie. *The Noble Savage: A Study in Romantic Naturalism*. 1928. Reprint. New York: Russell and Russell, 1961.

Foley, William E., and C. David Rice. *The First Chouteaus: River Barons of Early St. Louis*. Urbana: University of Illinois Press, 1983.

Folmer, Henry. "The Mallet Expedition of 1739 through Nebraska, Kansas, and Colorado to Santa Fe." *The Colorado Magazine* 15, no. 5 (September 1939): 163–73.

———. *Franco-Spanish Rivalry in North America, 1524–1763*. Glendale, CA: Clark, 1953).

Frégault, Guy. *Le XVIIIe siècle canadien. Etudes*. Montréal: HMH, 1968.

———. *Iberville le Conquérant*. Montréal: Fidès, 1968.

Franklin, Benjamin. "Information to Those who Would Remove to America." *Benjamin Franklin, Writings*. Edited by J. A. Leo Lemay. New York: The Library of America, 1987, 975–83.

Gallup, Andrew, ed. *The Celoron Rexpedition to the Ohio Country, 1749: The Reports of Pierre-Joseph Céloron and Father Bonnecamps*. Bowie, MD: Heritage Books, 1997.

Gabriel, Louis-Jaray. *L'Empire français d'Amérique (1534–1803)*. Paris: Armand Colin, 1938.

Garnier, Michael. *Bonaparte et la Louisiane*. Paris: Kronos, 1992

Gass, William. *The Journals of the Lewis and Clark Expedition* vol 10. Edited by Gary E. Moulton, Lincoln: University of Nebraska Press, 1966.

Giraud, Marcel. *Le Métis canadien*. Paris: Travaux et mémoires de l'institut d'ethnologie, vol. 15, Institut d'ethnologie, Université de Paris, 1945. Reprint: *The Métis in the Canadian West* . Translated by George Woodcock. Edmonton: The University of Alberta Press, 1985.

———. *Histoire de la Louisiane*. Paris: Presses universitaires de France, 1953

Goubert, Pierre. *L'Ancien Régime*. Paris: Colin, 1969.

Greer, Allan. *The People of New France*. Toronto: University of Toronto Press, 1997.

———. *Mohawk Saint: Catherine Tekakwitha and the Jesuits*. Oxford: Oxford University Press, 2004.

Hafen, Leroy R., ed. *French Fur Traders and Voyageurs in the American West*. 1965. Lincoln: University of Nebraska Press, 1997.

Hamelin, Jean. *Economie et société en Nouvelle-France*. Québec: Presses de l'Université Laval, 1970.

Hamilton, Edward P. *Adventure in the Wilderness: The American Journals of Louis Antoine de Bougainville 1756–1760*. (Norman: University of Oklahoma Press,1964.

Havard, Gilles. *Empire et métissages: Indiens et Français dans le Pays d'En Haut, 1660–1715*. Sillery, Quebec/ Paris: Septentrion/ Presses de l'Université Paris-Sorbonne, 2003.

Hebard, Grace Raymond. *Sacajawea, A guide and interpreter of the Lewis and Clark expedition with an account of the travels of Toussaint Charbonneau, and of Jean Baptiste, the expedition papoose*. Glendale, CA: The Arthur Clarke Company, 1957.

Helvetius, Charles André. *Traité sur l'homme*. Paris, 1772.

Hennepin, Louis. *Description de la Louisiane, nouvellement découverte au Sud Ouest de la Nouvelle France par ordre du Roy, avec la carte du pays, les mœurs et la manière de vivre des sauvages*. Paris: Sébastien Huré, 1683. English edition: *A Description of Louisiana*. Translated by John Gilmary Shea. 1880. Reprint. Ann Arbor: University Microfilms, 1966.

———. *Nouvelle découverte d'un très grand pays situé entre le Nouveau Mexique et la mer glaciale. Avec les cartes et les figures nécessaires et de plus l'histoire naturelle et morale et les avantages qu'on peut tirer par l'établissement de colonies le tout dédié à Sa Majesté britannique Guillaume III*. Utrecht: Guillaume Broedelet, 1687. English edition: *A New Discovery of a Vast Country in America*. London: For M. Bentley, J. Tonson, H. Bonwick, etc., 1698.

———. *Voyage curieux du Révérend Père Hennepin*. Amsterdam: Pierre Vander, 1704.

Henry, Alexander. *Travels in Canada and the Indian Territories between the Years 1760 and 1776, by Alexander Henry, Fur Trader*. Edited by James Bain. Toronto: George N. Morang, 1901. Reprint, Chicago: R. Donnelley and Sons, 1921.

———. *Alexander Henry's Travels and Adventures in the Years 1760–1776*. Edited by Milo M. Quaife. Chicago: The Lakeside Press, 1921.

Hinderaker, Eric. *Elusive Empires. Constructing Colonialism in the Ohio Valley, 1673–1800*. Cambridge: Cambridge University Press, 1997.

———. *Essays on New France*. Toronto: Oxford University Press, 1987.

Houck, Louis. *The Spanish Regime in Missouri*, 2 vols. Chicago: R.R. Donnelley, 1909.

Howard, Harold P. *Sacajawea*. Norman: University of Oklahoma Press, 1971.

Howard, Joseph K. *Strange Empire: A Narrative of the Northwest*. New York: William Morrow and Co., 1952. Reprint. Saint Paul: Minnesota Historical Society Press, 1994.

Hughes, Thomas, S.J. *History of the Society of Jesus in North America, Colonial and Federal.* 2 vols. New York: Longmans, Green and Co. 1917.

Hunt, George T. *The Wars of the Iroquois.* Madison: University Press of Wisconsin, 1940.

Innis, Harold A. *The Fur Trade in Canada—An Introduction to Canadian Economic History.* New Haven: Yale University Press, 1930.

Jackson, Donald, ed. *Letters of the Lewis and Clark Expedition with Related Documents, 1783-1854.* 2 vols. Urbana: University of Illinois Press, 1978.

Jacquin, Philippe. *Les Indiens Blancs: Français et Indiens en Amérique du Nord, XVIIe–XVIIIe siècles.* Paris: Payot, 1987.

————and Daniel Royot. *Le Mythe de l'Ouest.* Paris: Autrement, 1993.

Jaenen, Cornelius J. *Friend and Foe: Aspects of French-Amerindian Cultural Contact in the Sixteenth and Seventeenth Centuries.* New York: Columbia University Press, 1976.

————. "Les Sauvages Américains: Persistence into the Eighteenth Century of Traditional French Concepts and Constructs for Comprehending Amerindians." *Ethnohistory* 29, no.1 (1982): 43–56.

————, ed. *The French Regime in the Upper Country of Canada during the Seventeenth Century.* Vol.16. Toronto: The Publications of the Champlain Society, Ontario Series, 1996.

Jefferson, Thomas. *The Writings of Thomas Jefferson.* Edited by H. A. Washington. Washington, D.C.: Taylor and Maury, 1854.

Jennings, Francis. *Empire of Fortune. Crowns, Colonies and Tribes in the Seven Years War in America.* New York: W.W. Norton & Co., 1988.

————. *The Ordeal of the Longhouse. The People of the Iroquois League in the Era of European Colonization.* Chapel Hill: University of North Carolina Press, 1992.

Jérémie, Nicolas. *Relation du détroit de la Baie d'Hudson.* Amsterdam: Bernard, 1720.

Jones, Landon Y. *William Clark and the Shaping of the West.* New York: Hill and Wang, 2004.

Joutard, Philippe, and Thomas Wien, eds. *Mémoires de Nouvelle France: de France en Nouvelle France.* Rennes: Presses universitaires de Rennes,2005.

Joutel, Henri. *Journal historiqe du dernier voyage qui fut de M. de la Salle.* Paris: Estienne Robinot, 1713. English edition: *Joutel's Journal of La Salle's Last Voyage.* 1714. Reprint. Albany: Joseph McDonough, 1906.

————. Relation d'Henri Joutel. Voyage de M. de la Salle dans l'Amérique septentrionale dans l'année 1685. In Margry, *Découvertes et Etablissements,* 3:88–534. Paris: D. Jouaust, 1879–88.

Kalm, Peter. *Travels into North America, containing its Natural History in General.* 3 vols. Warrington, 1770–71. *Voyage de Peter Kalm au Canada en 1749.* Translated and edited by J. Rousseau and G. Béthune, Montreal: Tisseyre, 1977.

Kavanagh, Martin. *La Vérendrye: His Life and Times.* Brandon, Manitoba: Martin Kavanagh. 1967.

Kellog, Louise Phelps. *The French Régime in Wisconsin and the Northwest.* Madison: State Historical Society of Wisconsin, 1925.

Lachance, André, ed. *Les Marginaux, les exclus et l'autre au Canada au XVII–XVIIIe siècles.* Montréal: Fidès,1996.

Lacoursière, Jacques, Jean Provencher, and Denis Vaugeois. *Canada-Québec: 1534–2000.* Sillery, Québec: Septentrion, 2000.

Lafitau, Joseph-François. *Mœurs des sauvages américains comparés aux mœurs des premiers temps.* Paris: Saugrain, C.E. Hochereau, 1724. English edition: *Customs of the American Indians Compared with the Customs of Primitive Times.* Translated and edited by William Fenton and Elizabeth Moore. Toronto: The Champlain Society, 1974.

————. *Mœurs des sauvages américains* (1724). 2 vols. Paris: Maspero, 1983.

La Harpe, Jean-Baptiste Bénard de. "Account of the Journey of Bénard de La Harpe: Discovery Made by Him of Several Nations Situated in the West." Translated and edited by Ralph A. Smith. *Southwestern Historical Quarterly* 62 (1958–59): 75–86, 246–59, 371–85, 525–41.

Lahontan, Louis-Armand de Lom d'Arc, baron de. *Nouveaux voyages de M. le Baron de Lahontan dans l'Amérique septentrionale qui contiennent une relation des différents peuples qui y habitent. La nature de leur gouvernement, leur commerce, leurs coutumes, leur religion et leur manière de faire la guerre. Tome premier. Mémoires de l'Amérique septentrionale, ou la suite des voyages de M. le Baron de Lahontan. Qui contiennent la description d'une grande étendue de pays de ce continent, l'intérêt des Français et des Anglais, leurs commerces, leurs navigations, les mœurs et les coutumes des sauvages. Avec un petit dictionnaire de la langue du pays. Le tout enrichi de cartes et de figures. Tome second: Supplément aux voyages du Baron de Lahontan. Où l'on trouve des dialogues curieux entre l'auteur et un sauvage de bon sens qui a voyagé. L'on y voit aussi plusieurs observations faites par le même auteur dans ses voyages. Tome troisième.* 3 vols. La Haye: Les Frères Honoré, 1703. English edition: *New Voyages to North America.* 1703. Reprint. Edited by Reuben Thwaites. Chicago: A. C. McClurg and Co., 1905.

————. *Oeuvres complètes.* 2 vols. Montréal: Presses de l'Université de Montréal, 1990.

Lalemant, Gabriel. *Relation des Hurons.* Paris, 1639.

Lanctot, Gustave. *Histoire du Canada.* 3 vols. Montreal: Beauchemin, 1967.

La Potherie, Claude-Charles Le Roy, Bacqueville de. *Voyage en Amérique; Contenant ce qui s'est passé de plus remarquable dans l'Amérique septentrionale depuis 1534 jusqu'à présent.* 4 vols. Amsterdam, 1723.

————. *Histoire de l'Amérique septentrionale.* 1722. Reprint, 4 vols. Paris, Brocas, 1753.

La Rochefoucauld-Liancourt, François Duc de. *Journal d'un Voyage en Amérique et d'un séjour à Philadelphie.* 1794. Paris: Droz,1940.

Larocque, François-Antoine. *Journal of Larocque from the Assiniboine to the Yellowstone.* 1805. Edited by Lawrence J. Burpee. Publication of the Canadian Archives, vol. 3, Ottawa: Government Printing Bureau, 1910, 1–82.

Laverdière, Camille. *Le Sieur de Roberval: Jean-François de Larocque,* Chicoutimi, Québec: Editions JCL, 2005.

La Vérendrye, Pierre Gaultier de Varennes de, *Journals and Letters of Pierre Gaultier de Varennes de la Vérendrye and his Sons, with Correspondence between the Governors of Canada and the French Court, touching the search for the western sea.* Edited by Lawrence J. Burpee. Publications of The Champlain Society, vol. 17. Toronto, 1927.

Le Clerq, Chrétien. *Nouvelles Relations de Gaspésie.* Paris: Aimable Auroy, 1665.

———— *Premier établissement de la Foy dans la Nouvelle France contenant la publication de l'Evangile, l'histoire des colonies françaises et les fameuses découvertes de La Salle,* 2 vols. Paris: Aimable Auroy, 1691. English edition: *First Establishment of the Faith in New France.* Translated by J. G. Shea. New York: J. G. Shea, 1881.

Lemay, J. A. Leo. "The Frontiersman from Lout to Hero: Notes on the Significance of the Comparative Method and the Stage Theory in Early American Literature and Culture." *Proceedings of the American Antiquarian Society* 88, no. 2 (October 1979): 187–223.

Léry, Jean de. *Histoire d'un voyage fait en la terre du Brésil, autrement dite Amérique.* La Rochelle: Antoine Chuppin, 1578.

Lescarbot, Marc. *Histoire de la Nouvelle France: Contenant les navigations et découvertes des Français faites dans les golfes et grandes rivières du Canada.* Paris: Jean Milot, 1609. English edition: *The History of New France.* Translated and edited by W. L. Grant, 1907–1914. Reprint. New York: Greenwood Press, 1968.

Letters of the Lewis and Clark Expedition, with Related Documents, 1783–1854. Edited by Donald Jackson. Urbana: University of Illinois Press, 1962.

Litalien, Raymonde. *Les Explorations de l'Amerique du nord.* Sillery, Quebec: Septentrion, 1993.

Loomis, Noel M., and Abraham P. Nasatir. *Pedro Vial and the Roads to Santa Fe.* Norman: University of Oklahoma Press,1967.

Lugan, Bernard. *Histoire de la Louisiane française,*1682–1804. Paris: Perrin, 1994.

McDermott, John F. *A Glossary of Mississippi Valley French, 1673–1850.* Washington University Studies, New Series, language and Literature, vol. 12. Saint Louis: Washington University, 1941.

———, ed. *The French in the Mississippi Valley.* Urbana: University of Illinois Press, 1965.

———. *Frenchmen and French Ways in the Mississippi Valley.* Urbana: University of Illinois Press, 1969.

Magnin, Frédéric. Mottin de La Balme. *Cavalier des deux mondes et de la liberté.* Paris: L'Harmattan, 2005.

Mandrou, Robert. *Les Français hors de France aux XVIe et XVIIe siècles.* Paris: Les Annales, vol. 5:4, 1959, 662–75.

Margry, Pierre, ed. *Découvertes et établisssements des Français dans l'ouest et dans le sud de l'Amérique septentrionale, 1614–1754, mémoires et documents originaux.* 6 vols. Paris: Jouaud, 1876–88. Volume 6 contains Céloron's journal and some papers on La Vérendrye.

———, ed. *Relations et mémoires inédits pour servir à l'histoire de France dans les pays d'outre-mer.* Paris: Challamel, 1867.

Martin, Calvin. *Keepers of the Game: Indian-Animal Relationships and the Fur Trade.* Berkeley: University of California Press, 1978.

Masson, L.R., ed. *Les Bourgeois de la Compagnie du Nord-Ouest: Récits de voyages, lettres et rapports inédits relatifs au Nord-Ouest Canadien.* 2 vols. Quebec: Imprimerie Générale A. Côte et Cie, 1889–90. Reprint in 2 vols. New York: Antiquarian Press, 1960.

Melville, Herman. *Moby-Dick.* 1850. (New York: Norton, 1967).

Membré, Zénobie. "Relation de la découverte de l'embouchure dé la rivière Mississippi dans le golfe de Mexique, faite par le Sieur De La Salle, l'année passée 1682," published in Raymond Thomassy, *Géologie pratique de la Louisiane.* Nouvelle-Orléans, 1860, 9–16.

———. *Narrative of the Adventures of la Salle's Party at Fort Crèvecoeur in Illinois from February 1680 to June 1681.* English version translated and edited by Joslin Cox. New York, 1905.

Millet, Pierre. *Captivity Among the Oneidas.* 1888. Reprint. New York: Garland, 1978.

Mirabeau,Victor Riqueti, Marquis de. *L'Ami des hommes ou Traité de la population,* Paris, 1755, 58, 59.

Montaigne, Michel de. *Essais.* 1582. 3 vols. Paris: Gallimard, Folio Classique, 1994.

Montesquieu, Charles-Louis de Secondat. *Lettres Persanes,* Paris, 1721. Reprint. Jean Starobinski, ed., Paris: Gallimard, 1973.

Moogk, Peter. "Reluctant Exiles: Emigrants from France to Canada before 1760" *William and Mary Quarterly* 46, no. 3 (1989): 475–90.

———. La Nouvelle France. *The Making of French Canada-A Cultural History.* East Lansing: Michigan State University Press, 2000.

Munro, William B. *The Seigniorial System in Canada: A Study in French Colonial Policy.* New York: Longmans, Green and Co., 1907.

Murat, Ines. *Napoléon et le rêve américain.* Paris: Fayard, 1976.

Naroll, Raoul. "The Cause of the Fourth Iroquois War." *Ethnohistory* 16, no. 1 (1969): 51–81.

Nasatir, Abraham P. *Before Lewis and Clark: Documents Illustrating the History of the Missouri,* 1785–1804. 2 vols. Saint Louis, MO: Saint Louis Historical Documents Foundation, 1952.

———. "Jacques D'Eglise." *Mississippi Valley Historical Review* 14 (1927): 47–71.

Nelson, W. Dale. *Interpreters with Lewis and Clark, The Story of Sacagawea and Toussaint Charbonneau.* Denton: University of North Texas Press, 2003.

Nute, Grace. *Caesars of the Wilderness.* St. Paul: Minnesota Historical Society Press,1978. Reprint. 1994.

Oglesby, Richard Edward. *Manuel Lisa and the Opening of the Missouri Fur Trade,* Norman: University of Oklahoma Press, 1963.

Otterbein, Keith F. "Hurons vs Iroquois: A Case Study in Intertribal Warfare." *Ethnohistory* 6, no.2 (1979): 141–52.

Palmer, Frederick. *Clark of the Ohio: A Life of George Rogers Clark.* New York: Dodd, Mead and Company, 1929.

Parkman, Francis. *France and England in North America: The Old Régime in Canada.* Boston, 1884.

———. *The Conspiracy of Pontiac and the Indian War after the Conquest of Canada.* 2 vols. Boston, 1886.

Pease, Thomas C., and Richard C. Werner, eds. *The French Foundations 1680–1693.* Collection of the Illinois State Historical Library, vol. 23. Springfield, Illinois, 1934. Contains Deliette, *Mémoires,* 302–20.

Peckham, Howard. *Pontiac and the Indian Uprising of 1763* (Princeton: Princeton University Press, 1947.

Perkins, Elzabeth A. *Border Life: Experience and Memory in the Evolutionary Ohio Valley.* Chapel Hill: University of North Carolina Press, 1998.

Perrin du Lac. *Voyage dans les deux Louisianes, et chez les nations sauvages du Missouri, par les Etats-Unis, l'Ohio, et les provinces qui le bordent, en 1801, 1802, et 1803, avec un aperçu des moeurs, des usages, du caractère et des coutumes religieuses et civiles des peuples de ces diverses contrées.* Paris, 1805.

Perrot, Nicolas. *Mémoire sur les moeurs, coutumes et religion des sauvages de l'Amérique septentrionale,* 1715. Edited by Père Tailhan. Paris: A. Franck, 1864. Reprint. Montreal: Elysée, 1973.

Peterson, Jacqueline, and Jennifer S.H. Brown, eds. *The New Peoples: Being and Becoming Métis in North America*. Winipeg: The University of Manitoba Press, 1985.

―――. "Prelude to Red River: A Social Portrait of the Great Lakes Métis," *Ethnohistory* 25, no. 3 (1978): 41–67.

Peyser, Joseph, ed. and trans. *Letters from New France: The Upper Country, 1686–1783*, Urbana: University of Illinois Press, 1992.

―――. *On the Eve of Conquest: The Chevalier De Raymond's Critique of New France in 1754*, East Lansing: Michigan State University Press, 1997.

Phares, Ross. *Cavalier in the Wilderness, the Story of the Explorer and Trader Louis Juchereau de Saint-Denis*. Baton Rouge: Louisiana State University Press, 1952.

Pike, Zebulon M. *An Account of Expeditions to the Sources of the Mississppi and through the Western Part of Louisiana . . . and a Tour through the Interior Parts of New Spain*. Philadelphia: C. and A. Conrad, 1810.

Pinot-Duclos, Charles. *Considérations sur les mœurs de ce siècle*. Paris, 1751.

Pomerleau, Jeanne. *Les Coureurs des bois. La traite des fourrures avec les Amérindiens*. Québec: J.C. Dupont, 1996.

Quaife, Milo. "Extracts of Mr. Evans' Journal," *Proceedings of the Wisconsin State Historical Society*, 63 (1915): 195–200.

―――. *The Western Country in the Seventeenth Century: The Memoirs of Lamothe-Cadillac and Pierre Deliette*. Chicago: Lakeside Press, 1947.

Radisson, Pierre-Esprit. *Voyages of Peter-Esprit Radisson, being an Account of his Travels and Experiences among the North American Indians from 1652 to 1684*. Edited by Gideon Scull. Boston: Prince Society Publications,1885. Reprint. New York: P. Smith, 1943.

Raudot, Antoine-Denis. *Relation par lettres de l'Amérique septentrionale, 1709–1710*. Edited by Camille de Rochemontiex. Paris: Letouzey et Ané, 1904.

Ray, Arthur J. *Indians in the Fur Trade: Their Role as Hunters, Trappers, and Middlemen in the Lands Southwest of Hudson Bay, 1660–1870*. Toronto: University of Toronto Press, 1974.

Raynal, Abbé Guillaume-Thomas. *Histoire philosophique et politique des établissements et du commerce des Européens dans les deux Indes*. 10 vols. Genève. 1781.

Rochemontiex, Camille de. *Relation par lettres de l'Amérique septentrionale 1709–1710*. Paris: Letouzey et Ané, 1904.

Rousseau, Jean-Jacques. *Discours sur l'origine et les fondements de l'inégalité*. Paris, 1755. Reprint. Paris: Garnier-Flammarion, 1971.

Roy, Georges P., ed. *Inventaire des ordonnances des intendants de la Nouvelle France, conservées aux archives provinciales de Québec*, 3 vols. Quebec, 1919.

Rumilly, Robert. *La Compagnie du Nord-Ouest, une épopée montréalaise*. 2 vols. Montreal: Fides, 1980,.

Sagard-Théodat, Gabriel. *Le Grand voyage du Pays des Hurons*. 1632. Paris: Tross, 1865.

Salisbury, Neal. *Manitou and Providence*. Oxford: Oxford University Press, 1987.

Sandoz, Mari. *The Beaver Men*. Lincoln: University of Nebraska Press, 1964.

Sayre, Gordon M. *Les Sauvages Américains, Representations of Native Americans in French and English Colonial Literature*. Chapel Hill: University of North Carolina Press, 1997.

Shea, John Gilmary. *The Catholic Church in Colonial days, 1521–1763*. New York, 1866.

Shortt, Adam. *Documents Relative to Money, Exchange and Finances of Canada Under the French Régime*, 2 vols. Ottawa, 1926.

Skarsten, M. O. *George Drouillard, Hunter and Interpreter for Lewis and Clark and Fur Trader, 1807–1810*, Glendale, CA: The Arthur H. Clark Co., 1964.

Sleeper-Smith, Susan. *Indian Women and French Men: Rethinking Cultural Encounter in the Western Great Lakes*. Amherst: University of Massachusete Press, 2001.

Smith, G. Hubert. *The Explorations of La Vérendrye in the Northern Plains, 1738–1743*. Lincoln: University of Nebraska Press, 1980.

Snelling, William Joseph. *Tales of the North West*. Boston: Hilliard, Gray, Little, and Wilkins, 1830.

Surrey, Nancy M. *The Commerce of Louisiana during the French Regime, 1699–1763*. New York: Longmans, Green & Co., 1916.

Sword, Wiley. *President Washington's Indian War: The Struggle for the Old Northwest, 1790–1795*. Norman: University of Oklahoma Press, 1985.

Tabeau, Pierre-Antoine. *Tabeau's Narrative of Loisel's Expedition to the Upper Missouri*. Edited by Annie Heloise Abel. Norman: University of Oklahoma Press, 1939.

Tassé, Joseph. *Les Canadiens de l'Ouest*. 2 vols. Montreal: Compagnie d'imprimerie canadienne,1882.

Texada, David K. *O'Reilly and the New Orleans Rebel*. Lafayette: University of Southwestern Louisiana, 1970.

Thom, James Alexander. *Sign-Talker: The Adventure of George Drouillard on the Lewis and Clark Expedition*. New York: Ballantine Books, 2000.

Thompson, David. *David Thompson's Narrative of His Explorations in Western America, 1784–1812*. Publications of The Champlain Society, Vol. 12. Edited by J. B. Tyrrel. Toronto: Champlain Society, 1916. Reprint. New York: Green Press, 1968.

———. *Travels in Western North America, 1784–1812*. Edited by Victor G. Hopgood. Toronto: Macmillan Company of Canada, 1971.

Thorp, Willard. "Cooper Beyond America," *New York History* 35, no. 4 (October, 1954): 522–39.

Thwaites, Reuben G. *Early Western Travels, 1748–1846; a Series of Annotated Reprints of Some of the Best and Rarest Contemporary Volumes of Travel, Descriptive of the Aborigenes and Social and Economic Conditions in the Middle and Far West, during the Period of Early American Settlement*, 32 vols. Cleveland, 1904.

———. *The Jesuit Relations and Allied Documents—Travels and Explorations of the Jesuit Missionaries in New France, 1610–1701*, 73 vols. Cleveland, 1904. Vols. 69 and 70 refer to the Illinois colony.

———. *Original Journals of the Lewis and Clark Expedition, 1804–1806, printed from the original manuscripts in the library of the American Philosophical Society and by direction of its committee on historical documents, together with manuscript material of Lewis and Clark from other sources—now for the first time published in full and exactly as written*. 8 vols. New York: Dodd, Mead & Co., 1904–5.

Trigger, Bruce G. "The Jesuits and the Fur Trade." *Ethnohistory* 5, no. 1 (1965): 166–77.

———. *The Hurons: Farmers of the North*. New York: Holt, Rinehart and Winston, 1969.

———. *The Children of Aataentsic: A History of the Huron People to 1660*. 2 vols. Montreal: McGill-Queen's University Press, 1976..

————. *Natives and Newcomers: Canada's Heroic Age Reconsidered.* Kingston: McGill-Queen's University Press, 1985.

Trudel, Marcel. *Louis XVI, le Congrès américain et le Canada, 1774–1789*, Québec: Les Editions du Quartier Latin, 1949.

————. *Initiation à la Nouvelle France.* Montreal: Holt, Rinehart and Winston, 1968.

————. *La Population du Canada en 1663.* Montreal: Fides, 1973.

————. *Histoire de la Nouvelle France.* 4 vols. Montreal: Fidès, 1966–97.

————. "L'affaire Jumonville." *Revue d'histoire de l'Amérique française,* 6 no. 3 (1952): 331–73.

Truteau, Jean Baptiste. "The Description of the Upper Missouri." 1796. Edited by Annie Heloise Abel, *Mississippi Valley Historical Review* 8 (1921): 157–79.

Utley, Robert M. *A Life Wild and Perilous, Mountain Men and the Paths to the Pacific.* New York: Henry Holt and Company, 1998.

Van Kirk, Sylvie. *Many Tender Ties, Women in the Fur Trade Society, 1670–1870.* Winnipeg: Watson & Dwyer, 1980.

Vaugeois, Denis. *America, l'expédition de Lewis et Clark et la naissance d'une nouvelle puissance.* Sillery, Québec: Septentrion, 2002.

Vincens, Simone. *Madame Montour et son temps,* Montreal: Québec Amérique, 1979.

Volney, Constantin de. *Œuvres complètes.* Paris: Didot, 1846.

Voltaire. *Essai sur les mœurs.* 1756. Paris, Garnier, 1990 .

Voorhis, Ernest. *Historic Forts and Trading Posts of the French Régime and of the English Fur Trade Companies.* Ottawa, Ontario, 1930.

Walthall, John A., and Thomas E. Emerson, eds. *Calumet and Fleur de Lys: Archaeology of Indian and French Contact in the Midcontinent.* Washington, D.C.: Smithsonian Institution Press, 1992.

Weber, David J. *The Spanish Frontier in North America.* New Haven: Yale University Press,1992.

White, Richard. *The Roots of Dependency: Subsistence, Environment and Social Change among the Choctaws, Pawnees and Navajos.* Lincoln: University of Nebraska Press, 1983.

————. *The Middle Ground, Indians, Empires and Republics in the Great Lakes Region, 1610–1815.* Cambridge: Cambridge University Press, 1989.

Williams, Helen Marie. *Souvenirs de la Révolution française,* Paris: Doudey Duprey, 1827.

Winsor, Justin. *The Mississippi Basin. The Struggle in America between England and France, 1697–1763.* Boston, 1898.

Wood W. Raymond. "David Thompson at the Mandan-Hidatsa Villages,1797–1798: The Original Journals." *Ethnohistory* 24, no. 3 (1977): 329–42.

————, and Thomas D. Thiessen. *Early Fur Trade on the Northern Plains, Canadian Traders Among the Mandan and Hidatsa Indians, 1738–1818.* Norman: University of Oklahoma Press, 1985.

Wrong, George M. *The Rise and Fall of New France.* 2 vols. New York, 1928.

Zitomersky, Joseph. *French Americans-Native Americans in Eighteenth Century French Colonial Louisiana.* Lund: Lund University Press, 1994.

————. "In the Middle and on the Margin: Greater French Louisiana in History and in Professional Historical Memory." *Le citoyen dans l'empire du milieu. Perspectives comparatistes*. Edited by Claude Féral. Saint-Denis: Alizés Presses de l'Université de la Réunion, 2001, 201–64.

Zoltany, Yves. "New France in the West." *Canadian Historical Review* 46, no.4 (1965): 301–2.

Index